The Russian R

The year 2005 marks the centenary of Russia's 'first revolution', that of 1905. Hundreds were killed and injured when, on 9 January, 'Bloody Sunday', Cossacks fired upon workers and their families who were marching peacefully to deliver a petition to Tsar Nicholas II in St Petersburg. This set off a wave of strikes, urban uprisings, peasant revolts, national revolutions and mutinies across the Russian Empire. Tsarism survived, but only after having made significant political and social concessions, and allowing the Russian people a 'dress rehearsal', in Lenin's words, for the revolutions of 1917. Thus, 1905 proved a crucial turning point in the demise of the autocracy and the rise of a revolutionary socialism that would shape Russia, Europe and the international system for the rest of the twentieth century.

The centenary of the revolution has prompted scholars to review and reassess our understanding of 1905. Recent opportunities to access archives throughout the former Soviet Union are yielding new provincial perspectives, as well as fresh insights into the roles of national and religious minorities and the parts played by individuals, social groups, political parties and institutions. *The Russian Revolution of 1905* brings together some of the best of this new research and reassessment. The volume includes thirteen chapters written by leading historians from around the world, together with an introduction by Abraham Ascher.

Jonathan D. Smele is Senior Lecturer in Modern European History at Queen Mary, University of London. **Anthony Heywood** is Senior Lecturer in History at the University of Bradford.

Routledge studies in modern European history

1 **Facing Fascism**
The Conservative Party and the European dictators 1935–1940
Nick Crowson

2 **French Foreign and Defence Policy, 1918–1940**
The decline and fall of a great power
Edited by Robert Boyce

3 **Britain and the Problem of International Disarmament 1919–1934**
Carolyn Kitching

4 **British Foreign Policy 1874–1914**
The role of India
Sneh Mahajan

5 **Racial Theories in Fascist Italy**
Aaron Gilette

6 **Stormtroopers and Crisis in the Nazi Movement**
Activism, ideology and dissolution
Thomas D. Grant

7 **Trials of Irish History**
Genesis and evolution of a reappraisal
Evi Gkotzaridis

8 **From Slave Trade to Empire**
European colonisation of Black Africa 1780s-1880s
Edited by Olivier Pétré-Grenouilleau

9 **The Russian Revolution of 1905**
Centenary perspectives
Edited by Jonathan D. Smele and Anthony Heywood

The Russian Revolution of 1905

Centenary perspectives

Edited by Jonathan D. Smele and
Anthony Heywood

Routledge
Taylor & Francis Group

LONDON AND NEW YORK

First published 2005
by Routledge
2 Park Square, Milton Park, Abingdon, Oxon OX14 4RN

Simultaneously published in the USA and Canada
by Routledge
711 Third Ave, New York, NY 10017

First issued in paperback 2012

Routledge is an imprint of the Taylor & Francis Group

© 2005 Jonathan D. Smele and Anthony Heywood selection and
editorial matter; the contributors their contributions

Typeset in Garamond by Wearset Ltd, Boldon, Tyne and Wear

British Library Cataloguing in Publication Data
A catalogue record for this book is available from the British Library

Library of Congress Cataloging in Publication Data
A catalog record for this book has been requested

ISBN 978 0 4156 5413 5

Contents

List of contributors   vii
Acknowledgements   x
Note on style   xi

1 **Introduction**   1
  ABRAHAM ASCHER

2 **Psychohistorical approaches to 1905 radicalism**   13
  ANNA GEIFMAN

3 **1905: the view from the provinces**   34
  BERYL WILLIAMS

4 **The 1905 Revolution in Russia's Baltic provinces**   55
  JAMES D. WHITE

5 **Finland in 1905: the political and social history of
  the revolution**   79
  ANTTI KUJALA

6 **Revolution and revolt in the Manchurian armies, as
  perceived by a future leader of the White movement**   94
  OLEG AIRAPETOV

7 **Retrospectively revolting: Kazan Tatar 'conspiracies'
  during the 1905 Revolution**   119
  CHRISTIAN NOACK

8 **Peasant protest and peasant violence in 1905:
  Voronezh province, Ostrogozhskii uezd**   137
  FRANZISKA SCHEDEWIE

 9 Jews and revolution in Kharkiv: how one
    Ukrainian city escaped a pogrom in 1905   156
    MICHAEL F. HAMM

10 Socialists, liberals and the Union of Unions in Kyiv
    during the 1905 Revolution: an engineer's
    perspective   177
    ANTHONY HEYWOOD

11 Kadet domination of the First Duma and its limits   196
    SHMUEL GALAI

12 Lenin and the 1905 Revolution   218
    CHRISTOPHER READ

13 Leon Trotsky and 1905   241
    IAN D. THATCHER

14 The 1905 Revolution on Tyneside   260
    DAVID SAUNDERS

    Index   279

Contributors

Oleg Airapetov, a specialist in Russian foreign policy and the country's military history of the late nineteenth and early twentieth centuries, is Senior Lecturer in the Department of History at Moscow State University. He is currently working on a study of the Imperial General Staff in the First World War. His publications include *Zabytaia kar'era 'russkogo Mol'tke': Nikolai Nikolaevich Obruchev (1830–1904)* (St Petersburg, 1998); *Generaly, liberaly i predprinimateli: rabota na front i na revoliutsiiu (1908–1917)* (Moscow, 2003); the edited collections *Poslednaia voina Imperatorskoi Rossii* (Moscow, 2002); and *Russko-Iaponskaia voina 1904–1905gg.: vzgliad cherez stoletie* (Moscow, 2004).

Abraham Ascher, Distinguished Professor Emeritus of History at the Graduate Center of the City University of New York, is the author of *Pavel Axelrod and the Development of Menshevism* (Cambridge, Mass., 1972); *The Revolution of 1905*, 2 vols (Stanford, 1988–92); *P. A. Stolypin: The Search for Stability in Late Imperial Russia* (Stanford, 2001); *Russia: A Short History* (Oxford, 2002); and *The Revolution of 1905: A Short History* (Stanford, 2004); he is also the editor of *The Mensheviks in the Russian Revolution* (Ithaca, N.Y., 1976) and *Studying Russian and Soviet History* (Boulder, 1987).

Shmuel Galai is Professor Emeritus of Ben-Gurion University of the Negev, Israel. His contribution to this collection forms part of his current project, a study of the Kadet Party from its inception to the Bolshevik seizure of power in October 1917. His book on *The Liberation Movement in Russia, 1900–1905* (London, 1973) was reissued in paperback by Cambridge University Press in 2002.

Anna Geifman, Professor of History at Boston University, is the author of *Thou Shalt Kill: Revolutionary Terrorism in Russia, 1894–1917* (Princeton, 1993) and *Entangled in Terror: The Azef Affair and the Russian Revolution* (Wilmington, 2000); she is also the editor of *Russia under the Last Tsar: Opposition and Subversion, 1894–1917* (Oxford, 1999). She has published many articles on Russian political and cultural history and is currently working on a volume of psychohistorical essays on political extremism.

Michael F. Hamm is Ewing T. Boles Professor of History at Centre College, where he teaches courses on Russia, the Soviet Union, modern Europe and the Middle East. He is the author of *Kiev: A Portrait, 1800–1917* (Princeton, 1993); and editor and part-author of *The City in Russian History* (Lexington, Ky., 1976) and *The City in Late Imperial Russia* (Bloomington, 1986), as well as the author of scholarly articles on Kyiv, Kharkiv, Riga and Kishinev.

Anthony Heywood is Senior Lecturer in History at the University of Bradford. His publications include *Modernising Lenin's Russia: Economic Reconstruction, Foreign Trade and the Railways* (Cambridge, 1999) and his biography of the eminent Russian transport engineer Iurii Vladimirovich Lomonosov is forthcoming as *Engineer of Revolutionary Russia* (Aldershot, 2006).

Antti Kujala is Senior Lecturer in Finnish and Russian History at the University of Helsinki. In addition to the books mentioned in the notes to his chapter in this book, his major publications include *The Crown, the Nobility and the Peasants 1630–1713: Tax, Rent and Relations of Power* (Helsinki, 2003) and *Miekka ei laske leikkiä: Suomi suuressa pohjan sodassa, 1700–1714* (Helsinki, 2001).

Christian Noack is Assistant Professor of East European History at Bielefeld University. His main fields of research are nationality questions in Eastern Europe, the Russian Empire and the Soviet Union and, currently, the history of travel and tourism in the USSR. His publications include *Muslimischer Nationalismus. Nationsbildung und Nationalbewegung bei Tataren und Baschkiren, 1861–1917* (Stuttgart, 2000).

Christopher Read is Professor of History at the University of Warwick. His publications include *The Stalin Years: A Reader* (Basingstoke, 2003); *The Making and Breaking of the Soviet System* (Basingstoke, 2001); and *From Tsar to Soviets: The Russian People and Their Revolution, 1917–1921* (London, 1996). His latest book is *Lenin: A Revolutionary Life* (London, 2005).

David Saunders is Professor of the History of the Russian Empire at the University of Newcastle upon Tyne. His publications include *The Ukrainian Impact on Russian Culture, 1750–1850* (Edmonton, 1985); *Russia in the Age of Reaction and Reform 1801–1881* (London, 1992); and about thirty academic articles.

Franziska Schedewie submitted her Ph.D. thesis, entitled 'Selbstverwaltung und sozialer Wandel in der russischen Provinz. Bauern und Zemstvo in Voronež, 1864–1914', at the University of Heidelberg in 2004. She is currently working at the University of Jena on a research project on Russian foreign policies under Alexander I and the relations between Russia and Weimar.

Ian D. Thatcher is Reader in Modern European History at Brunel University and the author of numerous academic articles and books, including *Leon Trotsky and World War One, August 1914–February 1917* (Basingstoke, 2000) and *Trotsky* (London, 2003). He also edited *Alec Nove on Economic Theory: Previously Unpublished Writings*, 2 vols (Northampton, Mass., 1998) and *Regime and Society in Twentieth-Century Russia* (Basingstoke, 1999).

James D. White is Professor of Russian and East European Studies and Head of the School of Slavonic, Central and East European Studies at the University of Glasgow. His publications include *The Russian Revolution, 1917–1921: A Short History* (London, 1994); *Karl Marx and the Intellectual Origins of Dialectical Materialism* (Basingstoke, 1996); and *Lenin: The Practice and Theory of Revolution* (Basingstoke, 2001).

Beryl Williams is Emeritus Reader in History at the University of Sussex. She is the author of *The Russian Revolution, 1917–1921* (Oxford, 1987; reissued and updated 1995) and *Lenin* (London, 2000), as well as numerous academic articles.

Acknowledgements

This volume is derived from some of the papers delivered at the XXXth Annual Conference of the Study Group on the Russian Revolution (SGRR), which took place at Nottingham on 3–5 January 2004, with the financial support of the British Academy, BASEES and the Institute for Russian, Soviet and Central and East European Studies, University of Nottingham.

Information regarding membership of the SGRR and its future conferences can be obtained from the group's website: http://www.basees.org.uk/sgrusrev.htm.

The SGRR's journal, *Revolutionary Russia*, has been published biannually since 1988. For general editorial matters, including the submission of articles, contact the editor (at the time of writing: Dr Jonathan D. Smele, Department of History, Queen Mary, University of London, London E1 4NS). Regarding subscriptions and the contents of past issues, see the publisher's website: http://www.tandf.co.uk/journals/.

Note on style

As this book is about events prior to the Bolsheviks' modernization of the Russian calendar in 1918, when dealing with events in the Russian Empire the 'old-style' Julian calendar (which, in the twentieth century, was thirteen days behind the Gregorian calendar used in the West) has been employed. When dealing with events outside of the Empire, the Gregorian ('new-style') calendar has been employed. When necessary for clarity, dates in both calendars are indicated. All Russian words (including names) have been transliterated according to the Library of Congress simplified system, except for Anglicized versions of common names that gained general acceptance and familiarity prior to the widespread adoption of that system (e.g. Trotsky, not Trotskii). Russian forms of non-Russian place names within the Russian Empire (e.g. Khar'kov) have been used in chapters dealing with affairs from an 'all-Russian' point of view, but the local form (i.e. Kharkiv) has been retained in chapters where the focus is on a specific non-Russian region.

1 Introduction

Abraham Ascher

As the title of this volume on the Russian Revolution of 1905 suggests, the book is intended to provide readers with new perspectives on what is generally considered to have been one of the critical junctures in modern Russian history and, in many ways, in the history of the twentieth century, aptly termed the 'age of extremes'. Initially prepared as papers for the XXXth Annual Conference of the Study Group on the Russian Revolution (at Nottingham, United Kingdom, on 3–5 January 2004), all the contributions except one were extensively discussed by a group of some forty scholars and then revised to take into account various criticisms and suggestions. The result, in my view, is a collection of highly interesting and stimulating chapters that shed light on an event that is still insufficiently understood.

My task in this introduction, it seems to me, is to help students of history derive maximum benefit from reading the book. I could best do this, I thought, by pointing out some of the scholarly controversies surrounding the Revolution of 1905, by showing how the essays fit into these interpretations and by raising general questions about them. Above all I would like to emphasize how the chapters collected here demonstrate that the discipline of History is not a closed book but, rather, an endless debate about the past.

Actually, the Revolution of 1905 has been a highly controversial topic from the moment it ended. Even the duration of the upheaval has been a bone of contention, and that is not surprising because this touches on all the questions in dispute. It is arguable that the event's proper title should be 'The Revolution of 1904–07', which, admittedly, is rather cumbersome. But a strong case can be made that the upheaval began late in 1904, when liberals, dismayed by the country's military defeats at the hands of the Japanese, engaged in widespread agitation against the autocracy, and that it did not end until June 1907, with the dissolution of the Second State Duma (the elected chamber of deputies). Historians who tend to downplay the agitation of 1904 and the conflicts in the two dumas, in 1906 and 1907, do so because they believe that it was not the liberals but the workers and, to a lesser extent, the peasants, who played the critical role in the revolution – two groups that were especially active in the opposition to the old order in the year 1905 itself. But there are two other reasons for the differing interpretations of the revolution: the incredible complexity of the events that comprised the upheaval; and the ambiguity of the outcome of 1905.

In the Soviet Union the standard interpretation of the revolution was based on comments Lenin made in 1920. He referred to it as a 'dress rehearsal', without which the 'victory of the October Revolution in 1917 would have been impossible'.[1] Lenin's aim, clearly, was to suggest the inevitability of 1917, since a dress rehearsal is always followed by the first performance. Furthermore, Lenin insisted that the upheaval began with Bloody Sunday on 9 January 1905, when government troops shot at peaceful demonstrators, killing 130 of them and wounding 299. He also contended that the proletariat was the driving force of events and that the Moscow uprising in December that year, led by the Bolsheviks and harshly crushed by the government, was the high point of the upheaval. In Lenin's view, the intransigence of the ruling class precluded any outcome other than the one that occurred – the defeat of the revolution. Lenin's analysis became the principal interpretation of 1905 in the Soviet Union and guided the work of Soviet historians for over seventy years. And the literature on the subject was vast: a scholarly bibliography of 1905 that was published as early as 1930 ran to 715 pages.[2]

In the West, there has also been strong interest in the revolution, especially during the past four decades or so, but the interpretations have been diverse. Broadly speaking, there have been four Western approaches. Social historians in the West and most historians on the left have been more subtle and open-minded than those who have followed the Leninist line, but they also tend to argue that the masses, and in particular the working class, were at all times the driving force of the revolution. Moreover, many of them also consider Bloody Sunday to have been the starting point of the upheaval and view the armed uprising in Moscow as one of its high points. Finally, these historians tend to dismiss as totally inadequate the concessions by the government and reject the possibility of Russia's peaceful transformation into a constitutional monarchy on the Western model.[3]

By contrast, conservative writers – and this would include some Russian émigré scholars and former tsarist officials – insist that it was the radicalism and intransigence of the opposition at every turn of the upheaval that undermined the chances of a peaceful resolution of the crisis. Only a monarchical order with a powerful tsar could maintain the Russian Empire as a viable state, they argue. Nicholas II, in this interpretation, had no choice but to act as he did.[4]

It has also been suggested – and this is the third Western interpretation – that there was no revolution at all in 1905.[5] Certainly, an orthodox Marxist might well dispute the designation, for political power was not transferred from one social class to another. Non-Marxists, who define a revolution as a fundamental change in the system of legality, might also hesitate to use the term, since the tsar's authority remained paramount, even though it was clearly reduced by the establishment of an elected parliament that exercised some legislative power. Yet it is understandable that the term should have been adopted by contemporaries and retained by political activists as well as historians. From mid-1904 until late in 1905, there occurred an assault on tsarist authority from below that was so massive, potent and successful that, to all appearances, the old regime was disintegrating. Civil order broke down and for several months the government seemed incapable of little more than biding its time until the outbursts of defiance, generally unplanned and unorganized, had spent themselves. So effective a challenge to the state's monopoly of power, even though temporary, may justifiably be characterized as a revolution.

The last interpretation I want to consider might be termed, for want of a better description, as broadly 'liberal'.[6] It depicts the revolution not as an event that made any one path of development inevitable, but rather as a critical juncture that opened up several alternative paths. Under intense pressure, initially from liberals among the nobility and professional classes for political change and then from other social groups – workers, peasants and national minorities – who were additionally interested in economic and social change, the autocracy appeared to suffer a loss of nerve. For an entire year, beginning in the autumn of 1904, the government oscillated between accommodation and repression; but neither policy succeeded in ending the unrest. On the contrary, the government's inconsistency was taken as a sign of weakness by the various groups within the opposition, encouraging them to step up their agitation. Indeed, had the opposition groups been able to collaborate fully, the outcome might have been quite different.

During the general strike in October 1905 – the high point of the revolution in the 'liberal' interpretation – the pressure from the mass movements became so acute that it drove the autocracy to the verge of collapse, and to many it now seemed possible that the old regime might actually be overthrown. Even though that prospect did not materialize, some institutional changes introduced during the period of unrest survived the failure of the revolution. Most notably, Russia retained an elected legislature with some real powers, as well as political parties speaking for various social and economic interests. In addition, despite many restrictions, trade unions, which had been legalized during the upheaval, continued to exist and there was considerably more freedom of expression after 1905 than had prevailed before that year.

This approach to the study of 1905, which stresses complexity and ambiguity, might seem to deprive the revolution of some of its excitement by not linking it directly to the more momentous revolution of 1917. Such an approach, however, yields better – and ultimately more exciting – history: it is closer to what actually happened. The individuals who participated in the mass movements of 1905 did not believe that they were merely preparing the way for the real event at some future date. They were trying to bring about far-reaching changes then and there. Furthermore, it is not certain that these endeavours were necessarily doomed to fail. On several occasions, the authorities considered daring reforms that at an earlier stage of the revolution would have satisfied enough of the opposition's demands to have brought the unrest to an end. However, the tsar and his advisers always offered concessions that were too niggardly; and they were always offered too late. There were also several fairly elaborate attempts to restore political stability by bringing liberals into the government, but in the end the differences between the authorities and the opposition proved to be too deep. The revolutionary period from 1904 to 1907 might even be designated as one of missed opportunities to end the upheaval by peaceful means.

Since 1991, Russia has found itself in the throes of yet another upheaval, one that has also been inspired to a considerable extent by the ideals that had animated much of the opposition in 1905: the rule of law, government by the people, individual rights and respect for the rights of ethnic and religious minorities. Thus, though aborted, the Revolution of 1905 may be said to have initiated a process of political, economic and social change that still has not run its full course. Even now, as I write these words in September 2004, President Vladimir Putin is taking steps to undermine some of the democratic reforms introduced after the collapse of Communism in 1991. It almost seems like a replay of the tsar's arbitrary measures in 1907, when he reneged on many of the reforms introduced in 1905 and 1906. The supporters of a liberal and democratic Russia continue to hope and believe that Mr Putin's measures will prove to be only a temporary defeat for their cause.

If one takes such a long-range view of Russian history, then the Revolution of 1905 can be seen not simply as a failure or as an event that was important because it led inexorably to 1917. On the contrary, 1905 should be viewed as an upheaval that opened up new possibilities for the country that were suppressed by the Bolshevik Revolution of 1917. After all, most countries undergoing transitions from absolutism to constitutionalism endured long periods of conflict; the path to what is generally referred to as modernity has rarely been smooth, almost never without many zigzags and major catastrophes. Just think of France from 1789 to 1905 (when the Chamber of Deputies passed a law separating church and state), Germany from 1848 to 1949, and the United Kingdom, long ago, in the seventeenth century.

It was with these thoughts that I examined the chapters prepared for this volume. More specifically, I asked myself several questions that may serve as guides: How did the chapters conform to, or modify, the five broad interpretations of 1905 I discussed above? Did they examine issues previously ignored or slighted? Did they offer new approaches? Were they based on sources not previously examined or previously available? Or did they perhaps reinforce positions advanced by other historians? And, finally, did they raise issues that in the end may be unanswerable but are nonetheless worthy of discussion?

The first thing I noticed was that seven of the chapters deal with developments in the provinces or among national and religious minorities – subjects that, it is fair to say, have not received sufficient attention in previous studies of 1905. Three focus on the liberals, who were so important throughout the upheaval that they deserve further scrutiny. One of these, the perceptive chapter by Anthony Heywood, concentrates on the liberals' activities outside the two capitals (St Petersburg and Moscow), in Kiev (Kyiv), and, in addition, touches on the political conduct of socialists in that city. Two chapters focus on the question that sociologists like to call 'human agency': I am referring to those devoted to Lenin and Trotsky. One is on military developments in Manchuria and their very important impact on a major participant in the events of 1917. Finally, the chapter by Anna Geifman suggests that a psychohistorical approach should be applied to the study of radicalism and revolutionary extremism. These categories are not perfect; there is, necessarily, a fair amount of overlap and some chapters deal with several aspects of the revolution. I want to emphasize that my comments on the contents of this volume are made in a friendly spirit and are designed to encourage discussion of difficult issues to which there are no easy answers.

Let me start with Professor Anna Geifman's thoughtful and interesting chapter. In emphasizing that Russian terrorists were psychologically impaired she has offered a novel approach to the study of early twentieth-century extremism in Russia. Additionally, of course, this is a subject that is relevant to present-day developments in many parts of the world. I myself think that the psychohistorical approach can be instructive in seeking to understand the extremists and, in particular, the terrorists; the few I have examined in detail were very troubled people. And it seems to me that Geifman is probably right in suggesting, by means of a quotation from Walter Laqueur, that 'objective circumstances *per se* are not a sufficient' condition for the escalation of violence. But I do have some doubts about the second part of the statement she quotes: that objective circumstances may 'perhaps not be . . . a necessary condition' for terrorist violence. Here I would raise several questions: Why was there so much more terrorism early in the twentieth century in Russia than elsewhere in Europe? Why so much more terrorism after 1905 than before that year? In this connection, a point made by Antii Kujala in his excellent analysis of conditions in Finland – a subject, by the way, that is too often slighted in Western studies of late Imperial Russia – is especially pertinent. Kujala points out that political assassinations in Finland were 'quite rare' prior to 1904 and became more frequent in the years from 1904 to 1908. Incidentally, immediately after the words quoted by Geifman, Professor Laqueur qualifies his own generalization. He states that 'The formation or existence of a revolutionary party needs definite ideological objectives and also a certain personality type.'[7]

I would also suggest that Professor Geifman may be exaggerating a bit in asserting that the terrorists were, to use a term she quotes from the novelist Andrei Bely, 'half-cracked'. The terrorists of early twentieth-century Russia by and large attacked people who occupied positions of authority or were in some way allied with the authorities: senior officials, senior military officers, policemen and capitalists. They did not, to the best of my knowledge, deliberately engage in random killings, although innocent civilians were often victims because they happened to be near the targets of attack. Can it therefore be said that the terrorists in Russia, however misguided and immoral they may have been, were as irrational as the term 'half-cracked' implies? The psychohistorical approach can be helpful in understanding extremists, but if it is applied without careful qualifications we run the danger of trivializing the deep social, political and economic conflicts and tensions in Russia early in the twentieth century, which, I am sure, was not Professor Geifman's intention.

The chapters on the provinces and minorities remind us once again that although developments in St Petersburg and Moscow were of fundamental importance in determining the course of the revolution, the upheaval was truly national in scale. This is demonstrated by Beryl Williams's informative and wide-ranging study of the latest literature on the causes of 1905, in which she also raises a challenging question about how to understand the upheaval. Can it be best understood by applying the general explanation of revolutions offered by Alexis de Tocqueville, who contended that they break out when economic conditions are on the upswing? Or are revolutions better explained by Karl Marx's claim that 'increasing misery' impels the masses to rebel against the prevailing political and social order? Dr Williams pays special attention to the claims of scholars who have argued over the past two decades or so that peasants in Russia were not as deprived economically as had previously been widely assumed and that 'nationality mattered more than class in the ethnically divided areas of the south, particularly in the Caucasus but also in Ukraine'. Moreover, these scholars contend that Russia was 'catching up fast' in industrializing the country and that 'over all, things may well have been improving, not getting worse'.

Professor James White, on the other hand, concentrates on the Baltic provinces – modern-day Estonia, Latvia and Lithuania – and provides a concise and reliable survey of the background and development of the revolution in this region. Especially valuable are his comparisons between events there and those in the heartland, which raises the thorny questions of the extent to which the unrest in the provinces simply echoed the upheaval in the heartland, most particularly in St Petersburg and Moscow, and also how, if at all, events in the provinces affected the course of the revolution as a whole. This is a subject of continuing interest to scholars.

Dr Oleg Airapetov points to yet another important aspect of the turbulence of 1905 in a region far from the heartland, the disintegration of the Russian army in Manchuria in February and March 1905. The war between Russia and Japan, begun in February 1904 and recklessly provoked by the tsarist authorities, had been a major cause of the unrest that spread across the Russian Empire late that year and continued to be a major factor in energizing the opposition to the autocracy throughout 1905. Airapetov's graphic account of the demoralization of the Russian army adds greatly to our understanding of the political crisis in St Petersburg in the autumn of 1905, when the old regime was brought to its knees. But what I found especially intriguing is Airapetov's revelation that General M. V. Alekseev's conduct in February 1917, when he was chief of staff to the tsar, was decisively influenced by his experience in 1905 when he was quartermaster-general of the Third Manchurian Army. Airapetov here has in mind Alekseev's cable to Tsar Nicholas II on 1 March 1917, in which he said that the army was very likely to react to events in St Petersburg – that is, it would disintegrate or join the opposition – and that therefore a government of national confidence (in effect, one responsible to the Duma) should be formed.[8] Not long after this cable, Nicholas abdicated, with consequences that are well known. It would be interesting to know how many more senior military officers were similarly affected by 1905. In drawing our attention to the influence that 1905 had on General Alekseev, Airapetov points to a fascinating link between 1905 and 1917, casting fresh light on how and why the old order collapsed so quickly once popular discontent manifested itself early in 1917.

Christian Noack's chapter, which at times reads like a detective story, describes the dubious claims of the Kazan police to have discovered (late in 1907) revolutionary and separatist conspiracies by Muslims determined to overturn the tsarist order during the previous period of revolutionary turbulence. In fact, as Noack points out, the Muslims, the largest minority (about 13 million people) in the Russian Empire, by and large shunned radicalism and their behaviour poses yet another challenge to the Marxist notion of class struggle as the driving force in history. For primarily religious reasons, Muslims rejected armed action against the authorities and, in fact, rejected the very idea of revolution. To engage in disorder against the authorities was considered a violation of Islamic principles. What Noack's chapter nicely exposes is the incompetence and clumsiness of the Russian police in seeking to level the charge of conspiracy on what was essentially a peaceful minority. In the end, the police only succeeded in 'reinforcing the Muslims' future revolutionary potential'. This was by no means the only incident of police conduct during the revolution that, instead of protecting the old order, made matters worse.[9]

No topic is more central to an understanding of the unfolding of the revolution than the role of the peasants, who, after all, comprised more than 80 per cent of Russia's population. In this field, Franziska Schedewie belongs to the revisionists (already mentioned by Beryl Williams) and, in a spirited and impressively documented chapter, rejects the argument that peasants in 1905 were driven by 'increasing impoverishment'. On the basis of her research (albeit limited, to be sure, to developments in one district in Voronezh province), she concludes that, insofar as peasants participated in the protest movement, they were not 'primarily revolutionary or even progressive' but were engaging in 'acts of social protest against the effects of modernization'. She also asserts that the disorderly in the countryside were peasants whose conditions were changing either for 'worse or for the better'.

It is a challenging thesis and, if further research in other areas of the Russian Empire bears out her claims, historians of Russia will have to rethink long-cherished views.

Michael Hamm tackles yet another highly charged and controversial issue, the pogroms carried out mainly (but not solely) against Jews in 1905. The debate owes its origins to the claims by the eminent Jewish historian, S. M. Dubnow, that 'mysterious emissaries from St Petersburg' had encouraged the violence against Jews in 1881 and 1882 and that, in 1905, the perpetrators of pogroms had obeyed a 'prearranged signal'. The impression left with readers was that the government had played a key role in the bloody events.[10] Historians have since challenged this interpretation.[11] We now know that even Alexander III, not noted for his sympathies for the Jews or any other minority, actually tried to put a stop to the pogroms of 1881 because he feared that the unrest would spread and lead to attacks on land-lords, government officials and, eventually, the highest authorities, including the tsar himself. During the 1905 Revolution, too, several senior officials (including prime ministers S. Iu. Witte and P. A. Stolypin) held on to Alexander's position, although it is true that on the local level many policemen and others in positions of authority looked the other way once the violence began and sometimes even encouraged the marauders. In his chapter on Khar'kov (Kharkiv), Michael Hamm mentions this scholarly debate and then describes the history of that city, which seems to complicate further the historians' inclination to offer generalizations about the pogroms. He shows how Khar'kov, which had a Jewish population in excess of 10,000, managed to escape pogroms in 1905 because local authorities, polit-ical activists and workers of the city's locomotive-building factory took measures to prevent violence against Jews.

The liberals, who played a major role in the revolution (and especially in the first two dumas) are well served in this volume. Shmuel Galai thought-fully examines the role of the Kadets (Constitutional Democrats) in the First State Duma and shows how deep the divide was between them and the government. Anthony Heywood, on the other hand, focuses on one large city, Kiev (Kyiv), and analyses, on the basis of newly discovered archival sources, the relationship between the liberal camp and the radical left, a theme also touched upon by Galai. Heywood is correct in stating that 'one of the regime's greatest fears was a revolutionary alliance of the liberal intel-ligentsia with the workers' and peasants' movements'. That alliance was crit-ical for the success of the general strike in October 1905 and, had it been maintained, could have had a profound impact on the course of events in 1906 and 1907, perhaps even assuring the success of the revolution. But Heywood makes an important point in noting that the alliance was always on shaky ground; in fact, even before the issuance of the October Manifesto the two groups in Kiev had moved apart because they could not agree on tactics or on ultimate goals. 'Class rivalry' took precedence over the commit-ment, shared by both movements, to dismantle the autocracy.

At the same time, as Galai points out, the divisions between the Kadets and the radicals hampered the former in their attempts to form a Kadet government, albeit that that was never a very likely prospect to start with. This touches on a very fundamental dilemma liberals faced throughout the period of upheaval. If they supported the radicals, who favoured violent revolution, the liberals ran the danger of bringing about one of two unpalatable outcomes: a crackdown by the authorities that would destroy the entire opposition movement; or success by the radicals, whose social and economic programme was unacceptable to the liberals. As has often been noted, it was a great misfortune for Russia that the bourgeois revolution, which is how the events of 1905 may be characterized, came at a time when there already existed a potent radical movement that was intent on playing a decisive role in political affairs.

Now a few words on the two engaging contributions dealing with human agency, both of which depict leading revolutionaries in a distinctly positive light. In his trenchant and provocative chapter, Professor Christopher Read tells us that Lenin loved being in the company of children and was quite modest, going so far as to describe himself in 1920 as essentially a revolutionary writer, theorist and teacher. But I wonder if he wasn't much more than that – even as early as 1900, when he was a dominant figure in the editing and distribution of the newspaper *Iskra*. In the performance of these tasks Lenin proved to be masterful in the creation of Social Democratic centres in Russia, which was a major political and organizational achievement. Lenin already, then, displayed the political acumen, tenacity and single-mindedness for which he later became famous as the leader of Bolshevism.

I suppose that one can agree with Professor Read that Lenin was not a 'monster', especially if he is compared to his successor, Stalin, or to Hitler. But as early as 1905 he demonstrated a ruthlessness that reasserted itself with full force when he became the leader of Russia. In a private letter of 11 February 1905, for example, he denounced comrades who had hesitated to organize circles in Russia to promote the Bolshevik cause and called for nothing less than their physical extermination. 'I am for the shooting on the spot of anyone', he wrote of the Bolsheviks, 'who presumes to say that there are no people to be had [who can promote Bolshevism]. The people in Russia are legion; all we have to do is to recruit young people more widely and boldly, more boldly and widely, and again more widely and boldly . . . This is a time of war.'[12] On the other hand, I think that Read is right in stating that there are 'strong elements of continuity' between Lenin's position on the desirability of a quick proletarian seizure of power in 1905 and his views in 1917. In fact, the notion that the proletariat would shed its blood in a revolution against the autocracy and then voluntarily make way for other classes, most notably the bourgeoisie, to take and hold on to power temporarily, always struck me as one of the less convincing tenets of Russian Marxism.

In his equally trenchant chapter on Leon Trotsky, Ian Thatcher argues — convincingly, in my view — that Trotsky's thinking and later conduct were deeply influenced by the events of 1905, and, in fact, that he was 'a product of 1905'. First of all, it was at the time of this upheaval that (together with Alexander Helphand) Trotsky developed the theory of permanent revolution, which, of course, became a guiding principle for the Bolsheviks in 1917. But it is perhaps worth noting that this theory was, from the beginning, based on a fundamental misconception of European socialism. Trotsky assumed that if the proletariat in Russia seized power and the international bourgeoisie then tried to crush the revolution, 'West European workers would take the side of Russian comrades'. This was a puzzling prediction: an examination of the comments by German socialists in the party press and at party meetings on the events in 1905, for example, indicates that the German socialist party — the most powerful of its kind in the world and the one that Trotsky believed would come to the aid of its colleagues in Russia — was actually very far from being committed to such a course. Despite their scorn for tsarism and their admiration for Russian revolutionaries, prominent spokesmen from all wings of the German Social Democratic Party voiced serious doubts about the tactics of their comrades in the East and rejected the notion that the strategies pursued by Russian socialists should be applied in Germany.[13] Indeed, Trotsky should not really have been surprised that, in the years from 1917 to 1920, the German left largely refused to emulate the Bolsheviks in attempting to seize power or even to come to their aid.

I also have a reservation about the soundness of Trotsky's understanding of the course of the revolution in 1905. Dr Thatcher indicates that Trotsky referred to the legislature promised in the October Manifesto as a 'consultative' body. If that is what Trotsky really believed, then he did not fully understand what had happened during the general strike in October 1905. The issuance of that document actually marked a decisive moment in the revolution. In granting that 'no law can become effective without the approval of the State Duma', Nicholas II did what he had vowed never to do: he abandoned the principle of autocracy. True, he soon changed his mind, but for a short while it looked as though Russia had undergone a true revolution. Was there any chance for the opposition to consolidate that huge achievement? That remains one of the key questions for historians.

The last chapter in the volume, Professor David Saunders's fascinating and highly original account of the Revolution of 1905 on Tyneside, in north-east England, does not deal with events in Russia itself, but it nevertheless touches on issues of direct relevance to developments there. The reaction of the West to 1905 is not a minor matter — and not simply because weapons were shipped from Western Europe to Russian revolutionaries. Russian leaders — Witte, Stolypin and the minister of finance V. N. Kokovtsov, to mention only a few — were very much concerned about how French, British and United States public opinion reacted to events in their country, in large measure because Russia badly needed loans from those countries. We know that the Russian government spent considerable sums of money to influence the French press, and it would be good to know to what extent, if at all, they also bribed the British and American press. Witte was certainly very cosy with the British journalist Edward J. Dillon, whose articles were so obsequious to Witte that another British journalist exclaimed that 'The man has no right to publish that unless he's paid for it!' And Dillon was rewarded handsomely: 'Already possessed of a Panhard,' a colleague noted, 'he suddenly appeared in a Rolls Royce.'[14] The whole subject of how the Russian authorities sought to influence Western public opinion deserves more study and Saunders's excellent chapter deserves much credit for having piqued our curiosity.

I hope that I have achieved my aim in this introduction; that is, to raise questions about 1905 that will encourage readers to think critically about that momentous event. One may not agree with all the interpretations offered by the thirteen other chapters in this volume, but there is no doubt in my mind that they are all significant contributions to historical scholarship and that they all demonstrate, once again, the point I made earlier — that History is an endless debate about the past. I would not have the slightest hesitation in assigning the volume to students or to anyone interested in gaining a deeper understanding of the twentieth century and, for that matter, our present era.

Notes

1 For Lenin's comments on 1905, see Robert C. Tucker (ed.), *The Lenin Anthology* (New York, 1975), pp. 278–92, 555–6 and *passim*.
2 Kommunisticheskaia Akademiia, *Pervaia russkaia revoliutsiia: Ukazatel' literatury* (Moscow, 1930).
3 See, for example: Walter Sablinsky, *The Road to Bloody Sunday: Father Gapon and the St Petersburg Massacre of 1905* (Princeton, 1976); Robert C. Weinberg, *The Revolution of 1905 in Odessa: Blood on the Steps* (Bloomington, 1993); John Bushnell, *Mutiny and Repression: Russian Soldiers in the Revolution of 1905–1906* (Bloomington, 1985); Laura Engelstein, *Moscow, 1905: Working-Class Organization and Political Conflict* (Stanford, 1982); Gerald D. Surh, *1905 in St Petersburg: Labor, Society, and Revolution* (Stanford, 1989); and Robert Edelman, *Proletarian Peasants: The Revolution of 1905 in Russia's Southwest* (Ithaca, 1987). The social historians have all benefited from a close reading of the magisterial four-volume work published by a group of Mensheviks: see L. Martov, P. Maslov and A. Potresov (eds), *Obshchestvennoe dvizhenie v nachale XX-go veka* (St Petersburg, 1909–14). The latter is not a systematic, chronological account of events during the revolution. Rather, it consists of detailed and scholarly studies of political parties, political developments, the working class, the bourgeoisie, the intelligentsia and the peasantry, to mention only some of the more important topics. Written from a Marxist and Menshevik perspective, the work is a gold mine of reliable information.
4 See, for example, S. S. Oldenburg, *Last Tsar: Nicholas II. His Reign and His Russia*, transl. by Leonid I. Mihalap and Patrick J. Rollins, 4 vols (Gulf Breeze, 1975–77); Dominic Lieven, *Nicholas II: Twilight of the Empire* (New York,

1993); V. A. Maklakov, *Vtoraia Gosudarstvennaia Duma (vospominaniia sovremennika)* (Paris, n.d. [1948?]); V. N. Kokovtsev, *Iz moego proshlogo: vospominaniia 1903–1919gg.* (Paris, 1933).

5 The point is made by John Keep in his *The Rise of Social Democracy in Russia* (Oxford, 1963), p. 150. However, Keep concluded that the term 'The Revolution of 1905' is too well established to be discarded.

6 For a more detailed statement of this position, see Abraham Ascher, *The Revolution of 1905*, 2 vols (Stanford, 1988–92), *passim*.

7 Walter Laqueur, *Terrorism* (Boston, 1977), pp. 145–6.

8 On this cable, see Richard Pipes, *The Russian Revolution, 1899–1919* (New York, 1990), p. 309.

9 For example, in 1901, the government adopted an experiment in police unionization, proposed by the police officer S. V. Zubatov. Government officials organized a series of 'police unions' that were designed to draw workers into organizations loyal to the government but, within two years, one of the police unions was believed to have been the moving force behind a general strike in Odessa, the first work stoppage of such dimensions in Russia. The experiment was immediately ended. However, in 1904, the minister of internal affairs, V. K. Plehve, at a loss as to how to defuse the protest movement of the working class, permitted Father Georgii Gapon to revive 'police socialism', with results, after the firing upon Gapon's followers on 'Bloody Sunday', that were far more explosive than those in Odessa. See Jeremiah Schneiderman, *Sergei Zubatov and Revolutionary Marxism: The Struggle for the Working Class in Tsarist Russia* (Ithaca, 1976).

10 S. M. Dubnov and G. Ia. Krasnyi-Admoni (eds), *Materialy dlia istorii antievreiskikh pogromov v Rossii* (Petrograd, 1919–23), Vol. 1, p. ix; S. M. Dubnow, *History of the Jews in Russia and Poland*, transl. by I. Friedlaender (Philadelphia, 1918), Vol. 2, pp. 247–8, 283; and Vol. 3, p. 127. See also Louis Greenberg, *The Jews in Russia* (New Haven, 1965), Vol. 2, pp. 23–4.

11 See, for example, I. Michael Aronson, *Troubled Waters: The Origins of the 1881 Anti-Jewish Pogroms in Russia* (Pittsburgh, 1990), pp. 15–17 and *passim*; John D. Klier and Shlomo Labroza (eds), *Pogroms: Anti-Jewish Violence in Modern Russian History* (Cambridge, 1992), p. 51; and Hans Rogger, *Jewish Policies and Right-Wing Politics in Imperial Russia* (Berkeley, 1986), p. 30.

12 V. I. Lenin, *Collected Works*, Vol. 8 (Moscow, 1977), p. 146.

13 See Abraham Ascher, 'German Socialists and the Russian Revolution of 1905', in Ezra Mendelsohn and Marshal S. Shatz (eds), *Imperial Russia 1700–1917: State, Society, Opposition. Essays in Honor of Marc Raeff* (DeKalb, 1988), pp. 260–78.

14 Bernard Pares, *A Wandering Student: The Story of a Purpose* (Syracuse, 1948), pp. 132–3.

2 Psychohistorical approaches to 1905 radicalism

Anna Geifman

Shifting the emphasis from ideological justifications for revolutionary activism to psychological conditions that contributed to the escalation of political violence in Russia after the turn of the twentieth century, this chapter analyses the impact of a rapid breakdown of traditional collective identities on the behaviour patterns of Russian radicals. It focuses on individual pressures and limitations, camouflaged motives and aberrant personality states as the driving forces behind extremist tendencies, and demonstrates that, as part of the turbulent individuation process, self-loathing and self-denial were often projected externally, manifesting themselves in aggressive and destructive political acts.

In considering revolutionary politics in late-imperial Russia, historians tend to take for granted that radical behaviour was principally a response to oppressive socio-economic and political conditions under the autocratic regime. Accordingly, scholars traditionally accept the extremists' justifications for subversive activities and focus on ideological viewpoints and controversies within the anti-government camp. They also typically ascribe primary importance for the growth and development of the opposition movement around the turn of the twentieth century to theoretical polemics regarding the most befitting revolutionary tactics.

Grievous economic conditions and complex relations among and within the newly emerging social groups during the initial phases of the country's industrialization indeed seemed to validate the radical socialists' claim that exploitation, competition and the alienation of individuals – those odious features of capitalism – would disappear only after the overthrow of the old regime. Likewise, the unexpected and devastating effects of the Russo-Japanese War and the generally inflexible policies of the autocratic government encouraged revolutionary action as a logical course. Yet, as Walter Laqueur has noted, despite their obvious importance, 'objective circumstances *per se* are not a sufficient, perhaps not even a necessary condition' for the escalation of political extremism and violence,[1] and the process of becoming a revolutionary is hardly self-evident. Ideological rhetoric notwithstanding, numerous extremists demonstrated not only the utter disregard for the interests of the people that they purportedly loved and sought to liberate, but also for the fundamentals of their own utopian doctrines. Significantly, by joining the radical camp, participants sought to undermine and overturn the world of which they were integral parts and thus, in effect, were engaged in self-destructive behaviour. In analysing the revolutionary process, therefore, it is methodologically misleading to rely primarily on the more than questionable *post factum* rationalizations offered by the radicals themselves in order to justify their involvement in extremist politics. A psychohistorical approach warrants a substantial shift in focus from the revolutionaries' ostensible ideological motives to the psychological environment that shaped and provided the venues for expression of personal needs, based on deeper and often aberrant inner states.

Against their penchant to bemoan the suffering masses, many of those who came to espouse the revolution around the turn of the century exhibited the type of mentality best summarized by the then popular motto 'the worse, the better' (*chom khuzho, tem luchsho*). In essence, they presupposed that further deterioration of Russia's domestic situation, including grave agrarian and urban problems intensified by the country's swift modernization, would contribute to the growing instability of the regime and benefit the revolutionary cause. In accordance with their assumption that people's proclivity for protest was directly proportionate to the degree of suffering, the radicals condemned any liberal measures aimed at helping the peasants during famines, arguing that such charities deviously helped the government to deal with general impoverishment and only strengthened the 'sickly regime'.[2] 'If, God willing,' wrote one revolutionary in a private letter, 'we have a bad harvest this year, you'll see what a game will begin.'[3] Similarly, the extremists considered any official action damaging to the welfare of the people to be propitious for the revolution. In this context, a typical reaction of radical émigrés to the news of Bloody Sunday is particularly revealing. One revolutionary recounted these early days in 1905: 'Surprisingly, no one among the Russians was depressed ... On the contrary, [they] were in a lively, uplifted mood. It was clear that 22 [9] January would be the signal for a victorious struggle.'[4]

Deeply felt compassion for the people's plight, therefore, was not necessarily among the primary stimuli for participation in revolutionary politics. Moreover, it is necessary further to question the radicals' motives, due to their propensity to discard their own fundamental theoretical principles for the sake of practical (or tactical) advantages, or to ignore ideology altogether. Initial signs of this tendency were already present in the nineteenth century. Yet, in comparison with most of their theory-oriented predecessors, for whom the intricate details of the revolutionary socialist dogma were essential both in forming their outlook and in guiding their activities, in the post-1900 era extremists evinced a considerably lower level of intellectual and ideological awareness. Their behaviour also demonstrated less inclination towards selfless idealism and dedication to the cause. By the outbreak of the 1905 Revolution, the prevalent prototype – branded by contemporaries 'the new type' or 'the new breed' of radical – dominated the anti-government camp numerically and in spirit, its psychology showing signs of 'liberation . . . from all moral restraints'.[5]

Indifference not only to conventional but also to revolutionary ethics was particularly common among the combatants (*boeviki*) involved in daily polit-ical assassinations and various forms of expropriation, including robbery, extortion and blackmail – acts that in the nineteenth century radicals had rejected with 'unconcealed feeling[s] of disgust'.[6] This new type of terrorism became 'so addictive that it was often carried out without even weighing the moral questions posed by earlier generations'.[7] In fact, it was often difficult to distinguish between an allegedly altruistic, politically motivated rebel and a common criminal, especially in cases involving individuals with lengthy his-tories of contact with the police authorities. Such a person might initially be arrested for felonious behaviour, then several years later be sentenced to a term of imprisonment for taking part in a terrorist attempt, and eventually end up in court again on rape charges.[8] Contrasting sharply with the traditionally accepted portrait of the selfless revolutionary idealist were – among innumerable other examples – members of an anarchist gang operat-ing in the Moscow area: a navy deserter, who claimed responsibility for eleven murders, although admittedly failing to grasp the meaning of the group's programme until his arrest; his girlfriend, a registered prostitute; another fugitive sailor, who had been sentenced to hard labour for taking part in killing a priest and robbing a church; and that convict's lover, a thief with a police record.[9] Overwhelming confusion between the activities of self-proclaimed 'freedom fighters' and common criminals, who used revolutionary rhetoric to justify pure banditry, became the theme of a contemporary joke:

'How does a murderer become a revolutionary?'
'When, Browning [pistol] in hand, he robs a bank.'
'How does a revolutionary become a murderer, then?'
'In the same way!'[10]

Theoretical incompatibility of party doctrines with terrorist ventures – as, for example, was the case with the Marxists – did not restrain any of the Social Democratic organizations operating in the Russian Empire after the turn of the century from supporting and often participating in individual acts of violence.[11] Nor did dogmatic discrepancies prevent extremists of various (and often rival) organizations from joining forces in preparation for political assassinations and expropriations. They frequently acted sponta-neously and indiscriminately, without sanction from the parties they claimed to represent.[12] More often than not, they were either illiterate or semi-literate, 'green youths, absolute babes in the political sense', according to one revolutionary; they had great trouble verbalizing (much less defend-ing) their 'extremely obscure perception of the revolution' and were unaware of the basic differences among party programmes.[13] The relatively few combatants who were sophisticated enough to develop a philosophical outlook typically considered debate over theory to be idle talk and an excuse to evade fighting. Convinced anarchist Fedor Nazarov, for example, found himself a member of the Socialist-Revolutionary Party's Combat Organization but 'in his views stood far from the PSR programme'; as did Boris Moiseenko, 'a man of independent and original opinions [and] from the party's point of view ... a heretic', who 'regarded conferences, meetings and congresses with badly concealed disdain. He believed in terror alone'. Likewise, the SR Abram Gots declared himself to be a follower of Immanuel Kant, while terrorist Mariia Benevskaia was an ardent Christian who never parted with the Gospels.[14] Thus, despite ideological squabbles among party leaders in Paris, Geneva and other centres of émigré politics, dogmatic controversies seem to be less than relevant for the numerous extremist practitioners operating inside Russia – a phenomenon suggesting that theoretical ideals might not have been the essential motives that had driven them to violence. Lofty rhetoric, to which their creed was often reduced, served as rationalization of the deeper drives that were instigating extremist behaviour.

'The degeneration of the revolutionary spirit', of which the radicals themselves were well aware,[15] occurred simultaneously with (and largely as a result of) the democratization of their ranks – something which presented a marked contrast to the situation in the nineteenth century, when the underground circles consisted predominantly of men from privileged society. By 1905, the overwhelming majority of the extremists issued from various new social groups, whose members suddenly found themselves out of place when the traditionally static autocratic system was undermined by intricate socio-cultural transformations – post-emancipation agricultural developments, industrialization, urbanization and the spread of education.

Amid rampant poverty, drunkenness and diseases in the cities' slums, typical of early phases of the industrialization, legions of industrial labourers became most susceptible to radical indoctrination. Young (and predominantly single) men from impoverished peasant families, who had migrated from the countryside, swarmed the cities as first generation proletarians and performed at least 50 per cent of all SR terrorist acts, with the percentage of worker-terrorists in other radical groups being even higher.[16] For their part, as a result of rapidly changing family relations, many young girls from various social strata could no longer be confined to the conventionally prescribed role of a woman at home, yet, as a rule, they found little opportunity to realize their intellectual or social ambitions.[17] The government's rigidly conservative policies with regards to higher education and career opportunities drove these women into the ranks of radical outcasts, the revolutionary milieu being the only one where females could feel almost equal to their male comrades, who gave them ample opportunity to assert themselves through taking part in dangerous underground operations. Women thus came to comprise approximately a quarter of all Russian terrorists and nearly one-third of the SR Combat Organization.[18] Finally, representatives of various minority groups within the Empire (including the traditional Jewish communities, the nationalities of the Caucasus, Poland and the Baltic provinces), who were all subject to varying degrees of national or religious discrimination, joined the Russian radical camp much more frequently than ever before. In sum, by the outbreak of the 1905 Revolution, the collective portrait of the revolutionary movement 'became as [socially] complex as the social structure of Imperial Russia itself'.[19]

'Things fall apart; the centre cannot hold.' Although written about Ireland, this line from W. B. Yeats's 'Second Coming' perfectly describes Russia at the turn of the twentieth century. Along with the long-term socio-economic processes that undermined traditional ways of life, old forms of communication and time-honoured customs and social practices were becoming impeded by a growing disregard not only for the official Ortho-dox Church but also for the very fundamentals of faith and Christian spiritu-ality. In many ways, the country was catching up with other European societies in renouncing organized religion and traditional communal and family forms of life, and in espousing individualism as a social norm. In other words, Russia was rapidly turning into a 'modern society', the main attribute of which was a special emphasis on the hitherto unrecognized powers and responsibilities of the individual.

The break with age-old communal traditions, based on co-operative culti-vation of land and on the Russian Orthodox adherence to *sobornost'* (conjoint God-worship), occurred too abruptly to allow a smooth transformation from collectivism to individualism. Scores of displaced and unsettled individuals – neophytes as far as urban life was concerned – experienced the new situ-ation as arduous and disheartening. Perhaps more consequential than miser-able economic conditions, psychological adaptation to the alien milieu and lifestyle was exceedingly slow. Many thousands had severed physical and spiritual ties with their indigenous communities, but only a few displayed the ability to function outside a collective and to react adequately to new obligations of life as 'I', not 'we'.[20]

Ordinarily, a turn-of-the-century 'modern Russian'[21] had no experience as a separated self. The traditional communal life spared him from angst-provoking attributes of individualistic existence – self-doubts and self-asser-tion; inner conflicts and consequences of their projections; the need for privacy and simultaneous fear of isolation. With the old defence mechanisms inefficacious outside of the commune, the individual lacked the means to deal with the anxiety (concomitant with alienation) that was inevitably invading his life. Increased competition that intensified interpersonal hostil-ity in a stratified, urbanized and mechanized environment reinforced fear, confusion and distress.[22] Life turned harsh, discomfiting and devoid of basic social security when traditional mores and ways of mutual assistance no longer provided rudimentary economic protection. Fast-paced city life, 'in which factories replaced cathedrals as the great monuments of a new society' and 'the instruments of technology had come between humankind and

God',[23] did not offer a relief for anxiety and the feelings of helplessness to the germinating self.[24] The 'I', isolated as it was from any accustomed communal ways, submerged into ego-dystonic confusion when forced by modern metropolitan life to face all the challenges of being an adult individual.[25]

Indeed, from the point of view of psychological development, many of the proverbially 'superfluous people' were infant-like: they exhibited discordant or fluid personalities, which lacked cohesiveness and distinct ego boundaries. Few found sufficient ego resources to face the demands that modern life made on their puerile, weak, maladjusted and often disturbed selves.[26] Estranged from their new environment and frustrated, some – primarily representatives of new social groups – engaged in extremist politics, since they 'could not envision a satisfactory place for themselves in the future, if Russia were to remain as it was'.[27] For many, including members of the intelligentsia, destructive behaviour, which often took the form of political action, became an outlet for inner tensions.

Along with other students of human behaviour, Karen Horney has noted 'the general principle of finding satisfaction' – that is, reducing the devastating effects of anxiety – 'by losing the self in something greater, by dissolving the individuality, by getting rid of the self with its doubts, conflicts, pains, limitations and isolation'. Nietzsche called this tendency 'liberation from the *principium individuationis*'.[28] Numerous unsettled personalities thus sought to escape the traumatic aspects of individualization and yielded to their urgency to abandon themselves by experimenting with 'alternative life-styles'. Literature of this period, from Mikhail Artsybashev's low-grade *Sanin* (1907) to Andrei Bely's phenomenal *Petersburg* (1913), illustrates a variety of fads and compulsions which entailed attempts to rescind people's tormented psyche – to dissolve or drown their nascent selves in alcohol or in drug-induced nirvana, in the hitherto unthinkable (and often blatantly perverse) 'uninhibited sexuality', and in toying with the occult and with superficial components of exotic cultures. These tendencies were among the essential features of the Russian Silver Age, a period of intense cultural vicissitude, intellectual turmoil and aesthetic decadence. It 'was as if something was in the air hovering over each and every one of us', poetess Zinaida Gippius remembered: 'People ... rushed about, never understanding why they did so, nor knowing what to do with themselves.'[29]

As part of the Silver Age, some of Russia's highly individualistic and cultivated minds demonstrated unprecedented spiritual energy. Like the rest of the country, they had to confront and cope with the challenges of modernization; yet the emotionally and spiritually strongest found this to be invigorating, rather than stifling, as they transmuted these challenges into sources of creativity and emotional release.[30] The era's feast of refinement, of vibrant intellect and spirituality, manifested itself in contemporary musical, artistic, philosophical and theological masterpieces – works of profound aestheticism, insight and courage. This, however, was the road of the chosen, the few who found requisite ego resources to uphold and nurture their selves, notwithstanding all the pressures of individualization. At the same time, for many vulnerable and 'undefined personalities', extravagant and sometimes-obsessive experimentation that aimed to fill the inner void became a way of life.

Erratic diversions, which changed at a whim in a kaleidoscopic fashion, had a characteristic ulterior purpose. Although the infantile personalities – 'the not staunch' and the 'half-cracked',[31] according to Bely's confession – rationalized their behaviour by extolling the sanctity of unique self-expression, they in fact realigned themselves with a new, non-conformist community, as a means of reducing individualization-related anxiety. As Bely put it: 'lonely paths amidst snow piles of misunderstanding' lead to places of refuge, in which 'everyone of the misunderstood finds an asylum where ... each, in his escape from his already remote place of origin, develops ... the cult of the new home'.[32] The 'border generation'[33] community thus reasserted the power of the collective 'we' over the painfully maladjusted 'I'.

Moreover, this new kinship yielded its own archetype to be admired and emulated. The 'beau ideal' was a person burdened by inner contradictions, 'of which the youth ... was proud, as if these were war wounds ... The divided, bizarre type ... was therefore customary among the best, most nervous and sensitive young people' of the time.[34] Many in the new generation, revolted by what they deemed the philistine values of the traditional culture, applauded 'to everything *"abnormal"*, *"odd"*, *"sick"*, and also expressed themselves anti-socially'.[35] According to the writer Aleksei Tolstoi, 'These were the days when love, and all sane and kindly emotions were regarded as commonplace and old-fashioned, when ... neurasthenia [was an attribute] of refinement ... People invented vices and perversions for themselves' – anything rather than be regarded as banal. 'Destructiveness was considered a sign of good taste',[36] and an inescapable 'sense of decay' accompanied the daring break with the old culture.[37]

Fascinated with a symbiosis of destructive energy and artistic ecstasy, people looked for and found 'poetry in death'[38] which contributed to the catastrophic increase in suicides in Russia around 1905 and a real 'suicide epidemic' in St Petersburg.[39] Similarly, in the process of searching for a 'different spirituality' and an iconoclastic ideology that was to become an invigorating guiding force and was to provide new meaning to their existence, many came to embrace the notion of socio-political revolution as a new faith.[40] Like the revolution in the arts, the all-out revolt against the traditional establishment was an integral feature of the Silver Age mentality: 'Circumstances were ideal. The pre-war years, the boiling pot ... Everything that declared itself as a protest was received with sympathy and curiosity; any scandal discharged the atmosphere and freshened stale air.'[41] 'Revolution was becoming the fashion',[42] remembered the SR party leader Viktor Chernov. According to the country's most renowned contemporary poet, Aleksandr Blok, 'one could already begin to sense the smell of burning, blood, and iron in the air'.[43]

The revolution also provided perhaps the most auspicious long-term solution for those incoherent and malfunctioning selves who sought to lose their feeble individuality in a new 'larger than life' experience by joining the cohort of enthusiastic devotees. For those who had experimented with various addictive fads to escape from themselves, participation in extreme political activism might have been analogous to narcotics or perhaps cheap-thrill entertainment – encompassing 'exaggerated gestures, flamboyant colours and noises, and . . . gripping, if garish' excitement. As one revolutionary declared, 'I cannot live peacefully. I like danger, so as to feel the thrill.'[44] His colleague admitted that his role in terrorist operations was just another 'very interesting game'.[45]

Yet the thrill generated by subversive action had one essential advantage over all other forms of marginal behaviours aimed at self-annulment. Unlike those engaged in other diversions, in which the individual must cope with nadirs between peaks of excitement, the revolutionaries could forever pursue their visionary ideals.[46] They were thus able to negate themselves entirely by becoming one with a new collective – the party – for the sake of a great common cause, affirmed by their recently acquired ideology.[47] Having submerged themselves in the stormy waters of revolutionary struggle, the proselytes did indeed behave 'selflessly', but only in the strict morphological sense of the word. Simultaneously, they began to operate under a 'delusion of . . . pseudo-greatness', which astonished even their own comrades.[48] This delusion could be sustained only in total isolation from life outside the radicals' tiny underground community – as if, as one young terrorist put it, 'the world did not exist'.[49]

Abandoning one's self in a 'new commune', a tightly knit revolutionary conspiracy, was an opportunity to forsake all normalcy. Indeed, this was an option exclusively for the individual whose abnormal emotional state coincided with and suited the aberrant climate within the terrorist cell. For, according to a renegade extremist leader, this was 'the life of a hunted wolf':

> The dominant awareness is that he must be prepared to perish not just today or tomorrow, but any second. The only hope of coping with this awareness is to push out of mind many matters which for someone who wishes to be a mature human being require thought. In this condition, an attachment of any seriousness and of any kind is a genuine misfortune. The study of any question . . . is unthinkable. A plan of action, minimally complex, minimally comprehensive, is not even allowed to enter one's mind. Apart from five to ten like-minded persons, one must deceive from morning to night literally everyone; one must hide from everyone, suspect in everyone an enemy.[50]

Although contributing to the underlying purpose of self-repudiation, life in the clandestine collective often proved insufficient to ease tormenting inner tensions, which led the radicals to seek escape through acts of physical self-annihilation and motivated numerous terrorist suicide attacks. In fact, terrorism offered an opportunity to flirt with 'the mysticism of death', quite in accordance with the ethos of the Silver Age – something that extremists acknowledged when referring to the 'suicidal urge' that was widespread in their ranks.[51] Some of the radicals had made one or more attempts on their own lives even prior to their involvement in revolution; and, for many who desired to die, a terrorist act presented an indirect way of doing away with their selves shredded by unresolved conflicts and distress.[52] This tendency was particularly widespread among the youngest (frequently adolescent) extremists who had contemplated killing themselves before becoming involved in political violence. Some of these were hysterical personalities, prone to 'nervous fits'; others exhibited more serious pathological behaviour and received formal treatment for psychological disorders. Medical experts declared many mentally unbalanced extremists to be not accountable for their actions, and one liberal psychologist recognized them as 'mad ones who choose the means of political assassination in order to end their lives'.[53] Such was the case of the unmistakably deranged Evstiliia Rogozinnikova, a young SR who, on 15 October 1907, wore thirteen pounds of nitroglycerin strapped to her body as she made her way into the offices of the St Petersburg Prison Department. She shot and killed its head, Maksimovskii, but was apprehended before she had a chance to perish by blowing up the entire building.[54] For her part, the SR Zinaida Konopliannikova, who assassinated Major-General Min on 13 August 1906, was so eager to end her deep torment that, according to an observer witnessing the last moments of her life, she 'went to her execution as one would go to a holiday festivity'.[55]

The radicals' emotional impairment and outright abnormality was often recognized even by their own comrades, who described them as 'turbulent and unbalanced', 'hysterical', 'completely abnormal' or 'crazy'.[56] It is also evident in frequent mental breakdowns and a large variety of diagnosed long-term psychological illnesses, including severe depression and paranoia, and in manic and unquestionably sadistic behaviour, marked by acts of striking and senseless cruelty.[57] Significantly, psychologically unstable revolutionary activists in Russia often gravitated towards terrorism – the most extreme form of political activism.[58] This observation finds strong support in the direct link – recognized since the nineteenth century – between mental imbalance and aggressive impulses.[59] Scholars agree that, although there is no specific psychological pattern, 'a particular personality constellation, a uniform terrorist mind . . . people with particular personality traits and tendencies are drawn disproportionately to terrorist careers'. As was the case elsewhere, in Russia 'individuals with narcissistic and borderline personality disturbances',[60] as well as people suffering from some anti-social personality disorder,[61] were strikingly common among the terrorists and, while the ones suffering from psychosis were exceptions, neurotics seemed to be the prevalent type.

The scope of this discussion hardly warrants a venture into the intricacies of the long-standing controversy about deep causes of ego pathologies, to which many psychologists attribute extremist behaviour.[62] Suffice it to note that the salient traits of the revolutionary personality were a narcissistic feeling that others were somehow 'less than human' and a collateral inability to recognize another person's existence as autonomous from one's own.[63] Regarding people exclusively as the means or the instruments to achieve his objectives, the archetypal rebel developed an extraneous attitude towards any single, nameless representatives of the ideational *narod* whose separate life contributed little, if at all, to 'historical progress' and the 'emancipation of the humankind'. In fact, the lack of ability to empathize with a human being-turned-object[64] might have been one reason why the extremists tended to validate their behaviour by accentuating the abstract notion of 'the masses', while employing complicated theories to justify the need for their liberation. A classic literary illustration of this psychological type is Dostoevsky's Ivan Karamazov, an iconoclast exasperated by the world's cruelty, who 'returns God His ticket' yet impatiently kicks away the defenceless, piteous man, who pleaded for a bit of his kindness.

Having thus dehumanized and objectified the individual, the radicals were intent upon asserting their *raison d'être* – the destruction of that world that they perceived as pernicious and incompatible with their own existence – and at anyone else's expense, if their objectives so required. A glaring, if extreme, example of this attitude was that of the SR Ekaterina Breshko-Breshkovskaia, venerated as an idol of the Russian revolution, who had abandoned her newborn son so as to be able to take part in activities aimed at bringing happiness to the people.[65] Such behaviour is understandable, if considered concurrently with the fact that people with personality disorders 'are very afraid of real, mature, intimacy ... emotional involvement, which is the result of interactions in constant and predictable (safe) proximity'. Numerous individuals with impaired psyche 'interpret intimacy ... as strangulation, the snuffing [out] of freedom' and 'are terrorized by it'.[66] They are thus incapable of either genuine emotional attachment and love (which are 'perceived as threats' to their undeveloped, perpetually puerile selves)[67] or for 'emotional life which ... appears to be shallow and reflects an absence of normal empathy for others'.[68]

Horney affirms that when a person is unable to assuage anxiety by means of emotional attachments and affection (however displaced, perverse, tentative or fake they may be), he is often driven to seek power and control, as a compensatory manoeuvre to alleviate tension. Investing in 'affection means obtaining reassurance through intensified contact with others, while striving for power ... means obtaining reassurance through loosening of the contact with others and through fortifying one's own position'. Yet, the neurotic quest for power as a protection, 'born out of anxiety' that is associated with feelings of inferiority, weakness and helplessness, serves also 'as a channel through which repressed hostility can be discharged'.[69] It is apparently more concordant with such a personality to turn anger into an instrument of self-mitigation rather than perpetually to repress it in an emotional relationship.

In other words, a hostile individual is better suited for a power game than for a game of love.

Moreover, 'striving for power serves as a protection against the danger of feeling or being regarded as insignificant. The neurotic develops a rigid and irrational ideal of strength which makes him believe he should be able to master any situation, no matter how difficult ... This ideal becomes linked with pride, and as a consequence the neurotic considers weakness not only as a danger but also as a disgrace.' As the next logical step there develops the 'desire to have control over others as well as over himself'. A medium for releasing underlying hostility, the tendency to dominate 'may be disguised in ... humanistic forms',[70] such as in taking the initiative in liberating the oppressed. In this case, rudimentary anger and aggression are externalized and expressed violently *vis-à-vis* designated oppressors. Detrimental external conditions facilitate the task of choosing targets of hatred required by the malignant inner state; but, quintessentially, socio-political reality is thus used as an alloplastic defence – to shift the darkness within (as well as the guilt and the blame for it) to the outside world.

Of course, not every Russian radical was mentally unbalanced, yet research on Russian terrorism yields ample evidence to demonstrate that emotionally damaged individuals employed sometimes-forceful arguments in support of revolutionary violence as sheer rationalizations of behaviour that was actually based on their inability to resolve their own inner conflicts, ubiquitous frustration and deep-seated anxiety. In the words of Jerrold Post, terrorists are 'driven to commit acts of violence as a consequence of psycho-logical forces, and ... special psycho-logic is constructed to rationalize acts they are psychologically compelled to commit'. Such individuals typically suffered from 'a damaged self-concept';[71] most frequently, at the root of their extremism was an all-pervading and relentless self-hatred – displaced and projected onto designated political enemies.[72]

For Fruma Frumkina, a physically deformed woman and a compulsively (and demonstratively) aggressive SR *boevik*, terrorist motives 'stemmed from a deep feeling of inadequacy and a desire to confirm her own importance as an individual'.[73] A confessional letter of another female terrorist, Lidiia Ezerskaia, revealed similar feelings of inferiority and boredom and a desperate need to relieve a depression resulting from a sense of personal triviality. Admitting that she had no talents and fearing that for her, at the age of 38, 'time was slipping away', Ezerskaia chose a sufficiently reactionary state official as a target for a terrorist act that was to give purpose to her otherwise empty life.[74] Another disgruntled and embittered individual, tormented by his meaningless existence, enunciated his motives for joining a terrorist group in St Petersburg: 'I am terribly fed up with my life. More than anything, I am sick of the way I lived before.'[75]

Historians have accentuated self-loathing and denial of one's identity as a driving force for radicalism in connection with the ongoing discussion about the participation of Jewish radicals in Russian revolutionary politics in numbers entirely disproportionate to their overall population in the Empire.[76] Thus, Leon Trotsky tried to dissociate himself from his traditional Jewish past and claimed that he did not understand Yiddish.[77] The Menshevik Lev Deich was even more direct in expressing Jewish self-hatred: 'We wanted the Jewish masses to assimilate as quickly as possible; everything that smelled of Jewishness called forth among many of us a feeling of contempt, if not more.'[78]

For their part, psychologists have stressed that fundamental discord, inducing hatred in the ailing self, as well as the hopelessness associated with the inability to find a solution for the inner *impasse*, are 'the basis from which envy is constantly generated. It is not so much an envy of something special, but what Nietzsche has described as *Lebensneid*, a very general envy of everyone who feels more secure, more poised, more happy, more straightforward, more self-confident.'[79] Inevitably, 'the neurotic will try to disguise the crudity of his begrudging attitude' and transform the diffused envy into a focused and justified one, directed at those who are perceived to have advantages.[80] This, in turn, may amplify the narcissistic feelings of personal deprivation, unhappiness and entitlement and cause them to become 'all-pervasive, demanding and aggressive' – such that they 'easily deteriorate' into open and unmitigated violence against others.[81] In this context, particularly revealing is the matter-of-fact reasoning of a young Russian revolutionary who planned an expropriation and counted on using half the loot to help the downtrodden proletarians and the other half to purchase for himself an estate abroad. He admitted that, 'as much as he sympathizes with the socialists . . . he considers their hope for a just social order totally unrealizable, [and] as much as he hates the bourgeoisie . . . he cannot help but envy it'.[82]

Vamik Volkan's research illuminates the relationship between internal psychological criteria, or the images of 'badness', and 'the need to have enemies'. In connecting intra-psychic dynamics and the process of projection, Volkan elucidates the tendency to relocate a sense of worthlessness to the 'outside', to some hated 'other', as a result of either dominating regression or a split in the self, which leads to weak differentiation between the inner and the outer. 'When kept inside, unintegrated bad units threaten the self's cohesiveness; when put out there at a safe distance and used for comparison with good self . . . they can enhance the sense of self.'[83] The revolutionary personalities, undermined by self-hatred and anxiety, thus doubtlessly sought to preserve their vulnerable selves via this process of externalization of intrinsic hostility.[84]

Many of those who suffered from devastating neurotic conflicts could rid themselves temporarily of distress by projecting onto others 'all the hated and devalued weakness within'. Unable to face subjectively perceived deficiencies and resultant self-loathing, in the pervading atmosphere of anti-government protest the revolutionaries easily found targets 'to blame and attack for their own inner weakness'.[85] They then welcomed any chance to express animosity by violent action sanctioned by loosely defined ideological beliefs, striking – randomly and *en masse* – against state employees, police and military officers, or anyone else labelled by their parties as an 'oppressor' or 'exploiter' and therefore a suitable target for assassination. Amid general violence and bloodshed in Russia during the first decade of the twentieth century – a period in which close to 17,000 people became victims of terrorist activities – it was common for the new type of radicals to fire or throw bombs into passing military and Cossack units or into their barracks, without provocation. Combatants on the streets for an evening's excursion would toss sulphuric acid in the face of the first uniformed street policeman or guard they encountered. 'Human life was cheapened' and soon 'was not worth a penny' to the assassins – or, as one revolutionary called them, the 'woodchoppers' (*drovokoly*). They even competed against each other to see who had committed the greatest number of robberies and murders, and often exhibited jealousy over others' successes. In the process that anarchist Iuda Grossman labelled 'a mechanical militancy', a postman would be killed for wearing a uniform, as would any 'bourgeois exploiter' because he was well dressed.[86] The displacement of malice and externalization of the urge to murder was evident in SR Lidiia Sture's repeated assertions that if she had not been able to enter a terrorist group she would have killed herself. Her colleague Frumkina, 'longing for terror' and self-confessedly unable to control herself, attacked literally every jailer at her hard-labour prison.[87]

The externalization of hostility further contributed to the radicals' yearning to lose themselves in the new revolutionary collective. According to James M. Glass, 'placing the self's internal sense of badness' outside, by defining the enemy, 'also strengthens group identity, since the hated other can be collectively shared and collectively destroyed'. The group then 'comes to see itself as exclusive, possessing a boundary the hated other may never pass or threaten . . . [T]he border separates the pure from the impure, . . . the polluted from the good', the saints from the villains.[88] This was exactly the case with the SR Combat Organization, which launched its large-scale terrorist campaign in 1902. Quickly, it turned into a sect, the members of which 'developed their own values and their own elitist *esprit de corps*' and conceived of themselves as the 'true bearers of Russia's revolutionary cross'. They not only committed terrorist acts in Russia's capitals, but also revered terror as a sacred thing.[89]

Volkan postulates that particular historical conditions may lead to 'group regression' and cause members of such groups to 'dehumanize' their enemies, to turn them into 'a stereotype of negative qualities' and 'non-human or inanimate suitable targets(s) of externalization'.[90] The Russian terrorists did precisely this, labelling targets of their attacks as 'beasts' and 'the watchdogs of the tsarist regime'.[91] In the process where an assailant 'group loses its own humanity in dehumanizing another', paradoxically, the attackers and their targets experience a psychological connection of 'shared anxiety'.[92] We thus return to the radical's anxiety, the ensuing pressure to invalidate or dehumanize the self and the related compulsion to undermine and annihilate the insufferable environment by means of political action: 'if we analyze the psychic reality of these men, we find that they were destroyers and not revolutionaries. They hated not only their enemies, they hated life itself'[93] — life, in which they felt alienated, superfluous, frustrated and angry, barely alive and miserable.

Psychologists, as well as fiction writers, have further noted the process of 'projection of various unendurable and repressed emotions onto nonhuman things', upon which a person 'can project various part aspects of himself, until such time as his ego is sufficiently strong to integrate them into his developing sense of self'.[94] Although this tendency is prevalent in children, the same phenomenon is evident in adults and may be attributable to the impaired revolutionary personalities — especially given their infantilism and thwarted states of autonomous ego-development. Individuals, whose malformed selves precluded adequate 'differentiation' from external stimuli,[95] thus extended their morbid (self-destructive) and mortal (aggressive) emotional states not only to their human enemies through the process of projective identification but also to their nonhuman environment,[96] which was then held to be wretched and deserving of destruction. Prominent British psychiatrist R. D. Laing demonstrates that the vacillating, split self is prone to project externally as aggression its own self-destructive attributes,[97] as does also Bely's radically minded protagonist, who refers to one of the most beautiful cities in the world as if it were a dismal and threatening place: 'Petersburg, Petersburg! Precipitating out as fog, you have pursued me ... Cruel-hearted tormentor! Restless spectre! For years you have attacked me.'[98] In line with Sam Vaknin's vivid description of the narcissistically disordered individuals, these lives are 'a reflection of ... [their] psychological landscape: barren, paranoiac, tormented, guilt ridden'. They feel 'compelled to do unto others' what they perpetrate unto themselves and gradually transform all around them into replicas of their aggressive, 'conflictive, punishing personality structures'.[99]

Simultaneously destructive and self-destructive, the revolutionaries were entangled in a vicious circle of hostility: projecting their deep-seated animosity, they also necessarily suffered from indirect (yet devastating) effects of self-loathing, since it was directed at their own insufferable world — a warped mental product of their impaired psyche.[100] The compounded hatred brought forth a subjectively unbearable situation, which (also subjectively) called for externalization — immediate direct action, aggression and the annihilation of the obnoxious environment. Having armed themselves with a variety of theoretical and ideological schemes, which rationalized their drives by delineating (and finding ways to correct) the fundamental corruption in the old order, the new believers set out on the path of destruction. As a culmination of this process, the smallest spark could start a conflagration of bottled-up rage, when external circumstances came to provide auxiliary impetus to the inner ones. These immediate socio-economic, political and military circumstances, such as defeat in the Russo-Japanese War and the events of Bloody Sunday in St Petersburg in January 1905, took the form of anti-government revolt. Its inmost purpose was to shatter to pieces the world to which the radicals did but could not belong because their own emotional world was so damaged. Thus, the fury that turned Russia into a revolutionary boiling pot in the initial years of the twentieth century first smouldered in the souls of the country's inhabitants.[101]

Notes

1 Walter Laqueur, *Terrorism* (Boston, 1977), p. 145.
2 O. V. Aptekman, 'Partiia "Narodnogo Prava"', *Byloe*, Vol. 7 (1907), No. 19, p. 189. See also G. Ul'ianov, 'Vospominaniia o M. A. Natansone', *Katorga i ssylka*, Vol. 89 (1932), p. 71.
3 'Iz otcheta o perliustratsii dept. politsii za 1908g.', *Katorga i ssylka*, Vol. 27 (1928), p. 156.
4 O. Piatnitskii, *Zapiski bol'shevika* (Moscow, 1956), p. 65.
5 Petr Struve, cited in A. Serebrennikov (ed.), *Ubiistvo Stolypina. Svidetel'stva i dokumenty* (New York, 1986), p. 319. See also A. Lokerman, 'Po tsarskim tiur'mam. V Ekaterinoslave', *Katorga i ssylka*, Vol. 25 (1926), p. 186.
6 'Iz obshchestvennoi khroniki', *Vestnik Evropy*, Vol. 9 (1906), pp. 422–3.
7 Norman M. Naimark, 'Terrorism and the Fall of Imperial Russia' (unpublished lecture at Boston University, 4 April 1986), p. 21.
8 E. Koval'skaia, 'Po povodu stat'i M. P. Orlova "Ob Akatui vremen Mel'shina"', *Katorga i ssylka*, Vol. 52 (1929), p. 164. For examples, see Anna Geifman, *Thou Shalt Kill: Revolutionary Terrorism in Russia, 1894–1917* (Princeton, 1993), p. 138; and *Gosudarstvennyi Arkhiv Rossiiskoi Federatsii (GARF), f.* 102 (DPOO), *op.* 1915, *d.* 12 (Chapter 6, pp. 1–2). Since any criminal behaviour destabilized the socio-political order, some radicals considered it 'socially progressive' and sometimes declared bandits to be 'the only true revolutionaries in Russia': P. P. Zavarzin, *Zhandarmy i revoliutsionery* (Paris, 1930), p. 180, cited in M. Slonim, *Russkie predtechi bol'shevizma* (Berlin, 1922), p. 47.
9 Zavarzin, *Zhandarmy*, pp. 180–1, 185.
10 *Sekira*, Vol. 12 (1906), p. 7, in Hoover Institution Archives, Stanford, Calif.: Boris I. Nicolaevsky Collection (hereafter HIA Nicolaevsky), box 436, folder 2.
11 The Social Democrats consistently violated their official stand that, in accordance with Marxist theory, 'using bombs for individual terrorist acts was out of the question since the party rejected individual terror as a means of struggle'. For detailed discussion see Geifman, *Thou Shalt Kill*, Chapter 3.
12 Ibid., Chapter 6.
13 Moskvich, 'K istorii odnogo pokusheniia', *Byloe*, Vol. 14 (1912), pp. 38–9. See also *Al'manakh. Sbornik po istorii anarkhicheskogo dvizheniia v Rossii* (Paris, 1909), pp. 45, 115; and Lokerman, 'Po tsarskim tiur'mam', pp. 186, 189.
14 Boris Savinkov, *Vospominaniia terrorista* (Khar'kov, 1926), pp. 40, 92, 194–6.
15 HIA Nicolaevsky, box 12, folder 1: Grigorii Gershuni, 'Ob ekspropriatsiiakh' (undated letter to comrades), p. 1. See also M. Rakovskii, 'Neskol'ko slov o Sirorskom', *Katorga i ssylka*, Vol. 41 (1928), p. 147; and Petr Kropotkin, *Russkaia revoliutsiia i anarkhizm. Doklady chitannye na s''ezde Kommunistov-Anarkhistov v oktiabre 1906 goda* (London, 1907), p. 40. SR terrorist leader Gershuni conceded that as many as nine-tenths of all expropriations were acts of common banditry. See HIA Nicolaevsky, box 12, folder 1: Unaddressed letter from G. Gershuni (23 February 1906).
16 Maureen Perrie, 'Political and Economic Terror in the Tactics of the Russian

Socialist Revolutionary Party Before 1914', in Wolfgang J. Mommsen and Gerhard Hirschfeld (eds), *Social Protest, Violence and Terror in Nineteenth- and Twentieth-Century Europe* (New York, 1982), p. 68 (Table 6.2). Naimark's figure is even higher: in his estimate, workers carried out some 70 per cent of SR terrorist acts: Naimark, 'Terrorism', p. 5.

17 Amy Knight, 'Female Terrorists in the Russian Socialist Revolutionary Party', *Russian Review*, Vol. 38 (1979), No. 2, pp. 144–5.

18 Laqueur, *Terrorism*, p. 121; Naimark, 'Terrorism', p. 5.

19 Norman M. Naimark, *Terrorists and Social Democrats: The Russian Revolutionary Movement under Alexander III* (Cambridge, Mass., 1983), pp. 241–2.

20 For an in-depth analysis of the role of the individual in the traditional Russian collective, and discussion of the relevant literature, see Daniel Rancour-Laferriere, *The Slave Soul of Russia: Moral Masochism and the Cult of Suffering* (New York, 1995), Chapter 9. For a revisionist approach, see Oleg Kharkhordin, *The Collective and the Individual in Russia: A Study of Practices* (Berkeley, 1999).

21 'Russian' here refers to any inhabitant of the Russian Empire, and the processes being described may be applied to representatives of the Russian Orthodox, Jewish and other ethnic and religious groups residing in the country. For stylistic purposes, the third person masculine is used throughout this chapter when referring to both males and females.

22 By virtue of their relocation to the city, the peasants might have felt 'anxiety over the loss of a cherished, omnipotent' unity with their familiar natural environment, which had been experienced as a 'harmonious extension' of their 'world-embracing' selves. Their agitation was likely to intensify still further as a result of their being overwhelmed by entirely foreign 'nonhuman material' in the urban setting. See Harold F. Searles, *The Nonhuman Environment* (New York, 1960), pp. 39, 19–20.

23 W. Bruce Lincoln, *Sunlight at Midnight: St Petersburg and the Rise of Modern Russia* (New York, 2000), p. 212.

24 Karen Horney notes that in modern Western-type societies there are very few, if any, means left to avoid anxiety through self-abrogation. Most importantly, the age-old possibility to dissolve one's individuality in the body of the Church (in the Russian case, in *sobornost'*) has largely lost attractiveness. Modern Western society provides no cultural means of relief for the psyche through self-negation; in fact, the process of fusing one's ego with a larger whole is constantly thwarted because the individualistic culture requires one 'to stand on his own feet, assert himself'. See Karen Horney, *Neurotic Personality of Our Time* (New York, 1937), pp. 278–9.

25 The newcomers to the city made attempts to simulate a comforting communal life: workers of the same trade, for example, united in the *artels*, where labour was performed in common and the profits shared by the participants. Similarly, students and workers of common geographical origins joined the so-called *zemliachestva* ('associations of the land'). These, however, were inadequate substitutions for the peasant economic and religious community and the traditional family structure.

26 Searles postulates that a final stage of human ego-development is connected to one's 'awareness of oneself as a living human *individual*, distinct from other human beings'. At the same time, he refers to individuals whose ego organization may be at a level 'comparable with so very primitive' infantile ego states (Searles, *The Nonhuman Environment*, pp. 43–4, 73).

27 Sherron Nay, 'The Maximalists' (unpublished manuscript), p. 29, cited in Anna Geifman (ed.), *Russia under the Last Tsar: Opposition and Subversion, 1894–1917* (Oxford, 1999), p. 14.

28 Horney, *Neurotic Personality*, p. 270.
29 Cited in Lincoln, *Sunlight at Midnight*, p. 212.
30 This tendency is consistent with Kernberg's finding that patients with 'higher sublimatory potential . . . who have been able to achieve some really creative development in a certain area of their life have a better prognosis than those who have no capacity in this regard'. See Otto Kernberg, *Borderline Conditions and Pathological Narcissism* (Northvale, N.J., 1997), pp. 252, 253.
31 Andrei Belyi, *Na rubezhe dvukh stoletii* (Chicago, 1966), p. 5.
32 Ibid., p. 4.
33 Ibid., p. 3.
34 Andrei Belyi, *Nachalo veka* (Moscow and Leningrad, 1933), p. 3.
35 Ibid.
36 Aleksei Tolstoi, *Ordeal* (Moscow, 1953), pp. 29–30.
37 E. Iu. Kuz'mina-Karavaeva, cited in Lincoln, *Sunlight at Midnight*, p. 210. The rebellion was admittedly nihilistic: 'We met under different banners; the banner that united us was the denial of life that had formed us and the struggle against [this] life': Belyi, *Na rubezhe*, p. 4. 'Breaking out of old patterns, whether individual or societal, is frightening, exhilarating, liberating, dangerous, and vitalizing', affirms psychologist James Bugental. Yet, 'breaking out . . . when done solely to break out, delivers only a brief jolt of energy and very quickly becomes deadening. Then we look for a bigger jolt, push the breaking-out further, risk losing the point of the whole thing. As with any act taken only in opposition to something else, it is still motivated by that something else, having no energy of its own.' See James F. T. Bugental, *Intimate Journeys* (San Francisco, 1990), p. 239.
38 Cited in Viacheslav Venozhinskii, *Smertnaia kazn'i terror* (St Petersburg, 1908), p. 28.
39 Roberta Ann Kaplan, '"A Total Negation of Russia": Russian Intellectual Perception of Suicide, 1900–1914' (unpublished paper, Harvard University, 1988), p. 32; Aleksei Nikolaevich Tolstoi, 'khozhdenie po mukam' (http://kulichki.com/moshkow/TOLSTOJA/hozhdenie1.txt). Fifteen hundred Petersburgers killed themselves in 1908 alone (Lincoln, *Sunlight at Midnight*, p. 208).
40 At the time when revolutionary bloodletting was becoming commonplace, a few among the literati felt that the impelling force behind it was deeper than all the politics: 'Some different higher principle is needed', said Blok, to replace the relinquished traditions and conventions. 'Since there is none, rebellion and violence of all sorts take its place.' See Alexander Blok, 'The People and the Intelligentsia', in Marc Raeff (ed.), *Russian Intellectual History: An Anthology* (Atlantic Highlands, 1978), p. 362.
41 Iurii Karabchievskii, *Voskresenie Maiakovskogo* (Munich, 1985), p. 86.
42 V. M. Chernov, *Pered burei* (New York, 1953), p. 169.
43 Cited in Lincoln, *Sunlight at Midnight*, p. 212.
44 G. Nestroev, *Iz dnevnika maksimalista* (Paris, 1910), p. 218.
45 Geifman (ed.), *Russia under the Last Tsar*, p. 8; International Institute of Social History, Amsterdam (IISH), *Arkhiv Partii sotsialistov-revoliutsionerov*, box 5, folder 518: 'Materialy o provokatorakh.'
46 Osip Mandelstam wrote:.

> We went insane from living indulgently.
> Wine before noon, by evening a heavy head.
> How can we sustain your feverish red.
> O drunken plague, and your vain revelry?

In Robert Tracy (ed.), *Osip Mandelstam's Stone* (Princeton, 1981), p. 131.

47   Historians have noted that, perhaps since the time of Bakunin, the notion of freedom in the mind of the Russian radicals was associated 'not with the *preservation* of individualism but rather its *total dissolution* in a collective form of unity that would free humankind from the suffering brought on by the selfish competitiveness of the capitalist bourgeoisie'. See Steven G. Marks, *How Russia Shaped the Modern World: From Art to Anti-Semitism, from Ballet to Bolshevism* (Princeton, 2004), cited from http://pup.princeton.edu/chapters/s7346.html (accessed February 2004).

48   IISH, *Arkhiv Partii sotsialistov-revoliutsionerov*, box 5, folder 518: 'Materialy o provokatorakh'. This attitude corroborates Alfred Adler's remark that 'behind everyone who behaves as if he were superior to others, we can suspect a feeling of inferiority which calls for very special efforts of concealment. It is as if a man feared that he was too small and walked on his toes to make himself seem taller.' See 'In the Words of Alfred Adler', http://www.tearsofllorona.com/adler.html (accessed March 2004).

49   Knight, 'Female Terrorists', pp. 152–3.

50   Lev Tikhomirov, quoted in Richard Pipes, *The Degaev Affair: Terror and Treason in Tsarist Russia* (New Haven, 2003), pp. 17–18.

51   Laqueur, *Terrorism*, pp. 127, 130, 135.

52   See, for example, Geifman, *Thou Shalt Kill*, p. 168. As Knight observes, 'Suicidal tendencies were part of terrorist mentality, for a terrorist act was often a suicide mission' (Knight, 'Female Terrorists', p. 150). For the same inclination among the nineteenth-century terrorists, see Pipes, *The Degaev Affair*, pp. 14–15.

53   Geifman, *Thou Shalt Kill*, pp. 321–2 (n. 96); IISH, *Arkhiv Partii sotsialistov-revoliutsionerov*, box 4, folder 346: clipping from *Russkoe slovo* No. 94 (25 April 1909); and Kaplan, '"A Total Negation of Russia"', p. 42.

54   Although obviously insane, Rogozinnikova was put on trial, during which she 'broke her silence only by periodic gales of laughter'. See P. G. Kurlov, *Gibel' imperatorskoi Rossii* (Moscow, 1991), pp. 90–1; and Naimark, 'Terrorism', p. 18.

55   Cited in Knight, 'Female Terrorists', p. 150.

56   Cited in Geifman, *Thou Shalt Kill*, pp. 170, 325 (n. 120). See also ibid., pp. 322–3 (ns 98, 100, 101).

57   For numerous examples, see ibid., pp. 166–72, 321–2 (ns 96, 98), 325 (ns 120, 121). Sometimes extremists were strikingly open about their true motives, as was one terrorist responsible for the death of nineteen police officers and gendarmes. He admitted after his arrest that 'in the beginning it was difficult for him to kill, but by the third or fourth time the act of taking a life was already making an unusually pleasant impression on him. Seeing the blood of his victim gave him a special feeling, and therefore he felt an increasing urge to experience this sweet sensation again. This is why he has committed so many murders, of which he does not repent in the least.' See P. P. Zavarzin, *Rabota tainoi politsii* (Paris, 1924), pp. 128–9.

58   Naimark, *Terrorists*, pp. 242–3.

59   Some terrorist leaders were aware of the connection between mental illness – or what they referred to as 'weak nerves' – and the proclivity for violence (Vera Figner, quoted in Pipes, *The Degaev Affair*, p. 17). Occasionally, party-affiliated 'head-hunters' even deliberately recruited mentally deranged individuals for combat work, a number of whom medical experts recognized as 'unconditional degenerates'. See Geifman, *Thou Shalt Kill*, p. 322 (n. 98).

60   Jerrold M. Post, 'Terrorist Psycho-Logic: Terrorist Behavior As a Product of Psychological Forces', in Walter Reich (ed.), *Origins of Terrorism* (Cambridge, 1990), pp. 27–8. According to Sam Vaknin, 'Terrorists . . . can be phenomenologically

described as narcissists in a constant state of deficient narcissistic supply.' See Sam Vaknin, 'Object Relations. The Psychology of Serial and Mass Killers', http://www.toddlertime.com/sam/matrix/killers.htm (accessed February 2004).

61 Kernberg stresses 'the continuum between the narcissistic personality and the antisocial personality', which, in his opinion, is 'an extreme form of pathological narcissism, with, among other features, a complete absence of an integrated superego'. See Kernberg, *Borderline Conditions*, p. 254.

62 Among other scholars, psychologists Jerrold M. Post, John W. Crayton and Richard M. Pearlstein analyse terrorism from the point of view of ego impairment. See the historiographical references and discussion in Rex A. Hudson, *Who Becomes A Terrorist and Why: The 1999 Government Report on Profiling Terrorists* (Guilford, Conn., 1999), pp. 31–2. Lloyd DeMause approaches the problem from the point of view of developmental injuries in 'The Childhood Origins of Terrorism', in *The Emotional Life of Nations*, http://www.psychohistory.com/htm/eln03_terrorism.html (accessed March 2004).

63 Sam Vaknin, *Malignant Self-Love*, http://samvak.tripod.com/faq21.html (accessed February 2004).

64 One of the most distinct traits of the narcissist is a lack of empathy: see Criterion 7 in *Diagnostic and Statistical Manual of Mental Disorders* (4th edition), DSM-IV (Washington, 1994), p. 661. The narcissist 'feels that no evil can be inflicted on machines, instruments, or extensions': http://www.toddlertime.com/sam/matrix/killers.htm (accessed February 2004); Sam Vaknin, 'The World of the Narcissist (Essay)', http://samvak.tripod.com/msla8.html (accessed February 2004).

65 Geifman (ed.), *Russia under the Last Tsar*, p. 7.

66 Sam Vaknin, 'Self Love and Self Destruction', http://samvak.tripod.com/7.html (accessed February 2004).

67 Vaknin, 'The World of the Narcissist'.

68 Kernberg, *Borderline Conditions*, p. 106.

69 Horney, *Neurotic Personality*, pp. 162–4, 166, 171.

70 Ibid., pp. 166–7, 174.

71 Post, 'Terrorist Psycho-Logic', p. 25.

72 Vaknin, *Malignant Self-Love*.

73 Knight, 'Female Terrorists', p. 153.

74 IISH, *Arkhiv Partii sotsialistov-revoliutsionerov*, box 1, folder 2: undated confessional letter from Lidiia Pavlovna Ezerskaia.

75 HIA, *Arkhiv Zagranichnoi Agentury Departamenta Politsii* (Okhrana Collection), box XXIVi, folder 1B: copy of a 14 March 1907 letter from a revolutionary in St Petersburg to Dmitriev in Geneva.

76 By 1901, almost 30 per cent of the individuals arrested for political crimes were Jews. In 1903, only 7 million of the 136 million inhabitants of the Russian Empire were Jewish (roughly 5 per cent), but the membership of the revolutionary parties was approximately 50 per cent Jewish. See Naimark, 'Terrorism', p. 4; and Leonard Schapiro, *Russian Studies* (New York, 1988), p. 266. Although many revolutionary leaders preferred not to use Jews as executors of terrorist acts, for fear of raising anti-Semitic sentiments, some Maximalist and anarchist groups did not have a choice: in their composition, they were almost entirely Jewish: Geifman, *Thou Shalt Kill*, pp. 34, 269–70 (n. 124).

77 Philip Pomper, *Lenin, Trotsky, Stalin* (New York, 1990), p. 90.

78 Henry J. Tobias, *The Jewish Bund in Russia* (Stanford, 1972), p. 18. For a general discussion of self-denial among the Jews, see Sander Gilman, *Jewish Self-Hatred* (Baltimore, 1986).

79 Horney, *Neurotic Personality*, p. 228.
80 Ibid., p. 182. See also Kernberg, *Borderline Conditions*, p. 106.
81 Vaknin, *Malignant Self-Love*.
82 V. I. Sukhomlin, 'Iz tiuremnykh skitanii', *Katorga i ssylka*, Vol. 55 (1929), p. 104. P. Murashev cites similar examples in 'Stolitsa Urala v 1905–1908gg.', *Katorga i ssylka*, Vol. 65 (1930), pp. 49, 51.
83 Vamik Volkan, *The Need to Have Enemies and Allies: From Clinical Practice to International Relationships* (Northvale, N.J., 1988), p. 33. For similar argument, see Julia Kristeva, *Strangers to Ourselves* (New York, 1991).
84 Scholars generally concur on the tendency to transform 'this internal turmoil into deep-seated aggression'. See, for example, Vaknin, *Malignant Self Love*.
85 Post, 'Terrorist Psycho-Logic', p. 31. In psychological terms, it is the Superego 'which is unpredictable, capricious, arbitrary, judgemental, cruel, and self-annihilating (suicidal). Externalising these internal traits is a way of alleviating internal conflicts and fears generated by this inner turmoil.' Such damaged self 'projects his civil war and drags everyone around him into a swirl of bitterness, suspiciousness, meanness, aggression and pettiness': http://samvak.tripod.com/faq21.html (accessed February 2004).
86 Further discussion and all citations are in Geifman, *Thou Shalt Kill*, pp. 21, 39–40, 137.
87 I. Zhukovskii-Zhuk, 'Pamiati Lidii Petrovny Sture', *Katorga i ssylka*, Vol. 19 (1925), p. 253 (cited in Knight, 'Female Terrorists', p. 153); Roizman, 'Vospominaniia o Frumkinoi', *Katorga i ssylka*, Vols 28–9 (1926), p. 383.
88 James M. Glass, *Psychosis and Power: Threats to Democracy in the Self and the Group* (Ithaca, 1995), p. 129.
89 Knight, 'Female Terrorists', p. 147. In general, the spirit of a religious order prevailed among the Russian extremists, as it does in other countries, where terrorist groups resemble sects or cults as much as ideological organizations. See Martha Crenshaw, 'Theories of Terrorism: Instrumental and Organizational Approaches', in David C. Rapoport (ed.), *Inside Terrorist Organizations* (London, 1988), p. 20. John W. Crayton suggests that the 'meaningful high ideals' of the political terrorist group 'protects the group members from experiencing shame' (cited in Hudson, *Who Becomes A Terrorist*, p. 31).
90 Volkan, *The Need to Have Enemies*, p. 120.
91 IISH, *Arkhiv Partii sotsialistov-revoliutsionerov*, box 3, folder 216. See also Geifman, *Thou Shalt Kill*, p. 134.
92 Volkan, *The Need to Have Enemies*, pp. 120–1.
93 Erich Fromm, *The Anatomy of Human Destructiveness* (New York, 1973), p. 279.
94 Searles, *The Nonhuman Environment*, pp. 79–80.
95 Ibid., p. 51.
96 'The sense of injury denies the neurotic the happiness of socialization, prevents his contact with society. It . . . hinders his spontaneity, the feeling of satisfaction . . . He is not destined to spread joy around himself' (Alfred Adler, *O nervicheskom kharaktere* (St Petersburg and Moscow), p. 129). One of Milan Kundera's characters expresses the same idea as follows:.

> [Y]ou are always living below the level of true existence, you bitter weed, you anthropomorphized vat of vinegar! You're full of acid . . . Your highest wish is to be able to see all around you the same ugliness you carry inside yourself. That's the only way you can feel for a few moments some kind of peace between yourself and the world. That's because the world, which is beautiful, seems horrible to you, torments you and excludes you.

See Milan Kundera, *The Farewell Party* (New York, 1977), p. 142.

 97 R. D. Laing, *Self and Others* (Harmondsworth, 1961), pp. 132–3.
 98 Andrei Bely, *Petersburg* (Bloomington, 1978), p. 148.
 99 According to Vaknin, the behaviour of such a person 'is dictated by forces that he cannot master. Most of the time he is not even conscious of why he is doing what he is doing ... Even when he can – he feels powerless to behave otherwise.' He 'is a pawn in the chess game played between the structures of his fragmented, fluid personality' (Vaknin, *Malignant Self Love*).
100 The 'internal agonizing conflicts lead the narcissist to hate his tormenting self. As a form of self-punishment, he then engages in self-destructive and self-defeating behaviours' (Vaknin, 'Self Love and Self Destruction'). It is worth mentioning here a clinically observed tendency on the part of those functioning either at a borderline or an openly psychotic level to blur the 'self–nonself limits, so that aggression is expressed indiscriminately against others or the self' (Kernberg, *Borderline Conditions*, p. 127).
101 'Pathological anger is neither coherent, not externally induced. It emanates from the inside and it is diffuse, directed at the "world" and at "injustice" in general. The personality disordered person is often able to identify the *immediate* cause of his anger. Still, upon closer scrutiny, the cause is found lacking and the anger excessive, disproportionate and incoherent ... While normal anger generates action directed at its source (or at least the planning or contemplation of such action) – pathological anger is mostly directed at oneself or even lacks direction altogether ("diffused anger").' For detailed discussion of pathological anger, see Vaknin, 'Object Relations'.

3   1905

The view from the provinces

Beryl Williams

New scholarship and increased access to archival sources since the collapse of the Soviet Union have enabled a rethinking of the period leading up to the Revolution of 1905 and of the revolution itself. This chapter looks at some of this new work with regard to the causes of the revolution and examines the year from the point of view of events in the provinces, especially the south and west of Russia, stressing the importance of local concerns and leaders and the importance of the idea of local self-government.

The end of the Soviet Union initiated a revival of interest in the last years of the tsarist regime, and the centenary of the Revolution of 1905 is a good moment to consider what has been achieved. It is still useful to describe 1905 as a 'revolution', although by most definitions of the term it does not qualify. Hannah Arendt's interpretation of revolution as a spontaneous, popular upheaval during which new forms of self-government or alternative political structures were developed from below, including factory committees, soviets and town councils, is perhaps most helpful.[1] Abraham Ascher's standard work on the Revolution of 1905 accepts the term as applicable, while Moira Donald has also recently made a convincing case for retaining it.[2] Moreover, 1905 is of interest for its own sake and not just as Lenin's 'dress rehearsal' for 1917. It raises questions pertinent to all revolutions: about causes and progress, the relationship of mass aspirations to party programmes, economic as opposed to political motivation, about spontaneity as opposed to organization and about the relationship of the periphery to the centre.

After decades of Soviet (and often Western) assumptions as to the inevitability of the collapse of the tsarist regime, the period centring on 1905 is now being radically reinterpreted, above all in the economic field. Enhanced availability of archives, especially provincial ones, is at last allowing detailed work to be done on local areas. This is especially important for 1905, when the periphery of the Empire was often more violent than the centre. Moreover, new interests – above all in the field of the new 'cultural history' – have shifted the focus of enquiry. The role of the political parties, so long the centre of concern, is now being played down in favour of the aspirations, discourse and actions of the popular movement itself.

Recent work has revised the traditional view that Russian agriculture was in crisis by the end of the century and that industry's phenomenal growth in the 1890s was at the expense of the peasantry and created a proletariat easily influenced by the revolutionaries. Although by no means universally accepted,[3] new work has complicated the picture and given a more positive account. It would now appear that Tocqueville may be more relevant than Marx in explaining the origins of 1905, and that the inverted 'J curve' described by J. C. Davies offers the best explanation as to why the revolution broke out.[4] Certainly Russia was more backward than the major European powers and the USA, but from the 1880s, when industrialization really took off, she was catching up fast. By 1905 Russia was one of the major economic powers, ranking fourth or fifth in the world, and was by then keeping up with her competitors' output. It was her population growth that kept per capita figures low. Her raw materials and wheat export capacity, together with her access to foreign loans, gave her capital to expand.

As early as 1977, James Y. Simms Jr wrote an article questioning the traditional picture of increasing peasant misery, and by the end of the 1980s others were coming to his support.[5] One expert has recently stated that the Russian economy by the early twentieth century had 'begun the process of overcoming its relative backwardness and was on the way to sharing the affluence of Western Europe and North America'. Moreover, with regard to agriculture he has declared that the 'empirical evidence does not support the notion of a deep agrarian crisis. In fact, on an economy-wide basis, Russian agriculture was growing per capita, peasant living standards and real wages were rising and exports were booming.'[6]

It is now argued that although between 1860 and the 1880s agricultural production was stagnant, from the 1880s to 1913 it grew rapidly (and at nearly double the rate of population increase), with a 73 per cent increase in grain production and a 47 per cent increase in the output of potatoes. There were only two brief periods, of four years each, which went against this trend: the first was the famine years of 1889 to 1892; the second was the revolutionary years of 1905 to 1908. Both of these downturns were caused by adverse weather conditions and a subsequent run of bad harvests (although in the second case the impact of the revolution itself was added to the consequences of drought in 1905). In both periods the state spent heavily on aid – partly, however, in the form of food loans, which needed to be repaid.

Also the picture varied considerably across the Empire. The traditional centre of Russian agricultural production, the central agricultural provinces and the Volga region, fared much worse than the newly prosperous areas of the south and west, and many of the accounts of rural poverty (from government statistics to the literary descriptions of the populist writers and Chekhov) came from these more deprived areas. Moreover, yields were higher on peasant than on landlord land. Landlords were selling or renting out land at a steady rate after 1861, and it was peasants who were buying it (with 27 per cent of landlord land passing into peasant hands between 1877 and 1905). The peasantry owned 66 per cent of all arable land in Russia by 1913, and rented more. Before the 1890s it was cheap to rent land and there was plenty of land on the market.[7]

Peasants, then, adapted to the new conditions of emancipation, industrialization and a market economy better than has been thought – or better than was thought by Lenin, the populists or the government at the time. Lenin divided his peasantry into 'rich', 'middle' or 'poor', on the basis of zemstvo statistics of the amount of agricultural land farmed by families as well as the military horse census. But, in a rapidly changing world, there were other ways of making a living than by farming, as peasants – who were not stupid and who had their own priorities – quickly realized. The peasants themselves often introduced new technologies and crops. The potato, sugar-beet (which became a major industry on the west bank of the Ukraine and was run by the nobility in plantations with hired wage labour), the growth of market gardening to feed the expanding towns and, above all, the development of railways to transport produce and people, all enabled those with initiative (and who lived in the right areas) to prosper.

Nothing has been blamed for the so-called 'backwardness' of Russian agriculture more than the preservation of the village commune and the traditional strip farming system it encompassed. Yet over these years communal farming proved surprisingly flexible. Four, rather than three, crops were introduced, with clover or grass for fodder on the fallow fields. Peasant communes grew cash crops for the market and wheat for export (once the railway to Odessa was completed), or sunflower seeds. This might mean that they ceased to concentrate on growing grain for their own subsistence and bought grain on the market, or did not keep many cattle, which needed expensive fodder to keep alive in the winter. The one area where there was undoubted decline over this period was in the number (although not necessarily the quality) of livestock.[8]

In the village of Viriatino, studied by a Soviet ethnological team in the 1950s, it was found that in the last decades of the nineteenth century men had been abandoning agriculture for the profitable carting trade and then migrating for six months of the year to the newly developed coal mines of the Donbass, living in dormitories and leaving their families in the villages. Their earnings, large parts of which they sent home, enabled those villagers to build new houses, to buy grain – and wheat, not rye, at that – and also furniture and shop-made clothes.[9] Communes, as a whole, could grow for the market on common land more easily than individual peasants, while their common pasture also enabled the preservation of livestock. Joint labour schemes, enforced by the commune on everyone once there had been a majority vote, enabled wells to be dug, land to be cleared, irrigation ditches extended and arrangements made to maximize efficiency. Thus, it was the vulnerable and isolated independent family farm that was more likely to fail when times were hard.[10]

The continuation of the communal system of landownership (and of the three-generational, joint family farm within it) enabled young peasant men to work in industry without losing their right to land or their ties with the villages. Lenin assumed that, once transformed into proletarians, peasants would become 'class conscious' and cut off from the 'idiocy' of rural life. But Russia was not like Western Europe. Young males married in the villages before they left, bringing daughters-in-law into the family unit as labourers, and then went as individuals into the cities (often to specific jobs in specific factories where Uncle Ivan was already established). They returned to help with the harvest and, when they retired or fell ill, they went back to the villages and their sons took their place. They remained legally peasants and members of the commune and still held land. Moreover, they were rarely allowed to just drift away and become permanent city dwellers. The commune, which granted internal passports and co-operated with the police in finding strays, could insist on a marriage before a young man left, supported the fathers' continued control over their absent sons, and insisted on payments being sent back regularly to the village. Between half and three-quarters of industrial earnings returned to the communes to help pay off taxes or redemption payments to the government or the landlords.[11]

By the 1890s there were obviously rich peasants, and poor ones – but that did not mean that there was class differentiation in the way that Lenin believed or that it was increasing, as he assumed. Teodor Shanin has argued that, as sons demanded their share of the land when they married and as peasants got into debt, there was a form of cyclical mobility. It is now believed that where families became increasingly poor it was likely to be because of a family break up, or a lack of sons, or illness.[12]

All this does not mean that Russian peasants were not poor, or that there were not areas where things were bad. But it does mean that, overall, things may well have been improving, not getting worse. There is no evidence that taxes were an overwhelming burden or that they prevented increased spending on consumer goods. Certainly redemption payments were in arrears, but this may have been because the peasants simply did not pay them in bad years.[13] Of course, peasants still perceived that they needed more land, that they were overtaxed and suffering from debt. Equally, the peasant dream of a *chernyi peredel*, of the land belonging entirely to those who worked it, remained and had a potent appeal, as all myths do.

Certainly, the peasant revolt in 1905 did not take place at a time of great hardship, although a drought later in the year had a considerable impact on the central agricultural provinces. Rather, it would appear that the peasantry took advantage of the government being in crisis to see what they could get away with. They had, they believed, succeeded in 1902–03 in forcing the cancellation of government pressure to pay arrears of debt that had built up during the years following the famine of the early 1890s. When, in 1904, debts on redemption payments were wiped out, following the birth of a male heir, the peasants unsurprisingly felt that revolt had paid off.[14] It was to succeed again in 1905, when, as a result of the revolution, more land was put cheaply on the market by panicking landowners and there were significant reductions in rent and the abolition of redemption payments.

If the existence of economic growth during the second half of the nineteenth century is still controversial, the arrival of depression by 1900 is not, and the revolution is best explained by this sudden downturn. Land prices rose sharply at the end of the 1890s. Landlords, who were attempting to restore their declining fortunes by more commercial practices, put 30 per cent less land on the market between 1895 and 1905 than in the previous ten years and sharply increased rents, leading to peasant revolt in 1902–03. Meanwhile, competition from North American wheat sold in Western Europe had an impact on the export trade.[15] All areas of the economy were affected. The St Petersburg metalworking industry saw a curtailment of government orders, and the closure of small firms led to unemployment. Real wages dropped and strikes increased. The railway industry was particularly badly hit and saw strikes in Rostov in November 1902, and across southern Russia the following year. The railways were to start the strike movement after Bloody Sunday. One driver stated that his earnings in 1900 of 100 roubles a month were 35 roubles lower than fifteen years previously.[16]

The depression hit the south of Russia hard. In the new industrial areas of the south and west, the numbers of industrial workers had increased three and a half times in a decade. Ekaterinoslav's population had more than trebled in twelve years from 48,000 in 1888 to 156,000 by 1900. The Donbass saw phenomenal rates of growth, but by 1903 only twenty-three of the thirty-five blast furnaces across the region were still working and mines were closing, sacking workers. Baku's oil boom saw the town's population grow from 14,000 in 1860 to 207,000 in 1900, with nearly 80,000 industrial workers in 1903, 30,000 of which were employed by the oil industry. The crash, when it came after 1900, was sudden and dramatic. An international slump in the oil industry led to firms laying off workers. One international company withdrew altogether and relocated to Egypt. The number of workers employed in the oil industry dropped by 10,000 in one year. Peasant workers returned to their villages to lead the revolt in 1902. Finally, the Russo-Japanese War led to the government banning cereal exports to the Far East, causing great hardship in towns like Odessa and Batumi.[17]

By the outbreak of the Russo-Japanese War, therefore, Russia was in a highly volatile situation, experiencing all the problems of rapid social and economic change. The 'real' working class (urban dwellers working in factories employing over twenty people), numbered no more than 1.6 million. Some factories, like the Putilov works in St Petersburg, could employ tens of thousands, but most industry remained in the countryside and in small artisan units. The fact that most workers remained legally peasants and still associated themselves with their villages, meant that proletarianization in the Western sense, so hoped for by Marxists, was minimal. Indeed, it has recently been argued that, rather than peasants being urbanized, the cities were actually swamped by peasant attitudes.[18] Two-thirds of St Petersburg's population and three-quarters of Moscow's were migrant peasants. The sugar-beet industry saw large numbers of migrant workers arriving seasonally for hire, sometimes organized in *artels*, with their own elected leaders who would bargain for the contract – and who were deeply resented by the local labour force for under-cutting wages. Local labourers were often women, getting a second (in this case meagre) income while their husbands worked their own land.[19]

In the towns, peasants replicated village organizations, loyalties and customs through the *zemliachestva* (societies of peasants from the same district), factory elders (recognized by the government in 1903) and mutual aid schemes of various kinds. Peasants brought the tradition of peasant revolt into the cities as readily as urban ideas penetrated the villages through returning workers or soldiers. Steve Smith has stressed the importance of 'craft' or 'shop consciousness' (even among the metalworking industries of St Petersburg) and the divisions among the workers themselves – between literate and skilled male metalworkers or printers and the unskilled foundry men or (the often female) textile workers.[20] As one worker later put it, 'the oddness of textile workers hit me in the eyes. Many of then still wore peasant clothes, they looked as though they had wandered into town by mistake . . . one never lost an opportunity to pour scorn on them.'[21]

Urban conditions were often terrible, especially in the small artisan workshops where government legislation did not apply. In some factories workers slept round the machines or in dormitories – sharing bunks on a shift system – and were paid partly in vouchers for the factory shops. But in others, both foreign- and Russian-owned, there were model employers who provided housing, leisure and education facilities and health care for their employees. Some Moscow industrialists spent heavily on such facilities and saw this as a religious duty and part of the paternalistic image of their role. The situation was very mixed and under constant change, which had major implications for the nature of the popular movement and the influences on it by 1905.

The early Bolshevik historian M. N. Pokrovskii wrote in 1920 about the 'colossal stream of the spontaneous movement of the masses'. Their spontaneity, however, could be turned in any direction and, he wrote, they were, on the whole, 'not capable of active revolutionary fighting'.[22] For Pokrovskii, it was the Bolsheviks who most successfully harnessed this spontaneity and made it 'conscious' and revolutionary, but Pokrovskii's claims may be questioned. His was the account often given by Bolshevik worker activists in the 1920s, when they wrote their memoirs, but these were written under the political constraints in the new regime and by workers (or, by then, ex-workers) who were far from typical. They also concentrated their accounts on the two capitals. If one looks away from St Petersburg and Moscow to the provinces and small towns, to the newly industrialized areas of south Russia, Ukraine, the Caucasus and other national minority areas (although this chapter will not examine Finland, Poland and the Baltic States), a picture emerges which is more spontaneous, more complex and more concerned with local issues. This view from the provinces is, therefore, more difficult to describe in terms of party programmes or influence. Indeed, it is difficult to ascribe much coherence to it at all.

Party activity was certainly widely present across the country and the Social Democrats had great influence among organized factory workers. However, they were not necessarily as dominant as many histories imply, and this chapter will look at other (non-Marxist and non-party) influences on local events. The Socialist-Revolutionary Party is now acknowledged to have been more of an urban than a rural party at this time, with its activists being workers or students and its bases being established in small towns – even if its aspirations and programme were aimed primarily at the country-side. Its members' militant and emotional appeal and their advocacy of armed struggle and terrorism were popular among newly urbanized peasants and railwaymen, and could lead to both rivalry and co-operation with local Bolsheviks. But it also had strongholds in large, mechanized factories and among skilled and literate workers (the Briansk engineering company's works in Ekaterinoslav and factories of the Urals, for example).[23] Maureen Perrie has estimated that its membership in 1905 was 45 per cent worker and only 7 per cent peasant,[24] while the SR Party's report to the Socialist International in Stuttgart in 1907 bewailed its failure to have much impact in the villages in 1905 outside its home base in the Volga provinces, and admitted that most of its activity was in the towns.[25]

The SR terrorist wing merged easily with the many anarchist groups in 1905, and the party's local branches often called for rural terror against landlords and advocated violence and arson. A high proportion of SR leaflets were devoted to explaining and justifying political assassinations. Anarchist groups were strong in many southern and western cities, springing up, as one activist claimed, 'like mushrooms after a rain'. Odessa was the scene of several trials of anarchists after the bombing of the main Libman café in the town in December 1905, and at least three of those found guilty were hanged. The town had both an anarcho-communist group (which operated a protection racket in the port under cover of 'expropriations') and a widely supported syndicalist movement under a man calling himself Daniil Novomirskii, which was behind some of the strikes of the year.[26]

If the SRs were an urban party, the Mensheviks in Georgia were a rural one, with widespread peasant support in Guria and elsewhere. Party lines and allegiances were fluid. Party support could shift and activists could change parties – and they frequently did. In the provinces, if not in the capitals, faced with practical problems and with worker hostility to the split, Mensheviks and Bolsheviks often worked together and there were frequent demands for unity and for a 'workers' party' which would unite all parties and stop factional divisions. In many provincial towns this was achieved in practice, with appeals to the population being signed by representatives of all local parties (including, sometimes, liberal groups). Nevertheless, the split among the Social Democrats rendered the party almost impotent in many areas at the beginning of 1905.

In St Petersburg this was particularly obvious. The secretary of the Bolshevik committee there recalled that 'workers were awaiting direction from our own party . . . but we wasted three-quarters of our strength and time on the fight with the Mensheviks'. Solomon Schwarz (who was then a Bolshevik) also admitted that in January 1905 the party was in 'an extremely sorry state . . . there was not a single worker among the members of the committee . . . Before January 9th the workers' feelings towards the committee were extremely hostile. Our agitators were beaten up, our leaflets destroyed.'[27] Nikolai Valentinov said, with regard to a strike in Kiev in 1903, that the workers' revolt presented the Bolshevik party with 'a sphinx of which he had no knowledge'.[28] All sources say that the revolutionary parties were unprepared for the revolt that broke out in 1905 and that workers and peasants were often hostile to them or, at best, apathetic.

In Voronezh, in February 1905, workers refused to add political demands inserted by agitators to the list of economic grievances presented to employers. Similar actions were reported coming from railwaymen in Saratov and St Petersburg: 'They didn't read this to us and we don't want it' was one comment.[29] Even as late as October (and in St Petersburg itself), the Soviet rejected the Social Democrats' political platform, saying that they were only interested in party not worker interests, and declared that 'there are no parties now'.[30] In September, in Moscow, political ideas unconnected with immediate strike issues aroused suspicion, socialist speakers were interrupted and workers would walk out of meetings in protest when party activists squabbled over methods.[31]

This does not mean that there were no external influences on the popular movement or that its demands were solely economic. Indeed, it is now argued that the old dichotomies of economic/political, spontaneous/organized must be abandoned.[32] What it does mean, however, is that to understand the popular movement one should look not only at the revolutionary parties. After all, if the number of factory workers in Russia was small (under 2 per cent of the population), the number of revolutionaries was even smaller. Parties could count on only a few hundred members – even in sizeable cities – and their support was volatile. In Iuzovka, as T. H. Friedgut has reminded us, there were 15,000 workers but only an estimated 500 of these had ever come into contact with a revolutionary by 1905.[33] Wladimir Woytinsky, then a Bolshevik student, described his culture shock in going into factories, and even more into villages, as an agitator in 1905.[34] Party activists found it difficult to penetrate the *zemliachestva* and workers were reluctant to listen to students who could not work a machine. Workers and peasants listened more to their own kind or to local leaders, whom they knew and trusted, and their demands and attitudes were not necessarily in line with party policies. One party activist in Ivanovo-Voznesensk wrote in May 1905, 'we feel we are on another planet'.[35]

It is now suggested that the experience of 1905 was only the first step in supplanting traditional attitudes with party-influenced concepts of class consciousness – a process that perhaps was not completed until 1917, if then. A. Buzinov wrote later that the word 'conscious' was first heard in the factories only in 1906.[36] Meanwhile, and unsurprisingly, what has been called 'naive monarchism' still prevailed in the villages in 1905. The decree of 18 February inviting communes to address petitions (*prigovory*) to the tsar led to an enormous and enthusiastic response. Demands flooded in, addressed first to Nicholas II himself and later to the Duma, which the peasants saw as some sort of charitable institution. The peasants' priority was for more land, the return of the lost lands (*otrezki*, or 'cut-offs') of 1861 and for a reduction in taxes, rents and redemption payments. A typical list of demands came from Nikolaev, in September 1905, when an estate manager was forced to sign a document fixing rents at six roubles per *desiatina* (that is, at one-third rather than one-half of income) and to be paid in kind not cash, rent for cottages to be three not five roubles a year and a ban on hired labour from outside the village.[37] The *prigovory* also demanded more education, an end to the war with Japan, controls over the police and other government officials, the abolition of the hated land captains and even a constitution. The authorities blamed intellectual outsiders for such political demands, but this was not necessarily the case. Peasants were by then sufficiently informed about the outside world, through newspapers and their neighbours who had worked in cities, to be aware of political developments in the urban areas. This politicization undoubtedly increased as the year continued.[38]

Peasant literacy was, of course, much lower than in the cities and David Moon and others have found that, although schools had been established in the villages, peasant children were normally withdrawn after one or two years of schooling and without obtaining a qualification. The peasants valued schooling for the practical advantages of basic literacy but were little influenced by broader educational ideas. Nevertheless, the peasants knew enough to insist on their views being accurately represented by those, often village schoolteachers, whom they asked to help them in drawing up the petitions.[39]

The All-Russian Peasant Union, created in July 1905 under the patronage of the Imperial Agricultural Society, rejected violence and urged change through legal means. It did, however, follow peasant demands closely, even to the extent of calling for the abolition of private landholding. The ancient peasant belief that land was like air or water and should be free to all who used it was deep-rooted and still dominant in 1905: 'Land is the mother of us all', was a common argument.[40] As peasant revolt escalated through the summer and autumn of 1905, absentee landlords and middlemen were particular targets, but the movement was more violent against property than against people. Arson attacks, or threats of them, took place not just against landlords' manor houses but also against machinery and commercial installations like flourmills and sugar refineries. The peasants also had a realization of legal niceties, destroying title deeds and insisting on managers and landlords signing new arrangements regarding rents and wages, although there was little outright seizure of land.

Peasant leaders came largely from within the community, often being returning soldiers or workers. There are reports of some dressing as 'generals', and there were widespread rumours that the tsar had sanctioned the action against landlords, especially after the issuing of the October Manifesto. Some peasants who were arrested as ringleaders or activists were respectable heads of families and village elders.[41] Some leaders were trusted local intellectuals or even gentry. In Sumy district, in Khar'kov province, a small landowner named A. P. Shcherbak, who had spent time in America, led the local collection of *prigovory* and attracted mass meetings of peasants, using local legal agricultural societies as a base and shunning revolutionaries or overtly political demands. He emphasized loyalty to the tsar and, although briefly arrested in the summer, by the autumn he was back in charge and Sumy was running itself, with villages setting up strike committees and militia, forcing the re-election of *volost'* administrators and driving out the local police.[42] Other so-called 'peasant republics' were set up in Saratov and Samara districts, where peasants collected taxes and maintained order themselves.[43]

The most famous example, however, was Guria, in Georgia, which became a *cause célèbre* and attracted considerable interest within Russia and from abroad. An area with exceptionally high land prices and where the Russian government owned a very large proportion of the land, it had suffered badly from competition from North America on the European grain market. Work in nearby Batumi had dried up by 1903, as a result of the depression, and workers had returned to their villages. Guria was Menshevik-influenced, but only as the result of local Mensheviks ignoring central party policies and putting local peasant demands at the forefront of their approach. Tsarist officials were driven out, the peasants demanding that they should be left to govern themselves. Despite this, it was still believed locally that they had the tsar's blessing. It being an area of exceptionally high literacy, the peasants in Guria certainly knew how to organize their own communities, although local teachers and priests co-operated with the movement. Women also participated in local village meetings and took an active role. Villagers refused to pay rents and taxes and elected their own local committees, with each group of ten houses sending one delegate. They ran their own courts and kept order, albeit with a good deal of intimidation.

Their demands, again, were a mixture of the economic and the political, although they were more radical than in many other places. They asked for redemption payments to be not just abolished but returned to the peasantry, for the confiscation of landlord, church and government land, for freedom of speech and assembly and for free compulsory education, for the abolition of the internal passport system and the standing army, and for the calling of a constituent assembly.[44]

Other localities saw a similar emphasis on local concerns mixed with a wider realization of more national issues. In right-bank Ukraine, with its wage-labour force in the sugar industry, strikes for higher wages and intimidation of imported migrant labour took precedence over land issues. Again, leadership came from local strike committees, formed here from the village *skhody* (assemblies).[45]

Turning to the towns, a similar picture emerges of local and national concerns. Worker demands show few signs of class-consciousness or understanding of party political programmes. It is now being argued that workers, like the peasants so many of them still partly were, preserved a mentality that was essentially paternalistic. Employers, like the serf owners of old, were expected to be good masters, to treat their workers with respect and to support them in hard times. Demands were first of all economic: for higher wages and lower hours and, above all, for an eight-hour day. Secondary demands were for rights of association, the right to strike, for legal trade unions, for permanently elected factory committees with the right to negotiate with bosses over hiring and firing arrangements and the fixing of wage rates (often referred to collectively as the establishment of a 'constitutional factory'). Third, there were demands for personal dignity: 'We are people too' meant not being addressed by the demeaning second-person singular, for an end to harassment (including sexual harassment) at work, for washing facilities, insurance schemes paid for by the employer, pension rights and educational opportunities.

Such demands show a concern for human rights, for liberty and equality within the system, rather than outright opposition to it. As Steve Smith has pointed out, *svoboda* (freedom) not socialism – a moral not a class imperative – was the prevailing language of the year 1905.[46] Typical was a Moscow baker, involved in the bakers' strike in April, who spoke not of class hatred but of the workers bearing themselves with pride and an increased sense of self-dignity: 'They turned out to be people', he said.[47] Mark Steinberg has also documented how printers were prepared to work with employers to achieve more dignity, equality and self-improvement within their industry.[48] There was certainly a realization on the part of the working class that the old estate system excluded 'the toiling people' from both individual and collective rights, and that it needed to be changed.

That these ideas were not just confined to the worker aristocracy was shown by the enormous popularity of the Zubatov movement before 1905, through which worker demands could be expressed within a legal and loyal framework, in places even including the right to strike. The Independent Jewish Labour Party, started by Zubatov in Minsk and Vil'na, often using former revolutionaries as activists, spread to Odessa and other southern towns and has been described as being the 'largest organized labour group in Russia' by 1903, coming close to becoming a legal political party. K. Shae-vich led a successful and non-violent general strike in Odessa in 1903, attracting huge crowds with a programme that explicitly rejected socialists and political demands.[49] The Zubatov movement, and Shaevich himself, became a victim of its own success by the end of 1903, but the ideas behind the movement had struck a chord with the working class. Gapon had some 20,000–25,000 members in his Assembly of Russian Working Men in St Petersburg in January 1905, at a time when the revolutionary parties in the capital could almost count their membership on the fingers of one hand. The British ambassador, writing home in disgust at the government reaction, was undoubtedly right to report that the authorities had grossly mishandled the situation and that the tsar had missed the best opportunity of his reign.[50]

Mutual aid organizations under local control were established in Khar'kov (under A. A. Evdokimov) as early as 1898, followed in Moscow by 1901. It has been argued that these anticipated the soviets in 1905. Workers in St Petersburg welcomed the Shidlovskii Commission, with its recognition of elected delegates from the factory floors after Bloody Sunday, and peti-tioned it to restore the Gapon organizations. In March 1905, 2,500 marchers presented a petition calling for legal trade unions, state insurance for accidents, the right to strike, shorter working days and equal labour rights.[51] There was still a belief that a petition to the tsar, the landlord or the factory owner, especially if that petition was backed up with the threat of force or a strike, would work. Frequently, in 1905, it did. Factory owners were often prepared to give way to demands in order to stop strikes and keep production levels up. The French consul in Baku was complaining by 1906 that local workers were being paid more than those in Marseilles.[52]

The educated intelligentsia had long been vocal in its support for more equal rights for all Russia's people. Moscow university professors drew up the statutes for the Moscow Society for Mutual Aid for the Workers of the Mechanical Trades in 1902, and gave public lectures on labour laws and housing projects in Europe in the many institutions for public self-education in Moscow and other provincial cities that existed by the end of the nineteenth century.[53] Moscow's city duma, controlled largely by philanthropically inclined members of its wealthy merchant community, established numerous welfare, charitable and educational schemes for the city's working class. The Museum of Aid to Labour was especially influential and helped establish trade unions in 1905. All sorts of voluntary associations proliferated in late tsarist Russia and, by 1900, it can be argued that there was a civil society in embryo, enabling workers to acquire the means of self-education and self-help through reading rooms, evening classes, public lectures and libraries.

In fact, the respectable working class was as likely to attend legal temper-ance societies as underground revolutionary meetings. One interpretation is that 'a lively, non-revolutionary civic life emerged in the largest cities' by the early years of the twentieth century and that this included certain parts of the working class, as indeed did the growing entertainment and consumer culture.[54] Literacy rates among male urban workers were over 50 per cent, with two-thirds of metalworkers able to read and write according to the 1897 census. And what they read were popular broadsheets, cheap thrillers and government and liberal newspapers more than revolutionary leaflets, which were badly produced and difficult to get hold of.[55]

It is now being suggested that the liberal movement had more influence on popular attitudes than has hitherto been realized. The Kadet programme was far more radical than its Western European counterparts; and the party called itself 'The Party of the People's Freedom' in Russia — a title with populist rather than liberal connotations. The Kadet leaders claimed to be an 'all-class' party and stressed their credentials as social reformers. It has been estimated that they had between 50,000 and 100,000 members by the end of 1905, with up to 350 local branches. They ran newspapers and called for land reform, a constituent assembly with universal male suffrage (with a strong pro-women lobby) and extensive social change. In many areas, they collaborated with local soviets and local socialists to put pressure on the government to grant reform and lived up to their slogan of 'no enemies on the left'. Some local branches, as in Vladimir, Tver and Kostroma, got significant popular support.[56]

Paul Miliukov's Union of Unions had 100,000 members by October 1905 and was both radical and non-party. Trade unions of all sorts proliferated, once they were legalized in October, and were often set up with intellectual help and support. There was widespread cross-class collaboration during the year, particularly before October. Doctors refused to collaborate with the government over the cholera epidemic, lawyers defended revolutionaries and white-collar members of trade unions supported general strikes. Some industrialists, like Savva Morozov and N. P. Shmidt in Moscow, gave money to Social Democrat funds, deliberately hired known party activists to work in their factories and paid strike pay (or, at least, refrained from lockouts). Both Shmidt and N. I. Prokhorov were killed by police action in Moscow in 1905. Others armed their own workers and formed militia against Black Hundred gangs.[57]

Concessions by both managers and the authorities, as the result of successful strike action, could result in the reduction of the appeal of the revolutionary parties. In Saratov, a railway strike in January 1905 led to an agreement for a nine-hour day, abolition of compulsory overtime, and pay increases. As a result, there was a firm rejection of 'narrow party or class hegemony' by the railwaymen.[58] The success of strikes could, however, lead to others following the same tactics, and the government imposed martial law on the railways after the Southern Railway Company got an eight-hour day, elected worker representatives and the promise of freedom of assembly the following month. The result was the foundation of the most successful trade union of the year, *Vikzhel*, but this remained firmly non-partisan and rejected Bolshevik calls for an armed uprising in the autumn. For the railway leaders, the October Manifesto had satisfied, at least temporarily, their demands for what were essentially civil rights.[59]

If this interpretation of popular demands is correct, there was some potential for a reformist policy of change in 1905. The demands voiced, however, from both workers and peasants, were certainly subversive of the old autocratic order and must be seen as containing broad political implications, even if they were presented as basically economic concerns. 'Political' did not, however, necessarily mean 'revolutionary' or even 'party-motivated'. Nevertheless, excessive government repression and the existence of right-wing parties and militias made peaceful change unlikely. The situation was too volatile to be easily controlled and the forces of law and order were, with a few local exceptions, clearly incapable of so doing. The result was an astonishing degree of self-government at a local level throughout the country. Although demands from the villages and the streets show a realization of wider concerns, and although protests were often sparked by events in the capitals, it can be argued that, in the provinces, local issues and local leaders were all-important. As one report by a party activist from Saratov put it, the local population 'went not for revolution but for leaders and for personalities'.[60]

These local leaders could be individuals like Shcherbak in Sumy (referred to above), or like the self-styled 'President' who gave the French consul safe passage on the strike-bound Ekaterinskaia railway in December 1905. He explained that strikers had taken over the railway line and were collecting fares and contributions for the strike fund. The 'President' added that he wanted a constitutional monarchy, on the English model, but that other members of the royal family, apart from the tsar, and all foreigners, should leave Russia or be killed.[61] They might also be former Zubatov activists, who, as Victoria Bonnell has pointed out, grew into 'the kernel of labor organizations everywhere'.[62] They could be anarchists (like Novomirskii, in Odessa) or syndicalists (like Evdokimov, in Khar'kov) who got local support by putting worker demands to the fore. By September 1905, with the Museum of Assistance to Labour in Moscow, Evdokimov was organizing the first All-Russian Conference of Representatives of Professional Unions. Another 'Economist'-inclined former Marxist, who left the party but retained local influence, was F. A. Kondrat'ev in Ivanovo-Voznesensk. There, as elsewhere, skilled workers were elected as deputies to factory committees and provided local leadership.[63] Members of political parties who got popular support often did so by abandoning the official party line which came down from St Petersburg or Geneva and by sticking firmly to local issues and economic grievances. They were sometimes expelled from their party for their pains.

The best example, in this regard, is Baku, where the brothers Lev and Ilia

Shendrikov were expelled as 'Economists' when the Baku Social Democrat committee was Bolshevized in early 1904. Concentrating on local grievances and economic issues, they founded the rival Association of the Workers of Balakhany and Bibi Eibat and organized the general strike in Baku in December 1904 (which should be regarded as the real beginning of the 1905 Revolution). By the end of 1904, they had 4,000 members, compared with about 300 for the official Social Democrat committee. They were to keep popular support in the oil fields until the end of the revolutionary year. The Shendrikovs negotiated and agreed with the oil magnates the first labour contract in Russian history, with a nine-hour day, sick pay, free fuel and elected factory delegates empowered to negotiate on behalf of the work-force. Demands included a constituent assembly, freedom of the press and trade unions and the right to strike. The brothers ran a democratic organi-zation, with full worker participation in local party affairs. By October, when they led the newly formed soviet, they had achieved 'considerable suc-cesses, including promises of housing and free oil and medical care from the employers. Ironically, their successes led to the failure of their strike call in November, by which time their followers saw no need for further action, and they lost power in the city by the end of the year. Some foreign firms, like Nobel, favoured attempting to stem the enormous losses faced by the indus-try during the year by concessions, although nothing could much alleviate the conditions of life in the oilfield, which were graphically described by all visitors as a version of hell.[64]

Nationality mattered more than class in the ethnically divided areas of the south, particularly in the Caucasus but also in Ukraine. Kiev was primarily a Russian and Jewish city, Tiflis a Russian and Armenian one. The new urban areas could be a separate and alien world to the local peasantry who came to work there and to man their growing factories. Both the oil and the coal industry in the Donbass operated on national and hierarchical lines. Man-agers and owners were often foreign and were resented as such (including Russians). Skilled workers and entrepreneurs were Russian, Jewish or Armenian, unskilled workers were local peasants or, in the case of Baku, were imported from Persia. National groups organized themselves, like the Armenian Dashnaks, on religious lines. As popular rejoicing at the October Manifesto drew huge crowds onto the streets across the country, patriotic demonstrations could quickly turn against Jews or other groups, like the Poles, seen as non-Russian. Clashes, between those who greeted the Mani-festo with loyal parades and those who supported the revolutionary groups, quickly turned violent.

Odessa was the scene of the most notorious anti-Semitic pogroms of 1905 and was the city where the authorities most obviously either supported or ignored the atrocities; but other towns saw similar events. Paradoxically, in Odessa, Social Democratic support was largely Jewish, while the Russian working class remained loyal to the former Zubatovite Independent Jewish

Labour Party. According to Robert Weinberg, the mass of Russian workers in Odessa remained untouched by Social Democratic ideas in 1905. Russian factory workers there could easily be recruited to join in anti-Semitic pogroms.[65] Similar 'patriotic' demonstrations, involving some (often unskilled) workers turning against Jews, were common across Russia: they involved workers in Ekaterinoslav, miners in Iuzovka and railwaymen across the country.[66] In the Caucasus, the victims could be Armenian rather than Jewish. A loyal group that was only pushed into opposition by the government's assault on Armenian church property, the Armenians, like the Jews, were both perpetrators and victims of violence. The local authorities in the Caucasus lost control of the situation to such an extent that the Mensheviks were given arms to protect the Armenian community in Tiflis in November.

The bewildering array of local right-wing and monarchist parties, which proliferated across the country after the October Manifesto, could also attract wide popular support. Tula, Kursk and Orel all saw significant support for local, moderate right-wing parties. The People's Party of Order in Kursk got some peasant support and had a membership of 1,500 by January 1906. Charismatic local leadership, concentrating on local problems, could again make a difference, as in the case of Count V. A. Bobrinskii in Tula. Extremist groups, organized in so-called 'Black Hundred' militias, could attract large numbers in some towns, as in Odessa. Disorder throughout the revolution was endemic and not necessarily 'conscious' or organized by anyone. Crime and violence rose sharply after Bloody Sunday and continued to do so into 1906. This could be, as Joan Neuberger suggests, a manifestation of generalized hostility to the government and respectable society, or it could be simply the result of a collapse in governmental authority and policing, or part of what was already widely seen as 'hooliganism'.[67]

If local issues and leaders were often only marginally connected with the policies and programmes of revolutionary parties, neither did these parties necessarily initiate or control the development of soviets across the country, or explain their enormous popularity. No local soviet was one-party controlled and their appeal lay more in the local control of their own affairs than in ideology: they ran their own militias and called strikes; they printed newspapers and controlled railways and postal services, bakeries and sanitation systems. Whether or not they developed into the leaders of armed uprisings and barricade fighting, for a few days or weeks in November and December 1905, many local soviets across the country became potential or actual governments at a local level, in charge of whole cities (or, at least, worker districts). Some, as with the peasant districts already considered, called themselves 'republics'.

The most radical soviets elected people's courts and revolutionary tribunals. Novorossisk, where the local garrison mutinied, saw the mayor and town duma submit to the soviet in December, with an armed militia of workers running the town and imposing discipline. In Khar'kov, the town soviet was a united front of various parties led by the Mensheviks, but got active support from the liberal town duma, which donated funds for a town militia. In Ekaterinoslav, the general strike saw barricades manned by men of all ages and classes, and the soviet had wide popular support. Chaired by two Mensheviks, the Pavlovich brothers, it was described as an 'all-party' body and even got support from the local factory administration. The fighting and strike committee that succeeded it in December, included engineers and members of the intelligentsia. The so-called Chechelev Republic (in that district of the town) organized and ran its own services, until it was forcibly suppressed at the end of the year.[68] Nizhnii Novgorod, Chita, Rostov and Krasnoiarsk were all under 'people power' for a while. A French report from Irkutsk talked of a 'committee of public safety' calling for the governor general to leave and for Siberia to become a self-governing republic under American protection.[69]

So how should we interpret the 1905 Revolution? It was a popular protest, but one stemming from a period of economic growth rather than one of increasing misery, a period when certain individuals and areas benefited but others did not, and a period during which attitudes and society were undergoing rapid change. It was a movement initiated by sudden depression and war rather than by fundamental economic causes. It was a popular movement more concerned with dignity, freedom and civil rights than with class hatred and socialism, or with the programmes of political parties whose activists were often seen as outsiders divorced from local concerns, and in which political and economic concerns were inextricably interlinked.[70] It was a revolution in which local issues and local desires for self-control and (in some areas) self-rule and local autonomy (if not necessarily, except in a small minority of cases, independence) were seen as most important.

As in earlier (and later) 'times of trouble', when central, autocratic authority was perceived to be weak, the Russian Empire began to fragment, with demands for local autonomy and a more federal system surfacing in the form of 'people power' across rural districts, national minority areas, provincial towns and worker districts alike. *Oblastnichestvo* (regionalism), as an alternative, non-centralist structure for Russia, harking back to an earlier vision of *Rus'*, was a central part of the populist movement, especially in Siberia and Ukraine. A professor of history at Kazan, in his inaugural lecture in 1861, had talked of 'not the idea of the state, nor that of centralization, but the idea of *narodnost'* and of regionalism'. Herzen had also argued that 'centralization is alien to the Slav spirit – federalism is far more natural to it', while the Siberian *oblastnik* N. Potanin stated at about the same time that 'every region ... from a cultural point of view has the right of independent development of its own resources'.[71] For the revolutionaries in 1905 it was the freedom to run their own towns and districts, with their own elected authorities, through a political system which left people at liberty from centralized control and from repression (whether from government officials or local employers) and a freedom that gave them what they perceived of as dignity and economic fairness, that, in essence, the revolution was all about.

Notes

1 Hannah Arendt, *On Revolution* (London, 1963).
2 Abraham Ascher, *The Revolution of 1905, Vol. 1: Russia in Disarray* (Stanford, 1988), p. 127; and Moira Donald, 'Russia 1905: The Forgotten Revolution', in Moira Donald and Tim Rees (eds), *Reinterpreting Revolution in Twentieth-Century Europe* (London, 2001), pp. 41–54.
3 See, for example, David Saunders, 'The Static Society: Patterns of Work in the Later Russian Empire', in Geoffrey Hosking and Robert Service (eds), *Reinterpreting Russia* (London, 1999), pp. 126–41.
4 J. C. Davies, 'Towards a Theory of Revolution', *American Sociological Review*, Vol. 27 (1962), No. 1, pp. 5–19.
5 James Y. Simms Jr, 'The Crisis in Russian Agriculture at the End of the Nineteenth Century: A Different View', *Slavic Review*, Vol. 36 (1977), No. 3, pp. 377–98; Robert Bideleux, *Communism and Development* (London, 1985); Heinz-Dietrich Löwe, *Die Lage du Bauern in Russland 1880–1905* (St Katharinen, 1987).
6 Paul R. Gregory, *Before Command: An Economic History of Russia from the Emancipation to the First Five-Year Plan* (Princeton, 1994), pp. 36, 54.
7 Stephen G. Wheatcroft, 'Crises and the Condition of the Peasantry in Late Imperial Russia', in Esther Kingston-Mann and Timothy Mixter (eds), *Peasant Economy, Culture and Politics in European Russia, 1800–1921* (Princeton, 1991), pp. 128–72; Judith Pallot, 'Agrarian Modernisation on Peasant Farms in the Era of Capitalism', in James H. Bater and R. A. French (eds), *Studies in Russian Historical Geography*, Vol. 2 (London, 1983), pp. 423–49; and Bideleux, *Communism and Development*, pp. 12–13.
8 Elvira M. Wilbur, 'Peasant Poverty in Theory and Practice: A View From Russia's "Impoverished Centre"', in Kingston-Mann and Mixter (eds), *Peasant Economy*, pp. 101–27; A. Baker, 'Deterioration or Development? The Peasant Economy of Moscow Province Prior to 1914', *Russian History*, Vol. 5 (1978), No. 1, pp. 1–23.
9 Sula Benet (ed.), *The Village of Viriatino: An Ethnographic Study of a Russian Village from before the Revolution to the Present* (New York, 1970), pp. 28–40, 67–73.
10 Robert Bideleux, 'Agricultural Advance under the Russian Village Commune System', in Roger Bartlett (ed.), *Land Commune and Peasant Community in Russia* (London, 1990), pp. 196–218; and Heinz-Dietrich Löwe, 'Differentiation in Russian Peasant Society: Causes and Trends, 1880–1905', in ibid., pp. 165–95.
11 Jeffrey Burds, 'The Social Control of Peasant Labour in Russia', in Kingston-Mann and Mixter (eds), *Peasant Economy*, pp. 52–100.
12 Teodor Shanin, *The Awkward Class: Political Sociology of Peasantry in a Developing Society. Russia, 1910–1925* (Oxford, 1972); Wilbur, 'Peasant Poverty'.
13 S. Plaggenborg, 'Who Paid for the Industrialisation of Tsarist Russia?', *Revolutionary Russia*, Vol. 3 (1990), No. 2, pp. 183–210.
14 Wheatcroft, 'Crises and the Condition of the Peasantry', pp. 166–71; Steven L. Hoch, 'On Good Numbers and Bad: Malthus, Population Trends and Peasant

Standards of Living in Late Imperial Russia', *Slavic Review*, Vol. 53 (1994), No. 1, pp. 41–75.

15 Roberta T. Manning, *The Crisis of the Old Order in Russia* (Princeton, 1982), pp. 20–1.

16 Henry Reichman, *Railwaymen and Revolution: Russia, 1905* (Berkeley, 1987), p. 85.

17 Theodore H. Friedgut, *Iuzovka and Revolution*, Vol. 2 (Princeton, 1994), p. 135; David Lane, *The Roots of Russian Communism: A Social and Historical Study of Russian Social Democracy, 1898–1907* (Assen, 1969), pp. 159, 176–7.

18 Saunders, 'The Static Society'; David Moon, 'Peasants into Russian Citizens? A Comparative Perspective', *Revolutionary Russia*, Vol. 9 (1996), No. 1, pp. 43–81.

19 See Robert Edelman, *Proletarian Peasants: The Revolution of 1905 in Russia's Southwest* (Ithaca, 1987), Chapter 2.

20 S. A. Smith, *Red Petrograd: Revolution in the Factories, 1917–1918* (Cambridge, 1983).

21 A. Buzinov, *Za Nevskoi Zastavoi* (Moscow and Leningrad, 1930), pp. 20–1.

22 M. N. Pokrovsky, *A Brief History of Russia*, Vol. 2 (London, 1933), pp. 117, 152–3, 216.

23 Christopher Rice, *Russian Workers and the Socialist-Revolutionary Party through the Revolution of 1905–07* (London, 1983), pp. 49, 124, 197.

24 Maureen Perrie, *The Agrarian Policy of the Russian Socialist-Revolutionary Party from its Origins through the Revolution of 1905–1907* (Cambridge, 1976), p. 186.

25 *Rapport du Parti Socialiste Revolutionnaire de Russie au Congres Socialiste International de Stuttgart* (Gand, 1907).

26 Paul Avrich, *The Russian Anarchists* (Princeton, 1967), pp. 42, 47–9, 61, 67–9.

27 Gusev in *Proletarskaia Revoliutsiia*, No. 2(31) (1925), p. 20; Solomon M. Schwartz, *The Russian Revolution of 1905: The Workers' Movement and the Formation of Bolshevism and Menshevism* (Chicago, 1967), p. 55.

28 Nikolai Valentinov, *Encounters with Lenin* (London, 1968), p. 96.

29 Kathleen Prevo, 'Worker Reaction to Bloody Sunday in Voronezh', in F.-X. Coquin and C. Gervais-Francelle (eds), *1905. La Première Révolution Russe* (Paris, 1986), pp. 165–78; Reichman, *Railwaymen and Revolution*, pp. 136–7.

30 Israel Getzler, 'The Bolshevik Onslaught on the Non-Party "Political Profile" of the Petersburg Soviet of Workers' Deputies, October–November 1905', *Revolutionary Russia*, Vol. 5 (1992), No. 2, pp. 123–46.

31 Laura Engelstein, *Moscow 1905: Working-Class Organization and Political Conflict* (Stanford, 1982), p. 207.

32 Joan Neuberger, *Hooliganism, Crime, Culture and Power in St Petersburg, 1900–1914* (Berkeley, 1993), p. 76.

33 Friedgut, *Iuzovka and Revolution*, Vol. 2, p. 154.

34 Wladimir S. Woytinsky, *Stormy Passage: A Personal History Through Two Russian Revolutions to Democracy and Freedom* (New York, 1961), pp. 21, 60–1.

35 S. Vorderer, '"All the Non-Working Rascals we will send to the Devil": Labor Activities and Revolutionary Culture in an Imperial Russian Textile City', in Nicholas S. Racheotes and Hugh Guilderson (eds), *Life Lines: Perspectives on Russian and European Peasant Culture, Society and Politics* (Boulder, 2001), pp. 142–63 (the quotation is on p. 149).

36 Buzinov, *Za Nevskoi Zastavoi*, pp. 101–3.

37 Public Record Office (National Archives), London: FO 181/857, Nikolaiev to St Petersburg (26 September 1905).

38 Maureen Perrie, 'The Russian Peasant Movement of 1905–1907: Its Social Composition and Revolutionary Significance', *Past and Present*, No. 57 (November 1972), pp. 123–55; Andrew Verner, 'Discursive Strategies in the 1905

Revolution: Peasant Petitions from Vladimir Province', *Russian Review*, Vol. 54 (1995), No. 1, pp. 65–90.

39 Moon, 'Peasants into Russian Citizens?'; Ben Eklof, 'Peasants and Schools', in Ben Eklof and Stephen P. Frank (eds), *The World of the Russian Peasant* (Boston, 1990), pp. 115–32.

40 Scott J. Serengy, 'Peasant and Politics: Peasant Unions during the 1905 Revolution', in Kingston-Mann and Mixter (eds), *Peasant Economy*, pp. 341–77; E. I. Kiriukhina, 'Vserossiiskii Krest'ianskii soiuz v 1905g.', *Istoricheskie zapiski* (1955), pp. 95–141.

41 Manning, *The Crisis*, p. 153; P. N. Pershin, *Agrarnaia revoliutsiia v Rossii: istoriko-ekonomicheskoe issledovani* (Moscow, 1966), p. 280.

42 Serengy, ' Peasant and Politics'.

43 Manning, *The Crisis*, p. 150.

44 Stephen. F. Jones, 'Marxism and Peasant Revolt in the Russian Empire: the Case of the Gurian Republic', *Slavonic and East European Review*, Vol. 67 (1989), No. 3, pp. 403–34; Archives du Ministère des Affaires Étrangères. Russie. Direction Politique, nouvelle série, 7. 1896–1914 (Paris): Tiflis to St Petersburg (29 March 1905).

45 Robert Edelman, 'Rural Proletarians and Peasant Disturbances. The Right-bank Ukraine in the Revolution of 1905', *Journal of Modern History*, Vol. 57 (1985), pp. 248–77.

46 S. A. Smith, 'Workers and Civil Rights in Tsarist Russia, 1899–1917', in Olga Crisp and Linda Edmondson (eds), *Civil Rights in Imperial Russia* (Oxford, 1989), pp. 145–70; Victoria E. Bonnell, *Roots of Rebellion: Workers' Politics and Organizations in St Petersburg and Moscow, 1900–1914* (Berkeley, 1983), p. 112.

47 P. Korolev, cited in Tim McDaniel, *Autocracy, Capitalism and Revolution in Russia* (Berkeley, 1988), p. 282.

48 Mark D. Steinberg, *Moral Communities: The Culture of Class Relations in the Russian Printing Industry, 1867–1907* (Berkeley, 1992); and Mark D. Steinberg, 'Vanguard Workers and the Morality of Class', in Louis H. Siegelbaum and Ronald G. Suny (eds), *Making Workers Soviet: Power, Class and Identity* (Ithaca, 1994), pp. 66–84.

49 Jeremiah Schneiderman, *Sergei Zubatov and Revolutionary Marxism: The Struggle for the Working Class in Tsarist Russia* (Ithaca, 1976), pp. 297–8, 321.

50 See Dominic Lieven (ed.), *British Documents on Foreign Affairs: Reports and Papers from the Foreign Office Confidential Print* (Frederick, Md., 1983), Part 1, Series A. Russia, Vol. 3: Harding to Lansdowne (27 January 1905); Doc. 18, No. 72.

51 M. K. Palat, 'Police Socialism in Tsarist Russia, 1900–1905', *Studies in History* (Delhi), Vol. 2 (1986), pp. 71–136.

52 Ministère des Affaires Étrangères. n.s., 7: Baku to St Petersburg (27 July 1906); Robert W. Rolf, *The Russian Rockefellers: The Saga of the Nobel Family and the Russian Oil Industry* (Stanford, 1976), p. 163.

53 Dimitry Pospielovsky, *Russian Police Trade Unionism: Experiment or Provocation?* (London, 1971), p. 78.

54 Joseph H. Bradley, 'Subjects into Citizens: Societies, Civil Society and Autocracy in Tsarist Russia', *American Historical Review*, Vol. 107 (2002), No. 4, pp. 1094–123; and Joseph H. Bradley, 'Moscow: From Big Village to Metropolis', in Michael F. Hamm (ed.), *The City in Late Imperial Russia* (Bloomington, 1986), pp. 9–42.

55 John Morison, 'Education and the 1905 Revolution', *Revolutionary Russia*, Vol. 1 (June 1988), No. 1, pp. 5–19.

56 Shmuel Galai, 'The Kadet Quest for the Masses', in Robert B. McKean (ed.), *New Perspectives in Modern Russian History. Selected Papers from the Fourth World*

Congress for Soviet and East European Studies, Harrogate, 1990 (London, 1992), pp. 80–98.

57 Iu. A. Petrov, 'Moskva Revoliutsionnera Dekabr' 1905-go goda. Repetitsiia grazhdanskoi voiny', *Otechestvennaia istoriia* (1996), No. 2, pp. 13–27.

58 J. Sanders, 'Lessons from the Periphery: Saratov, January 1905', *Slavic Review*, Vol. 46 (1987), No. 2, pp. 229–44.

59 Walter Sablinsky, 'The All-Russian Railway Union and the beginning of the General Strike in October 1905', in Alexander and Janet Rabinowitch with Ladis K. D. Kristof (eds), *Revolution and Politics in Russia: Essays in Memory of B. I. Nicolaevsky* (Bloomington, 1972), pp. 113–33.

60 Sanders, 'Lessons from the Periphery', p. 243.

61 Ministère des Affaires Étrangères. n.s., 3: Droujkowka to St Petersburg, No. 5 (13 February 1906).

62 Bonnell, *Roots of Rebellion*, p. 127.

63 Vorderer, 'All the Non-Working Rascals'; Avrich, *Russian Anarchists*, pp. 77–8.

64 G. L. Keenan, 'La Grève générale de décembre 1904', in René Girault *et al.* (eds), *Sur 1905* (Paris, 1974), pp. 51–97; Ronald G. Suny, *The Baku Commune 1917–1918: Class and Nationality in the Russian Revolution* (Princeton, 1972), p. 41; Lane, *Roots*, pp. 182–3; *The Petroleum Review* (9 September 1905).

65 R. Weinberg, 'Workers, Pogroms and the 1905 Revolution in Odessa', *Russian Review*, Vol. 46 (1987), No. 1, pp. 53–75; and R. Weinberg, 'Social Democracy and Workers in Odessa', *Carl Beck Papers in Russian and East European Studies*, No. 504 (1985).

66 Friedgut, *Iuzovka and Revolution*, Vol. 2, p. 149; Charles Steinwedel, 'The 1905 Revolution in Ufa: Mass Politics, Elections and Nationality', *Russian Review*, Vol. 59 (2000), No. 4, pp. 555–76.

67 Don C. Rawson, *Russian Rightists and the Revolution of 1905* (Cambridge, 1995), pp. 78, 83, 106; Neuberger, *Hooliganism*, pp. 77–8, 89, 107.

68 Oskar Anweiler, *The Soviets: The Russian Workers', Peasants' and Soldiers' Councils, 1905–1921* (New York, 1974), pp. 61–2; Lane, *Roots*, pp. 169–74; Ascher, *The Revolution of 1905*, Vol. 1, pp. 291–2.

69 Ministère des Affaires Étrangères. n.s., 2: Irkutsk to St Petersburg, No. 149 (24 November 1905).

70 Linda Edmondson, 'Was there a Movement for Civil Rights in Russia in 1905?', in Crisp and Edmondson (eds), *Civil Rights*, pp. 263–86.

71 Franco Venturi, *Roots of Revolution: A History of the Populist and Socialist Movements in 19th Century Russia* (London, 1960), p. 199; Aleksandr Herzen, *Selected Philosophical Works* (Moscow, 1956), p. 478; Dimitri von Mohrenschildt, *Toward a United States of Russia: Plans and Projects of Federal Reconstruction of Russia in the Nineteenth Century* (London, 1981), p. 85.

4 The 1905 Revolution in Russia's Baltic provinces

James D. White

The events in Russia's Baltic provinces did not meet Lenin's definition of the 1905 Revolution as a 'dress rehearsal' for the October revolution of 1917 because, during the First World War, much of the territory in question was under German military occupation and not in a position to participate in the great upheaval in Russia. To that extent, the revolution in the Baltic provinces is a feature peculiar to the 1905 Revolution and is worthy of study on that account. The scope of the present chapter is an examination of the developments in those provinces of the Russian Empire that would later constitute the Baltic states of Estonia, Latvia and Lithuania, focusing in particular on the workers' and peasants' movement and on the part played by national aspirations.

Baltic characteristics

Social and economic conditions in the Baltic provinces differed from those in the Russian heartland in a number of respects. The most fundamental one was that landowners and peasants belonged to different nationalities. In the *Baltikum* (that is, Estland, Livland and Kurland), the landowning class consisted mainly of the German aristocracy, descendants of the Teutonic knights, who still in the twentieth century referred to themselves as a *Ritterschaft* ('corporation of nobles'). In Estland and northern Livland, the peasants were Estonian; in southern Livland and Kurland, they were Latvian. In the Lithuanian provinces of Vil'na and Kovno, the landowners were either Polish or Russian and the peasants were Lithuanian.

Also, the agrarian structure in the *Baltikum* was more polarized than in Russia proper. Landed estates were, on average, much larger than those in the rest of European Russia. Whereas in European Russia a landed estate averaged 496 *desiatinas*, in the *Baltikum* the average size was 2,255 *desiatinas*[1] – 1,923 *desiatinas* in Livland,[2] 1,768 *desiatinas* in Estland[3] and 2,660 in Kurland.[4] In the Lithuanian provinces, however, the average size of a landed estate was only 406 *desiatinas*, indicating that the Polish *szlachta* (nobles) were not far removed from the local peasantry.[5]

In Estland, Livland and Kurland, the liberation of the peasantry without land and other reforms, carried out between 1816 and 1819, had brought about a stratification of the peasantry that was more radical than elsewhere in European Russia. Characteristic of the Baltic countryside was the large numbers of landless farm labourers. Kurland had the greatest proportion of these (72 per cent), followed by Livland (66 per cent)[6] and Estland (59 per cent).[7] The liberation of the peasants in the Lithuanian provinces, on the other hand, had been carried out against the background of the 1863 Polish insurrection, when the Russian government had favoured the peasants at the expense of the Polish landowners. Consequently, in the Lithuanian provinces there were considerably fewer landless peasants: 24 per cent in the province of Suvalki and 9.7 per cent in the province of Vil'na.

In the Baltic provinces there was no peasant commune (*mir*) like that in Russia. Peasant settlements in the Lithuanian provinces, Kurland and the Latvian part of Livland were individual farmsteads, whereas the Estonians tended to congregate in villages.[8] There was, consequently, no mechanism in the Baltic region to retard the growth of economic inequality among the rural population. Those peasants who owned land tended to have relatively large amounts of it. Thus, in Livland, Kurland and Estland 97.8 per cent of peasant holdings were over ten *desiatinas*, whereas only 1.5 per cent were under five *desiatinas*. In the Lithuanian provinces, 77 per cent of peasant holdings were over ten, and only 4 per cent under five *desiatinas*. In the northern industrial region of Russia, by contrast, only 28.4 per cent of peasant holdings exceeded ten *desiatinas*, whereas 16.8 per cent were under five *desiatinas*.[9]

The migration of large numbers of landless peasants contributed to the growth of urbanization in the Baltic region, as they moved into the towns in search of employment. In 1867 Riga had a population of 103,000; by 1897 it was 282,000.[10] The seaport of Libau (Liepāja) experienced a similar growth in population in the same period. In 1863, it stood at 10,000; by 1881, it had climbed to 29,600; by 1897, it stood at 64,000.[11] Reval (Tallinn), which had still been a quiet provincial town in the mid-nineteenth century, serving as a holiday resort for the inhabitants of St Petersburg, became a thriving seaport by the end of the century, especially after the opening of the Baltic Railway. In 1871, Reval's population was 28,850; by 1881, it was 46,236. The population of Vil'na (Vilnius), meanwhile, rose from 60,500 in 1861 to over 154,000 in 1897.[12]

Urbanization had the effect of raising the proportion of Latvians and Estonians in Baltic towns. In Riga, for example, in 1867, out of a total of 103,000 inhabitants, 24 per cent were Latvians, 43 per cent were Germans, 25 per cent were Russians, and 5 per cent were Jews; by 1897, out of a total population of 282,000, 42 per cent were Latvians, 25 per cent were Germans, 17 per cent were Russians, 6 per cent were Jews, and 5 per cent were Poles. Most of the incoming population had been Latvian peasants from Livland and Kurland.[13] The increase in Reval's population also had its source in the peasantry of the surrounding countryside. In 1871 Reval's population consisted of 32.2 per cent Germans and 48.9 per cent Estonians;

in 1881, 20 per cent were Germans and 57.9 per cent Estonians; in 1897, 15.9 per cent were Germans and 62.7 per cent were Estonians.[14] Vil'na and Kovno (Kaunas), however, throughout the nineteenth and early twentieth centuries, had a minority of Lithuanians, most of the urban population consisting of Jews, Poles and Russians.[15] Vil'na was within the Pale of Jewish settlement, so that its small-scale industries had a plentiful supply of labour to hand. Lithuanian peasants, therefore, tended to go further afield to find employment – to Riga, Libau, Mitau (Jelgava) or St Petersburg.[16] They might even emigrate to find employment in the mines and steelworks of Lanarkshire or the meat-canning factories of Chicago. Thus, whereas the growth of trade and industry in the 1880s and 1890s made Riga more Latvian and Reval more Estonian, it did not make Vil'na more Lithuanian.

Industry in the Baltic provinces developed rapidly from the 1870s onwards, stimulated by railway construction and the increasing importance of the Baltic ports for Russia's trade. The industrialization of the Baltic was also furthered by the Russian government's policy of erecting high tariff barriers to raise revenue and to foster native industry. Rather than halting imports, however, the new high customs duties encouraged foreign firms, particularly German ones, to set up branches in the Baltic provinces.[17] When Sergei Witte was minister of finance in the 1890s, this tendency was positively encouraged. Foreign investment fostered the development in Riga of metalworking and railway-wagon building. The demand for electrical tramway systems in Russian cities gave rise to firms in Riga specializing in electrical engineering. Riga factories also supplied the Russian market with cement and other building materials.[18] The chemical industry was a particularly successful one in Riga, with the manufacture of dyes, rubber goods and asbestos.

Reval also benefited from the Russian demand for railway rolling stock, which was behind the establishment of the Dvigatel firm in 1898. The electrical industry was also developed in Reval, with the opening the following year of the Vol'ta firm, which produced electric motors for the Russian market.[19] Textiles were produced by the Kreenholm mills near Narva, which in 1900 employed 5,400 workers.[20]

Industry in the Lithuanian provinces was less well developed than in the neighbouring *Baltikum*. The main branches of industry were primarily those associated with agriculture and forestry, such as flour-milling, brewing, tobacco-processing, leather-working and saw-milling. The textile industry was also important in Lithuania, but only branches of it (such as hosiery and garment-making) that were not in competition with the great textile centres of Russia and Poland. It was in industries like these that many of Vil'na's Jewish population found employment.[21]

The politics of the Baltic provinces

In the political developments leading to the 1905 Revolution, the defining one was the Polish insurrection of 1863. This was an episode that shook the tsarist empire to its foundations and demonstrated to its rulers the potential vulnerability of their realm. At its height, the rebellion threatened to spread from Poland to Russia's internal provinces and the tsarist regime was forced to resort to desperate measures. To deprive the Polish rebels of peasant support, the Russian government offered the peasantry of the Lithuanian and Belorussian provinces a more generous land reform than that promised to them by the Polish insurgents. The provisions of the Emancipation Statute of 1861 were altered to give the peasants of these provinces more land, on better conditions, than had previously been intended. Even landless peasants were supplied with small allotments, on comparatively favourable terms, since it was believed that this was the social group that was most likely to side with the insurgents. Moreover, peasants in the Lithuanian and Belorussian provinces were not deprived of the use of meadows, forests and streams, as was the case in Russia proper (and which would be a serious source of grievance there in years to come).[22]

The agrarian legislation implemented in the Lithuanian provinces was successful in halting the rebellion in that area. But the Russian government did not stop there: in order to wean the Lithuanian peasants away from the baneful Polish and Catholic influence, the government banned the printing of books and newspapers in the Roman alphabet, and decreed that publications in Lithuanian should be in the Cyrillic script. This prohibition was a highly objectionable one for Lithuanians, especially for the clergy, for whom the Roman alphabet had a religious significance and who regarded texts in Cyrillic as ungodly. In the event, books were printed in Roman characters in neighbouring East Prussia and brought into Lithuania by *knygnešiai* ('book smugglers'). The prohibition had thereby caused even the most conservative elements in Lithuanian society to become law-breakers.

The effects of the Polish rebellion of 1863 on the *Baltikum* were more indirect, but no less profound. Government thinking on the policies to adopt in Poland had been heavily influenced by the group of conservative Slavophile thinkers led by M. N. Katkov and P. M. Leont'ev, who published the semi-official newspaper *Moskovskie vedomosti*. In Katkov's eyes, what had brought about the Polish insurrection were the 'centrifugal tendencies' inherent in the Russian government's willingness to allow a measure of self-government to national groups. Here Katkov had in mind not only the Poles and the Finns but also the Baltic Germans, who had their own provincial assemblies. The cure for these centrifugal tendencies was for the government to treat all national groups the same. Katkov thoroughly approved of the Russification policies applied to the Poles after 1863. But although the Baltic Germans were in his sights for the same treatment, it was to be only in the reign of Alexander III that such a policy was implemented.[23]

In the meantime, an alliance was formed between the Slavophiles and the Latvian national movement, the 'Young Latvians' (*Jaunlatvieši*), who saw the Baltic Germans as the oppressors of the Latvian peasantry. In the extensive polemic that raged in the 1860s between the Slavophiles and the ideological representatives of the Baltic Germans, the Young Latvians weighed in on the side of the Slavophiles. The Slavophiles had every reason to look favourably on the Latvians – not least since, in the 1840s, as a protest against Baltic German oppression, Latvian and Estonian peasants had converted in large numbers from Lutheranism to Russian Orthodoxy. Courting the Slavophiles brought great dividends to the Young Latvian movement. In the 1860s, with something approaching official approval, the Latvian newspaper *Pēterburgas Avīzes* (St Petersburg News) was allowed to appear in the capital. As Krišjānis Valdemars, the Young Latvian leader, explained:

> It is extremely fortunate that Katkov and Leont'ev, these two prominent Russian public figures, deviate, one may say, from the conservatism of their newspaper, and in Baltic affairs support the current that is directed against the interests and aspirations of our privileged Germans. But these same Germans have enormous power ... What can the forces of the poor Latvians and Estonians do against them? Liberal and independent Russian newspapers can do little to help them because they have no influence on the government. Therefore, wise Latvian intellectuals must use for the good of their people the influential *Moskovskie vedomosti*, whose powerful voice is heard in both far and high places...[24]

The publication of *Pēterburgas Avīzes* was a major landmark in the development of the Baltic national movements, and was to serve as a model for later publications to follow. Valdemars, in fact, even managed to organize the intervention of Katkov's *Moskovskie vedomosti* on behalf of the Estonians, to enable the newspaper *Sakala* (edited by Carl Jakobson) to appear in 1877 in the teeth of Baltic German opposition.

To those members of the Lithuanian national movement, such as Jonas Basanavičius and Jonas Šliūpas, who were in touch with the Young Latvians, it seemed that if they were to side with the Russian government against the Poles (as Valdemars and Jakobson had allied with the Russian government against the Baltic Germans), they might be allowed to publish a newspaper in the Roman alphabet. In 1884, Šliūpas duly presented a memorandum to the governor-general of Warsaw, arguing that if the Lithuanians were allowed the use of the Roman alphabet all anti-government activity in Lithuania would cease, book smuggling would stop and there would take place a 'spiritual communion with Russia'.[25] However, a lack of enthusiasm by the Russian authorities prevented any such bargain being struck. In any case, at the time Šliūpas was negotiating with the Russians, *Auszra* (Dawn), the first newspaper of the Lithuanian national awakening, was already being printed in Prussia and then smuggled across the border in the traditional manner for Lithuanian publications.[26]

By the time *Auszra* ceased publication in 1886 it was clear that any overtures to the Russian authorities to allow the legal publication of a Lithuanian newspaper were doomed to failure and that the Lithuanian national movement would not be able to enjoy the privileged position of the Young Latvians.[27] *Auszra's* successor, *Varpas* (The Bell), which appeared between 1899 and 1905 (under the editorship of Vincas Kudirka), accordingly adopted an increasingly critical stance towards the government. By the turn of the century, *Varpas* was looked upon practically as a socialist journal, many of its contributors at that time belonging to socialist groups in Lithuania. The non-socialist *varpininkai* formed themselves into a separate party in 1902, the Lithuanian Democratic Party, which resolved to campaign for national autonomy and an elected assembly in Vilnius. The evolution of *Varpas* reflected the close relationships that existed between the national and socialist movements in Lithuania.

After the accession to the throne of Alexander III in 1881, the Russification of the Baltic provinces, which the Slavophiles had long advocated, was implemented. The process, which was encouraged by Alexander's mentor, Konstantin Pobedonostsev, the procurator of the Holy Synod, was to continue for the entire reign. The first measures were to strengthen the position of the Russian Orthodoxy in the Baltic provinces in relation to the Lutheran Evangelical Church. Primary education was removed from the jurisdiction of the Lutheran Church and placed under the control of the Russian Ministry of Education. In 1887, Russian replaced Latvian and Estonian as the language of instruction for primary schools in the Baltic provinces. The prestigious *Gymnazia* for the children of the German nobility were closed; and, in 1889, the process of Russification of the University of Dorpat was begun. In 1893, the town of Dorpat itself was renamed Iur'ev (in independent Estonia it became Tartu). The Russian police and judicial systems were also introduced into the Baltic provinces in 1888 and 1889. With the accession of Nicholas II, however, the Russification policies were relaxed and, on the eve of the 1905 Revolution, the Baltic Germans were hoping that they might recover some of the privileges they had lost.[28]

One gains the impression from recent histories of Latvia and Estonia that the Russification process was one in which the Latvians, Estonians and the Germans suffered alike – that Russification affected all the national groups equally. One might even be led to believe that the antagonism between Latvians and Estonians, on the one hand, and Germans, on the other, was a minor one, and that the real divide was between these three Baltic nationalities and the Russian government.[29] These conceptions, however, are not supported by the contemporary evidence and were probably arrived at by projecting backwards the political alignments among Baltic émigrés in the period after the Second World War. In fact, the main target of Russification was the privileged status of the Germans in the Baltic provinces. Moreover, despite the fact that the Latvians and Estonians suffered from the imposition of Russian as a language of instruction in primary schools, the Baltic Germans saw them as accomplices of the Russian government in the anti-German campaign. The siege mentality of the Germans, as well as the social stratification, helps explain the degree of ferocity that the 1905 Revolution would attain in the Baltic area.

Socialism in the Baltic provinces underwent a very different evolution from that in Russia. There were several reasons for this. One was that the relative isolation of the Baltic provinces cut them off from intellectual developments in the rest of the country. The Russian language was not widely known and, since educated Latvians and Estonians would know German rather than Russian, it was natural that knowledge of socialism should come through German rather than Russian sources. Moreover, as there was no peasant *mir* in the Baltic provinces, the current of thought represented by Chernyshevskii and Herzen, which proposed to base the future socialist society on that institution, had no appeal in the Baltic. Finally, since radical Latvians and Estonians tended to see the Russian government as a real or potential ally, rather than as an adversary, the terrorist tactics of the People's Will had little resonance among them. Thus, when socialist doctrine came to the Baltic provinces, it came as Social Democracy.

The first Baltic socialist group appeared in Vil'na in about 1887. Its members included a number of intellectuals (such as Leo Jogiches [Tyszka], Tsemech Kopelzon and Wacław Sielicki) who were influenced by the Polish socialist party, 'Proletariat'.[30] The composition of this group was multinational, but, as propaganda activities were extended among the local workers, this early unity was lost. Propaganda in Jewish workers' circles was carried out in Russian, while Polish was used in groups containing Polish and Lithuanian workers. One of the lasting achievements of 'Proletariat' had been the production of socialist literature written specially for workers, some of which had been translated into Russian.[31] Very few of the Jewish workers in Vil'na, however, could read Russian, although they were eager to learn the language for professional advancement.[32] The intellectuals who ran the study groups for Jewish workers, notably Julius Martov and Alexander Kremer, decided that a wider audience could be reached if, instead of conducting propaganda in Russian among workers in study groups, one were to address larger, more informal meetings using agitational literature in Yiddish.[33]

This idea was abhorrent to the members of the Jewish workers' circles, who felt themselves to be betrayed by the intelligentsia and deprived of the opportunity to acquire Russian culture.[34] The new tactic was defended, however, in a pamphlet written by Kremer entitled *On Agitation* and published in Geneva in 1896. The essay subsequently exerted a profound influence on Social Democracy throughout Russia. The production of agitational literature for Lithuanian workers did not meet with the same negative response with which Jewish workers greeted literature in Yiddish, but it led to serious divisions within Social Democracy in Lithuania.

In 1893, Alfons Morawski and Andrius Domaszewicz (both of whom belonged to the local gentry and were graduates of Russian universities) took over the workers' propaganda circles in Vil'na. They were joined in 1895 by Stanisław Trusiewicz, a member of 'Proletariat'. None of this group could speak Lithuanian and, initially, they confined themselves to distributing Polish socialist literature and to organizing Polish-speaking workers.[35] In order to reach Lithuanian workers, Domaszewicz and his associates formed an alliance with the *Varpas* group to publish Social Democratic literature in Lithuanian.[36]

In 1895, the Domaszewicz group expanded considerably with the influx of students from the secondary school in Vil'na, among whose number was Feliks Dzierżyński.[37] In the same year, the group held a conference – in which the publications' committee from *Varpas* took part on an equal footing with the Social Democrats – to draw up a programme.[38] The programme that emerged had the same kind of nationalist overtones as that of the Polish Socialist Party (PPS) drawn up two years previously. It called for the formation of an independent democratic republic, consisting of Lithuania, Poland and other countries, based on a free federation. The implication was that this would be a federation without Russia, since little faith was placed on the revolutionary potential of the Russians.[39] In 1896, the Social Democratic group constituted itself into the Lithuanian Social Democratic Party (LSDP) at a congress held on 1 May.[40]

At this congress, Trusiewicz objected that the party programme was a travesty of socialism, that collaboration with the *Varpas* group had diverted the Social Democrats from their real purpose and that, whereas it was incumbent upon the party to oppose the PPS, the LSDP was actually following its example. Trusiewicz, therefore, dissociated himself from the LSDP and, within weeks of the founding congress, he established his own Social Democratic group – the Workers' Union in Lithuania (Związek robotniczy na Litwie).[41] In 1900, the Workers' Union joined the party recently formed by Leo Jogiches and Rosa Luxemburg, the Social Democracy of the Kingdom of Poland (SDKP), to form the Social Democracy of the Kingdom of Poland and Lithuania (SDKPiL).[42]

As the LSDP gained wider support, it also became more Lithuanian (as opposed to Polish) in character. And, since relatively few Lithuanians were urban workers, the LSDP began to draw its support increasingly from rural districts. This tendency was strengthened in 1899, when Domaszewicz, Trusiewicz and most of the old leadership were arrested and were succeeded by people of Lithuanian peasant origin.[43]

The fact that Vil'na's working class was mainly Jewish ensured that the Bund would be a leading political force in the city. But the Bund's espousal of Jewish nationalism generated dissenters and these gravitated towards the RSDLP. Vil'na, consequently, had a variety of socialist parties and groups – some of them of all-Russian or even international significance. But as none of them was adapted to lead the revolutionary movement in the Lithuanian provinces as a whole, co-operation between them was necessary if the movement was to succeed. As it emerged, this co-operation would be only partially attained.

Latvian Social Democracy was also closely connected with the national movement, though in the Latvian provinces Social Democracy was based on a large Latvian working class. The earliest working-class organizations in the Latvian towns were not political but were concerned with providing workers with mutual aid, education and entertainment. The earliest of these mutual aid societies appeared during the 1860s and by 1890 there were 250 of them in Riga alone. These societies became the forum for Social Democratic agitation by the radical Latvian intelligentsia at the turn of the century.[44]

In 1886, the Riga Mutual Aid Society for Latvian Artisans began to publish the newspaper *Dienas Lapa* (Daily News), which, under the editorship of Peteris Stučka (a graduate in law of St Petersburg University), became the rallying point for the Latvian Social Democratic movement known as the 'New Current' (*Jauna strava*).[45] Besides Stučka, the chief representatives of the New Current were the poet Janis Pliekšans (better known as Rainis), F. Roziņš, J. Jansons-Brauns, P. Dauge and other of the more radical Latvian students at the universities of St Petersburg, Moscow and Dorpat.

Dienas Lapa maintained a lively interest in the German workers' movement, carrying regular reports and editorial comments on the subject. Events in Germany received more attention from *Dienas Lapa* than the revolutionary movement in Russia. After Rainis became editor of *Dienas Lapa*, in 1891, the paper began to pay even more attention to the German Social Democratic movement, reporting extensively the speeches of August Bebel and Paul Singer. In August 1893, Rainis attended the Third Congress of the Socialist International at Zurich. He took the opportunity of visiting Bebel, who provided him with a large amount of socialist literature to take back to Riga. In the autumn of 1893, after Rainis's return from Zurich, *Dienas Lapa* began to disseminate Marxist ideas and the first workers' circles began to appear in Latvia. In 1897, mass arrests took place of people active in the New Current and *Dienas Lapa* was closed down. Almost all of the most prominent figures in the New Current – including Stučka, Rainis and Jansons-Brauns – were sentenced to internal exile. Some, such as F. Roziņš and D. Bundža, managed to escape abroad, to Britain and the USA, where they set about producing Latvian language journals to promote Social Democracy.[46]

Between 1903 and 1905, the leadership of the Latvian Social Democratic movement passed to students at the Riga Polytechnic. They succeeded in establishing workers' Social Democratic groups, so that by 1905 there were 116 such groups in Riga alone. By the summer of 1905, the Latvian Social Democratic Party had over 1,000 members. The Riga students were also successful in extending Social Democratic propaganda to the countryside,[47] thus rendering Social Democracy in the Latvian (as in the Lithuanian) provinces a peasant as well as a workers' movement.

Among the Estonians there was no parallel with the New Current. In the 1890s the most radical group involving Estonian intellectuals was that associated with the writer Eduard Vilde at Dorpat University. The group, which had some acquaintance with Marxism, included Latvian and Russian students.[48] In 1901, Vilde and Konstantin Päts collaborated in producing the newspaper *Teataja* (The Herald) which highlighted social issues and which advocated support for the Russian democratic movement in the hope that its victory would bring benefits to the Estonians. This orientation was contested by the Estonian liberals, whose views were reflected in the newspaper *Postimees* (Postman). This was edited by Jaan Tõnisson and Villem Reiman, who believed that Estonians should avoid involvement in Russian affairs.[49] In the period preceding the 1905 Revolution, there was no indigenous Estonian Social Democratic movement. The Social Democratic group that was established in Reval, in 1904, consisted largely of Russians.

The beginning of the revolution

In September 1904, the Latvian Social Democratic Party and the Jewish Bund had come together to form a Federative Committee of socialist organizations in Riga. When news of Bloody Sunday in St Petersburg of 9 January 1905 reached Riga on the following morning, the Federative Committee, in conjunction with the Russian Social Democratic Labour Party, called an eight-day general political strike in Riga from 12 January. The workers from the main Riga factories came out on the appointed day and were joined by workers in Libau, Mitau and Windau (Ventspils). The strikes were accompanied by mass demonstrations that condemned not only the tsarist autocracy but also Russia's war against Japan and the conscription it involved. Events at first proceeded smoothly, with good-natured processions of workers carrying red banners and singing revolutionary songs in Latvian and Russian. But on 13 January demonstrators were fired on by troops; seventy of them were killed and some 200 more were wounded. Demonstrators trying to escape the gunfire were drowned in the river Dvina. The event brought about a hardening of attitudes on the part of the socialist parties, making them determined to respond in kind to any future attack and, consequently, to encourage the workers to acquire weapons.[50] From this point onwards, the use of firearms was to become a characteristic of the revolution in Livland and Kurland.

Also fuelling the strikes in January were the economic grievances of the Riga workers and these were reflected in the demands that the Federative Committee put forward in its leaflets. These included demands for an eight-hour working day, double rates of pay for overtime, the resolving of disagreements between management and workers by elected commissions, the ending of the system of fines and the improvement of hygiene conditions. The demands were not acceded to – the management even refused to reduce the working day to ten hours and made no concessions on wage rates. As a result, the strikes were renewed in February, this time with more success: the working day was reduced, on average, by one hour and an average wage increase of 10 per cent was obtained.[51]

In February and March 1905, the strike movement began to spread into the countryside, first in the district around Riga and then in an ever-widening area. The peasant demands were primarily economic – such as increases in wages, reduction of the working day to ten hours in summertime and to eight hours in winter, free time on public holidays and the abolition of child labour. The strikes of farm labourers were often accompanied by demonstrations at which the Latvian Social Democrats would speak and distribute their leaflets, encouraging the peasants to demand civil rights and the convocation of a constituent assembly. Notably, a demand that the Latvian Social Democrats did not advance was for the division of landed estates among the peasantry. The Latvian Social Democrats, like their comrades in the Estonian and Lithuanian movements, did not favour the division of large agricultural estates among the peasantry, the policy advocated by their Russian counterparts.[52]

A convenient and effective forum in Livland and Kurland for Social Democrat speakers to address the agrarian population was outside the churches. The use of the churches for this purpose served to emphasize that the Latvian peasants regarded the Lutheran Evangelical Church as the instrument of the German barons, especially since the pastors were often baronial appointees. The German landowners, for their part, used these 'church disturbances' to justify the formation of local *Selbstschutz* ('self-defence') militias to protect their interests – or, as one German writer put it, 'so that seven hundred years of German culture should not fall victim to the people'.[53] The policy of the Baltic Germans was to fight, rather than make any concessions to their farm labourers, whose economic position, they would argue, was by no means impoverished.

In Reval there had been a general strike, accompanied by mass demonstrations, in response to the events of Bloody Sunday in St Petersburg, but by 15 January things had almost returned to normal. In the course of the strike, the workers had put forward demands similar to those of the workers in Riga. The response of the authorities, however, was rather less implacable than that given to workers in Livland and Kurland. The Estland governor-general, A. V. Bel'gard, said that he could see no reason why the working day should not be reduced to ten hours and that the workers that he had met had presented a perfectly reasonable case for their demand. The governor-general's approach alarmed the Baltic Germans, who put pressure on the Russian government to have him recalled. On the day that Bel'gard left Reval, several thousand workers turned out to thank him for his humane treatment and accompanied him to the railway station with a torch-lit procession in his honour, much to the annoyance of the Reval Committee of the RSDLP.[54]

Unlike in neighbouring Livland, the urban strike movement in Estland did not spread rapidly to the countryside, though the example of Livland was much in the minds of both the peasant population and the authorities. At the end of March 1905, the governor of Estland, A. N. Giers, reported to A. G. Bulygin, the minister of the interior, that some demands of an economic character had been put forward by labourers on some landed estates.

There were, however, no peasant disturbances on any major scale, although his informants feared that the influx of outside agitators might ignite the discontent that certainly existed among the Estonian peasantry. Besides low wages and high rents, Estonian peasants resented the exclusive hunting and fishing rights which the Baltic German landowners enjoyed, the denial to them of the right to cut wood (even on the land which they rented), and the unpaid labour they were expected to perform on the maintenance of roads and bridges.[55]

One factor in the low level of militancy among Estonian peasants was that the Estonian liberals, grouped around the newspaper *Postimees*, responded positively to the tsar's manifesto of 18 February which invited petitions to be presented 'for the improvement of the state and the nation's well-being'. *Postimees* published a draft petition, which it suggested might be used as a model, and organized an extensive campaign amongst the Estonian peasants to encourage them to make the most of the opportunity. The draft petition included such proposed reforms as the extension of rights of land use, the limitation of the arbitrary powers of the landowners in fixing land prices and rents and the reorganization of local government. It also demanded that Estonian should be the language of instruction in Estonian primary schools. The peasants themselves, especially the landless ones, were quite capable of modifying the draft petitions and adding more radical demands – such as that for social insurance and state subsidies for consumer goods.

The liberal St Petersburg Latvian newspaper *Pēterburgas Avīzes* printed a draft petition similar to the one in *Postimees* and Latvian peasants also sent petitions to the government. The Latvians' petition campaign, however, was overshadowed by the strike movement and more militant forms of political activity in which they had the backing of the Social Democrats, who disapproved of the loyal format which the petitions took. On the other hand, the fact that the petition campaign was an official one alarmed the Baltic Germans, who sought to moderate it by publishing draft petitions of their own. The Germans were quite ready to countenance the use of Estonian or Latvian in primary schools, but they vehemently opposed demands for universal suffrage in elections to local government institutions.[56]

News of Bloody Sunday reached Vil'na on the evening of 10 January 1905 and a united committee of the LSDP, the Bund, the RSDLP and the PPS organized a political strike in protest to begin on the following day. The strike, which lasted until 17 January, brought out most of the Vil'na workers, but the organizers were unable to put forward any coherent demands. Moreover, because the strike involved mostly Jewish workers, who had no links with the agrarian population, the strike in Vil'na did not spread to the countryside.[57]

In 1904 the prohibition on the use of the Roman alphabet had been lifted, allowing newspapers to be published legally in Lithuania. One of the first newspapers to appear was the liberal *Vilniaus Žinios* (Vilnius News), edited by Petras Vileišis.[58] In February, it gave a stimulus to the peasants' petition campaign by printing a petition that Lithuanians based in St Petersburg had presented to Count Witte, asking that national, cultural and economic restrictions be removed from the Lithuanians and that Lithuanian should be used in administrative institutions and in primary and secondary schools. They wanted Lithuanians to be allowed to establish economic, industrial, charitable and other kinds of societies. The Lithuanian peasants responded enthusiastically and, encouraged by the agitators from the LSDP, put forward demands to reduce taxes, to improve primary education and to use Lithuanian in schools, local government and the judiciary. The authorities were alarmed that the peasants did not confine their discussions to measures that might improve their own economic position, but were venturing to pronounce on matters pertaining to the constitution of the Empire.[59]

The spring and summer of 1905

After the mass strikes and street violence of January and February 1905 there was a brief period of relative calm in Livland and Kurland. But by March the peasant movement in the two provinces had become increasingly active. A Latvian Social Democratic Labour Party leaflet of the time mentions that there had been widespread agrarian strikes, demonstrations and meetings and that the German landowners had felt themselves sufficiently threatened to send away their wives and children and to station troops on their estates. The violent behaviour of the soldiers had antagonized the peasants even more and there had been instances of peasants setting fire to mansion houses. The LSDLP leaflet went on to stress that the destruction of property should be avoided: it did not harm the landowners, because their property was insured, but it would discredit the peasants themselves and give their enemies the pretext to accuse them of vandalism and arson.[60] How much attention the Latvian peasant paid to these injunctions would be shown later in the year.

The leaflet also included a list of suggested demands for the peasants to put forward. These largely coincided with those that had appeared in the draft petition published in *Postimees* and *Pēterburgas Avīzes*.[61] Among them were the convocation of a constituent assembly; freedom of speech, the press and assembly; the right to strike and to form trade unions; inviolability of the person and residence; abolition of internal passports; and abolition of special peasants' courts and the introduction of the same system of justice for all. There were also a number of demands in the religious sphere, such as the right to run Church affairs, the right of parishes to appoint clergymen, and the transfer of the right to register births, marriages and deaths to the local authorities. In education, the leaflet demanded compulsory schooling for children aged from six to sixteen years; teaching in primary schools to be in the native language; that religion be taught only to those who desired it; and that primary and secondary education should be run by the local authorities.

In the spring and summer of 1905, economic strikes spread throughout the Baltic provinces. In industry these were exacerbated by the factory owners' attempts to revoke the concessions they had made in February. Political strikes also broke out in Riga in July and August (on the latter occasion when the government announced the mobilization of reservists). Encouraged by the LSDP, the Latvian peasants went on strike for higher wages, shorter hours and payment for female labour (since the contract they had with the landowner stipulated that the wife of a farm labourer should work 30–40 days a year without payment). In Livland, where there was more uniformity in the economic position of the peasants, householders and farm labourers acted in concert; but in Kurland, where the peasantry was more differentiated, the landless labourers took the lead in the peasant movement and put forward more radical demands. As tensions between peasants and landowners increased in the summer of 1905, many landowners abandoned their estates and sought refuge in the towns. On 6 August, martial law was declared in Kurland. This only served to inflame the situation and to encourage the peasants to put up armed resistance. In all forms of peasant action it was the Latvian peasants who were the most militant; Estonian and Lithuanian peasants were on the whole considerably more moderate. Anonymous leaflets addressed to the Estonian peasants during the summer reproached them for failing to follow the example of their Latvian counterparts.[62]

Vincas Kapsukas, a Lithuanian Social Democrat who organized peasant strikes in the Lithuanian countryside in 1905, believed that the relative inactivity of the Lithuanian peasants was due to several causes. One was the fact that they did not suffer from acute land hunger, having received more generous allotments of land after the 1863 Polish uprising than peasants in Russia proper. Another was that those peasants who were landless (and therefore likely to be more militant) had already emigrated. The dispersal of the Lithuanian proletariat to other towns also meant that Lithuanian peasants were deprived of the workers' influence. Spreading the revolutionary message to the Lithuanian countryside had, consequently, to be done by LSDP propagandists, the Bund having relatively little influence outside the larger towns. According to Kapsukas, the peasant movement in the Lithuanian provinces was led by the wealthier peasants. These had been previously involved in the national movement and had acquired some political awareness. For this group, it was not land that was the main issue but the limitation of their civil rights and national oppression. Peasants of this category had taken an active part in the petition campaign in the spring of 1905. They initially aligned themselves with the liberals, but in the course of the year they became more receptive to Social Democratic propaganda.[63]

In Vil'na and Kovno provinces there were strikes by farm labourers for higher wages and demands for the closure of taverns. The greater intensity of the movement in Kovno province was probably due to the influence of events in the neighbouring Kurland. In the Lithuanian provinces, however, there were demands for the removal of Russian schoolteachers and officials and their replacement by native Lithuanians. The peasant movement in the Lithuanian provinces tended to be directed more against the government's Russification policies than against the local landowners.[64]

The October strikes

A new phase in developments in the Baltic provinces in 1905 accompanied the publication of the tsar's manifesto on 17 October and the general strike in Russia. On 15 October, Riga's Federative Committee ordered the workers to begin a general political strike. By 17 October, the strike had spread to all the enterprises in the city, so that when news of the tsar's manifesto reached Riga, it was amidst mass meetings and demonstrations. A meeting called by the Federative Committee on 18 October refused to recognize the manifesto until civil rights had been granted, political prisoners had been released and Cossack and police patrols removed from the streets. The strike continued until 24 January, with daily demonstrations and meetings addressed by speakers (some of them women) in Latvian, Russian, German, Lithuanian, Polish and Yiddish, reflecting the varied national composition of Riga's working class.[65]

In Vil'na the railway workers' strike escalated into a general strike that began on 14 October. The week-long general strike was organized by a united strike committee that consisted of representatives of the LSDP and the Bund. On 16 October, a mass demonstration was held to request that the governor-general remove the Cossack patrols from the city. Troops fired on the demonstrators, leaving three people dead and thirty injured, all of the casualties being Jewish. The funeral of the victims, which took place the following day, was the occasion of a mass demonstration against the tsarist regime, at which speeches were made in Lithuanian, Yiddish, Polish and Russian. On 21 October, the last day of the general strike, government troops again opened fire on demonstrators, killing seven and injuring fifty. The carnage ensured that, in the days that followed, the general strike would find support in Kovno and towns throughout the Lithuanian provinces.[66]

In Reval the general strike took a remarkably similar form. There the workers offered to keep order, in return for the release of political prisoners and the removal of military patrols from the city. The governor-general agreed but, although the prisoners were released, the patrols remained. A protest meeting held on 16 October was fired on by troops, resulting in ninety deaths and 200 people injured. The official explanation was that the officer in charge of the troops had been drunk. As in Vil'na, the publication of the tsar's manifesto on 17 October was overshadowed in Reval by the aftermath of a recent massacre of workers. Despite the furious response of the Social Democrats and the continuation of the general strike until 25 October, the Estonian liberals were able to diffuse the situation by calling for a commission of enquiry into the episode to find the guilty parties.[67] Many workers, however, concluded that they now needed to arm themselves and attempted to find weapons on the estates of the German landowners – even if, on occasion, this might involve the destruction of the estate in question.[68]

Whereas in Russia the October general strike prompted the formation of soviets, this was not the case in the Baltic provinces: only in Reval was a Soviet of Workers' Deputies established at the end of November.[69] According to Kapsukas, all the Social Democratic parties in Lithuania and Western Belorussia, especially the Bund, were against the formation of soviets. Their argument was that, since 90 per cent of the local workers belonged to socialist parties, it was not necessary to create soviets to organize the working class. It was a different matter in Russia, where most of the workers were unorganized. Similar reasoning prevented Social Democrats in Latvia from following the Russian example.[70]

Two congresses took place in Riga during November that marked the beginning of a new phase in developments in Livland and Kurland: one was the Congress of Primary Schoolteachers and the other was the Congress of Volost Representatives. About a thousand delegates attended the Congress of Schoolteachers, which took place from 10–14 November. Schoolteachers were amongst the most radical groups in Latvian society and many of them were members of the Social Democratic Party. Among the congress's resolutions were that schoolteachers should ignore the existing school authorities and free the primary schools from bureaucratic control, and that teaching should be in the native language, Russian being a taught subject. The schoolteachers' congress also resolved that the teaching programme should be broadened to include economic and legal sciences, that the teaching of religion should not be compulsory and that education should be separated from both the Church and the state. But the teachers' congress did not confine itself to purely educational matters and expressed the view that, when local self-government had been reorganized, all peoples in the Russian Empire, including the Latvian people, would unite, 'where possible, in a single self-governing union'.[71] The resolutions clearly reflected the popular mood, because one finds them repeated or referred to in the demands of Latvian institutions of local self-government in November 1905.[72]

The Congress of Volost Representatives from Livland and Kurland met on 19–20 November. The purpose of the thousand or so deputies was the reorganization of local government in the two provinces. The existing structure, the congress thought, was unsatisfactory because it supported the power of the German barons. Hence, it would be necessary to dissolve the old volost institutions and hold elections to new executive committees (*ricibas komitejs*) based on democratic principles. Among the functions of a local executive committee were: to boycott the government and its officials and refuse to carry out their orders, especially those concerned with the transport of soldiers, Cossacks, dragoons and police officers; to pay the salaries of teachers, secretaries and members of the committee; to look after the schools (in which teaching by the new programme should be intro-

duced); to see to it that the local forests were not destroyed by the landowners; to supervise the closure of taverns; to ensure that the economic position
of farm labourers on the estates and farms should be improved; and to keep
the peace and take charge of self-defence. The congress stressed that the
executive committees were only interim institutions that would function
only until such time as the constituent assembly of the Russian state was
convoked. On the question of the future of self-government, the congress
adopted the same formula as the Congress of Schoolteachers had done previously: that 'every people, including the Latvian people, will unite, where
possible, in a single self-governing union'.[73]

Within a month, 430 executive committees had been set up in Livland
and Kurland. Reports from local tsarist officials, complaining about the
actions of the executive committees, indicate that the resolutions of the Congress of Volost Representatives were being carried out on the ground. The
tsarist authorities were powerless to prevent the establishment of the new
institutions because of the mass peasant support which they enjoyed and the
ability of the local militias to put up a stiff resistance to any troops that were
then quartered in the provinces. The governors-general were acutely aware
that it was useless to confront the executive committees with anything less
than major troop formations.[74]

The tsar's manifesto of 17 October, granting new political freedoms (including that of assembly), also made possible some political initiatives by the
liberal groups in the Baltic provinces. In October the group associated with
Vilniaus Žinios organized elections for an assembly to be held in Vil'na. The
assembly, chaired by Basanavičius, duly met on 21–22 November and was
accorded the title the 'Great Vilnius *Sejm*'. All parties and groups were
represented – the two existing parties, the Lithuanian Democratic Party and
the Lithuanian Social Democratic Party, being joined by two new creations,
the Christian Democrats and the Peasants' Union. Delegates attended from
Lithuanian communities in Russia, Latvia and East Prussia. Greetings were
sent from Lithuanians in the USA and Scotland. The resolutions of the *Sejm*
included the demand for Lithuanian autonomy and a national assembly in
Vilnius. It was thought that these objectives should be pursued in concert
with other peoples in the Russian Empire. The means employed to achieve
them should be strikes, the boycotting of Russian schools, non-payment of
taxes and the refusal to supply recruits for the Russian army.[75]

Following the manifesto of 17 October, the group associated with *Postimees* founded the Estonian National Progressist Party. This party, which
was headed by Tõnisson, adopted a programme similar to that of the Kadets
in Russia.[76] It was the Progressist Party that was instrumental in organizing
the Congress of People's Representatives that met at Dorpat from 27 to 29
November. The assembly quickly divided into two groups: the liberal followers of Tõnisson and the radical democratic camp headed by Peter Speeks,
the editor of the newspaper *Uudised* (News). Of the 800 delegates, the

radicals were in a large majority. The groups met separately – the liberals in the 'Bürgermusse', and the radicals in the university assembly hall, or Aula. Among the 'Bürgermusse' resolutions were demands for a constituent assembly, Estonian autonomy and a constitutional monarchy with a representative assembly. The Aula resolutions also called for a constituent assembly and Estonian autonomy, but in addition demanded the overthrow of the tsarist government, the formation of committees of local self-government, the boycott of government institutions, the closure of taverns, refusal to provide recruits for the army, non-payment of taxes, teaching in schools to be in Estonian, the abolition of the army and the arming of local militias. The radicals also advocated that the privileges of the landowners be abolished, but they did not demand the confiscation of their estates.[77]

In the wake of the congress, over fifty local self-governing committees were set up in the volosts of Estland and northern Livland. Even where such committees were not established, the existing tsarist officials were removed and replaced by elected representatives. It was at this time that a soviet was created in Reval, though it proved to be of short duration because of the arrival in the city of punitive units of the tsarist army.

The winter of discontent

At the end of November and the beginning of December, clashes began to occur between the local militias and the troops based on the baronial estates. On 30 November, a particularly bitter engagement took place at Tuckum in Kurland, where peasant militiamen – only 200 of whom had firearms – attacked soldiers and dragoons who had run riot in the town. The militiamen managed to inflict a number of casualties on the regular troops, obliging their commander to conclude a truce. This, however, was broken, allowing the local landowner, Baron von Recke, to kill some fifty Tuckum inhabitants, some of them women and children.[78] A few days later, the town of Talsen was subjected to a barrage of artillery fire to subdue its defenders. In the first days of December pitched battles also took place at Windau and Hasenpoth (Aizpute) in Kurland.[79]

The response of the peasants was to burn the manor houses of the Baltic German landowners. The extent of the destruction is summarized in Table 4.1. A Duma commission, which compiled the figures and looked into the question in 1908, commented that in the uezds of northern Livland, which was inhabited by Estonians, the scale of destruction was less than in southern Livland, which was inhabited by Latvians. To the commission this implied a greater militancy among the Latvians than among their Estonian neighbours. The commission was also impressed by the fact that although the number of destructions in Kurland and Livland was more or less equal (229 and 230 respectively), the monetary value of the damaged caused was greater (by 777,000 roubles) in Kurland than in Livland. The explanation the commission offered for this was 'the extreme bitterness of the Kurland

Table 4.1 Attacks on estates in the Baltic provinces and damage caused

	Number of attacks on estates	*Damages (in millions of roubles)*
Kurland	229	5.01
Southern Livland	183	3.83
Total	412	8.84
Northern Livland	47	0.41
Estland	114	2.80
Total	161	3.21

Latvians against their landowners, whose property they strove to destroy come what may'.[80]

In the wake of the Vilnius *Sejm*, the Lithuanian peasants, especially those in Kovno province, began to reorganize their local government institutions, expelling Russian officials and installing Lithuanians in their place. The new authorities ceased paying taxes to the government, organized armed militias, closed down taverns and reorganized the schools, making Lithuanian the language of instruction.[81]

By the end of 1905, the ending of hostilities with Japan had enabled the Russian army to come to the rescue of the beleaguered German barons, and a number of punitive expeditions were sent into the Baltic provinces. The Baltic German press encouraged Russian military intervention by asserting that the Latvians and Estonians intended to establish independent republics.[82] The punitive expeditions acted with great ferocity towards the Latvian and Estonian populations. The barons supplied them with 'proscription lists', all of the people named thereon being put to death without trial. As the expeditions proceeded through the country, from 10–30 people were shot in each village and hundreds more were flogged. The members of peasants' executive committees, people's militias and all who were suspected of being agitators were hanged.[83] These routine executions were often accompanied by more selective atrocities perpetrated by both the Russian forces and the Baltic Germans. Between December 1905 and May 1909, about 700 people in the Latvian and Estonian provinces were condemned to death by military tribunal; over 8,000 more were imprisoned and exiled to Siberia.[84]

In the Lithuanian provinces the punitive expeditions dispersed the local authorities that had been established by the peasants and restored the tsarist institutions. They shot or arrested without trial those whom they suspected of being involved in revolutionary activities, often burning their houses. Many peasants were flogged or sent to Siberia for their involvement with the new democratic institutions. By 1906, about 2,000 people had been arrested in Vil'na province and about 800 in Kovno province.[85]

The disturbances in the Baltic provinces had caused the alliance between the Baltic Germans and the Russian government to become closer and to bring about a relaxation of the Russification measures directed against the Germans. In May 1905, the use of German was once more permitted as a language of instruction in Baltic private schools. In November the Livland *Ritterschaft* sent a memorandum to the minister of the interior arguing that the Russification policy and not the agitation of the Social Democrats was responsible for the current crisis. Such policies should therefore be revoked in the interests of social stability. The petitions of the Baltic Germans were sympathetically received by the government and, as the countryside was pacified, new concessions were made to the Germans in the sphere of local government and education.[86] Relations with the Latvians and Estonians, however, were embittered and would be a lasting legacy of the events of 1905.

Conclusion

The 1905 Revolution in the Baltic provinces consists of many interwoven threads, imparting to it a complex dynamic. Some of the driving forces behind the Baltic revolution were the same as the revolution in the neighbouring Russian provinces. In Russia, as in the Baltic provinces, the revolution was fuelled by a variety of grievances, some against the tsarist regime and some against the landowning class or the business community.

But there were also features that were common to the 1905 Revolution in the Baltic area as a whole. These concerned the native inhabitants' desire to assert their national identity by making their language the recognized one in the spheres of culture, education, local administration and the judiciary. They also included aspirations to establish national representative assemblies that would be based on democratic principles.

A third dimension embraces those features of the 1905 Revolution that were specific to each of the three different peoples. A major factor in this regard was the historical heritage of the territories: their division into the German Lutheran and Polish Catholic realms. This heritage was integrated into the national self-identities with the emergence of the three national movements in the second half of the nineteenth century. Although the Latvians and the Estonians had imbibed their national ideology from German thought, they saw the Germans as incomers and oppressors. The antagonism towards the Germans was a prominent feature, particularly of the Latvians' national movement. Lithuanians did not have a comparable antagonism towards the Poles, although the secular wing of the Lithuanian national movement sought to distance itself from Polish culture and Roman Catholicism. And because Lithuanian peasants had gained land at the expense of the Poles after the 1863 rebellion, they were less inclined to seize Polish estates in 1905.

Amongst all three Baltic peoples socialist ideas had emerged at the same time as national awareness, and the national and social movements were closely associated. But in both its national and socialist currents, the Latvians showed more radicalism than the Estonians. Politics among the Estonians took a liberal rather than a socialist direction. One may observe that this tendency was encouraged for a time by the judicious rule of tsarist officials in Estland. Among Lithuanians, socialism had to compete with Roman Catholicism as a national ideology – one that endorsed conservatism rather than revolution. This factor also acted in 1905 to moderate the revolutionary upsurge in the Lithuanian provinces.

The revolutions in all the Baltic provinces suffered the same fate of being crushed by military force. They share this fate with the revolution in Russia as a whole. But whereas the revolution in Russia reappeared again in 1917, with renewed vigour, that in the Baltic was smothered by German occupation. But did the Baltic revolution of 1905 really lead to nothing? The answer must be that it did, in fact, re-emerge – though in other forms. What succeeded the 1905 Baltic revolution was the foundation of the independent Baltic republics in 1918, and also the not inconsiderable contribution made by the three Baltic peoples to the formation of the Soviet state. The 1905 Revolution in the Baltic is, consequently, a landmark both in the emergence of the Soviet regime and in the development of the Latvian, Estonian and Lithuanian nations.

Notes

1　S. M. Dubrovskii, *Sel'skoe khoziaistvo i krest'ianstvo Rossii v period imperializma* (Moscow, 1975), p. 98.
2　'Lifliandskaia guberniia', in *Entsiklopedicheskii slovar'*, Vol. 17 (St Petersburg, 1904), p. 845.
3　'Estliandskaia guberniia', in ibid., Vol. 41, p. 117.
4　'Kurliandskaia guberniia', in ibid., Vol. 17, p. 86.
5　Dubrovskii, *Sel'skoe khoziaistvo*, p. 98.
6　Ia. P. Krastyn', *Revoliutsiia 1905–1907 godov v Latvii* (Moscow, 1952), p. 21.
7　*Istoriia Estonskoi SSSR*, Vol. 2 (Tallinn, 1966), p. 85.
8　L. C. D. Bray, *Essai critique sur l'histoire de la Livonie* (Dorpat, 1817), p. 61; 'Lifliandskaia guberniia', p. 844.
9　P. P. Maslov, 'Razvitie zemledeliia i polozhenie krest'ian do nachala XX veka', in L. Maslov (ed.), *Obshchestvennoe dvizhenie v Rossii v nachale XX-go veka*, Vol. 1 (St Petersburg, 1909), p. 26.
10　*Istoriia Latviiskoi SSR*, Vol. 2 (Riga, 1954), p. 159.
11　Ibid., p. 78.
12　V. K. Iatsunskii, 'Znachenie ekonomicheskikh sviazei s Rossiei dlia khoziaistvennogo razvitiia gorodov Pribaltiki v epokhu kapitalizma', *Istoricheskie zapiski*, Vol. 45 (1954), pp. 131, 134.
13　A. Mierna, 'Rigas teritorija un iedzivotaji 1860–1917 gada', in *Riga, 1860–1917* (Riga, 1978), p. 21.
14　R. Pullat, 'Tallinna elanikkonna kujunemine aastail 1871–1917', *Eesti NSV Teaduste Akadeemia Toimetised. Ühiskonnateaduste seeria 3* (1964), pp. 204–9.
15　V. Merkys, *Razvitie promyshlennosti i formirovanie proletariata Litvy v XIX v.* (Vilnius, 1969), p. 364.
16　A. Šapoka (ed.), *Lietuvos istorija* (Vilnius, 1990), p. 667.
17　Joachim Mai, *Das deutsche Kapital in Russland, 1850–1894* (Berlin, 1970), p. 102.

18 M. I. Kozin, *Ocherki ekonomicheskoi istorii Latvii, 1860–1900* (Riga, 1972), p. 394.

19 A. Köörna, *Suure Sotsialistliku Oktoobrirevolutsioon majanduslikud eeldused Eestis* (Tallinn, 1961), p. 19.

20 T. Karjahärm and R. Pullat, *Eesti revolutsionnitules, 1905–1907* (Tallinn, 1975), p. 29.

21 Merkys, *Razvitie*, p. 368.

22 P. A. Zaionchkovskii, *Otmena krepostnogo prava v Rossii* (Moscow, 1968), pp. 214–24.

23 V. A. Tvardovskaia, *Ideologiia poreformennogo samoderzhaviia* (Moscow, 1978), p. 65.

24 G. Libermanis, *Jaunlatvieši* (Riga, 1957), pp. 132–3.

25 Vincas Kapsukas, 'Iš Aušros archivų', *Raštai*, Vol. 10 (Vilnius, 1971), pp. 470–9; Jerzy Ochmański, *Litewski ruch narodowo-kulturalny w XIX wieku* (Białystok, 1965), pp. 148–9; Michał Römer, *Litwa: Studium o odrodzeniu narodu Litewskiego* (Lwów, 1908), pp. 130–2.

26 Ochmański, *Litewski ruch*, p. 136.

27 Römer, *Litwa*, p. 164.

28 Alexander von Tobien, *Die livländische Ritterschaft in ihrem Verhältnis zum Zarismus und russischen Nationalismus* (Riga, 1925), pp. 496–500; E. Seraphim, *Baltische Geschichte im Grundriss* (Reval, 1908), pp. 387–403.

29 Andrejs Plakans, *The Latvians: A Short History* (Stanford, 1995), pp. 101–2; Toivo U. Raun, *Estonia and the Estonians* (Stanford, 1991), pp. 66–7.

30 V. Merkys, *Narodnikai ir pirmieji marksistai Lietuvoje* (Vilnius, 1967), pp. 119–25.

31 Zygmunt Łukawski, *Polacy w rosyjskim ruchu socjaldemokratycznym w latach 1883–1893* (Cracow, 1970), pp. 123–5.

32 Iu. Martov, *Zapiski sotsial-demokrata* (Berlin, 1922), pp. 187–8.

33 Ibid., pp. 226–7.

34 Ibid., p. 229.

35 Vincas Kapsukas, 'Trumpa Lietuvos Social-Demokratų Partijos istorija', in *Raštai*, Vol. 7 (Vilnius, 1964), p. 548.

36 Ibid., p. 553.

37 Merkys, *Narodnikai*, p. 119.

38 Steponas Kairys, *Lietuva budo* (New York, 1957), pp. 243–4.

39 Zigmas Angarietis, *Lietuvos revoliucinio judėjmo ir darbininkų kovos istorija* (Smolensk, 1921), p. 179.

40 Kairys, *Lietuva budo*, p. 274.

41 N. Michta, and J. Sobczak, 'Stanisław Trusiewicz (Kazimierz Zalewski)', *Z pola walki*, Vol. 1(69) (1975), pp. 111–12.

42 Walentyna Najdus, *SDKPiL a SDPRR, 1893–1907* (Wrocław, 1973), pp. 73–7.

43 Ibid., p. 557; Vincas Kapsukas, '1905 metai Lietuvoje ir Vakarų Baltarusijoje', *Raštai*, Vol. 12 (Vilnius, 1978), p. 537.

44 P. Dauge, *P. Stučkas dzive un darbs* (Riga, 1958), p. 52.

45 Ibid., p. 51.

46 K. Lander, 'Ocherki iz istorii latyshskogo naroda', *Russkaia mysl'*, Vol. 10 (September 1906), p. 31.

47 Ibid.; *Ocherki istorii Kommunisticheskoi partii Latvii, Tom 1: 1893–1919* (Riga, 1962), p. 83.

48 H. Moosberg, 'Marksistlikud ringid Tartu ülikoolis ja veterinaaria instituudis XIX saj. 80–90-ndel aastal', *Eesti NSV ajaloo küsimüsi*, Vol. 2 (1961), p. 219.

49 Evald Uustalu, *The History of the Estonian People* (London, 1952), pp. 146–7.

50 *Revoliutsiia 1905–1907gg. v Latvii: dokumenty i materialy* (Riga, 1956), pp. 7–27.
51 Lander, 'Ocherki', p. 36.
52 Brūno Kalniņš, *Latvijas sociāldemokratijas piecdesmit gadi* (Stockholm, 1956), p. 44; Ia. P. Krastyn', 'K voprosu ob agrarnoi politike Kommunisticheskoi partii Latvii', *Voprosy istorii KPSS*, Vol. 4 (1959), pp. 72–87.
53 A. Transehe-Roseneck, *Die lettische Revolution*, Vol. 2 (Berlin, 1907), pp. 178–87.
54 *Revoliutsiia 1905–1907gg. v Estonii: Sbornik dokumentov i materialov* (Tallinn, 1955), pp. 52–4.
55 Ibid., pp. 92–3.
56 R. Sh. Ganelin, 'Petitsii estonskikh, latviiskikh i litovskikh krest'ian po ukazu 18 fevralia 1905g.', *Vspomogatel'nye istoricheskie distsipliny*, Vol. 18 (1987), pp. 199–202; Karjahärm and Pullat, *Eesti revolutsionnitules*, pp. 60–1.
57 *Revoliutsiia 1905–1907gg. v Litve. Dokumenty i materialy* (Vilnius, 1961), pp. 94–6; A. Tyla, *1905 metų revoliucija Lietuvos kaime* (Vilnius, 1968), p. 60.
58 Römer, *Litwa*, pp. 317, 329.
59 Tyla, *1905*, p. 65.
60 *Revoliutsiia 1905-1907gg. v Latvii*, pp. 119–21.
61 Ganelin, 'Petitsii', p. 207.
62 *Revoliutsiia 1905–1907gg. v Estonii*, pp. 200, 241.
63 Kapsukas, '1905 metai Lietuvoje ir Vakarų Baltarusijoje', pp. 537–8; Leonas Sabaliūnas, *Lithuanian Social-Democracy in Perspective, 1893–1914* (Durham, N.C., 1990), p. 58.
64 B. B. Veselovskii, V. S. Golubev and V. G. Groman (eds), *Agrarnoe dvizhenie v Rossii v 1905–1906gg.* (St Petersburg, 1908), p. 399.
65 J. Bērziņš, 'Rīgas rūpniecibas strādnieku streiku kustiba 1905. gadā', in *Latvijas stradnieki un ziemnieki 1905–1907. g. revolūcijā* (Riga, 1986), pp. 54–8.
66 Vincas Kapsukas, 'Kas darosi mūsų miestuose ir sodžiuose', *Raštai*, Vol. 2 (Vilnius, 1961), p. 375; *Revoliutsiia 1905–1907gg. v Litve*, p. 189; J. Jurginis, V. Merkys and J. Žiugžda (eds), *Lietuvos TSR istorija*, Vol. 2 (Vilnius, 1963), p. 327.
67 *Revoliutsiia 1905–1907gg. v Estonii*, pp. 259-61; Karjahärm and Pullat, *Eesti revolutsionnitules*, p. 95.
68 *Istoriia Estonskoi SSSR*, p. 432.
69 T. Kar'iakhiarm, J. Krastins and A. Tyla, *Revoliutsiia 1905–1907 godov v Pribaltike* (Tallin, 1981), pp. 54–5.
70 Kapsukas, '1905 metai Lietuvoje ir Vakarų Baltarusijoje', p. 556; Brūno Kalniņš, 'The Social Democratic Movement in Latvia', in Alexander and Janet Rabinowitch, with L. K. D. Kristof (eds), *Revolution and Politics in Russia* (Bloomington, 1972), p. 140.
71 *Revoliutsiia 1905–1907gg. v Latvii*, pp. 260–3.
72 Ibid., pp. 153, 156, 159, 172.
73 Ibid., pp. 164–8; A. Puļķis and I. Ronis, 'Revolucionārā kustiba Latvijas laukos 1905. gadā', in *Latvijas stradnieki un ziemnieki 1905–1907. g. revolūcijā* (Riga, 1986), pp. 110–11.
74 *Revoliutsiia 1905–1907gg. v Latvii*, pp. 168–9.
75 Römer, *Litwa*, pp. 386–93; Pranas Čepėnas, *Naujųjų laikų Lietuvos istorija* (Chicago, 1977), pp. 339–46.
76 Karjahärm and Pullat, *Eesti revolutsionnitules*, pp. 100–1.
77 Ibid., pp. 113–16; Raun, *Estonia and the Estonians*, pp. 84–5; *Istoriia Estonskoi SSSR*, pp. 443–5; Transehe-Roseneck, *Die lettische Revolution*, pp. 401–2.
78 *Revoliutsiia 1905–1907gg. v Latvii*, pp. 327–31.

79   Piotr Łossowski, 'Powstania rewolucyjne w guberniach nadbałtyckich Rosji w 1905 r', *Z pola walki*, Vol. 18 (1975), No. 2(70), pp. 36–8.

80   *Revoliutsiia 1905–1907gg. v Latvii*, pp. 196–8; Toivo U. Raun, 'The Revolution of 1905 in the Baltic Provinces and Finland', *Slavic Review*, Vol. 43 (1984), No. 3, p. 461.

81   Čepėnas, *Naujuju*, pp. 360–1.

82   *Appeal to the Civilised World against the Bestialities in Lettonia and Esthonia* (May 1906), British Library: Call Number: 1850.b.45.

83   Ernest O. F. Ames, *The Revolution in the Baltic Provinces of Russia: A Brief Account of the Activity of the Lettish Social Democratic Workers Party* (London, 1907), p. 66.

84   H. Kruus, *Grundriss der Geschichte des estnischen Volkes* (Tartu, 1932), p. 189; Kalniņš, 'The Social Democratic Movement in Latvia, p. 141.

85   Čepėnas, *Naujuju*, p. 375; Jerzy Ochmański, *Historia Litwy* (Wrocław, 1967), p. 218.

86   Seraphim, *Baltische Geschichte*, pp. 405–9.

5 Finland in 1905

The political and social history of the revolution

Antti Kujala

This chapter seeks to explore Finland's status within the Russian Revolution of 1905. The autonomy and political freedoms granted for Finland placed the Finns in a position different from that of all the other inhabitants of the Russian Empire. There was a constant clash between the empire-encompassing viewpoint of the Russian revolutionary parties and Finnish particularist interests. As a result of the repressive integration policy of the imperial government in the years 1899 to 1905 the Finnish political culture and political parties started to approach their Russian counterparts, but the freedom enjoyed by Finland, as of the autumn of 1905, reversed this trend almost completely.

By the beginning of the twentieth century, the Finnish political system and the structure of the country's society retained some old Swedish features (the Diet, the fairly few restrictions imposed on civic activities, the freedom of the peasants) which made the country differ from Russia. However, the inadequate operative capacity of the political system (the emperor was the major obstacle of reforms) and the problematic issues in the social structure (the large role still played by agriculture, rural over-population and the undeveloped labour market conditions) were factors promoting instability, associating Finland with Eastern Europe to a greater extent than Scandinavia.

The passive resistance against the government's integration policy and the revolutionary events of 1905 politicized the Finnish society, involving also the landless population of the rural areas, much more thoroughly than would have been the case in the absence of such policy.

Economic and social changes behind political developments

External impulses have greatly – but not fully – conditioned the development of Finnish economy, society and politics. Finland's connection to the Russian market and the economic policy of the Empire constituted the decisive conditions for the launch of the Finnish industrialization process towards the end of the nineteenth century, while the birth of the Finnish state was based on the status of the Finnish provinces, ceded by Sweden in 1809, within the Russian Empire. The Finnish declaration of independence in 1917 was a part of the Russian Revolution.

Despite the ongoing industrialization, primary production (agriculture and forestry) still accounted for about 40 per cent of Finnish GDP in the years preceding the First World War. The share of processing industries was about one-fourth and that of services one-third of GDP. During the years 1890 to 1913 the growth of the Finnish economy was more rapid than during the period of sluggish growth from 1860 to 1890.

In 1900 the Finnish population totalled about 2.7 million, 87 per cent of whom still lived in the rural areas. However, a certain small share of the rural population worked in non-agricultural industries. In 1910, the majority of industrial workers lived in rural municipalities around the larger cities (thus, in practice, belonging to the urban population) or in industrial centres in rural areas. The concentration of the working classes in large cities and population centres gave them a greater social and political impact than their numbers would otherwise have suggested. The peasants were divided into the landowning and landless farmers (tenant farmers and cottagers), and there was still a large stratum of agricultural labourers under the actual farmers. The so-called 'landless population issue' concerned the problems of the tenant farmers and the agricultural labourers, both dependent on the landowning peasants. The landless population accounted for over 60 per cent of the people involved in agriculture, and almost as many as 50 per cent of them (that is, those people involved in agriculture) could be classified as agricultural labourers.

The Finnish population grew in the period 1860 to 1910 by about 69 per cent, while the corresponding growth in Sweden during this period was 43 per cent. The industrial workers accounted for 12 per cent and urban population for 15 per cent of the Finnish population in 1910, while the corresponding percentages in Sweden were 32 and 30, respectively. The urban population accounted for 56 per cent of the entire Swedish population growth in the period 1860 to 1910, whereas the same figure in Finland was only 27 per cent. Thus, most of Finnish population growth took place within the agricultural sector. The cornerstones of Finnish society were of Scandinavian nature, but the large proportional growth of the landless population and the proletarization of tenant farmers (not necessarily in absolute terms but in relation to the landowning peasants), combined with the low productivity of agriculture, were features that distinguished Finland from Scandinavia and Western and Central European countries. Again, the Finnish pattern was one more associated with Eastern Europe. This is true despite the fact that serfdom had never existed in Finland, nor any collective forms of land use, as in Russia (except for the period characterized by the harvesting of burn-beaten lands in Eastern Finland).

Finland's special status was not only based on legislation but also had an administrative and economic basis. The mutual relationship between the

Finnish and Russian customs areas was defined in terms which were disadvantageous to the subjugated country, whilst providing the maximum benefit to Russia. Paradoxically enough, this arrangement proved in some cases to be a determinant motor for the development of Finnish industry. Russian exports to Finland were mainly free of customs duties, while Russia protected itself against Finnish competition through the sorts of tariffs and import restrictions that might be imposed on foreign imports. However, Russia ensured its access to the most necessary Finnish products through customs duties that were lower than those on foreign imports. It also had some duty-free export quotas.

The profitability of the trade between Russia and the Grand Duchy was based on the difference between the high Russian customs duties and the much lower Finnish duties. The low Finnish customs duties imposed on Western raw materials and machines decreased the Finnish production costs, ensuring the Finnish producers a competitive edge over the Russians (despite the Russian customs duties imposed on Finnish goods), while the high Russian duties on Western goods increased the production costs of the Russian producers. This customs policy was particularly advantageous to the Finnish paper industry; its exports to Russia accounted for 95 per cent of all Russian paper imports and for between a quarter and one-third of all Russian paper consumption before the First World War. Other industrial sectors were much less competitive. The Russian customs policy forced them to remain on the domestic market, thereby limiting their growth potential. Finland was able to export its sawn timber, wood-pulp and agricultural products only to Western and Central Europe. Indeed, sawn timber accounted for some 40–50 per cent of total Finnish exports in the decades preceding the war. The capital-intensive forest industry dominated the Finnish industrialization process and employed a relatively low number of people. Thus, the Russian customs had a narrowing impact on the Finnish industrial structure, contributing to the fact that Finland remained dependent on agriculture. However, as the country was quite agrarian in the first place, this decelerating impact was ultimately fairly marginal.

Finland could not protect itself against cheap Russian grain. In order to keep the level of industrial wages low, while still providing the workers with purchasing power, the country also allowed grain to be imported from abroad. The cheap imported grain, combined with the decrease in the prices of agricultural products, forced farmers to take up animal husbandry. The landowners sought compensation for the flow of cheap Russian and foreign grain by increasing the rents and day-labour imposed on the tenant farmers. The rental burden of the tenants was 30–40 per cent of the net production of the land they farmed. Unlike the landowning farmers, the landless population did not benefit from the proceeds of the sale of timber to the forest industry. The socio-economic contrasts in the rural areas, therefore, became increasingly stark.

Significant parts of Russian industry deemed Finland to be too dangerous a competitor and would not accept the merger of the two customs areas. Russia had thus created a mechanism that in the end – by the turn of the century – became an obstacle for the creation of a joint Finnish–Russian customs area.[1]

Finnish autonomy

A new idea took root in Finland during the course of the nineteenth century, suggesting that the country had its own constitution based on Swedish fundamental laws dating from the reign of Gustav III (1771–92). According to this view, the Russian tsars, in vowing to observe Finland's fundamental laws, shared legislative power with the Finnish Diet, thereby making the tsar (referred to as the 'emperor' in Finnish usage) a constitutional ruler in Finland, even though he was an autocrat in Russia. This idea was based on modern parliamentary thinking and, in reality, had no place in a situation where Finland had been annexed by force of arms to the Russian Empire in 1809. Nevertheless, this Finnish interpretation helped the country develop as a separate state and one that became increasingly distinguished from Russia.

Because of the divergence between Finnish and Russian interpretations, all efforts to update the old Swedish fundamental laws to correspond to the new political situation failed. Not a single Russian emperor between 1809 and 1917 gave a final answer to the question of what parts of the old laws they considered as being still in force. The result was that Finland lacked an agreed-upon and precise constitution.

In practice, the emperors, particularly Alexander II and Alexander III, observed the decrees of the Gustavian fundamental laws as far as possible. The new Diet Act of 1869 brought an important addition to Finland's administration, but so did the institutions created by executive measures by the emperor – such as the Senate, which acted as Finland's domestic government, and the system for presenting Finnish affairs in St Petersburg headed by the minister secretary of state for Finland. The members of the Senate and the minister secretary of state were the emperor's official Finnish advisers (and were appointed by him) and, in general, their influence in the administration of the country was more significant than that of the Diet. The Diet was divided into four estates until 1906, and members represented these estates. Suffrage was neither universal nor equal. The majority of the population did not have the right to vote.

Finland's political system was therefore defined, *de facto*, by a system for balancing Finnish and Russian interests formed by the institutions of both countries in handling Finnish affairs. The establishment of this practice gave rise to the idea, encouraged in Finland, that Finland had her own constitution.

The Russian emperors voluntarily accepted the established political system in Finland as long as the benefits of doing so – above all, the preservation of the country as a peaceful corner of the Empire – outweighed the disadvantages. They even encouraged the development of Finnish, the language of the majority of the population, and Finnish-language culture, towards a point where it would reach equality with Swedish. The emperors believed that the rise of Finnish nationalism would eliminate the basis for any political separatism aimed at reuniting the country with Sweden. Separatist activity, indeed, remained a mere curiosity in Finland throughout the nineteenth century.[2]

Administrative integration, 1899–1905

With the 'February Manifesto' of 1899, Nicholas II reduced the Finnish Diet to the status of an advisory body for the enactment of imperial legislation, laws which were to be implemented in both Finland and Russia, or those to be implemented only in Finland but which touched on imperial interests. Up to that point, the Diet had had the right to alter and reject legislative proposals that it deemed unacceptable and to determine the final content of legislation. The emperor had only the power either to pass the law or leave it unratified. The February Manifesto thus eliminated the Diet's say in imperial affairs. From then on, the Diet had the right to submit statements on proposals for imperial legislation, but these statements were not in any way binding for the emperor or the Russian State Council.

Most Finns considered the February Manifesto to be a gross violation of Finland's fundamental laws and as being virtually equivalent to a *coup d'état*. From the imperial viewpoint, however, the emperor had merely enacted a new system of legislation, as, in his opinion, he was entitled to do.[3]

The Russian government primarily needed the February Manifesto to put an end to Finland's own army and to introduce Russian-style conscription. The manifesto was issued to induce the reluctant Finnish Diet to accept the reform. If it would not submit, it would simply be bypassed. This confrontation demonstrated that the system for balancing mutual interests that had operated up until then no longer functioned. This was due to both the modernization of Russia's administration and to the rise of mass political activity in both Finland and Russia, which prevented officials from finding solutions agreeable to both countries as they had before.

The February Manifesto gave rise to peaceful opposition in Finland, but Governor-General N. I. Bobrikov (1898–1904) began to repress it heavy-handedly. At the same time, he began to integrate Finland's administration into that of the Empire. From the Russian government's standpoint, these moves meant the suppression of a rebellious Finnish separatist movement. Bobrikov was blind to the fact that the majority of Finns had been completely loyal to the emperor and the Russian Empire up until then. As Sergei Witte observed in his memoirs, Bobrikov imagined that he had been sent to Finland to put down a revolt, but in reality he provoked one.[4] In this regard, the Russian government's policy on Finland can be seen as a self-fulfilling prophecy.

The Finnish constitutionalists (comprising the Swedish Party and the Young Finns) called on young men of conscription age to boycott the draft that was to be implemented under the new conscription legislation. This boycott was the most noteworthy form of the passive resistance that developed across the country in response to Russian moves. The constitutionalists also developed an underground resistance movement, the *Kagal*, despite their generally conservative political and social leanings.

In the spring of 1903, the emperor issued a special degree granting Bobrikov a range of extraordinary powers to allow him to eliminate the opposition that had emerged. Under these new powers, a significant number of the leaders of the constitutionalist opposition were ordered into foreign exile. Bobrikov then tried to rule Finland with the help of the conciliation-minded Old Finns. Unlike the constitutionalists, the representatives of this party remained in the Senate. The Swedish Party and the two groupings within the Finnish Party were spokesmen for the upper ranks of society (the educated class and the middle class), the Old Finns for the wealthy peasants.

The Finnish Active Resistance Party, a small clandestine organization, came into being in the autumn of 1904. Unlike the constitutionalists, the Activists were prepared to resort to armed struggle and terrorist acts against the Russian authorities and to join forces with the Russian revolutionary movement. Many of the Activists were intellectuals from the higher social strata, with the majority of them having Swedish as their mother tongue. The Activist Party was revolutionary in political terms, but it had no social programme. Privately, though, the Activists were more progressive than the constitutionalists. The Finnish Workers' Party, meanwhile, was established in 1899, in response to workers' issues, the struggle for voting rights and the defence of Finland's political autonomy. In 1903 the party adopted a Social Democratic platform, changing its name to the Finnish Social Democratic Party. Unlike in Russia, the workers' organizations and newspapers were functioning legally.

In spite of the many actions initiated by Bobrikov, the fact remains that his integration policy failed to progress more than half way. When he was felled by an assassin's bullet on 16 June 1904 (n.s), Finland was still far from having the status and conditions of a Russian province.[5]

Passive resistance and the popular masses

The alienation of the tenant farmers and agricultural workers from the landowners and the Finnish state that served their interests was shown by the unwillingness of these strata to subscribe to the popular petition against the February Manifesto, which was signed by over half a million citizens (that is, by more than one in five Finns). The landless rural population was also far more willing to accept and participate in the Russian-style military conscription. That is to say, that faced with social and economic agonies the landless population put their faith in the 'good emperor', who they hoped would put the self-serving Finnish upper class in its place and implement a general land reform. But, as in Russia, only a few years later this naive monarchism would be replaced by political radicalism, as the tenant farmers started to strike against their masters during 1903.

By the turn of the century, the Russian revolutionaries began to take notice of the situation of the Finnish landless population, advising the Finnish constitutionalists, then in political opposition, that they should try to solve this problem. Otherwise, they argued, the Russian government would exploit this weak spot of the Finnish society, seeking to gain the acceptance of the landless people by presenting a quasi-reformist programme (in the tradition of the partly successful action taken by the imperial government after the 1863 revolt in Poland and Lithuania).[6] However, it was virtually impossible for the constitutionalists, and the Swedish Party in particular, to accept the idea that both the landless population issue and the suffrage question called for an immediate and thorough solution. That would not only challenge their liberal ideology (for example, with regard to their desire to protect the freedom of contract against regulation, as far as the land question was concerned) but would also involve the fact that the leading, Swedish-speaking stratum of society – which dominated two of the four estates in the Diet, as well as the administration until the turn of the century (and the economy far beyond that) – had more to lose than the others.

The passive resistance conducted by the constitutionalists against the government did, however, shake the traditional trust in authority shared by the popular masses. It turned out that the uneducated rural masses did lend a more attentive ear to those originating from the urban working class who were agitating for a boycott of conscription than they did to the students and other upper-class exponents of resistance. The passive resistance policy of the constitutionalists, therefore, launched a radicalization process in the countryside and among the popular masses in general. In fact, this process began to escape the control of the constitutionalists: the movement for passive resistance turned against its initiators.

Had it not been for the autonomy issue of the early twentieth century and the events of the year 1905, the Finnish labour movement would probably have remained a fairly insignificant social phenomenon, since the size of the Finnish industrial and urban working population was so small. But these issues and courses of events also had a politicizing effect on the Finnish countryside, and made the landless population, already faced with hardships, identify itself with the labour movement. Consequently, by international standards, the Finnish Social Democratic Party attained an exceptionally large degree of popular and electoral support, starting with the first election by universal and equal suffrage for the unicameral parliament in 1907, in which the SDP gained 37 per cent of the votes and 40 per cent of the seats, on a 71 per cent turnout. In Sweden, with no similar political crises, it took the labour movement decades longer to win such considerable support among the agricultural labourers.

During the very first years of the new century, the attitude of the Finnish Workers' Party (renamed the Social Democratic Party as of 1903) towards the Russian government was, however, far from unequivocal. Focusing on domestic social conflicts, some of the labour leaders utilized the tactical permissiveness of the Russian government to ensure the legal operative framework for their movement. The leadership of the workers' movement was well aware of the fact that the Russian government wanted it to refrain from resistance activities. In 1902 and 1903, part of the movement even accepted assistance provided by the Russian government for the unemployed and took a negative stand on the conscription boycott. These characteristics had a counterpart in the Russian police-run workers' movement (the Jewish Independent Labour Party and, particularly, the *Zubatovshchina*, named after Chief of Police S. V. Zubatov). Subsequent assumptions of innate and *ab initio* anti-government attitudes within the Finnish workers' movement are, therefore, unfounded.

The ideology of the Russian government included a strong belief in the idea that tsarism corresponded not only to the real interests of the Russians but also to those of the other peoples of the Empire. The government saw as its enemies only the agitators, who were blinded by foreign heresies and who were represented in Russia itself by the socialists and by separatists among the minority peoples. In Finland, separatism was allegedly personified by the upper-class Swedish Party. Thus, Governor-General Bobrikov regarded this party (together with its ally, the Young Finns) as Russia's main enemy. The Finnish-speaking common people, he held, would naturally remain Russian-minded, as long as Swedish-speaking agitators were not permitted to lead them astray. The government also applied this schematic and distorted concept to the Finnish workers' movement, thereby underestimating its ability to enter into independent political action until the great strike of 1905.

In Finland, the government interfered much less with free civic activities than in Russia. Indeed, in Finland, civic activities had traditionally been very little regulated – and not even Bobrikov was able to destroy the country's European character (including the tradition of freedom of assembly). In fact, it did not take more than a year after Bobrikov's death for the strong Russian control instituted by him to lapse. The attitudes of the Russian government towards the Finnish workers' movement contained elements of paternalism, belittlement and the course of *divide et impera*. For these reasons, the movement was allowed to operate publicly and legally in Finland. The need to maintain law and order, however, was the ultimate concern of the Russian authorities in defining policies *vis-à-vis* the Finnish workers' movement, and the various petty restrictions placed by the Russian authorities on the normal and legal activities of the movement turned workers against the government in 1903 and 1904. In fact, the radicalization of the workers' movement's moods and politics had already started around the beginning of 1904 – well before the losses encountered by the government in the war in the Far East had begun to make themselves felt in the political power relationships in Russia. The new radicalism of the workers' movement, in other words, was initially of domestic origin.

The integrationist and restrictive policy of the Russian government introduced the seeds of revolutionary radicalism into the originally rather moderate workers' movement in 1904 and 1905. These seeds were then spread by worker activism (notably by the participation of individual Social Democrats in the work of the Activists). Thus, the revolutionary position (which until as late as 1918 involved only part of the movement) came into the Finnish workers' movement by way of passive and active resistance to the Russian government's integrationist policy and not from the struggle for voting rights or from any other class conflict involving workers and the domestic bourgeoisie. However, in the long run, radicalism directed against the Russian authorities also engendered radicalism on the domestic front.[7]

The year 1905 in Finland: a revolution?

The 1905 events in Russia are generally seen as a revolution, albeit an interrupted (or uncompleted) revolution. However, the events of the same year in Finland are generally not classified as a 'revolution' in Finnish historical writing.[8] But what was the true state of affairs?

One point worthy of consideration is that, throughout Finnish history, political assassinations have been quite rare; but the period 1904 to 1908 constitutes a significant exception in this respect. The year 1904 saw one political murder (with the assassination of Governor-General Bobrikov) and one attempted murder. The following year there were five murders (an Old Finn procurator, a lieutenant-colonel of the Russian gendarmerie and two police officers; moreover, a worker-activist who had inspired suspicion among his own was also assassinated). There were also three murder attempts (the assistant to the governor-general and two governors, all of them Russians). The political murders of 1906 to 1908 were no longer associated with the operations of the Activists and worker-activists but were committed by socialist and anarchist groups, some of the deaths being the by-products of robberies or of revenge exacted against members of the movement.

The mass demonstrations of the year 1905 offer even more convincing evidence for the existence of a revolution. The following discussion limits itself to the demonstrations organized in Helsinki, although where nationwide events were concerned this is indicated. Demonstrations for universal and equal suffrage were organized in Helsinki on 19 February and 14 April 1905, with permission having been obtained for them from the Russian government. (Governor-General I. M. Obolenskii was naturally not at all unhappy about national discords, and that is also precisely the reason why he expressly avoided interfering with a paper industry strike that assumed quite extensive dimensions.) On 19 February 9,000 persons participated in the demonstration, while the number on the streets on 14 April ranged between 10,000 and 36,000. The former demonstration was nationwide, as was the third demonstration, on 4 June, which gathered between 7,000 and 10,000 demonstrators in Helsinki. This demonstration was organized without permission from the authorities, but the Russian government dared not prevent it (or the other unauthorized demonstrations in Helsinki, for that matter) – even though it would have been possible to do so with the help of the Russian troops stationed in the capital. The demonstration was also partly against the government.

There were also a number of other anti-government demonstrations – all of them, naturally, unauthorized. On 24 and 25 January there was a protest against the events of Bloody Sunday in St Petersburg, with 5,000–10,000 participants on the first day and 5,000 on the second. The police interfered on this occasion. The action had nationwide dimensions. On 9 April there was a demonstration against the fact that the police force had to a considerable degree been turned Russian, with 25,000–30,000 demonstrators participating in the action. Considering the fact that Helsinki only had about 100,000 inhabitants, between one-quarter and one-third of the city's population therefore participated in the demonstration. On 6 August there was a march against the state of emergency in every part of Finland, with 20,000 people on the streets in Helsinki. During the great strike from late October to early November, there were again huge demonstrations and popular assemblies all over Finland on a daily basis.

Comparable mass demonstrations have taken place in Finland only in 1917 and 1956, the year of the general strike. Thus, there can be no doubt that the Finnish events of 1905 were, indeed, a revolution. In fact, for Finland, the year 1905 was a more genuine revolution than that of the February Revolution in 1917, when Russian soldiers and sailors took the lead and the Finnish population remained as spectators. The year 1905 was a true popular revolution: unlike in 1917 and 1918, the whole population participated, not just the workers and the rural people who supported the Social Democrats.

The exceptional character of the years 1905–07 is also reflected in the number of labour disputes. There were thirty-six serious labour disputes in 1904, ninety-three in 1905, 174 in 1906, 176 in 1907, and 128 in 1908. In relation to the events in the political sector, however, the strikes in industry, construction and the harbours were secondary. This also applies to the movements of the tenant farmers.

In Finnish research, the 1905 events have, thus far, been generally described as representing more or less separate, independent outbursts. My own investigations, however, suggest that the Activist Party and the collaborating Social Democratic worker-activists were behind most of the demonstrations in the country, as well as being responsible for all the political murders. No revolutionary party elsewhere in the huge Russian Empire was able to steer the revolution, but this was what happened in Finland.[9]

The 1905 street-level revolution in Finland consisted of a series of actions by the Activists and the worker-activists, counter-measures by the Russian government and respective escalation, without either party seeing the possibility to launch extensive violent actions. The government certainly had the capacity to start an armed conflict, by using the Russian troops at its command, but the opposition did not have such forces. However, thanks to the peaceful character of Finnish political culture, as well as to the composure and prudence of Governor-General Obolenskii, the threshold for initiating violent actions remained high. The deepening of the Russian foreign and domestic political crisis was also an essential ingredient in the development of events in Finland, since the Finns alone could not have challenged the government. Nevertheless, events took their own independent course in Finland. Russian events provided a decisive impulse only twice. The first occasion, as we have seen, was in late January (subsequent to Bloody Sunday); the second was in October 1905. Prior to October, the escalating revolutionary process of the spring and summer of 1905 had peaked, with the revolution taking a break in the Grand Duchy. By introducing new troops in Finland in September, the government had demonstrated to the Finns that it still remained in control, and the mass movements had temporarily ceased. Thus, the subsequent great strike in Finland would probably not have been possible without the influence of the October general strike in Russia. Still, we can assert that the conditions for the great strike had already matured over the year due to the domestic events in Finland.[10]

The Activists had some contacts with their Russian sister organization, the Socialist-Revolutionary Party, but no true co-ordination of the activities was possible due to the occasional character of the contacts and the separate nature of the groups' actions.[11] Therefore, the Finnish great strike burst out only on 30 October, the very day that marked the end of the Russian general strike. Moreover, in Finland the great strike remained a peaceful, mass demonstration that – with the exception of the Old Finn senators who collaborated with the Russian government – involved almost all strata of society. The Social Democrats and the Activists regarded the great strike of October–November 1905 as a revolution similar to the French Revolution of 1789; for the constitutionalists, though, the events did not mark a revolution but, rather, the restoration of legality.

The great strike induced Nicholas II to issue the so-called 'November Manifesto' on 4 November, cancelling the political state of emergency in Finland that had been instituted by Governor-General Bobrikov. The manifesto also opened the way towards a unicameral parliament, elected by universal and equal suffrage, as well as securing freedom of association, assembly, speech and the press. Finally, it promised parliament the right to control the legality of the action of the members of the government (that is, the Finnish Senate). The emperor could approve these issues since he had just promised to give the Russians their Duma and full political and civil rights. The strike, thereby, put the constitutionalists into power, and they had no further reason to fight the government. Consequently, on 6 November 1905, the Social Democrats had to call off the strike, without achieving their main demand – the summoning of a national assembly that would reform parliament and issue a new constitution.

The November Manifesto also assigned the Diet the task of parliamentary reform. The Diet did not have the confidence of the workers but it did, however, take care of the issue, much in line with demands of the Social Democrats. The outcome of the great strike, therefore, sharpened the Social Democrats' attitude towards the constitutionalists who, according to the SDP, had stolen the victory gained through the strike. Domestic political issues were now increasingly reflected in political radicalism and social conflicts became more acute – but not as acute as later observers would suggest through the prism of the 1918 Finnish Civil War.

The consequences of the 1905 events

In the summer of 1906, the emperor adopted the Finnish parliamentary reform. Without the uncertainty surrounding the situation in Russia itself, this would not have been possible. By consenting to reform, Nicholas tried to preserve peace in at least one corner of his restless empire. Women also received the right to vote, becoming the first to do so in Europe.

Although the freedoms of association, assembly and the press were established constitutionally in Finland, only the possibility to practise freedom of assembly was made concrete by law. With the state of emergency regulations in force in Russia, civil and political rights were to a large degree restricted. In Finland, however, political freedom increased considerably. By introducing Russian control over civic activities, Governor-General Bobrikov had drawn Finland closer to Russia from a political culture standpoint. The country, which had had no clandestine revolutionary organizations and no terrorism before 1899, learned to act in an increasingly Russian manner. From 1905 onwards, though, Finland started to deviate from Russia in this respect.

As a result of this favourable development, Finland's political movements began to draw away from Russia's revolutionary parties. In spite of the Duma reform, the political changes brought the latter far fewer possibilities for public and legal action than were obtained by their Finnish counterparts. Prior to the great strike, the Finnish Social Democratic Party had not had any real contacts with its Russian sister party – and still, in 1906 to 1907, the relationship was only formal. Indeed, the Finns looked instead to the German Social Democratic Party as a model, not the corresponding Russian party. Party secretary Yrjö Sirola, one of the later founding fathers of the Communist Party of Finland (1918), said in 1907 that he was really tired of the Russian revolutionary movement: 'I am sure it will lead to nothing', he predicted. The Finns thus wanted to follow their own path, even if the parties and the people in general were not particularly separatist or anti-

Russian. The general wish was that the democratic process in Russia would make such political relations possible as would allow Finland to enjoy the right to self-determination in its own affairs.

The weakening of the Russian revolutionary movement after 1905 and the strengthening of the government's position gradually prevented all revolutionary actions in Finland. The majority of the Social Democratic Party put all its faith in the unicameral parliament, only to be disappointed, in the post-1907 period, as the desired reforms could not be attained through parliamentary action: if the bourgeois parties themselves did not constitute a sufficient obstacle to reform, the emperor still had the power to ratify or refuse to ratify the bills that had been approved by parliament. The SDP constituted a radical opposition, but not one that would resort to anything other than legal measures. The Russian government regarded Finnish Social Democrats as assistants to the Swedish and Young Finn parties until early 1917. From the Russian perspective, this view was not as peculiar as it seemed to the Finnish parties, all of which tended to insist upon the significance of their own peculiarities and differences.

The Finnish Social Democratic Party and the Activists refused to participate in the mutiny of the Russian soldiers in the Sveaborg fortress off Helsinki in 1906. Only a small fraction of the extremists joined the revolutionary sailors of the Russian navy, and the revolt was put down in less than three days without inspiring a revolution in Russia, as the rebels had mistakenly imagined it might. After this event, the revolutionary action of the Finnish extremists degenerated into bank robberies and other similar, separate actions, as was the case in all other parts of the Russian Empire. The defeat of the revolution gradually deprived these activities of any true foundations or significant degree of popular support.[12]

A more comprehensive workers' trade union organization came to be properly established only in the more liberal atmosphere created by the great strike, when there was less need to respect the patriarchal power of the employers than there had been in the past. Under Bobrikov's rule, it had been impossible to found new workers' associations, let alone trade unions. However, worker associations and union branches could be established as branches of pre-existing and similar associations, and – despite his best efforts – Bobrikov was not able to suppress this evasive tactic.

Due to their post-strike confidence and inexperience, the workers and the union branches overestimated their own capacities and launched ill-thought-out labour actions that resulted in losses. These setbacks tamed the general enthusiasm to join the unions. In fact, it became the major – almost the only – task of the unions to try to prevent rash strikes. Thus, the workers' political movement was thriving, thanks to the universal and equal suffrage, but the union movement remained weak. Due to their sheer poverty, the workers could not afford to make union payments and the rate of organization remained low. In 1907, the Social Democratic Party had 82,000 members and in the parliamentary elections of the same year gained

330,000 votes. Yet, at the end of that year, the central organization of the trade unions had only 26,000 members. By contrast, in other Nordic countries (and in Germany) the number of people organized in trade unions was far higher than the number of the members of the Social Democratic parties.

As the trade unions were weak and could not provide the peace and stability in the workplace and the labour market in which the employers were interested, the employers failed to renew the collective contracts that had become common in 1906 and in 1907.[13] In fact, normal Western labour market relationships were created in Finland only after the Second World War. The underdeveloped labour market conditions constituted a similar societal factor promoting instability, as did the over-population in agriculture or the inadequate operative capacity of the political system. All these issues were a reflection of Finland's status in the grey area between Western and Eastern Europe.

The years 1905 to 1907, then, witnessed at the very least a sort of a partial revolution in Finland. With the possible exceptions of 1917 and the decade after 1945, never has the political activity of the citizens been so high. But the objectives of the popular masses were realized only in part and the outcome did not at all meet with their expectations. The upper strata of the society were disappointed with the common people, whom the educated classes had previously idealized; now they deemed their actions to be little better than pure hooliganism. However, it is common that the upheavals of history produce changes that are quite different from those imagined by their advocates. And, ultimately, the years 1905 to 1907 gave birth to the Finnish political system (that is, the democratic parliamentary and party system) that – albeit with some modifications dating from 1917–18 and 1944 – has survived to the present day.

Notes

1 See, in particular, Pertti Haapala, *Kun yhteiskunta hajosi: Suomi 1914–1920* (Helsinki, 1995).
2 Robert Schweizer, *Autonomie und Autokratie: Die Stellung des Grossfürstentums Finnland im russischen Reich in der zweiten Hälfte des 19. Jahrhunderts* (Giessen, 1978); Osmo Jussila, 'The Russian Government and the Finnish Diet: A Study of the Evolution of Political Representation, 1863–1914', in Geoffrey Alderman (ed.), *Governments, Ethnic Groups and Political Representation: Comparative Studies on Governments and Nondominant Ethnic Groups in Europe (1850–1940)*, Vol. 4 (Dartmouth, 1993).
3 Osmo Jussila, 'The Historical Background of the February Manifesto of 1899', *Journal of Baltic Studies*, Vol. 15 (1984), No. 2–3, pp. 141–7.
4 Sidney Harcave (ed.), *The Memoirs of Count Witte* (Armonk, 1990), p. 258.
5 Tuomo Polvinen, *Imperial Borderland: Bobrikov and the Attempted Russification of Finland, 1898–1904* (London, 1995); Steven Duncan Huxley, *Constitutionalist Insurgency in Finland* (Helsinki, 1990); William Copeland, *The Uneasy Alliance: Collaboration between the Finnish Opposition and the Russian Underground,*

1898–1904 (Helsinki, 1973); Antti Kujala, 'March Separately – Strike Together: The Paris and Geneva Conferences held by the Russian and Minority Nationalities' Revolutionary and Opposition Parties, 1904–1905', in Akashi Motojirō, *Rakka ryūsui: Colonel Akashi's Report on His Secret Cooperation with the Russian Revolutionary Parties during the Russo-Japanese War*, edited by Olavi K. Fält and Antti Kujala (Helsinki, 1988), pp. 85–167; David Kirby, 'The Finnish Social Democratic Party, 1903–1918' (University of London Ph.D. thesis, 1971); Maurice Carrez, 'La classe ouvrière finlandaise entre 1880 et 1920' (Université de Paris VII Ph.D. thesis, 1987). The new-style (n.s.) calendar was used in Finland. The old style (o.s.) was used only by the Russian administration in the Grand Duchy. In this chapter all dates concerning events in Finland are given according to the new-style calendar.

6 *Letuchie listki*, No. 46 (10 August 1899, o.s.), p. 12; Åbo Akademis Bibliotek, J. N. Reuter Letter Collection, Vol. X: P. Kropotkin to Reuter (8 December 1899, n.s.).

7 Antti Kujala, *Venäjän hallitus ja Suomen työväenliike 1899–1905* (Helsinki, 1995), *passim*. See also Antti Kujala, 'Otnoshenie pravitel'stva Rossii k rabochemu dvizheniiu Finliandii v 1899–1905gg.', *Studia Slavica Finlandensia*, Vol. 12 (Helsinki, 1995), pp. 54–64; and [Iu. O. Martov], 'Russkie bona-partisty v Finliandii', *Iskra*, No. 37 (1 April 1903, o.s.), p. 1. On the attitude of the Russian government to the masses in Russia and in Finland, see Jeremy Schneiderman, *Sergei Zubatov and Revolutionary Marxism: The Struggle for Working Class in Tsarist Russia* (Ithaca, 1976), pp. 19–23, 56–9 and *passim*; and Osmo Jussila, 'Förfinskning och förryskning: Språkmanifestet år 1900 och dess bakgrund', *Historisk Tidskrift för Finland*, Vol. 65 (1980), pp. 1–17.

8 There are some exceptions: see Viljo Rasila, 'Suomen poliittisen historian vuodet 1905–1919', in *Suomen poliittinen historia 1905–1975* (Porvoo, 1980), pp. 11–15; and Risto Alapuro, *State and Revolution in Finland* (Berkeley, 1988), pp. 114–15. On the definition of revolution, see Charles Tilly, *European Revolutions, 1492–1992* (Oxford, 1996), pp. 1–20, 216–18.

9 See Kujala, *Venäjän hallitus*, pp. 344–411

10 Ibid.; and Antti Kujala, 'Finland and the Russian Revolution of 1905', in John Morison (ed.), *Ethnic and National Issues in Russian and East European History* (Basingstoke, 2000), pp. 105–8. The events of the year 1905 in Finland have been studied from the Soviet perspective in M. N. Vlasova, *Proletariat Finliandii v gody pervoi russkoi revoliutsii (1905–1907)* (Petrozavodsk, 1961), and A. Ia. Ovchinnikova, *Revoliutsionnaia Rossiia i Finliandiia 1905–1907* (Tallinn, 1988).

11 Antti Kujala, 'The Russian Revolutionary Movement and the Finnish Opposition, 1905: The *John Grafton* Affair and the Plans for an Uprising in St Petersburg', *Scandinavian Journal of History*, Vol. 5 (1980), No. 4, pp. 257–75; Kujala, 'March Separately', pp. 137–66.

12 Antti Kujala, *Vallankumous ja kansallinen itsemääräämisoikeus* (Helsinki, 1989), pp. 127–309; and Antti Kujala, 'Finnish Radicalism and the Russian Revolutionary Movement, 1899–1907', *Revolutionary Russia*, Vol. 5 (1992), No. 2, pp. 174–88. On Russian–Finnish relations in the period 1907 to 1916, see Antti Kujala, 'The Policy of the Russian Government Toward Finland, 1905–1917', in Mary S. Conroy (ed.), *Emerging Democracy in Late Imperial Russia* (Niwot, Colo., 1998), pp. 147–97.

13 On the trade union movement, see Pauli Kettunen, *Poliittinen liike ja sosiaalinen kollektiivisuus* (Helsinki, 1986), pp. 50–83; and Kari Teräs, *Arjessa ja liikkeessä: Verkostonäkökulma modernisoituviin työelämän suhteisiin 1880–1920* (Helsinki, 2001), *passim*.

6 Revolution and revolt in the Manchurian armies, as perceived by a future leader of the White movement

Oleg Airapetov (translated by David Fairhurst)

General Mikhail Vasil'evich Alekseev, chief of staff of the Imperial Headquarters during the First World War and one of those military leaders who advised Nicholas II to abdicate in February 1917, is renowned in émigré and Soviet history as the man who organized the White movement in South Russia during the Russian Civil War. However, his first contact with the chaos of revolution was in Manchuria, in 1905. His experience there is of importance not only for an estimation of what really happened in the Russian armies fighting against the Japanese but also for an understanding of how Alekseev later reacted to the revolutionary events of 1917 and after. Specifically, this chapter examines how senior Russian officers criticized the errors of the government and the army in 1905, in relation to the mutinies among Russian forces around Siping after the battle of Mukden and how they struggled against the army's disintegration.

'They all wanted to go home.'
(A British journalist referring to Russian troops at the time of the Battle of Mukden)[1]

General Mikhail Vasil'evich Alekseev (1857–1918), chief of staff at the Russian Supreme Command Headquarters during the First World War, is in many ways a symbolic figure in the work of Russian émigré and Soviet historians. This is due to his role in the events of February 1917, and his part in organizing the anti-Bolshevik movement in South Russia at the beginning of 1918. He was also, though, a witness to revolution and revolt in the Russian army in Manchuria in 1905. His views of the army mutinies and of the government's response to them are the subject of this chapter. The main sources used in writing it were documents obtained from the general's own archives, which are currently located in the Manuscript Section of the Russian State Library in Moscow. A significant amount of material from these documents was included in a biography/memoir of Alekseev written by the general's daughter, which was recently published in Russia.[2]

The general's first experience of a spontaneous revolution, in Manchuria in 1905, is interesting not only because it helps us to understand what was actually happening within the Russian army that fared so badly in its clashes with the Japanese in north-east China, but also because it helps to explain Alekseev's actions during the February Revolution. At the time of the Russo-Japanese War of 1904–05, Alekseev was quartermaster-general (equivalent today to chief of the operational staff) of the Third Manchurian Army and witnessed at first hand the breakdown in discipline among the Russian troops, which was followed by unrest among the reservists and soldiers on active service.

This process of disintegration began during the final stages of the Battle of Mukden, in February and March 1905. The fighting ended in a disorderly retreat, during which the army's discipline broke down completely.[3] The Russian army withdrew in utter confusion. The 'Mukden disaster' – or, to be more precise, the defeat at Mukden which ended in the fiasco on the Mandarin Road – is interesting for several reasons, and had many consequences. Most significantly, the Mandarin Road threw together people whose personal relationships would become extremely important in the period 1914 to 1918. Mention needs only to be made of the names Alekseev, Ruzskii, Kornilov, Denikin and Markov. The events in February 1905 made those who took part in the fighting at Mukden extremely critical, not only of the army but also of the way that the state was being run. Any defeat causes those concerned to think about reform, but the extent of the political changes under consideration by senior military officers at this time indicates how great a catastrophe the defeat was for the losing side. The Battle of Tsushima took place on the anniversary of Nicholas II's coronation and the tsar made note of this obviously unhappy coincidence in his diary.[4] His feelings are made most plain, though, in an entry he made two years later, on 14 (27) May 1907: 'An unforgettable day, forever overshadowed by the terrible loss of the fleet at the Battle of Tsushima!'[5] Alekseev's memories of the Russo-Japanese War, though, unlike the monarch's, were mainly centred on Mukden. The general's own 'February' thoughts went a great deal further than just military reform. Moreover, the events of 23–27 February 1905 remained for a long time the darkest period in his life and his reflections on Mukden allow us better to understand his actions as chief of staff at Supreme Command Headquarters during the same period in 1917.

The mass of troops retreating from Mukden (more than 300,000 men were involved) had not been given food of any description, let alone a hot meal, for several days. Their regular supplies had been interrupted even before the Battle of Mukden had all but been ended by Kuropatkin's improvised 'troop formations' and, after 25 February, when Kuropatkin gave the order to send the baggage train north, the troops were completely cut off from food supplies.[6] The over-exertion began to take its toll, as men fell asleep on the march, collapsing from exhaustion by the side of the road.[7] An army store had earlier been set up in the rear at T'ieh-ling and the approaches to the town had been reinforced. But the troops still had to reach it. All along the Mandarin Road the men had discarded everything that they felt they no longer needed. Their worn out and starving animals were certainly of no more use to them.[8]

Many of the stores along the road had been burned and neither food nor fodder from what remained of them could be handed out to the retreating troops without an order from the commanders. This was not forthcoming, as the General Staff had lost control over both the troops and the rear. The stores were set alight as the Japanese approached and the hungry soldiers could see the smoke from the fires. Nevertheless, largely thanks to the detachment assembled by Alekseev, the retreating troops suffered fewer losses than before. Order was maintained on the railway and among this rearguard. As they retreated, the troops blew up bridges and ripped out railway tracks. Meanwhile, the telegraph operators stayed at their posts until the final moment, leaving with the last remaining soldiers and destroying everything that they were unable to take with them. This allowed communications to be kept open, although there were no personnel in the rear who could take advantage of this.[9] By 5.00 p.m. on 27 February, the columns of troops had reached T'ieh-ling, where Alekseev was met by the commander of the armies, General A. A. von Bil'derling, and army chief of staff General F. V. Martson. However, the atmosphere in T'ieh-ling precluded any chance of restoring order and discipline.

Colonel D. P. Parskii, who had arrived with Alekseev, noted:

> There was terrible disorder in the town, especially around the main railway station, from where the wounded were sent north, and at the supply depots. There were crowds of men who must have belonged to various units, many of them were probably deserters, who, it is said, were sometimes intercepted far beyond T'ieh-ling. Later, those who were here on the final day of the battle told of the excesses which had taken place in the town — the deserters were forcing themselves onto the trains at the expense of the wounded, the supply depots were raided, officers were often assaulted when they attempted to put a stop to what was going on and restore order, etc. Such was the response to the Mukden disaster in the rear![10]

Not since Peter the Great's defeat against Sweden at Narva in 1700 had Russian officers lost control over their men under such tragic circumstances. The officers' natural reaction to this was to attempt to reverse the effects of both liberal reform and the almost universal enthusiasm for Populism.

On hearing, in the summer of 1905, of the mutiny on the battleship *Prince Potemkin-Tavricheskii*, Alekseev was reminded of Colonel Timofeev, mortally wounded by rebellious Russian troops during the retreat from Mukden:

> The sailors on the *Potemkin* and those brutal cowards [who had murdered Timofeev] were of the same mould. Both were the products of a

breakdown in discipline. Thanks to Dragomirov's leniency, we began putting the common soldiers on a pedestal. The officers were humiliated, the ordinary ranks indulged. We forgot that the troops require a firm hand, instruction and correction.[11]

Alekseev was referring here to General M. I. Dragomirov (1830–1905), the commander of the Kiev Military District from 1889 to 1905. Dragomirov had a reputation similar to General Suvorov's, but he managed, strangely, to combine that with an admiration for the ideas of Alexander Herzen (at least until 1863) that actually inspired him to make a show of upbraiding his officers in front of the troops. As Russian society traditionally made a link between the 'serf–landowner' relationship and that of the 'ordinary soldier–officer', this attitude was bound to be popular. But the Populist idea of repaying a 'historical debt' to a people that had been exploited for centuries and the related notion of the ordinary soldier's gradual emancipation were clearly unsuitable for the army. The war put the whole Dragomirov inheritance into question. At least, this is what those who, like Alekseev, took part in the war believed.

By 9 (22) March 1905, the army had arrived at Siping, almost 200 kilometres north of Mukden.[12] On the 4 (17) March, Kuropatkin was relieved of his post as supreme commander and replaced by General N. P. Linevich, who was already seventy years old and who had graduated from the military academy back in the time of Nicolas I. The soldiers called him 'the old dad'. Of course, the problem was not actually Linevich's age, but that – at least in the opinion of Alekseev – he was 'not of the first order' as a commander. Alekseev made an extremely accurate and fair assessment of the new supreme commander's abilities: 'He's got a decent enough brain, but it's more suited to commanding a division.'[13] At the same time, Linevich faced an immensely difficult task – to restore the troops' faith in their commanders and to remould three armies into a force that would give the Japanese something to reckon with. 'Linevich inherited a tough assignment', noted Dr E. S. Botkin at the beginning of April:

> Rumour has it that there are only 180,000 men left from all the armies. This is still a very rough estimate, of course, as they are still finding units. The losses – naturally also approximate – are reckoned to be as many as 107,000! The sick and wounded are put at up to 65,000, the dead at around 20,000. The rest are missing or captured! One artillery battery is considered to be completely lost, despite there being relatively few of its guns left on the field – thirty-one. Japanese losses are thought to be approximately 120,000.[14]

The Third Army also received a new commander, infantry general M. I. Bat'ianov.[15] This means that, during the active fighting, its previous commanders – A. V. Kaul'bars and von Bil'derling – had lasted no more than ten weeks each. There were to be no further changes in the armies' command, but only because conditions made this impossible. 'The wild confusion that marked the entire leadership of Kuropatkin and his staff', noted Alekseev ten days after the changes, 'has been passed on as a dismal inheritance to the new commanders.'[16]

It is interesting that, at this point, the German General Staff did not think that Russia had lost the war. 'General Kuropatkin', recalled Bernhard von Bülow, 'made some serious mistakes, but he showed exceptional energy in his counter-attacks. Our General Staff believes that it was Russia's staying power that proved decisive.'[17] To this we could add the Supreme Command's staying power. But then, suddenly, this was gone. And, although the army greeted the replacement of the supreme commander with joy, it had suffered too many defeats. A significant number of the officers and men had lost their belief in victory. The army was capable of defence, but not of going over to the attack.[18]

Yet, on more than one occasion the Russian soldiers revealed an amazing capacity to recover their morale following a defeat. They held on to their self-belief, but did not always trust those who led them and, more importantly, who sent them into battle. Kuropatkin took good care of his men, who realized and appreciated this, and they were even prepared to forgive him for the defeats. However, the army had no command system in place to bring the gritty qualities of the peasants and Cossacks into play. The time of panic and confusion had passed, but the commanders and troops had lost their faith in final victory. As an officer in one of the Cossack regiments commented:

> Our army was so stuck in the fatal habit of retreating when 'outnumbered by the enemy to a more advantageous position' that, in most cases, our commanders pulled the troops back too soon. In fact, Supreme Commander Linevich's report that 'the army is itching for battle' was very inaccurate. The impunity of some generals and the weaknesses in the top command were completely demoralizing our forces.[19]

According to one contemporary report, this is what happened again this time, after Mukden: 'Yet again that which foreigners find so amazing – the Russian ability to bounce back – became evident. The gloom of Mukden began to fade; thousands of those believed missing in action reappeared; it became more and more obvious that the Japanese were either disinclined or unable to attack us.'[20] In fact, no one on either side was planning an offensive. As the pre-revolutionary military researcher E. Tettau noted:

> If we simply consider the logistics, i.e. the sizes of the armies, the amount of guns, arms and ammunition, the positions of the forces, etc., there was undoubtedly a chance [of a successful attack]. But there was no self-belief, nor faith in the armies or commanders. It is very likely

that this lack of faith was also affecting the men at the top, which probably explains why the former supreme commander made no further attempt to take the fight to the victorious enemy, even though the logistics of the Siping position offered our best opportunity in the campaign, and even though the whole of Russia, from the tsar down to every last peasant, was desperate for a victory.[21]

Tettau called Siping 'the graveyard of the attacking spirit'. But at least the newly reorganized troops did everything possible to prevent a successful Japanese offensive. In the Second Army's sector alone, ninety-five fortified positions, 100 bridges and 450 kilometres of roads were constructed, sixty villages were converted into strong points and the defensive barriers erected were spread over 350,000 square metres.[22] The first thing that Linevich did on completion of this work, however, was to order reconnaissance for a new defensive line deep in the rear, along the Sungari river. Even though the Siping positions had become unassailable from the front, there was no guarantee that a repeat of Liao-yang and Mukden could be avoided if they were bypassed on the flanks.[23] The reconnaissance effort, in which Alekseev took part, was made more difficult by the absence of maps: tellingly, headquarters had been unable to contemplate the war moving so far north and so had not prepared them.[24]

The only sensible change made, which had provided a solution to problems in the Russian rear, was the recruitment of units from among the local *Hung hu tze* (bandit-partisan) bands. Alekseev viewed the *Hung hu tze* as a product of the social system: 'When the robber-bureaucrats disappear, maybe the *Hung hu tze* will go with them. But the latter live exclusively off the Chinese. It is only recently that the Japanese have started recruiting and organizing them, directing them against us', he wrote.[25] In fact, small groups of these so-called 'Redbeards' were used by the Japanese, and sometimes they took it upon themselves to attack isolated Russian soldiers and small foraging parties operating away from the front line.[26]

The Chinese, especially in the countryside, were suffering as a result of the activities of the two opposing armies. Whole villages were pressed into the construction of fortified positions, and fear of espionage was rife. According to Alekseev, however, even at Siping the Chinese continued to help unmask Japanese spies.[27] The *Hung hu tze* were trained by a staff officer of the Third Army. Subsequently, several officers and warrant officers were reassigned to these units and soon a force of around 400 *Hung hu tze* was gathered, which was sufficient to ensure proper order in the rear.[28] Nevertheless, in practice, it is true to say that armies usually only resort to the use of such 'contracted units' if they are losing their belief in victory.

Never again in the war did events on the front line depend so much on the army's morale. Reinforcements were by now beginning to arrive in Manchuria: after Mukden, 194 battalions, forty-eight companies, 916 guns and 496 machine-guns were dispatched to the army in the field. By the beginning of September 1905, when the armistice was signed, 130 battalions, forty-eight companies, 468 guns, 332 machine-guns and ten and a half battalions of engineers had arrived at Siping.[29] However, along with material aid, these troops were bringing with them news from a country already gripped by revolution. The mood changed, even among the officers – especially among those who had joined up during the war. Alekseev was particularly alarmed by the increase in pacifist sentiments:

> It is a *disease*, which saps will and character, a disease we have nurtured ourselves ... The internal agitation is aiding the efforts of the *pacifists*. What does it matter to these people that the current situation represents the beginning of Russia's disintegration? They only want to see the back of an unpleasant situation. Success requires persistence, staying power, belief in one's own abilities, the willingness to make sacrifices. Who would credit Russians today with these higher civic qualities? Victory *will be ours* if we can see this thing through.[30]

The Japanese army at Siping was in no hurry to go on the offensive, but Linevich, like his predecessor, believed defence to be the only possible course of action. After the fortifications had been constructed and a possible escape route had been prepared, the new supreme commander of the Manchurian armies ordered the chiefs of staff to make plans only for a *counter*-attack against the Japanese. The staff of the First Army, under Kuropatkin, managed to distinguish themselves in the writing of all sorts of such plans but, according to Tettau, the only report worthy of note was that of the quartermaster-general of the Third Army:

> General Alekseev did not agree at all with the idea of attacking only after an enemy offensive had been repulsed and believed that there was no sense in drawing up fully detailed plans based on such a premise. Approximate plans [he argued] can be formulated if you prescribe your own will to the enemy, if you assume that he will act only in accordance with your own moves. If, indeed, you delay your own offensive until the completely unpredictable moment when your opponent's attack breaks down, it will be impossible to foresee when you should attack, especially because you cannot predict what the troop positions and prevailing circumstances will be at the end of the battle.[31]

Alekseev was very active. He pinned hopes of a way out of the crisis on a possible Russian attack and breakthrough, if only on dry land: 'We need a victory,' he wrote on 27 April (9 May) 1905, 'without it Russia's future will be very bleak.'[32] In his opinion, defeat was also dangerous because it would make another war inevitable. The country's weakness would invite new attacks and there would certainly be no more strength to repulse them than there had been in 1905.[33] There is a rational core to these arguments. The idea of striking back springs not so much from the desire to settle scores with a victorious neighbour, as from the fear of an internal threat, the realization of one's own weakness. The example of France after 1871 was very revealing. Of course, Japan could not become as much of a threat to Russia as Germany was by now to Russia's ally, but a weak Russian army could provoke war in Europe. Alekseev was constantly haunted by this thought, even in August 1905 when there was no longer hope of a victorious conclusion to the war. He was already thinking about the future: 'How will the army feel if there is an armistice? It will not believe itself capable of victory in a future war. "What is to become of us?" – This is the thought that will take root in all our hearts.'[34]

Before leaving the peace conference at Portsmouth, New Hampshire, in September 1905, Sergei Witte met Grand Prince Nikolai Nikolaevich the younger, who also believed that the Russian army had been pressed into a coiled spring, which, on being released, could drive the Japanese right back to Kwantung. In order for this to happen, however, there was a need for materials and a willingness to make sacrifices. Moreover, without a fleet it would be impossible to strike the Japanese a decisive blow and win the war.[35] But with the defeat of the Russian Baltic Fleet at Tsushima, on 14–15 (27–28) May 1905, all hope of such an outcome had disappeared.

'The first news of the defeat in the Korean Strait', *Morskoi sbornik* (The Naval Journal) informed its readers in June 1905, 'came to Russia by way of disturbing and tentative reports and rather confusing rumours, but by the next evening all doubt had evaporated and it became absolutely clear that our fleet had been utterly defeated.'[36] The first official telegrams from Linevich arrived in St Petersburg on 18 and 19 May (31 May and 1 June).[37] Nevertheless, the army in Manchuria did not receive news of the disaster straight away. As one volunteer recalled:

> The only newspaper that we received regularly, the *Vestnik Man'chzhurskikh armii* [The Manchurian Armies' News], prepared us by degrees for this tragic news. It simply printed a short telegram about a naval battle underway off the Japanese coast, in which the Japanese were purported to have suffered huge losses. Nothing was said about the losses on our own side. And it was only on the seventh day that they published news of Russia's terrible defeat. The last remaining hope of winning the war was gone.[38]

The *Vestnik Man'chzhurskikh armii* was, indeed, slow in providing information. On 15 (28) May, with reference to a source in London, the newspaper wrote that, according to unofficial information, a large naval battle, in which the Japanese had allegedly been defeated, had taken place off the coast of Formosa (Taiwan). Three days later came the first mention of the Battle of Tsushima, the outcome of which was supposedly yet unknown – although among the probable Russian losses was named the battleship

Borodino, while Japanese losses were estimated to be high. In fact, the commanders already knew what had happened. On 19 May (1 June) the *Vestnik* admitted that the Russian fleet had lost the battle, but did not yet reveal the full scale of the defeat – and only on 23 May (5 June) did the newspaper provide a comprehensive account of what had taken place.[39] It was impossible to cover up the events, or their magnitude.

Alekseev had been investing a great deal of hope in the fleet, believing that a victory at sea could raise the army's spirits. These hopes were not realized, but even this defeat, surprisingly, did not provoke any particular reaction among the ordinary soldiers. The troops obviously had very little empathy with the sailors and could hardly imagine the nature and scale of the events. The officers and generals were a different matter.[40] The news of the defeat of Admiral Rozhestvenskii's squadrons dashed all hopes that the situation would improve. Alekseev wrote: 'Our naval forces were completely destroyed in the defeat and without them – even if victories on land should follow – there is no prospect of any real results. Indeed, only if the Japanese were cut off from their escape route home could we have any hope of finally forcing them to seek peace.'[41]

Russia's final great defeat in the war came with the Japanese campaign on the island of Sakhalin. On 7 June 1905, Lieutenant-General Haraguchi's Thirteenth Division landed on the island with around 10,000 troops, thirty-six field guns and twelve machine-guns. The Japanese units were mostly made up of aged reservists, as the best soldiers had already been sent to Manchuria. However, their landing was supported by the Japanese fleet and they were able to seize the initiative. Moreover, the Japanese had twice as many troops on Sakhalin as the Russians and eight and a half times as many big guns, while the Russians had no machine-guns and were scattered around the island. Finally, the Russian units had been simply thrown together: as much as half the garrison was made up of former convicts, who had been given concessions for helping to defend the island.[42] Poorly prepared for combat, these volunteer units fled in large numbers when the first shots were fired. On 1 August, Lieutenant-General M. N. Liapunov, the military governor of Sakhalin, surrendered. During the fighting, 800 of the island's defenders had been killed and 4,540 taken prisoner, while the Japanese suffered losses of just thirty-nine dead and 121 wounded.[43] Thus, the war began and ended in failure. This was bound to affect the mood of the Russian people and this, in turn, was passed on to the troops.

The Russian army was not even much strengthened when reinforcements arrived in the Far East, as events in the rear were having an increasingly detrimental effect on the front line. The troops had practically nothing to do on the journey and their most common request, whenever the train stopped, was for something to read. This of course provided a wonderful opportunity for the dissemination of revolutionary propaganda.[44] 'The reinforcements arriving from Russia', a Cossack officer noted, 'were extremely demoralized and were weighed down with leaflets.'[45] This is not at all surprising: after all, the trains bringing up the reinforcements were passing through Siberia, a region crawling with anti-government elements even before the Revolution of 1905. It was only on 6 (19) May 1905 that the minister of war decided to impose order on the troop trains heading to Manchuria. Typically, however, action was taken only when the problem had already got out of hand: 'In view of the disorder caused by the lower ranks en route to the Far East, drills and lectures are to be introduced at the stops for units travelling by train, regulations are to be observed, all leave and absences are prohibited, and it must be impressed upon the commanders that the trains are also in effect mobile barracks.'[46] Unfortunately, such sensible ideas were only put into practice when it was no longer possible to alter anything at the front. No one, or at least almost no one, still believed in victory.

'Were our army not corrupted by the idea that the whole of Russia is yearning for peace', wrote Alekseev in June 1905, 'and that it is *pointless* and *hopeless* to fight on, then our position in Manchuria would have to be considered very sound and solid ... [All would be well] provided other people were in charge. [But] Russia has scraped the bottom of the barrel for this war and has put what it found there at the head of its armies.'[47] General Linevich made absolutely no attempt to launch attacks during the peace talks, even though this would have made a big difference to their outcome.[48] As previously, morale was high among the Cossack officers, whose units were constantly in direct contact with the enemy and who had not lost faith in themselves or in victory. But the mood was completely different among the main force, the infantry, whose officers were far from ideal. In July Alekseev wrote: 'I have been obliged to meet several of the ne'er-do-wells sent to reinforce our *so-called* infantry regiments, those sent against their will from Russia, believing that they may kill, but not be killed, and preferring any kind of peace to a short continuation of the war.'[49] The information that was arriving directly (via correspondence) and indirectly (via newspapers and rumours) with the army from a country gripped by revolution had a demoralizing effect on these men. Alekseev himself was shaken when, in the summer of 1905, even the boys of the third form at the First Classical Grammar School in St Petersburg, where his son Nikolai was a pupil, tried to organize a strike against the teaching of Latin. Nikolai refused to join his classmates, much to the pleasure of his father, who took more than a dim view of strikes: 'Why, only a real contagion could inspire such an epidemic of strikes. Russian decrepitude, our natural predilection for laziness, has become all-pervasive and now everyone has started going on strike. Those who were leading the strikes had a clearly defined objective: to shut down the factories producing ships, guns and ammunition.'[50]

In my view, Alekseev's attitude towards the first Russian revolution, in 1905, is extremely important for an understanding of the role he played in the second, in February 1917. He was not wholeheartedly against the revolution; in fact, he was in favour of the institutions that only a revolutionary shock could jolt into existence. Alekseev was an advocate of a parliamentary monarchy, but only on the condition that the parliament would be made up not of politicians, who would fight against the government, but of experts, who would assist it. This sort of Utopian vision is very typical of a member of the army top brass, being a demand first and foremost for calm and stability on the home front and, second, for the rear's satisfaction – quickly and in full – of the army's requirements. Only those political tendencies that would satisfy these two requirements were acceptable to Alekseev. As a professional soldier, he saw everything in terms of the interests of the army at the front; he judged any event according to how it would affect the path to victory. On one hand, Alekseev was extremely critical of the press – the liberal, as well as the revolutionary. It was simply a source of irritation to him: 'In peacetime our press kept quiet, it ignored the army and when it did put the spotlight on someone from the military, then it always did so in an absurd, foolish manner. The average Russian not only dislikes the army, he sees it as a kind of evil, which only deserves to receive [into its ranks] the dregs of the intelligentsia.'[51] On the other hand, Alekseev was constantly vexed by the lack of professionalism of the officials in St Petersburg and their detachment from the real needs of the army: 'Let them take a look at what is required here and then they will understand that it is difficult to wage war with officers who do not provide the troops with those means to fight which are made available to the enemy – an enemy that scorns death and is very much in tune with the ideals it is fighting for.'[52] His condemnation of the government grew, as the army's failures mounted up. During the time Alekseev was at the front, the government failed to undertake any action that did not provoke his harsh criticism. He was especially irritated when the initiation of peace talks was made public – and not simply because he was, in principle, against making peace before the Russian side had achieved some successes. Rather, he was convinced that official announcements on the opening of peace negotiations with the Japanese had deprived the army of its will to continue the war.[53]

Alekseev had not changed his views even by mid-August 1905:

> Is it really possible that our spineless ruling clique – at all ranks and levels – is washing its hands of everything and allowing such humiliating concessions to be made? Come what may [they appear to be saying], at least the war will be off our backs and then we can get on with our internal shenanigans ... We've become soft from the top practically right down to the bottom; especially at the top.[54]

However, his criticism of the government and the court did not yet also extend to the monarch himself. He blamed not Nicholas II but those surrounding the tsar:

> These people could bring about disaster, through their vanity and their ignorance of Russia; they will harm the tsar, as they have already

harmed the country. They have become weak and tired and want to be rid of the war as soon as possible. It is like a millstone around their necks.'[55]

It must be pointed out, though, that Aleekseev was in no way a supporter of an absolute monarchy. This is well indicated by his attitude towards the first plans to introduce a consultative parliamentary chamber in 1905, the so-called Bulygin Duma.

The Bulygin rescript was signed by the tsar on 18 February (3 March) 1905. The troops in the Far East heard about it during the final phase of the Battle of Mukden, when the *Vestnik Man'chzhurskikh armii* of 21 February (6 March) published Nicholas's announcement: 'From this day forward, continuing the work of my royal predecessors – to unite and to build Russia, and with God's help, I intend to engage the most worthy men, entrusted and elected by the people, to participate in the drafting and discussion of legislation', said the tsar.[56] However, this news did not at all lift the spirits of the army or even provoke any particular interest. On 13 (26) July 1905, Alekseev wrote down his own feelings on the subject:

> They are also going about the matter of [summoning] the people's rep-resentatives in the wrong way. They are trying to play an ill-advised and dangerous game. They made promises and acted correctly at a critical time: it was long overdue. But now, it seems, they are regretting their promises and want to renege on them, by making the future assembly a consultative one. What use will that be? Who on earth will be satisfied with such an absurd creation? Indeed, from afar it seems that everyone is now pinning their hopes on this very assembly.[57]

On 21 August (3 September) 1905, a telegram from Nicholas II was read out to the troops, informing them that the preliminary peace conditions offered by the Japanese side at Portsmouth had been accepted.[58] On 5 September, the Treaty of Portsmouth was signed and the Russo-Japanese War was ended. The headquarters of the Russian army in Manchuria greeted this news with relief. But 'Those who had some wits about them', noted Alek-seev, 'all hung their heads, realizing that a state which is incapable of demonstrating the ability to concentrate its moral, spiritual and physical forces is weak and spineless. A country that does not taste the sweet fruits of victory during a war loses for a long time one of its most important military values – its belief in itself, its strength and its abilities.'[59] The war with the external enemy, therefore, was over. At Siping the Japanese duly offered an armistice and on 31 August (13 September) it was signed. Representatives of the Russian and Japanese command – Major-General V. A. Oranovskii and Major-General Yasumasa Fukushima respectively – met in the 'no-man's land' between the two armies. The Japanese were late, forcing the supreme commander's quartermaster-general to stand around waiting for the victors.[60] In accordance with the terms of the armistice, military action ceased from noon on 3 (16) September. The servicemen of both armies were forbidden from visiting each other's positions; at the same time, the forward posts began to be dismantled and reconnaissance operations were discontinued. The armies left the fortified positions for their camps.[61] Alekseev's fears were soon confirmed – at the same time, incidentally, as his false hopes that the emergence of a legislative Duma would help bring calm to the country were dashed. In fact the complete opposite was the case.

In November 1904, Witte had been irreconcilably opposed to Prince Sviatopolk-Mirskii's proposals for the inclusion of elected members in the State Council. On his return from America a year later, however, he no longer believed that a constitutional set-up had necessarily to entail Russia's ruin.[62] 'The constitution was promised and proclaimed; all that remained was to deliver on that promise', recalled a leading Kadet. 'But then came the time of reckoning. All the qualities of the Liberation Movement which had brought it victory turned out to be liabilities when it was time to make use of the triumph.'[63] It was certainly not only the radical parties that were interested in continuing the revolution, or, if the worst came to the worst, in making use of its continued existence to fight the government. In fact, the liberals, unlike the revolutionaries, were not so united in their final goals. Sometimes they imagined them in a completely unrealistic way. 'They often talked about the Western European order', noted another Kadet, referring to the elections to the first State Duma. 'At the same time the speakers demonstrated that they were all out of touch, and for some reason New Zealand was mentioned especially often. Quite simply, something quite chaotic and extremely exciting was happening . . . The mood was such that they preferred making a din and holding demonstrations to actually doing anything.'[64] The result of the election was also no surprise to some observers. 'It was an assembly of savages', noted S. E. Kryzhanovskii, the deputy minister of internal affairs:

> It seemed that Russia had sent all its wild elements to St Petersburg, full of envy and malice. If we accept the idea that these people actually represented their nation and its 'innermost aspirations', then it must be accepted that, for at least another hundred years, Russia can be held together not by internal bonds but by external force only and that her only salvation will be in an enlightened dictatorship.[65]

The events in Manchuria were no exception in this turmoil. There was a complete lack of calm in the Far East, where the local political opposition was also engaged in agitation, chaos, uproar and demonstrations. After the Manifesto of 17 October 1905, a significant number of exiles at the rear of the army were freed and the revolutionary propaganda only intensified. 'There was terrible pressure on the troops', recalled General L. N. Sobolev:

> This was bolstered by the awful news coming from Russia, very much of which was exaggerated and invented. All communications between

Russia and the army were severed, all rail transport came to a standstill; the postal service and money transfers were interrupted; the telegraph operators were only allowing through those reports that furthered the cause of the revolution. The transport of the reservists back home was halted. The army was in an agitated state. For a moment, many feared that order could not be maintained among the troops.[66]

As soon as they heard about the peace treaty, the troops, especially the mobilized reservists, expected to return home. They simply could not understand why they were still in the army. On top of this, rumours about what was happening back home in Russia gradually reached the army in the Far East and caused unrest in the ranks. As a result, 'Voices were raised to the effect that "the soldiers should go 'on strike'" and demand that the commanders send the mobilized units back to Russia immediately.'[67]

The order for demobilization, however, had not been given even by the end of September. On 14 (27) September, Alekseev noted with alarm: 'It is strange that St Petersburg has not issued a timetable for sending the troops home. They [i.e., the troops] wait and wait.'[68] It was only on 1 (14) October that the tsar ratified the Treaty of Portsmouth and another four days elapsed before the manifesto on peace with Japan appeared.[69] On 1 (14) October the army learned of the Imperial Order for the immediate demobilization of the officers and the lower ranks in the reserves, along with that of the former convicts who had served just two or three months less than a full year. This was due to begin in Manchuria and in the units stationed within the Empire following the ratification of the peace. News of this reached Siping on 5 (18) October.[70] But instead of returning home, the army was seized with unrest in the far rear – in Chita and even in Harbin – which had begun before the manifesto was issued on 17 October. On 15 (28) October the telegraph operators in Chita went on strike, supported by other railway workers; together, the demonstrators attempted to seize control of the weapons stores. They were dispersed with gunfire, but at 2.00 p.m. the army's communications with the town (and, consequently, with Russia), were severed. Supreme Commander Linevich issued an order to protect railway and telegraph office property and sent Colonel Zakharov with two companies of railway troops to the border station Manchuria. Zakharov's task was to restore rail and telegraph links with Chita and Irkutsk. On the following day, 16 (29) October, workers on the Chinese Eastern Railway also went on strike. However, as Zakharov succeeded in arresting some of the telegraph operators at Manchuria railway station and in replacing them with troops, the situation was improved to a certain extent.[71]

At this time, military censorship, introduced by order of Vice-Admiral E. I. Alekseev and dating back to measures of February–April 1904, was still in operation for all reports concerning the army and for private telegrams and letters sent abroad.[72] At the same time, communications between the Far East and the rest of the country had not yet been restored.

Consequently, on 17 (30) October, General Alekseev, who was now busy planning the army's evacuation, noted with irritation:

> Even the *Vestnik Man'chzhurskikh armii* does not inform us of what is happening in Russia — some sort of bacchanalia of strikes [seems to be going on]. The most recent news was simply that Moscow is completely cut off from all reports, because there are absolutely no trains arriving or departing. Will they really allow this to happen to St Petersburg as well? Authority has completely collapsed, and no one can be found at the moment who will take decisive action.[73]

The weakness of the highest authority in Manchuria — the supreme commander — caused the hardliners to lose their self-belief, whilst spurring the supporters of revolution into action. The decisive measures envisaged by Alekseev to end the disturbances included the wide use of military force (including even naval vessels) and the death penalty for active strikers.[74] Indeed, the strikers well understood the language of force and were apt to bow to it. For example, when, at Manchuria station, the strike committee attempted to halt a train carrying former convicts, the latter threatened to make short work of them and, as a result, the train was allowed to continue on its way with the minimum of delay. The men on the train were exiles from Sakhalin — mainly criminals given an amnesty for taking part in the island's defence, who were now returning from Japanese captivity. It should be pointed out that there was strict discipline on the train,[75] but it is nevertheless noteworthy that even such insignificant forces as these were sufficient to put the railway back in operation, even if it was only when such a train was passing through.

There were certain schedules and phases of demobilization to be observed. Priority went to the sick and wounded (who had suffered most from the strikes, as some of the hospital trains had been held up between stations, where it was impossible even to get hold of food), those returning from Japanese captivity, and reservist officers. Earlier, on 8 (21) October, the supreme commander issued an order to send officers, lower ranks and officials attached to the Manchurian army back to their own units in Russia, admittedly on condition that this would not hinder the demobilization.[76] The best troops were needed to fight the revolution and to train the autumn intake of recruits. However, without doubt this order was a mistake, provoking dangerous discontent among the ordinary ranks in the reserves, who had been yearning for home and who were anxious for demobilization to get underway. The situation was even more dangerous when set against the background of events in Manchuria and Siberia.

On 21 October (3 November) the circum-Baikal railway line was put out of operation and the authorities in Irkutsk and Harbin made an unsuccessful appeal to the army commanders in Manchuria for troops. Linevich, however, was not even in a position to control events in Harbin. On 24 October

(6 November) the striking telegraph operators at the railway stations were joined by the railway workers.[77] It was obvious that Linevich was no more able to intervene decisively on the 'home front' than he had been in Manchuria. In order to do have done so, he especially needed information on what was happening to the west of the Urals, but his headquarters had only a very vague idea about events in European Russia. On 23 October (5 November) Alekseev wrote:

> On arrival in Yao-ming, new reports: Moscow has declared its own government; in Russia a constitution has been proclaimed, but Moscow has already rejected it and is demanding recognition of both its own hegemony and of that of its rulers. There are no telegrams; no one has heard any encouraging news; the supreme commander is receiving short telegrams via Peking.[78]

The situation could have changed dramatically. Around noon on 5 November news still managed to reach Harbin of the manifesto of 17 (30) October. The telegraph operators had temporarily called off their strike to pass on this message. There was no guarantee, however, that the strikers had not deliberately passed on false information. Along with the manifesto came news of a change in the command of the troops in Moscow. Alekseev's reaction to this message was more than definite:

> Political freedom, while it has come as something of a surprise, is a good thing, but what pitifully bewildered people it is who are proclaiming this manifesto, heralding this freedom!!! ... What is being created in Russia? Is it still alive? Have the Jews and Armenians divided it up? ... After all, these will be our future leaders, deciding our fate. Indeed, this is how the liberalism of Russians differs from the liberalism of level-headed Europeans, in that the latter accept the idea of nationalism, they love their homeland; they care about its reputation and welfare. Our liberals are harming Russia, working for its fall and humiliation. All these attempts to discredit the army and its officers are exactly to the same purpose; with no reliable armed forces the state will quickly fall apart![79]

By evening, around 3,000 telegraph operators were marching through the streets of Harbin, carrying red banners. Meanwhile, workers at Manchuria station appealed to Linevich to release the activists Zakharov had arrested. He agreed.[80] This only intensified the unrest. The telegraph office was out of action, while the Supreme Command did nothing towards obtaining news by any alternative route – via China, for instance. At army headquarters rumours spread that Moscow was in flames and that more than 40,000 people had been killed or wounded in the city. One can only imagine the form these rumours took on after they had reached the ears of the ordinary soldiers![81]

At the same time, much depended on the mood of the lower ranks – especially on that of the most numerous force, the infantry. The unrest in Moscow was marked by the active participation of a few with the passive support of the majority. The troops, meanwhile, hesitated. This hesitation lasted until the Semenov Guards appeared in the city. 'The strength of the insurrection', noted S. P. Mel'gunov, who witnessed the Moscow events, 'lay of course in the unreliability of the troops. It was necessary to confine all infantry units to their barracks.'[82] There was a similar situation at Siping, with the exception that there were no barracks and that, of course, the Guards were not able to reach Manchuria within twenty-four hours. On 7 (20) November the army newspaper published the text of the manifestos of 17 (30) October and 3 (16) November. These concerned the halving of the redemption payments levied on the peasants after the 1861 reform – to take effect from 1 (14) January 1906 – and the complete cancellation of payments from 1 (14) January 1907.[83] The reason for publishing these two documents together is obvious, but they still failed to have an immediate effect. Every day fresh rumours spread among the troops – of an uprising in Finland, of tens of thousands killed in street fighting in St Petersburg, and so on. At the same time, the army was disintegrating, due especially to the activities of the former convicts, the group closest to the intelligentsia. On 28 October (10 November) Aleekseev noted: 'Discipline, already breaking down, is being eroded even further as the ignorant masses see freedom in the "cosy relationship" between every soldier and his superiors. Those who are consciously corrupting the army know that this is the best way to diminish respect for our armed forces.'[84]

On 30 October (12 November) 1905 unrest broke out in Vladivostok. The city was bursting at the seams with returning POWs and demobilized reservists. Both groups were unable to get home. Both were forced to wait, already halfway towards becoming civilians again. Obviously, the lack of discipline, the fact that order could not be restored quickly in such difficult circumstances, and the temptations of the city, were all taking their toll. The demobilized men began selling their personal effects. This led to scuffles in the market place between the former soldiers and sailors and the Chinese stall-owners, which soon erupted into unrest throughout the city. Troops had to be brought in to quell the disorder. The extent of the trouble can be gauged by the number of casualties. The action taken to restore order cost the lives of one officer and thirteen soldiers, while six officers and twenty-two men were injured. Among the crowd, two soldiers, thirteen sailors, six civilians and three 'foreigners' were killed, while thirty-two soldiers, fifty-two sailors, twenty-two civilians and twelve 'foreigners' were injured (as far as can be judged, the 'foreigners' were mostly Chinese). It took until 1 (14) November to put a stop to the riots.[85] On 5 (18) November Linevich issued order No. 2433 to the troops. Actually, it was not so much an order as an appeal to the soldiers to maintain their discipline. The temporary halt in demobilization was explained by the railway strike, he said. At the same time, the schedule for demobilization, which depended exclusively on the troops' original call-up dates, was announced. The first to be sent home were to be those called up from the beginning of the war until 31 August 1904; next in line were those enlisted from 1 September 1904 until 28 February 1905; and, finally, came the turn of all the others. The journey home was organized as follows: each train was supposed to hold 1,200 men plus three officers (the train commander and two subordinates).[86] The order did not even mention the penalties for infringements of discipline.

The authorities' reaction to revolutionary activities in the army was basically to try to mollify the troops. In 1905, the Ministry of War increased the soldiers' daily rations and improved their kit. This was in response to 'economic demands', but, as one pensive eyewitness pointed out, it happened 'only because material issues were more within the grasp of the masses than the nuances of the law, despite the root of the unrest being in the latter. The troublemakers knew this very well and it was on this that they based their successful political propaganda among the troops.'[87] This post-1905 account, by M. V. Grulev, is backed up by Alekseev's correspondence of the time, which took up an extremely negative position towards the Harbin press – the only one available in Manchuria. This (in Alekseev's words) 'Jewish press' had openly provoked the soldiers to disobedience:

> Of course, the men took this on board and the result is already making itself felt. A firm hand is needed, but our 'firm' hands are too involved in playing some kind of game. You are witness to the collapse of the old order, but you feel that the 'disorder' will continue, that these gentlemen are incapable of bringing about the *new* order.[88]

It is astonishing that a man who had held such opinions in 1905 resorted, in 1917, to associating with the very people he had never believed able to establish order, when fearful that the same events would be repeated.

In order to suppress the strikes, which Linevich finally decided to do in mid-November 1905, there was a need for reliable troops. The strikers were threatening armed resistance. Obviously, the reservists, who had stronger links than other troops to civilian life and who were yearning to go home as soon as possible, could not be used. Therefore, on 3 (16) November, the supreme commander ordered General P. A. Pleve, the commander of the Thirteenth Army Corps, along with a Colonel Zakharov, to go to Chita and then on to Irkutsk to restore order. In response to this, rail transport was interrupted three days later.[89] Demobilization became impossible, and even the movement of passenger trains beyond Chita (no more than two of which were running each day) depended on the mood of the engine drivers. The troop transports, meanwhile, stood totally motionless and, by the end of November, not one reservist had left Manchuria.[90]

The tsar himself had approved the timetable for the return of units from the Far East. However, General F. F. Palitsyn, the chief of the General Staff, was in no hurry to send away his best fighting corps, as he did not really trust the Japanese to keep to the terms of the peace. Yet, according to the timetable, the First and Thirteenth Army Corps were due to be dispatched first, in order to strengthen the troops in the Moscow and St Petersburg Military Districts in the struggle with the revolutionaries.[91] This led to an extremely explosive situation in Manchuria: the rank-and-file soldiers did not understand why, as Alekseev wrote, 'the corps which are made up fully of reservists and which arrived here in August–September 1904 have to make way for those who were disembarked in the same months of 1905 and who are mainly conscripts'.[92] The reservists, mostly peasants from the European part of the Russian Empire, wanted to go home; and this desire was only increased, of course, by rumours about what was happening in the countryside or about the changes that were planned. When his loved ones are threatened by danger, it is natural for a man to want to be with them. The officers were also worried about their families, especially those who had come to the Far East from the disturbed Kingdom of Poland.[93]

At the Manchurian army's headquarters, the idea was put forward of transporting some of the demobilized troops home by sea, but this suggestion did not initially receive support in St Petersburg. 'They do not understand', wrote Alekseev at the end of December 1905, 'that 400,000 reservists have become like hysterical, spineless, weak-willed old women, with only one thing in mind – to go home.'[94] Later, however, the authorities had to resort to this extraordinary and expensive measure after all. The number of officers and men designated for transport home by ship was constantly increasing – at first it was 40,000, then 60,000, later 80,000 and finally 100,000. But there were not enough ships for so many soldiers. The five vessels of the Volunteer Fleet that were suitable for transporting troops were completely tied up in bringing POWs from Japan to Vladivostok. By the beginning of February 1906, they had ferried ten generals, two admirals, 1,066 officers, 51,330 soldiers and 8,783 sailors over to Russia.[95] The evacuation of these men by rail was also far from being well organized, immediately exacerbating the problems on the Trans-Siberian Railway. While in captivity, the officers and men had been held in various camps; and the troops on the returning trains were also distributed fairly randomly, regardless of their proper units and commanders. The number of officers was often insufficient; moreover, they were often completely unfamiliar with their new charges. So, for example, one train, with 600 sailors on board who had been under the command of Rear-Admiral Nebogatov, was commanded by three officers from Port Arthur – a senior lieutenant and two midshipmen. With the unrest in Vladivostock having only been put down just before the POWs returned from captivity, one officer recalled:

It was impossible for us to establish any kind of communication with this unfamiliar command, which in the mutinous mood of the time threatened to cause complete anarchy on the train. And, in fact, sensing the absence of a firm hand on the railway line, the men soon lost their discipline completely: they became drunk, stole food from the station buffets, threatened the station-masters and once they even tried to leave the train by force, accusing the railwaymen of holding up the train and completely disregarding the station-master, who said that he could not allow us to continue, as there was another train heading towards us on the same line.[96]

The only assistance the officers received, until they met up with Meller-Zakomel'skii's expedition (on which see pp. 114–15), was from forty sailors from the coastal defence battleship *Admiral Ushakov*, who had maintained their cohesion and discipline under the command of their boatswain.[97]

The Russian army commanders had never evacuated POWs before, at least not in such numbers. Moreover, the experience of the last war, against Turkey in the 1870s, was of no use: back then, the remaining Russian troops were brought out of the Balkans still in good order. In 1905, the evacuation was lagging far behind the demobilization, which unavoidably made the situation in the rear of the army more difficult. At the same time, it was also impossible to halt the return of the enlisted reservists in such perilous circumstances – to have done so would have been to have risked losing control over the troops. On 4 (17) November in Vladivostok the reservist 'non-border region and Priamur region troops' began to be demobilized by order of the supreme commander. These immediately numbered 5,000 men. The *Vestnik Man'chzhurskikh armii* reported: 'The troops greeted the news with joy. The city is quiet. There is not a single restaurant left open. The port is full of foreign ships; there are also Russian vessels. Disembarkation [of the POWs brought from Japan] has not yet taken place.'[98] This soon did begin, however; otherwise, it would have been impossible for the military authorities to retain control over the city. In order to transport the reservists it was necessary to use practically all the available Russian, German, Belgian and British vessels. On the night of 4 (17) February 1906, the first troop ship arrived in Odessa: the *Burma* brought home 1,850 men. By February 1906, 12,146 men were supposed to have been transported back on Russian ships, together with 73,486 under foreign flags.[99]

By April 1906, when the situation on the railways finally stabilized, more than 120,000 men and 1,500 officers had been brought by seventy ships from Vladivostok to Odessa.[100] This undoubtedly helped to ease conditions in Manchuria. The more rapidly that the older reservists left the army, the easier it was to maintain control over the troops. The period from November 1905 to January 1906 was especially difficult for the army. The communications system and the railway were almost completely out of action. Wild rumours, which could not be verified, were circulating among the troops that the British had landed at Odessa, that British ships were anchored at Kronstadt, that several German divisions had entered Warsaw, that 20,000 people had been killed during the unrest in Moscow, and so on.[101] Meanwhile, large numbers of demobilized reservists were continuing to assemble at Siping. In order to ease the pressure, the commanders allowed those who wished to do so to remain in Manchuria or in Siberia. Nothing at all was said, however, about how these people were supposed to find new occupations in order to earn a living. It was clear that the railway could not provide enough vacancies: the loss of the war meant that the extent of the Russian-controlled network had contracted and, consequently, there was already a problem in finding work for the former employees of the South Manchurian Railway who had worked in the areas captured by the Japanese. On 19 November (2 December), the army began to be withdrawn from the former front line to Harbin and, two days later, five troop trains set off from there to Russia.[102] The most difficult period following the end of military action was drawing to a close.

At the same time Alekseev was forming an idea of how to end the crisis. For him, the ideal solution would have been the granting of concessions from the upper levels of Russian society, accompanied by the harsh suppression of those who had preached anti-patriotic messages. The general blamed both the imperial government and its opponents, including the liberals, for the emergency. Alekseev reacted to the news that 'civil liberties' had been declared on 21 November (4 December) 1905 in the following manner: 'This declaration has been wrenched out, when the tsar should have granted it earlier and of his own accord. A revolution from above is always less painful than one from below. What bloodshed would have accompanied the emancipation of the serfs, if it had been carried out in their name.'[103] Once the revolution had begun and blood was already being spilt, however, the general did not waver in his attitude towards events. At the end of 1905 and the beginning of 1906 he was in favour of the most harsh and rapid response to the revolution:

> With the Jews and Poles at their head, our revolutionaries march with a spring in their step towards the destruction of the state's integrity. But this integrity will be paid for *in rivers of blood – not in that of the revolutionaries, but in that of true Russians.* Hundreds of thousands will perish defending Russia's dignity, but they will defend it in vain. Would it not be better for ten thousand revolutionaries to fall?[104]

It was not only the revolutionaries, therefore, who were able to use 1905 as a rehearsal.

The commanders at Siping, meanwhile, still did not have reliable communications with St Petersburg via Russian territory. The reservists, returning home after the defeat, were causing trouble on the railway. The Ministry of War was planning to send out two punitive expeditions simultaneously to restore order on the Trans-Siberian Railway. The plan was drawn up by Palitsyn. In order to inform Linevich, the ministry set up three alternative lines of communication in mid-November 1905 – by courier via Omsk and

Peking and by telegraph via Europe, America and Japan. On 23 December 1905 (5 January 1906), an officer wearing civilian clothes arrived at Linevich's headquarters from Omsk. He was carrying a telegram from Nicholas II advising of General P. K. von Rennenkamf's appointment to the post of commander of the Trans-Siberian Punitive Expedition. On 2 (15) January the first train set off for Russia.[105] At the same time, General A. N. Meller-Zakomel'skii's detachment set out to meet Rennenkamf. Both had reputations as energetic military men, Meller having already distinguished himself in suppressing an uprising in Sevastopol in November 1905. Alekseev was pleased. Events were unfolding as he had wished: 'I wonder when the strike leaders will go on strike, those who represent various unions of unions, unions of engineers...? Maybe a strike like that would erase all but the ruins and memories of such unions.'[106]

The units set aside for the expedition were not large in number. Meller had only a reinforced company of household troops from the Lithuanian regiment and two field guns. Rennenkamf's detachment could also be fitted on to one train. Nevertheless, by the beginning of February 1906, thanks to the energy of these two men, order was restored on the Siberian railway. Meller's detachment played the major role. 'The task, which had seemed so difficult and dangerous', recalled A. F. Rediger, 'was performed smoothly and simply, with only negligible forces. The main credit in this operation should go to him [i.e., Meller-Zakomel'skii], as it was entirely thanks to his butcher's instinct that it was possible to club and slash so systematically along the whole route, visiting holy terror on all the rebels and strikers.'[107]

The success of the detachments can be measured by the extent to which the railway was put back in operation. In October 1905, the line had carried no more than one train per day. The strike had hit the railway hard – the trains were unable to return from beyond the Urals, the stations did not receive any coal, etc. By the beginning of 1906, the line was able to carry up to five troop trains per day (and that does not include the forty-one hospital trains). Between 1 (14) November 1905 and 8 (21) January 1906, 3,576 officers and 273,322 men had been transported along this route.[108]

The generals, having lost a war with an external foe, suddenly became convinced that it was possible to defeat – and with surprising ease – the enemy within. The main requirement for this task was officers and warrant officers who could also persuade the 'young' soldiers (that is, the conscripts) to fall in behind them. The enlisted reservists had been the main actors in the mutiny. The commanders had lost control of them twice – during the defeat at Mukden and after the armistice. As early as 1905, the revolutionaries began to take notice of the homesick soldiers, but the latter had been disarmed and brought under control with surprisingly small forces. Most importantly, this took place before they had come into contact with the radicals, who were ready to offer the soldiers, when still armed, simple and attractive solutions to their peacetime problems, in accordance with Lenin's well-known formula, 'an imperialist war should be turned into a civil war'.

Acknowledgement

The author and editors would like to thank the Department of History, Queen Mary, University of London for providing funds for the translation of this chapter.

Notes

1   F. McCullagh, *With the Cossacks. Being a Story of an Irishman Who Rode With The Cossacks Throughout the Russo-Japanese War* (London, 1906), p. 226.
2   V. [M.] Alekseeva-Borel', *Sorok let v riadakh russkoi imperatorskoi armii: General M. V. Alekseev* (St Petersburg, 2000). This book contains a publication of part of Alekseev's archive (without commentary), together with some personal reminiscences of him by his daughter, which makes it extremely useful for historians.
3   For more details, see O. R. Airapetov, 'Russkaia armiia na sopkakh Manchzhurii', *Voprosy istorii* (2002), No. 1, pp. 64–82.
4   *Dnevniki Nikolaia II* (Moscow, 1991), p. 315.
5   Ibid., p. 366.
6   N. [N.] Ianushkevich, 'Organizatsiia i rol' intendantstva v sovremennykh armiiakh na voine', *Voennyi sbornik* (1910), No. 4, p. 135.
7   A. I. Gusev, 'Iz dnevnika korpusnogo kontrolera (v russko-iaponskuiu voinu 1904–1905gg.)', *Voennyi sbornik* (1911), No. 11, p. 204.
8   A. I. Gusev, 'Iz vospominaniia uchastnika russko-iaponskoi voiny', *Voennyi sbornik* (1910), No. 9, p. 87.
9   Ibid.
10 D. [P.] Parskii, *Vospominaniia i mysli o poslednei voine (1904–1905gg.)* (St Petersburg, 1906), p. 69.
11 *Otdel Rukopisei Rossiiskoi Gosudarstvennoi Biblioteki* (Manuscript Section of the Russian State Library, hereafter *OR RGB*), f. 855, kart 1, ed.khr. 35, l. 37.
12 *Russko-iaponskaia voina v soobshcheniiakh v Nikolaevskoi Akademii General'nogo shtaba* (St Petersburg, 1907), Part 2, p. 236; L. N. Sobolev, *Kuropatkinskaia strategiia. Kratkie zametki byvshego komandira 6-go Sibirskogo Armeiskogo korpusa* (St Petersburg, 1910), p. 152; Parskii, *Vospominaniia*, p. 75.
13 *OR RGB*, f. 855, kart 1, ed.khr. 36, l. 19-ob.
14 E. S. Botkin, *Svet i teni russko-iaponskoi voiny 1904–5gg. (Iz pisem k zhene)* (St Petersburg, 1908), p. 79.
15 Parskii, *Vospominaniia*, p. 89.
16 *OR RGB*, f. 855, kart 1, ed.khr. 34, l. 5.
17 B. Bülow, *Vospominaniia* (Moscow and Leningrad, 1935), p. 301.
18 *OR RGB*, f. 855, kart 1, ed.khr. 34, ll. 8, 12.
19 E. Stepanov, 'Iz vospominanii kazach'ego ofitsera', *Vestnik russkoi konnitsy* (1911), No. 9, p. 359.
20 Botkin, *Svet i teni*, p. 82.
21 A. Vineken, 'Iaponskaia kavaleriia v minuvshuiu kampaniiu 1904–1905gg.', *Vestnik russkoi konnitsy* (1910), No. 1, p. 9.
22 E. Tettau, *Ot Mukdena do Portsmuta* (St Petersburg, 1914), pp. 11, 13.
23 Parskii, *Vospominaniia*, pp. 77, 80, 90.
24 *OR RGB*, f. 855, kart 1, ed.khr. 34, l. 15.
25 *OR RGB*, f. 855, kart 1, ed.khr. 35, l. 4.
26 N.V. Voronovich, *Potonuvshii mir. Ocherki proshlogo 1891–1920* (Moscow, 2001), pp. 79–80.
27 *OR RGB*, f. 855, kart 1, ed.khr. 35, l. 3-ob.

28 Parskii, *Vospominaniia*, p. 92.
29 Tettau, *Ot Mukdena*, p. 7.
30 *OR RGB, f.* 855, *kart* 1, *ed.khr.* 34, *l.* 50-*ob.*
31 Tettau, *Ot Mukdena*, pp. 37–8.
32 *OR RGB, f.* 855, *kart* 1, *ed.khr.* 34, *l.* 56.
33 *OR RGB, f.* 855, *kart* 1, *ed.khr.* 34, *l.* 50-*ob.*
34 *OR RGB, f.* 855, *kart* 1, *ed.khr.* 36, *l.* 17-*ob.*
35 I. N. Danilov, *Velikii kniaz' Nikolai Nikolaevich* (Paris, 1930), p. 71; S. Iu. Witte, *Vospominaniia* (Moscow, 1994), Vol. 2, pp. 379–80.
36 'Khronika voenno-morskikh deistvii na Dal'nem Vostoke', *Morskoi sbornik* (1905), No. 6, p. 220.
37 Ibid., p. 221.
38 Voronovich, *Potonuvshii mir*, p. 85.
39 *Vestnik Man'chzhurskikh armii*, No. 257 (15 May 1905), p. 1; No. 260 (18 May 1905), p. 1; No. 261 (19 May 1905), p. 1; No. 265 (23 May 1905), p. 1.
40 Parskii, *Vospominaniia*, p. 94; *OR RGB, f.* 855, *kart* 1, *ed.khr.* 43, *l.* 72.
41 *OR RGB, f.* 855, *kart* 1, *ed.khr.* 34, *l.* 1-ob.
42 For every month they served, a year was deducted from their sentences. Those who had already served out their sentences, but had still been forced to live in exile, were offered permission to go home if they volunteered.
43 S. Ursyn-Prushinski, 'Boi na ostrove Sakhalin vo vremia russko-iaponskoi voiny', *Kraevoi biulleten'* (Iuzhno-Sakhalinsk) (1995), No. 3. pp. 59, 66, 77.
44 Parskii, *Vospominaniia*, p. 96.
45 Stepanov, 'Iz vospominanii', p. 361.
46 *Vestnik Man'chzhurskikh armii*, No. 259 (17 May 1905), p. 1.
47 *OR RGB, f.* 855, *kart* 1, *ed.khr.* 35, *l.* 27.
48 Witte, *Vospominaniia*, Vol. 2, p. 414.
49 *OR RGB, f.* 855, *kart* 1, *ed.khr.* 36, *ll.* 3-3ob. Author's emphasis.
50 *OR RGB, f.* 855, *kart* 1, *ed.khr.* 34, *l.* 70-*ob.*
51 *OR RGB, f.* 855, *kart* 1, *ed.khr.* 35, *l.* 25.
52 *OR RGB, f.* 855, *kart* 1, *ed.khr.* 34, *l.* 13.
53 *OR RGB, f.* 855, *kart* 1, *ed.khr.* 35, *l.* 29-*ob.*
54 *OR RGB, f.* 855, *kart* 1, *ed.khr.* 36, *l.* 14-*ob.*
55 *OR RGB, f.* 855, *kart* 1, *ed.khr.* 35, *l.* 42-*ob.*
56 *Vestnik Man'chzhurskikh armii*, No. 198 (21 February 1905), p. 1.
57 *OR RGB, f.* 855, *kart* 1, *ed.khr.* 35, *l.* 52-*ob.*
58 Voronovich, *Potonuvshii mir*, p. 95.
59 *OR RGB, f.* 855, *kart* 1, *ed.khr.* 36, *l.* 35.
60 'Russkoe voennoe obozrenie. Deistviia v Manchzhurii', *Voennyi sbornik* (1905), No. 10, pp. 244, 247.
61 *Vestnik Man'chzhurskikh armii*, No. 367 (2 September 1905), p. 1.
62 S. E. Kryzhanovskii, *Vospominaniia. Iz bumag S. E. Kryzhanovski, poslednego gosudarstvennogo sekretaria Rossiiskoi imperii* (Berlin, n.d.), p. 26.
63 V. A. Maklakov, *Vlast' i obshchestvennost' na zakate staroi Rossii (Vospominaniia sovremennika)* (Paris, 1926), Part 3, p. 403.
64 S. I. Shidlovskii, *Vospominaniia*, (Berlin, 1923), Part 1, pp. 102–3.
65 Kryzhanovskii, *Vospominaniia*, p. 82.
66 Sobolev, *Kuropatkinskaia strategiia*, p. 268.
67 Voronovich, *Potonuvshii mir*, p. 95.
68 *OR RGB, f.* 855, *kart* 1, *ed.khr.* 36, *l.* 65.
69 'Russkoe voennoe obozrenie', *Voennyi sbornik* (1905), No. 11, p. 273.
70 *Vestnik Man'chzhurskikh armii*, No. 398 (3 October 1905), p. 1; No. 400 (5 October 1905), p. 1.

71 *Russko-iaponskaia voina. Iz dnevnikov A. N. Kuropatkina i N. P. Linevicha* (Leningrad, 1925), pp. 110–11; Tettau, *Ot Mukdena*, p. 75.
72 *Otchet o primenenii tsenzury na teatre voiny* (Compiled by the Censorship Department of the Supreme Command, edited by the Quartermaster-General) (Harbin, 1905), pp. 1–4.
73 *OR RGB, f.* 855, *kart* 1, *ed.khr.* 37, *l.* 14-*ob.*
74 *OR RGB, f.* 855, *kart* 1, *ed.khr.* 37, *ll.* 14-*ob*, 15.
75 Voronovich, *Potonuvshii mir*, p. 98.
76 *Vestnik Man'chzhurskikh armii*, No. 413 (18 October 1905), p. 1; 'Obzor voennykh sobytii s 12 noiabria po 13 dekabria', Appendix 3 ('Russkoe voennoe obozrenie'), *Voennyi sbornik* (1906), No. 1, pp. 241–3.
77 *OR RGB, f.* 855, *kart* 1, *ed.khr.* 37, *l.* 19; *Russko-iaponskaia voina. Iz dnevnikov A. N. Kuropatkina i N. P. Linevicha*, p. 113.
78 *OR RGB, f.* 855, *kart* 1, *ed.khr.* 37, *l.* 19-*ob.*
79 *OR RGB, f.* 855, *kart* 1, *ed.khr.* 37, *ll.* 19-*ob*, 20.
80 Tettau, *Ot Mukdena*, pp. 75–6.
81 *OR RGB, f.* 855, *kart* 1, *ed.khr.* 37, *l.* 17.
82 S. P. Mel'gunov, *Vospominaniia i dnevniki* (Paris, 1964), p. 169.
83 *Vestnik Man'chzhurskikh armii*, No. 417 (7 November 1905), p. 1.
84 *OR RGB, f.* 855, *kart* 1, *ed.khr.* 37, *ll.* 22; 24; 24-*ob.*
85 *Vestnik Man'chzhurskikh armii*, No. 417 (7 November 1905), pp. 1–2.
86 Ibid., p. 1.
87 M. [V.] Grulev, *Zloby dnia v zhizhni armii* (Brest-Litovsk, 1911), pp. 2, 4.
88 *OR RGB, f.* 855, *kart* 1, *ed.khr.* 37, *l.* 26-*ob.*
89 E. Tettau, *Ot Mukdena*, p. 75.
90 *OR RGB, f.* 855, *kart* 1, *ed.khr.* 37, *ll.* 30, 38-*ob*, 45-*ob.*
91 A. [F.] Rediger, *Istoriia moei zhizni. Vospominaniia voennogo ministra* (Moscow, 1999), Vol. 1, p. 512.
92 *OR RGB, f.* 855, *kart* 1, *ed.khr.* 37, *l.* 33.
93 *OR RGB, f.* 855, *kart* 1, *ed.khr.* 37, *l.* 32-*ob.*
94 *OR RGB, f.* 855, *kart* 1, *ed.khr.* 38, *l.* 13-*ob.*
95 'Obzor boevykh deistvii s 13-go ianvaria po 13-e fevralia', Appendix 5 ('Russkoe voennoe obozrenie'), *Voennyi sbornik* (1906), No. 3, pp. 244, 247.
96 B. P. Dudorov, *Admiral Nepenin* (St Petersburg, 1993), p. 135.
97 Ibid., p. 136.
98 *Vestnik Man'chzhurskikh armii*, No. 420 (10 November 1905), p. 1.
99 'Obzor boevykh deistvii s 14 dekabria po 12 ianvaria', Appendix 4 ('Russkoe voennoe obozrenie'), *Voennyi Sbornik* (1906), No. 2, p. 237; 'Obzor boevykh deistvii s 13-go ianvaria po 13-e fevralia', Appendix 5 ('Russkoe voennoe obozrenie'), *Voennyi sbornik* (1906), No. 3, pp. 248–9.
100 Tettau, *Ot Mukdena*, p. 96.
101 *OR RGB, f.* 855, *kart* 1, *ed.khr.* 38, *ll.* 19-*ob*, 48.
102 *Vestnik Man'chzhurskikh armii*, No. 433 (23 November 1905), p. 1.
103 *OR RGB, f.* 855, *kart* 1, *ed.khr.* 37, *l.* 50.
104 *OR RGB, f.* 855, *kart* 1, *ed.khr.* 38, *l.* 48-*ob.*
105 *Russko-iaponskaia voina. Iz dnevnikov A. N. Kuropatkina i N. P. Linevicha*, pp. 124, 126; Rediger, *Istoriia moei zhizni*, Vol. 1, p. 521.
106 *OR RGB, f.* 855, *kart* 1, *ed. khr.* 38, *ll.* 1, 51.
107 Rediger, *Istoriia moei zhizni* (Moscow, 1999), Vol. 1, pp. 521–2.
108 'Obzor voennykh deistvii s 12-go noiabria po 13-e dekabria', Appendix 3 ('Russkoe voennoe obozrenie'), *Voennyi Sbornik* (1906), No. 1, p. 241; 'Obzor voennykh deistvii s 14-go dekabria po 12-e ianvaria', Appendix 4 ('Russkoe voennoe obozrenie'), *Voennyi sbornik* (1906), No. 2, p. 237.

7 Retrospectively revolting

Kazan Tatar 'conspiracies' during the 1905 Revolution

Christian Noack

Muslim political mobilization caused little trouble to the authorities during the 1905 Revolution. Nevertheless, from 1907 onwards Kazan's police retrospectively 'uncovered' widespread revolutionary and separatist Muslim conspiracies that were said to have proliferated during the revolutionary period. This chapter pursues the fabrication of this narrative and discusses its basic components. It then examines the grounds on which the authorities grew suspicious about their actually quite loyal Muslim subjects; and, finally, it analyses that suspicion's effects on Russian–Muslim relations, as well as on inner-Muslim developments.

In October 1907, Kazan's gendarmes reported to the police department of the Ministry of the Interior on their recent findings about Tatar political activities in 1905 and 1906:

> At the time when the second State Duma was convened, a peculiar Tatar revolutionary organization appeared, with no affiliations to the Russian Social Democratic Workers Party or to the Party of Socialists-Revolutionaries. This new organization is led by some of the Muslim mullahs and merchants; that is, Tatars with progressive orientations. Using the favourable circumstances, the organization planned to overthrow autocracy in Russia and to establish a democratic republic, with a constituent assembly and the separation of all Russian Muslim Tatars into a particular federation, and the expulsion of all Russians from the Tatar environment, as happened in Finland.[1]

Thankfully, the reporting officer concluded, this revolutionary organization had not yet spread its harmful agitation beyond the confines of Kazan guberniia. As leaders of the conspiracy, the gendarmes singled out the Kazan mullahs Abdulla Apanaev, Salikhdzhan and Galimdzhan Galeev, all of whom they proposed to banish from Kazan guberniia.

The gendarmes perceived the emergence of this revolutionary organization as organically linked to the activities of two Tatar *shakird* (student) associations, 'Islakh' ('Reform') and 'Berek' ('Unity'), on which they had already reported earlier in 1907.[2] While 'Islakh' was seen as a student organization, pursuing purely educational purposes, 'Berek' was understood as its radical offspring that pursued the political objectives already cited above, such as the extension of Muslim political participation, the overthrow of autocracy and the creation of a parliamentary republic. The police notified the ministry that 'Berek' had so far found no significant support among the local Muslim population and had hence resolved to limit its activities to cautious and clandestine work among the peasantry in some of the Tatar districts of Kazan guberniia. It was reported too that, in investigating the case of 'Berek', the police had not been able to trace its leaders, but had learned about the above-mentioned conspiracy.

Three months later, Kazan governor M. V. Strizhevskii added evidence in a secret letter to the Ministry of the Interior's police department. Apart from the mullahs mentioned above, the Tatar novelist Gaiaz Iskhaki (who was also erroneously identified as being a mullah) was now added to list of leading conspirators.[3] More importantly, the governor accused all of them of having misused the Third Muslim Congress, in Nizhnii Novgorod in August 1906, to form a clandestine revolutionary organization. In addition to that, the governor tried to clarify the links between the mullahs and the student organizations. As early as 1905, he wrote, the former had supposedly used their prominent position within the Tatar community to organize meetings in their mosques and *madrasas* (Islamic schools) in order to 'unify the Muslim population in the combat against the existing state order' and to assert the necessity of separating the Tatars 'within a particular state'. To achieve these ends, they had founded student organizations that were to disseminate their ideas among Muslim youth. The police believed that 'Berek', in particular, served as a '*kuznitsa kadrov*' – a 'forge' for converting progressive students into revolutionary agitators. Its programme was accordingly labelled as an 'echo of the Muslim Congress'. The local administration boasted that it had impeded the spread of Tatar revolutionary propaganda when it closed courses for village teachers in Galimdzhan Galeev's *madrasa* in May 1907 and rounded up an illegal and 'clearly revolutionary congress of *shakirds* and teachers' near Kazan the same month: 'Since then, no further evidences of any anti-governmental activities by "Islakh" and "Berek" have been reported.'[4]

It thus took Kazan's local administration only half a year after Stolypin's *coup d'état* of 3 June 1907 to develop a narrative of Tatar revolutionary activities between 1905 and 1907 that depicted practically any political expression by the local Muslim population as part of one extensive, separatist conspiracy. This narrative would prove to be quite persistent and to have far-reaching consequences for Russian–Tatar relations up to 1917, although it heavily contradicted the evidence on Muslim political activities available for contemporaries and collected by the police before 1907.

This is rather surprising, as the Russian authorities traditionally regarded the Empire's Muslims as loyal subjects of the tsar, except for brief periods during the Crimean War and the Russo-Turkish campaign of 1877–78. And, indeed, there was little basis in fact to revise these views during the 1905 Revolution. With the exception of Baku, where bloody clashes between Armenians and Muslims with thousands of victims occurred first in 1903–04 and then continued through 1905–06,[5] Muslim communities throughout the Empire refrained from revolutionary violence. When the revolution brought liberalization and participatory politics to the provinces, Muslim elites rallied around an Empire-wide political movement ('Ittifak') instead.

Political mobilization became visible first and foremost among Tatars and Bashkirs, the Muslim communities that had settled in the heartland of European Russia, in the Volga Basin and the Ural mountains.[6] In comparison to the urban centres and the western and southern peripheries of the Empire, the political situation remained rather stable in the Volga–Urals region. Peasant unrest ravaged the countryside here to a far lesser degree than in other parts of central Russia. Still, Kazan, with its university and factories – and even, though to a lesser extent, provincial capitals like Ufa and Orenburg – witnessed a temporary breakdown of authority during the October strikes of 1905. In Kazan, for example, deputies of the city duma felt compelled to organize a citizens' militia to preserve law and order in the chaotic days that followed the publication of the October Manifesto. Only on 21 October 1905, after the declaration of martial law, could regular troops restore the governor's authority by the use of force. Between 20 and 40 militiamen were killed when the governor, P. Khomutov, ordered the storming of the duma building. Authorities temporarily retreated in Ufa too, leaving the streets to railway workers who beat several people to death during a 'patriotic' mass demonstration on 22 October. Police and military detachments reinforced authority here only by 24 October.[7] Later in 1905, fairly isolated armed upheavals organized by local Bolsheviks during the December railway strikes were quickly smashed both in Kazan and Ufa.[8]

The Muslim inhabitants of Kazan and Ufa, therefore, witnessed euphoria, mass meetings, strikes and violence during summer and autumn 1905, but largely remained bystanders. Only individual Tatars had participated in the disarmament of police units and the formation of a militia in Kazan in October 1905.[9] The majority of Muslim residents, however, chose to follow the cities' *ulema* (communities of legal scholars) and the Tatar bourgeoisie in organizing a demonstration of loyalty to the autocracy. This demonstration was, incidentally, led by that very Galimdzhan Galeev who later found himself listed among the incriminated 'revolutionaries'. In Ufa, Mufti Sultanov likewise addressed a patriotic mass meeting.[10] It seems, then, that even during the 'days of freedom' Social Democratic and Socialist-Revolutionary propaganda did not resonate much among the Muslim population. Certainly, revolutionary circles rounded up by the police in the winter of 1905–06 included very few Muslim members.[11]

In the long run, however, the local Muslim elites proved remarkably capable of exploiting the political changes to advance their own agenda. Political assemblies had been organized in Kazan and other Muslim centres in the Volga–Urals by influential merchants and mullahs from the end of 1904. As respected members of the local Muslim elite, they convened meetings in their private homes and in Kazan's mosques that may arguably be described as Tatar equivalents to the Russian banquet campaign. These meetings were instrumental for the preparation of the three All-Russian Muslim Congresses held in 1905 and 1906. Apanaev, Galeev and other Kazan-based merchants and mullahs participated in the work of these congresses and paved the way for the future establishment of a Russian Muslim political party, the Ittifak. The emerging Tatar press and to a lesser degree even Russian papers, covered these issues from 1906 onwards. Closely following the course of events, the Ministry of the Interior should thus have been well aware of the fact that Muslim political aspiration from 1905 to 1907 hardly ever went beyond Kadet-style liberalism.[12] Neither the congresses' agendas nor the draft party programme of Ittifak contained separatist or revolutionary demands. With regard to the question of autonomy, the Muslims claimed autonomous control only over their spiritual and educational institutions.[13]

We may assume that this too was well known to the Kazan police. In order to sustain the credibility of their conspiracy narrative they resolved, as we have seen, to allude to the 'secret discussions' that had allegedly been organized on the occasion of the Third Muslim Congress. In fact, the congress had witnessed open clashes between the representatives of the liberal majority and some younger leftist intellectuals instead. The question at stake had been the issue of whether the Muslims should form one single national movement or establish several class-based parties. Finally, the congress voted for the formation of one, Empire-wide Muslim party with a liberal profile.[14]

How much basis in fact was there to the reported co-operation between radicals and liberals, then? And to what extent, if ever, could Muslim radicals influence the course of events in larger scale? To the 'left' of the liberal Muslim mainstream there existed only a few small groups and circles. Although it sympathized with socialist ideas, even the small faction of the so-called 'Tatar *trudoviki*' in the Second State Duma had no organizational links with Russian groups or parties.[15]

To the extent that it spread at all, radicalism remained verbal among Kazan's Muslim teachers and students. Like other academic institutions throughout the Empire, Kazan's university became the most important location for the political mobilization, co-ordination and radicalization of the protest movement during late summer and autumn of 1905. Although only a few individual Muslims enrolled as teachers or students there, news from university meetings almost instantly reached the Muslim population too. The Kazan Tatar Teacher School, which had university professors among its instructors, served as the main link between the university and the Muslim community. Its Muslim students, again, maintained close relations with the pupils of the cities' *madrasas*. They passed on the sort of ideas that were developing simultaneously among their Russian counterparts and influenced them with their 'European' habits.[16] As among university students, the style of dress of the Russian worker became fashionable among *shakirds*: 'they let their hair grow and dressed in a red *rubakha* [shirt] tied by a big belt', noted one source.[17] This deliberate and unveiled *urusenie* ('Russianism') shocked Muslim society probably no less than did the educational demands the *shakirds* were putting forward. They had opted for a thorough secularization of the curriculum, the participation of teachers and pupils in discussing matters of instruction and administration and, finally, for the public founding of (and public control over) the formally 'private' religious institutions. Like Russian students and pupils, the *shakirds* of Kazan's reformed *madrasas* frequently went on strike to sustain their demands.[18]

In addition, the radicalized teachers and students used the newly acquired freedom of expression to establish a number of short-lived newspapers and journals. The most outspoken among them was *Tang juldyzy* (The Morning Star) published by the writer Gaiaz Iskhaki. Its adherents, the '*tangchylar*', flirted with revolutionary and Populist ideas and they even pretended to represent a Tatar branch of the PSR. Yet despite this verbal and habitual radicalism, Iskhaki and his friends supported the moderate position the liberals put forward at the Third Muslim Congress. It is probable that some of Iskhaki's followers had initiated the formation of the Tatar student association Berek, which had, as the aforementioned police report correctly stated, mustered little sympathy among fellow students. Incidentally, Berek's programme raised the same educational questions that had been brought up by the more influential Islakh, but added the conviction that these ends could only be achieved after the abolition of autocracy and the establishment of constitutional order.[19]

Islakh, on the other hand, had probably had a clandestine existence since 1901. During the 'days of freedom', it developed from a purely literary circle into a Muslim student organization that demanded reforms of the reformed *madrasas*. Islakh also hosted an inter-regional meeting of *shakirds* in May 1906, which supported the demands listed above and called for the establishment of a broader Muslim student association.[20] These proposals, to be sure, met with limited comprehension among the city's secular Tatar elites and, understandably, even less among the reform-minded *ulema*. The students' propositions were ignored by Galimdzhan Galeev, who repeatedly tried to banish the most outspoken *shakirds* from his 'Mukhamadiia' *madrasa*. In reaction to this, Islakh organized a school boycott and solidarity strikes among other Muslim schools of the city.

Kazan's gendarmes, who kept a close eye on what was happening in the university and other institutes of higher education in the city, must have been well aware of the situation in the Muslim schools – not least because they were called in several times to the Tatars' teacher-training school and to Mukhamadiia to restore order.[21] Indeed, the first reports on the Muslim students' efforts to organize an all-Russian congress of *shakirds* (in order to discuss educational problems and general matters pertaining to the role of students in the Muslim movement) had already been sent from Kazan to St Petersburg in May 1906.[22] The police continued to survey Muslim student activities from then on.

Probably alarmed by the *shakirds'* conduct, the local administration also refused to legalize congresses of Muslim teachers. The latter, who essentially shared the educational reform programme put forward by the students, had formed their own union in 1906, and worked on a national curriculum themselves. Unhampered by the police, their first inter-regional conference in Kazan had drawn up a programme for elementary schools in August 1906, and scheduled a second conference for May 1907. Unlike the *shakirds*, the teachers enjoyed support from the majority of reformed mullahs and the commercial Tatar bourgeoisie. Among them, the Galeev brothers and Apanacv actively supported the preparations for the teachers' congresses. When, in May 1907, the authorities repeatedly refused to permit their meeting, the teachers tried to convene illegally in a nearby village, but the police prevented them.[23] There is no evidence for any participation of Islakh (as an organization) in the preparation of the teacher courses and the teachers' congress in 1907, nor any mention of Berek activists – although it seems that a secret meeting of *shakirds* had immediately preceded these gatherings.[24]

Having rounded up most of the Russian revolutionary underground in late 1905, and largely suppressed peasant unrest by 1906, the local authorities were, by 1907, ready to cope with minor evils like the Muslim political mobilization. As we have seen, they basically blended three major, separate constituents into one comprehensive narrative: the overtly political activity of the liberal Muslim movement, the largely habitual and verbal radicalism of the *shakirds*, and the organizational efforts of Muslim teachers. They told the story of a 'revolutionary conspiracy' that embraced virtually all the mobilized strata of the Muslim population: the urban elites (mullahs and merchants), the teachers and the *shakirds*.[25] But why were the local authorities so concerned in the first place about Muslim conspiracies, when the Muslims' conduct had generally proved to be so loyal?

Of course, even the formative phase of the Muslim movement had already been viewed with suspicion – when not actively obstructed – by the Russian authorities. While it had been necessary to convene the First Muslim Congress (in Nizhnii Novgorod in August 1905) clandestinely, the changed legal environment meant that the government grudgingly consented to its follow-ups in St Petersburg and Nizhnii. Apparently, the local authorities in Kazan were not willing to acquiesce with the course of events and searched for evidence that would personally implicate Kazan's leading Muslim activists in a 'conspiracy'. In order to achieve this, in December 1906 – long before the teachers' congress was held – they had already secretly ordered additional investigations against Abdulla Apanaev, Galimdzhan Galeev and the Kazan publicist Khadi Maksudi.[26] The dodging of the ban on the teachers' congress, then, probably served to provide an already long-awaited legal pretext for their incrimination.

Second, the elections to the First and Second State Dumas had shown the capability of the mobilized Muslim elites to benefit from autocracy's political concessions. Except for in Ufa province, Muslims made up minorities and were largely outnumbered by the Russian population in the respective administrative units. Their representatives, however, had long since been accustomed to holding minority positions in the local zemstvo assemblies and city dumas. As a result, they had developed considerable voting discipline in order to maximize Muslim influence in such elected bodies.[27] In Ufa, Muslims even managed to secure an absolute majority of provincial delegates to the new national assembly. Twenty-five Muslim deputies were elected to the First State Duma, and thirty-six to the Second.[28] The Duma elections clearly displayed the cleavages among the Russian electorate, while Muslims were capable of mobilizing and organizing their voters very efficiently. This ability of the Muslims to monitor and even to dominate the electoral process certainly concerned the Russian authorities. Already, during the State Duma elections, they had tried to obstruct the balloting of individual Muslim candidates.[29] As Charles Steinwedel concluded, 'After 1905, the content of Muslim group interest may not have changed substantially, but the new institutional means available for the expression of these interests ... gave their activity new implications to some, though certainly not all observers.' What was happening was that the Russian authorities (and even parts of educated Russian society) began to perceive Muslims as a potentially subversive political rather than religious group. Russian publicists, politicians and bureaucrats increasingly regarded Muslim political mobilization as being opposed to what they thought to be the 'public interest'.[30]

Third, the police had probably been worried about student political activity in general during 1905. Kazan's university had served as a public forum for protest and provocation during September and October of that year and, without any doubt, the *shakirds'* conduct and outlook had been inspired by the Russian students. But if Kazan's authorities had not been suspicious of the local Muslim elite's political conduct before, it would have made little sense to hold them responsible for their students' (and, partially, their teachers') supposed radicalism. Hence, if we take the repeated conflicts between the *shakirds* and the reform-minded *ulema* into account – clashes that the local police itself had experienced – we may assume that the conspiracy theory was constructed deliberately and in the very face of the evidence at the police's disposal.[31]

Finally, the police proved to be more concerned with the liberals rather than the radicals. In May 1908, both the Galeev brothers and Apanaev were exiled to Vologda *guberniia*, together with the merchant Kazakov.[32] The

Kazan affair, however, proved to be only a prelude to an even harsher perse-
cution of Muslim activists by Kazan's authorities from 1908 onwards.[33] The
following section will discuss how Russian officialdom's overtly and deliberately distorted (re-)construction of Muslim political mobilization between
1905 and 1907 had a political impact on Russian–Muslim relations between
1907 and 1917.

The suspicious attitude that the Russian authorities displayed towards the
progressive Muslim elites was fuelled by an anonymous denunciation of
twelve mullahs addressed to the Ministry of the Interior in August 1908.
The content of this letter related perfectly to the 'facts' the police already
had recorded and added further evidence on the nature of the presumed
Muslim 'revolutionary conspiracy'. In it, above all, Galeev's *madrasa*
Mukhamadiia was depicted as a revolutionary stronghold, responsible for the
formation of *mugallimy* ('young teachers') – 'a particular association of revolutionaries' that dispersed among the Muslim settlements, trying 'to incite
the rural population against the government'. These teachers were said to
have infiltrated schools in order to agitate among the Muslim youth and to
drive a wedge between the ordinary people and the mullahs. The authors of
the letter even accused these teachers of distributing arms among the
Muslim communities. Both Ittifak and Islakh were mentioned as organizations backing the pursuit of these 'teacher-revolutionaries'. Added to this,
the informers singled out reform-minded Muslim individuals throughout
the Volga-Urals region whom they blamed as supporters. Finally, the
authors tried to explain why the conspirators succeeded in mobilizing large
parts of the Muslim population during the 1905 Revolution:

> Many Muslims joined the Muslim union because they considered it to
> be a useful enterprise, but they were deceived and had no idea about its
> real bad business. The basic ideas and attitudes were only known to its
> leaders, a few people and some bystanders. The others did not know and
> followed, and were cheated.[34]

The twelve signatory mullahs appealed to Stolypin to continue the persecu-
tion of the progressive elements with the Muslim community, since banning
the Galeevs and Apanaev had, as they put it, 'only removed one revolutionary tree from Kazan, but not its poisonous roots that thrive untouched.
These branches are the *mugallimy*.'

   Oddly enough, Stolypin, in his role as minister of the interior, had
already (in February 1908) ordered the educational administrations of
provinces with Muslim populations 'to collect carefully and secretly
information about the emerging class of *mugallimy* – private teachers'.[35]
Meanwhile, the revolutionary events in the Ottoman Empire and in Persia
had added to the sensitivity of Russia's ruling elite, as did the preparations
for a Muslim World Congress under the auspices of the Crimean Tatar

Ismail Bey Gasprinskii, the *spiritus rector* of Russia's Muslim movement. Against this background, it is hardly surprising that the police, taking into account both Stolypin's order and the above-mentioned denunciation, began to describe the reported Muslim activities as being not merely 'revolution-ary' and 'separatist' but as 'pan-Islamist' too.

The chief of Kazan's gendarmes, for instance, reported on 9 January 1909 to the police department on 'the idea of pan-Islamism, which had been transferred from Turkey to Russia'. The report reiterated the already familiar story about the *mugallimy* acting as agents of the Muslim elite, infiltrating and converting Muslim schools into instruments of propaganda, etc. Equally, 'pan-Islamism' was identified as the final aim of Muslim political aspirations. First, the pan-Islamists would allegedly awake national feelings among their compatriots, then they would obtain national autonomy for their territories and then, finally, they would unite them with Muslim territories in the Caucasus and Turkestan 'until an all-Turkish republic has been accomplished'. Besides the fact that this 'plot' would have been rather better described as 'pan-Turkic', the police habitually failed to deliver con-crete evidence of its existence. Rather, they simply claimed to cite 'one orator' at some 'unofficial meeting'. The following deliberations of the police chief deserve to be quoted in full, since they clearly demonstrate the force's preoccupation with the conspiracy narrative rather then with reporting the facts:

> Such are the dreams of the Russian pan-Islamists. Certainly, they do not utter them in public, but the idea is secretly embedded in the souls of each of them. In order to convince oneself about this fact, one has necessarily *to observe every feature of Muslim public life* and to be able to *determine the main principle lying behind it.* It is true that not too long ago it was not worth while to think really seriously about pan-Islamism, for it did not possess so much importance. But in recent years it has significantly advanced in the sense of spreading, and its supporters, playing on the religious feelings, try by all means to manipulate the ignorant Tatar masses.[36]

In other words, facing a highly dangerous national and revolutionary con-spiracy, the local authorities no longer had to bother to *prove* the treacherous quality of the Muslim reform movement. Since they already *knew* about it, they were able to detect it behind any seemingly harmless Muslim endeav-our. For the police, the identification of the 'pan-Islamist' movement with Kazan's politically mobilized Muslim elite was already beyond question.[37]

In a letter to Stolypin sent a week later, Governor Strizhevskii added copious interpretation of the conspiracy of the Muslim bourgeoisie, teachers and *shakirds* that had been unveiled the year before, portraying it as being directly linked to the newly detected phenomenon of 'pan-Islamism'. Regardless of the ban on the Galeevs and Apanaev, he wrote, progressive elements continued to teach in Kazan's leading *madrasas*. Thus, the governor concluded, education 'persisted to be influenced by the young Muslim progressive party', among which 'pan-Islamism was gaining ground'. Like the gendarmes, Strizhevskii qualified it as a recent phenomenon and, in order to prevent its further dissemination, he ordered the local school inspectors to keep a close eye on the teaching in the Muslim *madrasas* and *maktabs* (primary schools), in addition to the more general observation of the Muslim movement being undertaken by the police.[38]

While the Ministry of the Interior was receiving such alarming missives from the authorities in Kazan, most of the reports sent back from various neighbouring regions inhabited by Muslims during 1909 denied systematic revolutionary agitation by Muslim teachers – or, at least, played it down.

The head of Ufa's corps of gendarmes, for example, did not refrain from the employment of the term 'pan-Islamist' in his account and supposed that these pan-Islamists aimed at 'a unification not only of Russia's Muslims but also of [Muslims] from all other countries, for political and economical interests'. Nevertheless, he questioned some of the earlier findings of his colleagues from Kazan. Above all, he doubted that the pan-Islamists shared a common platform. Instead, he distinguished two competing categories of 'pan-Islamists'. The first group, according to his report, consisted of 'young Tatars or [Tatar] teachers, shop assistants and salesmen' who were said to have 'imitated the tactics of our [Russian] revolutionaries' and published several newspapers, practically all of which had ceased to exist by the end of 1909. The other wing was reported to have consisted of the local Muslim upper class, 'teachers, mullahs, advocates, merchants and others'. This wing was said to have been to all intents identical with the liberal Muslim movement, plus Islakh.

However, singling out Zia Kamalutdinov's *madrasa* 'Galia' as a revolutionary stronghold, Ufa's police distorted reality in a similar manner to that in which their colleagues from Kazan had done before them. Like Galeev's Mukhamadiia, this recently founded (1906) reformed *madrasa* had, in fact, suffered from a series of school strikes caused by the *shakirds'* frustration over the limitation of educational reforms. (Protests and strikes actually continued in Ufa well into the second decade of the twentieth century.)[39] Likewise, the 'pan-Islamist' character of the liberal Muslim movement seemed self-evident to Ufa's gendarmes, particularly since some of its protagonists (such as Gasprinskii, Iusuf Akchurin and Gaiaz Iskhaki) had left Russia (albeit temporarily) for Turkey and had advanced theories of a common Turko-Tatar historical descent. Before listing some of the local Ufa protagonists, the gendarmes affirmed that the 'pan-Islamists' had been relatively popular only in 1905 to 1906, while at present their activities had practically ceased. Just to be on the safe side, though, Ufa's governor, A. S. Kliucharev, conceded that he 'actually found it difficult to deny categorically the possibility of revolutionary propaganda among Muslims'.[40]

Further to the south and east, the police were apparently even less concerned. There were no references to the terms 'pan-Islamism' or 'pan-Islamist' in the report sent to St Petersburg by Orenburg's governor-general in September 1909,[41] and the same seems to be true for the accounts dispatched from Simbirsk and Saratov provinces around the same time.[42] While the police in Saratov and Simbirsk were not even able to confirm revolutionary agitation among Muslims during the period 1905 to 1907, Orenburg's governor had observed at least some futile leftist propaganda by individual residents. Moreover, none of the departments referred to any revolutionary influence from Persia or Turkey on their Muslim subjects. In addition to that, it should be mentioned that the Russian authorities of Orenburg, Saratov and Simbirsk quite correctly interpreted the denunciation of the twelve mullahs: they linked its origins to social tensions within the Muslim communities that had been caused by *jadid* educational reforms rather than by political objectives. The incriminated teachers, they reported, were the first generation of graduates from the few reformed *madrasas*. Their higher teaching qualification and their educational ethos were said to be viewed with distrust by members of the traditional *ulema*, who regarded the schools as mere extensions of their mosques and feared for their hitherto unlimited control over them — not least because the schools provided an important source of income for the *ulema*. The mullahs, the reports attested, were exploiting the suspicions of the Russian authorities for their own ends.[43]

As suggested above, the whole narrative of the Muslim 'revolutionary conspiracy' relied heavily upon a (more or less) deliberate misinterpretation of the facts of Muslim political mobilization between 1905 and 1907. Taking into account the lack of hard evidence, however, its authors, as we have seen, created a self-fulfilling prophecy: the very fact that the Muslim population, as a whole, continued, on the face of things, to behave loyally proved only that some of them were intriguing in secret.

However, the obvious geographical restriction of this Muslim conspiracy to the perception of Kazan's and (to a lesser degree) of Ufa's authorities, could not prevent their narrative from becoming the canonical interpretation of the 'Muslim Revolution of 1905'. A circular issued by the police department of the Ministry of the Interior on 18 October 1910 summarized the official governmental position as follows:

> The main principle that binds the pan-Islamist movement together and that, so to speak, forms its soul, is the political and economic unification of the whole Muslim world under Turkish leadership, towards the aim of the establishment of an all-Turkic Republic. At present, leading Turkish and Russian Muslim publicists increasingly search to distinguish tribes of their own race in order to incite them with hatred against Russia and to lead them into a future common Muslim federation.[44]

The circular went on to identify pan-Islamism with the progressive camp, almost literally repeating the above-cited passages on the two factions of influential 'teachers, mullahs and merchants', on the one hand, and 'teachers, shop assistants and salesmen' on the other. Still, any precise definition of what was to be denoted by 'pan-Islamism' was avoided. As noted above, hardly any efforts were made to distinguish 'pan-Islamism' from 'pan-Turkism'.[45] 'Pan-Islamism' became a synonym for any kind of separatism and, added to this, it was increasingly seen as primordial in Muslim political thought. This attitude, too, proved to be quite enduring. In fact, it survived the demise of the old regime to be revived under Soviet auspices when Stalin unleashed his infamous anti-religious campaigns.[46]

The Muslim conspiracies, however, did not exclusively trouble the police. Motivated by the actual (if generally exaggerated) influence that Muslim culture and Islam displayed on other, non-Russian people, Orthodox representatives had called for containment since the days of N. I. Il'minskii's missions to Central Asia of the previous century. Forced only temporarily to retreat during the 1905 Revolution, these circles began to reiterate their claims – and received growing support among governmental authorities – after Stolypin's ascent to power. This chorus of confessional and secular 'anti-Islamism' reached its climax with the notorious 'Special Meeting for the Elaboration of Measures to Counteract the Tatar-Muslim Influence in the Volga Region' of January 1910.[47] Stolypin did not participate in this personally, but he showed deep concern during the preparations for the meeting and ensured the attendance of influential representatives of the Church hierarchy, the Ministry of the Interior and the Ministry of Education.

Taking the existence of Muslim irredentism as given, this conference tried to convert attitudes into policies – at least as far as educational and religious matters were concerned. The conference opted for a further restriction of the (already limited) responsibilities of the Muslim spiritual board in Orenburg and took a clear stance against reforms in Muslim schools. It plainly accused the Muslims of abusing the exceptional status of their *madrasas* and *maktabs*:

> Under the pretext that the rational study of religion – Islam – demands it, subjects having nothing to do with religion have been introduced: arithmetic, the history of Turkey and its geography. At the same time, Russian language, Russian history and Russian geography have been completely ignored and the artificially constructed Pan-Turkic language [i.e., that developed by Gasprinskii and used by several Tatar periodicals] has been disseminated.[48]

Hence, all matters of general education were to be banned from the Muslim confessional schools. But, just as prior to 1905, Russian officialdom failed to grant viable alternatives, in the form of state-sponsored schools that would offer Tatar-language teaching and that would take the religious needs of the Muslim population into account. And, once again, as had been the case in the late nineteenth century, it failed to implement the announced sanctions effectively. Muslim participation in politics was marginalized and the reform movement in the schools was hampered – but it was certainly not reversed. In fact, under such pressure, Muslim eagerness to seek new allies even grew and, in some regions, local zemstva began to sponsor Muslim schools.[49]

As Robert Geraci put it, the power of 'nostalgia' had driven the Russian authorities into an 'impasse'[50] – and one that they would not be able to withdraw from until 1917. In denying Muslim modernism and reformism the opportunity of any legal development within the frameworks of the Empire, they forced the Muslim elites deeper and deeper into the enemy camp – a strategy that had few tangible political advantages.

As unfortunate as this strategy proved to be for Russian–Tatar relations, it proved to be even more disastrous for the Muslim reform movement itself. In the case of Kazan (where the persecutions started earlier and were conducted more systematically than elsewhere), the arrest and banishment of the Galeevs and Apanaev dealt a very serious blow to the mobilization of local Muslim community. Above all, Galimdzhan Galeev (1857–1921) and Abdulla Apanaev (1862–1918) had been hugely important figures in the local Muslim elite. Galeev (or 'al-Barudi' as he is generally referred to) founded the famous Mukhamadiia *madrasa* in the early 1880s and was able to secure the financial support from some of Kazan's richest merchants for his school, which was certainly the best built and best equipped in the city. From the 1890s, Galeev carefully introduced reforms in his *madrasa*. It would be an oversimplification to describe Galeev's convictions as being merely conservative, but during October 1905 he strongly disapproved of the conduct of Kazan's city duma and had marched at the head of a demonstration that displayed loyalty to the tsar. And he was certainly not among the most progressive members of the central committee of Ittifak elected at the Third Muslim Congress. Abdulla Apanaev, meanwhile, belonged to a wealthy and important local dynasty of merchants. He directed another reformed *madrasa* in Kazan's Tatar *sloboda* (suburb) and was even more actively involved in public endeavours than was Galeev. Apanaev had been an active member on the boards of several Muslim charity societies, had issued his own Tatar newspaper, *Azat* (Freedom), in 1906, and also held responsible posts in the developing Muslim movement. More importantly, he had been elected *kadi* (judge) to the Muslim Spiritual Assembly in early 1907, which promised a greater influence for the progressive party on the religious board.[51]

The exile of Apanaev and the Galeevs from Kazan only added to the 'brain drain' that the city's reformist elites had already suffered. Some prominent local leaders (such as Sadri Maksudi and Said-Girei Alkin) had moved to St Petersburg as elected deputies or members of the bureau of the

Muslim faction of the State Duma. Others (such as Jusuf Akchurin) were driven out of the country. Kazan thereby lost, for the time being, its role as the pre-eminent political centre of the Muslim political movement to St Petersburg and, to a degree, to Orenburg. While the Muslim liberals in their St Petersburg base became detached from their roots in the Volga–Urals region, the political vacuum that occurred in Kazan grew perceptibly – particularly after 1910. This finally paved the way for a younger, more radical and more Russified Tatar intelligentsia to come to prominence in Kazan. When the 'old' liberal elites tried in 1917 to revive the Muslim movement in a top-down approach from St Petersburg, they instantly found themselves exposed to a 'generation conflict' and were soon ousted by the newcomers. To the surprise of the older generation, the overwhelmingly socialist convictions of these younger leaders no longer deprived them of support among a wide cross-section of the local Muslim population.[52]

To measure these consequences on a more general level, one has to take into account the impact the 1905 Revolution had on developments within Muslim society. In fact, only the gradual inclusion of Muslims and (other non-Russians) in the expanded political space during 1905 had provided Muslim reformism with the *raison d'être* it had essentially lacked before that year. Renewal through modernization and Westernization had simply made little sense in the pre-revolutionary imperial context – a context that had provided hardly any perspectives of integration and social ascent for Muslims, even for those willing to adopt certain Russian customs and habits. Consequently, two separate worlds had developed during the era of Pobedonostsev, and a majority of the Muslim elites had opted to preserve Muslim communal cohesion by ignoring the hostile environment as far as possible. Reformism arose and developed only in the niches that were provided by the incompetent and incomplete implementation of Russian politics. Jadidism can certainly be traced back to the 1880s, but its reported success before 1905 is largely a myth that grew up in retrospect.[53]

The reformist message acquired plausibility and significance only in 1905 and 1906, when first the Muslim elites and then certain other groups (townspeople, students, teachers) encountered opportunities to take a share in public life and politics on an almost equal footing with the Russians. During those years, in the changed circumstances, social and political mobilization of the individual for the sake of the whole community appeared to be a more appropriate means to secure communal cohesion and identity. More and more people ceased to understand 'being a Muslim' simply in terms of self-affirmation as part of a different, ahistorical and stable local population. Rather, they came increasingly to conceive of 'being a Muslim' as meaning participation in a dynamic and developing 'imagined community'.[54] Reformism became politicized and the Muslim movement acquired nationalist qualities, even if its political programme remained largely confined to matters of Muslim emancipation and of confessional and cultural autonomy.[55]

With Stolypin restabilizing autocratic power in Russia, the Muslims (like the Jews and other confessional and national minorities) found themselves exposed to growing political discrimination. Anti-Islamic stereotypes re-emerged and the retrospective condemnation of Muslim reformism as a whole slammed shut a door that had just gradually opened. Indeed, the Jadid option of modernization through Westernization was not only denounced by state politics but also increasingly contested within the Muslim community itself. Reformism found itself caught between Scylla and Charybdis: between renewed Muslim traditionalism and young, leftist radicalism. Ultimately, then, the story of the 'Tatar Revolution of 1905', as narrated by Russia's authorities, grotesquely exaggerated Muslim participation in the revolution whilst at the same time reinforcing the Muslims' future revolutionary potential.

Notes

1 For the report, see 'Donesenie nachal'nika kazanskogo gubernskogo zhandarmskogo upravleniia v departament politsii, 3 oktiabria 1907g.', in *Natsional'nye dvizheniia v period pervoi revoliutsii v Rossii* (Cheboksary, 1935), pp. 237–9 (here p. 238).

2 'Donesenie kazanskogo gubernatora v departament politsii, sekretno, 2 maia 1907' and 'Prilozhenie: Programma soiuza shakirdov "Bregi"', in ibid., pp. 235–7.

3 The *guberniia* administration had already exiled all these alleged leaders by this time.

4 'Kazanskii gubernator v departament politsii, sekretno, 5 ianvaria 1908g.', in *Natsional'nye dvizheniia*, pp. 237–41.

5 Tadeusz Swietochowski, *Russian Azerbaijan, 1905–1920: the Shaping of National Identity in a Muslim Community* (Cambridge, 1985), pp. 37–63; J. Baberowski, *Der Feind ist überall. Stalinismus im Kaukasus* (Munich, 2003), pp. 77–83.

6 They were the largest groups in the *guberniias* of Kazan (1897: 630,000 or 29 per cent of the total population), Ufa (1897: 1,100,100 or 50 per cent) and Orenburg (1897 360,000 or 22 per cent).

7 On Kazan see Kh. Kh. Khasanov, *Revoliutsiia v Tatarii 1905–1907gg.* (Moscow, 1965), pp. 132–9; Kh. Kh. Khasanov, *Kazan v gody pervogo shturma Tsarizma* (Kazan, 1985), pp. 105–7; G. Ibragimov, *Tatary v revoliutsii 1905 goda* (Kazan, 1926), pp. 71–2. On Ufa see Charles Steinwedel, 'The 1905 Revolution in Ufa: Mass Politics, Elections, and Nationality', *Russian Review*, Vol. 59 (2000), No. 4, pp. 555–76.

8 Khasanov, *Kazan v gody*, p. 140; Ibragimov, *Tatary*, pp. 80–1; R. M. Raimov, *Revoliutsiia 1905–07gg. v Srednem Povol'zhe i Priural'e* (Moscow, 1955), pp. 739–52; Steinwedel, 'The 1905 Revolution in Ufa', p. 566.

9 R. R. Salikhov and R. R. Khairutdinov, *Respublika Tatarstan: Pamiatniki istorii i kul'tury tatarskogo naroda. Konets XVIII – nachalo XX vekov* (Kazan, 1995), pp. 122–4.

10 L. K. Klimovich, *Islam v tsarskoi Rossii. Ocherki* (Moscow, 1936), pp. 47–8; Khasanov, *Revoliutsiia v Tatarii*, pp. 142–3; Ibragimov, *Tatary*, p. 226; Steinwedel, 'The 1905 Revolution in Ufa', p. 564.

11 Ibragimov, *Tatary*, pp. 75–83. Also *National'nyi Arkhiv Respubliki Tatarstan* (NART), f. 199, d. 622, l. 439; and d. 906, ll. 117–18ob.

12 Police reports on the Muslim congresses are reprinted in *Natsional'nye*

dvizheniia, pp. 215–30. Finally, all efforts to register the Muslim party 'Ittifak' were thwarted by the government on the grounds that its programme listed the establishment of a constitutional monarchy as one of the party's goals. See Alfred Levin, *The Third Duma: Election and Profile* (Hamden, Colo., 1973), pp. 56–7.

13 See M. Bigi, *Islahat esaslary* (Petrograd, 1917), pp. 220–33. The programme of the Muslim faction in the Duma, which differs slightly to the party programme of 'Ittifak' that was prepared for the Third Muslim Congress, has been reprinted in *Politicheskaia zhizn' russkikh musul'man do fevral'skoi revoliutsii* (Oxford, 1987), pp. 67–84.

14 The Muslim political movement has been broadly covered in the existing literature. See. A.-A. Rorlich, *The Volga Tatars: a Profile in National Resilience* (Stanford, 1987), and A. Kanlidere, *Reform within Islam: the Tajdid and Jadid Movement Among the Kazan Tatars (1809–1917). Conciliation or Conflict?* (Istanbul, 1997). The most important source is Bigi, *Islahat esaslary*. For recent publications, see also L. A. Iamaeva, *Musul'manskii liberalizm nachala XX veka kak obshchestvenno-politicheskoe dvizhenie. Na materialakh Ufimskoi i Orenburgskoi gubernii* (Ufa, 2002); and D. M. Usmanova, *Musul'manskaia fraktsiia i problemy svoboda sovesti v Gosudarstvennoi Dume Rossii 1906–1917* (Kazan, 1999).

15 'Trudoviki' (or 'Labour Party') was the name adopted by Populist delegates to the State Duma. On the 'Muslim *trudoviki*' see Ibragimov, *Tatary*, pp. 219–22 (which is rather polemical in content); and D. M. Usmanova, 'The Activity of the Muslim Faction of the State Duma and its Political Significance in the Formation of a Political Culture Among the Muslim Peoples of Russia', in M. Kemper *et al.* (eds), *Muslim Culture in Russia and Central Asia from the 18th to the Early 20th Centuries*, Vol. 2 (Berlin, 1998), pp. 417–55 (especially pp. 422–3).

16 T. Ia. Kurbanov, 'Tatarskie uchitelia i tatarskaia uchashchaiasia molodezh' Povolzh'ia i Priural'ia v period burzhuazno-demokraticheskoi revoliutsii 1905–1907gg.', in *Iz istorii pedagogiki v Tatarii, Vyp. 1* (Kazan, 1967), pp. 10–74 (especially pp. 17–23). Cf. the description by Ibragimov, in *Tatary*, pp. 179–94.

17 Ibragimov, *Tatary*, p. 191. On the Russian role model in general, see Susan K. Morrissey, *Heralds of Revolution: Russian Students and the Mythologies of Radicalism* (Oxford, 1998), pp. 99–123.

18 Kurbanov, 'Tatarskie uchitelia', pp. 25–7.

19 On Berek, compare Ibragimov, *Tatary*, p. 184; and Kurbanov, 'Tatarskie uchitelia', pp. 45–7. See also 'Progamma soiuza shakirdov "Bregi"', in *Natsional'nye dvizheniia*, pp. 236–7. The self-claimed 'Socialists-Revolutionaries' resolved, in the best Populist tradition, for 'going to the people': NART, *f.* 199, *d.* 676, *ll.* 134–134ob.

20 Ibragimov, *Tatary*, pp. 186–7; Kurbanov, 'Tatarskie uchitelia', pp. 44–5.

21 Ibragimov, *Tatary*, pp. 187–9; Kurbanov, 'Tatarskie uchitelia', pp. 27–30.

22 'Soobshchenie Kazanskogo gubernatora v departament politsii, sekretno, 5 maia 1906g.', in *Natsional'nye dvizheniia*, p. 235. See also Kurbanov, 'Tatarskie uchitelia', pp. 44–5. Note the interconnectedness of academic and political goals, which was typical for Russia's student bodies.

23 Kurbanov, 'Tatarskie uchitelia', pp. 55–65.

24 Ibragimov, *Tatary*, p. 187; Kurbanov, 'Tatarskie uchitelia', p. 45. Ibragimov suggests that the leading protagonists of Islakh were already preoccupied with the publication of the newspaper *el-Islakh* that appeared between 1907 and 1909.

25 The Muslim peasantry on the Middle Volga had remained relatively passive during the 1905 Revolution. See Christian Noack, *Muslimischer Nationalismus im*

Russischen Reich. Nationsbildung und Nationalbewegung bei Tataren und Baschkiren 1861–1917 (Stuttgart, 2000), pp. 233–6.

26 *NART, f.* 1, *op.* 6, *d.* 372.

27 L. Häfner, 'Stadtdumawahlen und lokale Eliten in Kazan' 1870–1913. Zur rechtlichen Lage und politischen Praxis der lokalen Selbstverwaltung', *Jahrbücher für Geschichte Osteuropas*, Vol. 44 (1996), pp. 217–52; R. Salikhov, 'Predstavitel'stvo tatar-musl'man v vybornykh organakh mestnogo samouprvaleniia v Kazani na rubezhe XIX–XX vv.', *Panorama-Forum*, Vol. 2 (1996), pp. 41–57; L. M. Sverdlova, *Na perekrestke torgovykh putei* (Kazan, 1991), pp. 37, 132–9. For reference to further sources, see Noack, *Muslimischer Nationalismus*, pp. 92–4.

28 *Musul'manskie deputaty Gosudarstvennoi Dumy Rossii, 1906–1917* (Ufa, 1998); Usmanova, 'The Activity of the Muslim Faction', pp. 441–9.

29 In Ufa *guberniia* one Muslim candidate was sacked from his post in the provincial administration, while a Muslim candidate from Kazan *guberniia* was arrested under a false pretext and released only after the elections. *NART, f.* 199, *d.* 369, *ll.* 4–5; Ibragimov, *Tatary*, p. 164; S. M. Iskhakov, 'Revoliutsiia 1905–07gg. i rossiiskie musul'mane', in *1905 god – nachalo revoliutsionnykh potrasenii v Rossii XX veka* (Moscow, 1996), p. 204.

30 Steinwedel, 'The 1905 Revolution in Ufa', pp. 571–6 (here p. 573).

31 Later and better informed reports correctly point out that the *shakird* radicalism owed much more to the Russian example: 'They [the students] began "to feel passion for the nation" more than others, under the influence of the inspired studentship [*ideinoe studechestvo*]': 'Doklad nachal'nika Kazanskogo zhandarmskogo upravleniia v departament politsii, 23 aprelia 1914 goda', in *Natsional'nye dvizheniia*, pp. 269–75 (here p. 271).

32 *NART, f.* 199, *d.* 372, *ll.* 1–7, and *d.* 676, *ll.* 8ob–9ob. Later, the government allowed the Galeevs to leave the country for Syria, while Apanaev was permitted to emigrate to Persia and Kazakov to Berlin.

33 Except for the cited cases, the majority of files opened against Tatars by Kazan's gendarmes (*NART, f.* 199) date from after 1907.

34 The letter appears in full in *Natsional'nye dvizheniia*, pp. 245–51; the quotation here is from p. 249.

35 *Rossiiskii Gosudarstvenyi Istoricheskii Arkhiv, f.* 821, *op.* 8, *d.* 826, *l.* 3, reprinted in M. N. Farkhshatov (ed.), *Samoderzhavie i traditsionnye shkoly bashkir i tatar v nachale XX veka* (Ufa, 2000), pp. 199–200. Stolypin particularly underlined the fact that some of these teachers had studied abroad 'in Turkey, Egypt and other Muslim countries': ibid., p. 199.

36 *Natsional'nye dvizheniia*, pp. 251–4 (author's emphasis). All quotations here are from p. 252.

37 Ibid., p. 249.

38 'Soobshchenie orenburgskogo gubernatora v departament politsii, 24 sentiabria 1909', in ibid., pp. 255–7.

39 See R. Majaczak, 'Notes sur l'enseignement dans la Russie musulmane avant la révolution', *Revue du Monde Musulman*, Vols 33–4 (1917–18), pp. 179–234 (especially pp. 201–7).

40 'Donesenie nachal'nika Ufimskogo gubernskogo zhandarmskogo upravleniia v departament politsii, sovershenno sekretno, 18 dekabria 1909', *Natsional'nye dvizheniia*, pp. 259–61; 'Svodka donesenii departamenta politsii o deiatel'nosti "mugallimov", 30 sentiabria 1909', in ibid., pp. 261–9 (here quoting p. 268).

41 'Soobshchenie Orenburgskogo gubernatora v departament politsii, 24 sentiabria 1909', in ibid., pp. 257–9.

42 While the use of the term by the Kazan police is accurately reported in the

svodka, there is, at least, no mention of it appearing in the reports from Saratov and Simbirsk provinces. See ibid., pp. 261–9.

43 Ibid., pp. 263–8.

44 *NART, f. 199, d. 771, ll. 232–232ob.*

45 Only from 1912 onwards, against the background of the Balkan Wars, did the latter term come to be broadly used in the Russian political and official vocabulary. For rare examples of a differentiated use see R. Mouchammetchine, 'L'apport de quelques sources russes officielles à l'historiographie du djadidisme chez les Tatars de la Volga', *Cahiers du Monde russe*, Vol. 37 (1996), No. 1, pp. 83–95.

46 See A. Arsharuni and G. Gabidullin, *Ocherki panislamizma i panturkizma v Rossii* (Moscow, 1931), *passim*.

47 Robert P. Geraci, 'Russian Orientalism at an Impasse: Tsarist Educational Policy and the 1910 Conference on Islam', in D. Brower and E. J. Lazzerini (eds), *Russia's Orient: Imperial Borderlands and Peoples* (Bloomington, 1997), pp. 138–61.

48 *Zhurnal Osobogo soveshchaniia po vyrabotke mer dlia protivodeistviia tatarsko-musul'manskomu vliianiiu v Privolzhskom krae*, p. 119, cited in Geraci, 'Russian Orientalism', p. 147. The assertion concerning the Muslim schools' ignoring of all things Russian is a distortion: see, for example, the curriculum of Mukhamadiia, as cited by V. M. Gorochov, *Reaktsionnaia shkol'naia politika tsarizma v otnoshenii Tatar Povolzh'ia* (Kazan, 1941), pp. 206–8.

49 This is above all true for Ufa *guberniia*, the only territory where the Muslim population constituted a majority and maintained a substantial representation in the zemstvo boards. See Noack, *Muslimischer Nationalismus*, pp. 436–7.

50 'They [the Russian authorities] became nostalgic for Muslims they could patronize rather than fear': Geraci, 'Russian Orientalism', p. 148.

51 On al-Barudi see N. Davlet, 'Galimdzhan Barudi', *Dukhovnaia kul'tura i tatarskaia intelligentsiia: istoricheskie portrety* (Kazan, 2000), pp. 68–71; on Apanaev, R. Salikhov, 'Imamy Safiulla Abdullin i Gabdulla Apanaev – ucheniki Sh. Mardzhani', *Sh. Mardzhani: nasledie i sovremennost'* (Kazan, 1998), pp. 179–85.

52 Noack, *Muslimischer Nationalismus*, pp. 487–98.

53 Western scholars like Rorlich (*Volga Tatars, passim*) or A. Bennigsen and C. Quelquejay in *Les mouvements nationaux chez les Musulmans de Russie. Le Sultangalievisme au Tatarstan* (Paris, 1960), tended to overestimate the pre-revolutionary success of the Jadids, as they relied either on contemporary Jadid sources (that is, usually, the Muslim press) or on the so-called 'new Tatar historiography' of the 1970s and 1980s that, in the wake of Iakha Abdullin's *Tatarskaia prosvetitel'skaia mys'l. Sotsial'naia priroda i osnovnye problemy* (Moscow, 1976), sought to rehabilitate jadidism. See Edward J. Lazzerini, ' "Tatarovedenie" and the "New Historiography" in the Soviet Union: Revising the Interpretation of the Tatar–Russian Relationship', *Slavic Review*, Vol. 40 (1981), No. 4, pp. 625–35. More sober evaluations of the pre-revolutionary success of reformed schools are provided by M. Farkhshatov, *Narodnoe obrazovanie v Bashkirii v pore-formennyi period* (Moscow, 1994), pp. 89, 94; R. Salikhov, *Tatarskaia burzhuaziia i natsional'nye reformy vtoroi poloviny XIX – nachala XX v.* (Kazan, 2000), pp. 58–102; and Dzh. Validov, *Ocherk obrazannosti i literatury u Volzhskikh tatar* (Moscow, 1923), p. 50. For further discussion of this point see Noack, *Muslimischer Nationalismus*, pp. 205–17.

54 On this issue see Benedict Anderson, *Imagined Communities: Reflections on the Origin and Spread of Nationalism* (London, 1983).

55 See Christian Noack, 'State Policy and its Impact on the Formation of a Muslim Identity in the Volga–Urals', in Stephané A. Dudoignon and Komatsu Hisao (eds), *Islam in Politics in Russia and Central Asia (Early Eighteenth to Late Twentieth Centuries)* (London, 2001), pp. 3–26.

8 Peasant protest and peasant violence in 1905

Voronezh province, Ostrogozhskii uezd

Franziska Schedewie

This chapter examines peasant riots in one of the most disorderly districts of Russia in the years 1905 to 1907. It presents a new approach, insofar as it connects the study of peasant participation in acts of violence and upheaval with the results of a close analysis of peasant participation in the institution of all-estate rural self-government, the zemstvo. This comparison of the different ways of interaction of peasants with non-peasant society supports the thesis that the peasant riots in Voronezh's Ostrogozhskii uezd were not primarily revolutionary or even progressive in character, but should be understood as acts of social protest against the effects of modernization.

'I am deeply convinced that, without the convocation of a new duma in the near future and the solution of the agrarian question, this summer will experience a *Pugachevshchina*, of which may God spare Russia.'[1] When the agrarian expert and liberal zemstvo activist D. A. Pereleshin published this warning in a Voronezh newspaper in the winter of 1906, peasant disorders were already under way. Thousands of peasants came up with increasingly bold claims against landlords and the authorities. They refused to pay taxes and dues, drove their cattle onto landlords' fields and plundered forests, orchards and stores. At the height of the disturbances, members of the peasant communities gathered at night and set fire to the buildings, stables and haystacks of the landlords' estates.[2] The shadow of a new *Pugachevshchina*, a seemingly universal peasant rebellion of a kind that had not been so feared since the eve of the Emancipation in 1861, was already taking shape.[3]

For a long time afterwards, the explanation for these disorders seemed to be a quite clear and uncomplicated matter. The 'agrarian question' constituted one of the major topics of discussion in government circles and society and was presumed to be central to the political crisis that unfolded at the beginning of the twentieth century. Many contemporaries agreed with Pereleshin and interpreted the peasants' riots as being the inevitable reaction to an increasing impoverishment of the village, caused by continued exploitation and the uneven distribution of resources and income, for which either recent government policies or the existing order as a whole were held to be responsible. In consequence – and also in view of the impact and significance that peasant disorders undoubtedly had on the outcome of the 1905 Revolution[4] – contemporaries and subsequent historians saw in these outbreaks of violence an essential part of a general revolutionary movement: an integral element in a universal, simultaneous upheaval of an emancipating society against the representatives of the old, anachronistic, autocratic order.

Recent research has challenged this straightforward explanation, mainly on the basis of a 'new economic history' of Russia that has rejected the grim picture of the ever-increasing misery of the peasantry.[5] The present chapter adds a new approach, as it looks at the peasant disorders from the perspective of peasant interaction with non-peasant society. In particular, it examines peasant participation in the institution of all-estate rural self-government, the zemstvo. This interest in the peasant riots of 1905 to 1907 grew out of a close study of peasants and the zemstvo in Voronezh province between 1864 and 1914.[6] The focus here will be on one district, Ostrogozhskii uezd, that, in 1905, not only counted among the most disorderly in Russia[7] but was also (like the rest of the province) considered to be one of the most 'backward' places in the country, in social and economic terms. The thesis of the chapter is, broadly speaking, that zemstvo participation (as it will be defined below) can be regarded as an indicator or barometer[8] for modernization[9] and 'progress' among the peasants, whereas their participation in the riots, in contrast, points to the influence of surviving elements of relative 'backwardness'. Correlating these two distinct ways of participation of the peasants in Ostrogozhsk will support the assumption that long-term (structural) as well as short-term (more incidental) factors together made up the motives for peasants either to take part in riots or not to do so. In particular, such motives result from a change in the character of social relations – most importantly, from the dissolution of customary bonds between peasants and landlords during a transition from traditional-paternalistic to modern-capitalist relations. That change was initiated by the terms of the Emancipation Edict in 1861, but it did not take place on a broad scale until four decades later. Agrarian protest from 1905 to 1907 will, therefore, not be regarded primarily as being of a 'revolutionary' or 'progressive' nature, but, on the contrary, as a peak of social protest of peasants against the effects of a modernization that they experienced as having a negative impact on their lives. At the same time, this does not mean that the peasants' protests did not or could not adopt revolutionary traits during the course of events or that they did not incorporate revolutionary slogans. In fact, a mixture of retrospective social protest and revolutionary upheaval was all the more likely because peasants, as much as they were attached to their village communities, did not live in isolation from the rest of the world.

The records of the zemstvo assemblies themselves reflect the disorders and thus provide one immediate means of access to the issue.[10] Landlords claimed compensation for destroyed property on their estates[11] and demanded from the assembly the moral, if not the material, support for petitions that they intended to send to the central government.[12] The peasants, too, submitted numerous petitions to St Petersburg in 1905,[13] often with the help of the zemstvo employees, the so-called 'third element'.[14] Large numbers of these petitions were composed at the zemstvos' variously named 'agronomic', 'economic' or 'agricultural' commissions or councils. These had been established on uezd level, as a kind of appendix to the yearly zemstvo assemblies, as early as the 1890s.[15] Around 1905, many of them were greatly expanded and, according to Boris Veselovskii, were composed of between fifty and sixty and sometimes even several hundred peasant representatives.[16] In Ostrogozhsk, according to the information of its own journal of 1905,[17] the agricultural commission consisted of a number of invited peasants, who were encouraged to discuss their needs and demands in the presence of the zemstvo board, the zemstvo agronomist and – theoretically – a number of deputies elected by the zemstvo assembly.[18] But it is not these recorded demands by peasants who were requested to attend these gatherings during the general political crisis that shall be considered here in detail. In Ostrogozhsk, each of the twenty-six volosts of the uezd was represented at the commission by one peasant deputy, regardless of whether or not his particular volost was among those in upheaval during 1905. It is, rather, the correlation between the significant local variations in the occurrence of disorders and the everyday participation of peasants at the zemstvo that will be the focus of this chapter.

Beryl Williams's chapter in this collection points to the work of Elvira Wilbur,[19] Heinz-Dietrich Löwe[20] and others who have ventured on a 'new economic history' of Russia. By taking into account the work of contemporary writers, like Aleksandr Chaianov or Fedor Shcherbina,[21] these authors were able to reverse the common conviction according to which certain factors were to be condemned as primarily responsible for the steady decline of the peasant economy that had rendered provinces like Voronezh so backward, in comparison with other regions of Russia, after 1861. Specifically, these factors (that at the same time established the close links between landlord and serf economy) were the leasehold of (estate) land by peasants and *otrabotka* (that is, the payment of dues in the form of labour). Both were often referred to in combination (by Veselovskii, for example) as 'leasehold slavery' ('*kabal'nyia usloviia arendy*').[22] In contrast to the implications of such phrases, the 'new economic history' of Russia has shown that these remnants of pre-capitalist relations, which continued for long after 1861, actually helped peasants rather substantially in keeping their economy stable and even in improving it, provided that the landlords preferred to rent out their land to the peasants, rather than keeping it for themselves and investing in an active estate economy. However, as global economic conditions changed around the turn of the century and favoured landlord grain producers more than they had in the prior decades, the peasants lost much of the land they had previously been able to use. Former agreements, like *otrabotka* or the division of the harvest, that were advantageous for peasants,[23] became obsolete. After four decades of stable – or even improving – conditions for the peasants since 1861, this reversal of developments struck their economy as a heavy blow.[24]

As one of the first proponents of such a 'new economic history', Elvira Wilbur concentrates especially on the so-called 'Russian revolutionary crisis' of 1905 and 1917, regarding which her book presents 'a call for a reappraisal'.[25] She questions the conventional view of peasant revolts arising as the result of a Malthusian crisis, as well as offering a critique of the traditional Marxist assumption of a new, exploitative peasant capitalism that was developing in the villages.[26] Instead, Wilbur concludes that, against the background of an emerging market economy and the parallel, continued presence of large landlord estates, the rioters were not primarily the poor – or, as Wilbur calls them, the 'pressed traditionalists'[27] (as distinguished from 'market traditionalists' or 'market modernizers',[28] who found themselves in an economically more secure or even promising position). The disorderly were, rather, those whose economic situation in 1905 was changing, or offered a prospect for change, whether for the worse or for the better.[29]

Wilbur's approach is based mainly on two analytical pillars and a large compilation of figures. On a synchronic level, for 1905–07 and 1917, she counts and locates all 'incidents of peasant protest' to be found in various Soviet collections.[30] She then correlates these incidents with a map of economic conditions that she drew in the first part of her book. This map, again on the synchronic level, is chiefly based on Fedor Shcherbina's famous study of peasant budgets, *Krest'ianskie biudzhety*, of 1900.[31] To complete the picture, Wilbur then adds data on landlord estates and market access in the form of nearby railway stations or local fairs.

Wilbur's 'mathematical' approach is very instructive and was helpful in my own inquiry into the zemstvo. For that purpose, however, it was necessary, in terms of the present study, to extend it in two ways: first, the perspective had to be shifted from the synchronic to the diachronic level; second, instead of looking only at economic conditions, social and also cultural backgrounds had to be taken into account and traced as 'socio-economic developments' over time (from the Great Reforms of the 1860s and even earlier until 1905 and beyond). Not only has this extended approach been useful for studying the activities of the zemstvos on the micro-level, it also turned out that it helps explain for 1905 what Wilbur does not explain (and did not intend to explain in the first place): why riots were more violent on some estates than on others. Why, in other words, some estates were hit with *podzhogi*,[32] while, on others, there occurred merely *potravy*.[33]

The sources for data on incidents of disorder in Ostrogozhskii uezd – not only for the revolutionary years but also for the whole period between 1861 and 1916 – are the well-known Soviet collections, as well as unpublished archival materials from Voronezh.[34] In order to trace socio-economic developments over the extended period, though, it is not enough to look into the zemstvo statistics that primarily offer the data for synchronic cross-sections. For longitudinal analyses, one has to make use of further material. For that purpose, the less well-known, yearly zemstvo journals (*zhurnaly zemskago sobraniia*) have proved to be of great value. Apart from supplying yearly statistical records on all matters of the zemstvos' agenda, these journals and their attachments contain copies of the correspondence between the zemstvos and peasants. Of particular importance are the collective applications – *prigovory* (resolutions), petitions and other requests that were submitted to the institution by peasant communities or brought forward, directly, by peasant deputies or authorized community members at the zemstvo assemblies.[35] These applications are highly interesting because many of them contain requests for socio-economic improvements that, in many cases, were proposed by the peasants on their own initiative.[36] From Ostrogozhskii uezd, 627 peasant applications were identified in all the available zemstvo journals between 1872 and 1914.[37] Of these, 600 concerned local concerns of villages or volosts;[38] ninety-three applications requested the opening of a new fair;[39] 144 concerned the building or repair of bridges and roads; and thirty-eight asked for a new school.[40] If one takes into account the particular situations of the localities from which these applications came,[41] and puts them in relation to the frequency and the contents of the peasants' applications, these applications turn out to be good indicators for the varying degrees of modernization in the villages. Likewise, they can be considered as indicators for the inclination of peasants to adopt modernizing measures and to take the initiative to turn to the zemstvo institution (and not to a landlord) for that purpose. Thus, the analysis for Ostrogozhsk and three other uezds of Voronezh[42] has shown that those most likely to address the zemstvo with applications were the inhabitants of villages that were comparatively prosperous and already possessed a rather diversified economic structure. These places usually had a good market access, either in the form of an important local fair or a nearby railway station or cattle track. In other words, it was especially those villages that owed their prosperity primarily to the market (with otherwise unfavourable conditions for a self-contained, agricultural economy) that had learned to turn to the zemstvo to secure and to enhance their own situation. The former state-peasant village of Roven'ki, in southern Ostrogozhskii uezd, is an illustrative example of that. There, conditions for agriculture were bad (like everywhere in the south of the uezd, beyond the river Chernaia Kalitva). Lying between the Central Black Earth region and the southern steppe, the area suffered from a harsh climate and chalky soil. But the cattle fair of Roven'ki was famous beyond the borders of the uezd and secured the local peasants a standard of living of such quality that, in the village, as one early Soviet historian remarked, 'even the poor peasant owned a cow'.[43] According to the zemstvo journals, the number of peasant applications from the volost of Roven'ki was as high as 45. On the other hand, even though there was an estate of a noble landlord, G. A. Firsov, nearby, the same peasant community engaged only four times in disorders (twice in the period 1905 to 1907) – and those were not of a serious nature – throughout the entire period under investigation.

Figure 8.1[44] shows all volosts of Ostrogozhsk and displays the number of their applications to the zemstvo versus incidents of peasant protest within them over four decades.[45] As the map indicates, disorders and applications were distributed very unevenly within the different volosts and across the uezd. Unlike the peasants of Roven'ki, some submitted few applications, but were rather inclined to upheaval. Who were they?

In Ostrogozhskii uezd, of all peasants in 1900, about 70 per cent were former state peasants, while 30 per cent were former serfs.[46] The establishment of landlord estates in the region was a late but extensive development.[47] The majority of these estates – and, consequently, most of the former serf villages – were concentrated in two parts of the uezd. One was the north eastern corner, next to the river Don and comprising the volosts Kolybel'skaia and Markovskaia. The second area was in the south and extended as a broad belt across the uezd, along the river Chernaia Kalitva, from Mar'evka in the west to Evstratovka and Semeiki in the east (excluding, however, the state peasant-dominated volosts of Staraia and Novaia Kalitva).

Peasants had come to this territory before the estates existed. The great majority of them were of Ukrainian Cossack origin and had moved to the area as free settlers in two great waves of immigration in 1652 and 1721. Of their leaders, some eventually became *pomeshchiki*, while the poorest Cossacks were soon turned into serfs. The bulk of the settlers eventually made up the large group of state peasants. *Pomeshchiki* from Central Russia and non-Russian nobles moved to the region, too. The estate economy expanded, as did the market for grain, and the accessibility of this market increased with the extension of the railway.

There exist some reports, in the narrative parts of the zemstvo statistics, of how the peasants themselves remembered the origins of their villages and their bonds to the landlords. 'Here you find people of every kind', declared the peasants of Semeiskaia volost: 'Some were bought by the landlord, others were moved here from other places, and yet others came by themselves.'[48] According to the peasants' own memory, the ancestors of some of them had moved onto estate land voluntarily, as they could not sustain themselves without the help of a patron. As the peasants remembered the early arrangements between their own ancestors and the *pan* (lord), the peasants merely paid a small sum of money (called *'chench'*),[49] or they worked a little for the landowner. It is questionable how these memories went together with other evidence, according to which some *pomeshchiki* appear to have simply annexed the land, regardless of whether it was already settled or not.[50] But the very fact that such positive memories existed – albeit not to the exclusion of negative ones[51] – indicates that the peasants conserved a vivid consciousness of their former state of freedom.[52] Likewise, the oral accounts of

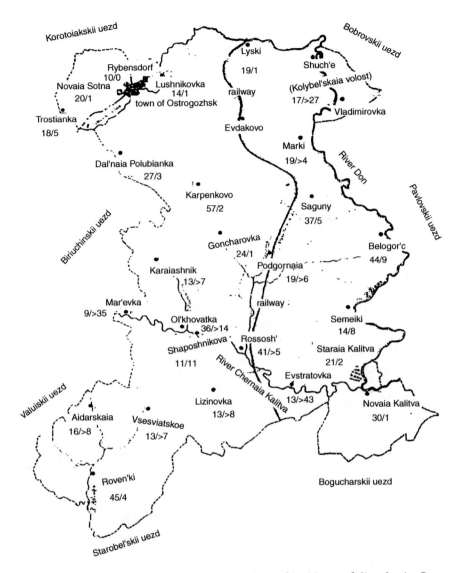

Korotoiakskii uezd

Bobrovskii uezd

Lyski
19/1

Shuch'e
(Kolybel'skaia volost)
17/>27

Rybensdorf
10/0
Novaia Sotna   Lushnikovka
20/1   14/1
        town of Ostrogozhsk

railway

Vladimirovka

Trostianka
18/5

Evdakovo

Marki
19/>4

River Don

Pavlovskii uezd

Dal'naia Polubianka
27/3

Biriuchinskii uezd

Karpenkovo
57/2

Saguny
37/5

Goncharovka
24/1

Belogor'c
44/9

Karaiashnik
13/>7

Podgornaia
19/>6

railway

Mar'evka
9/>35

Ol'khovatka
36/>14

Semeiki
14/8

Rossosh'
41/>5

Shaposhnikova
11/11

River Chernaia Kalitva

Staraia Kalitva
21/2

Evstratovka

Valuiskii uezd

Lizinovka
13/>8

13/>43

Novaia Kalitva
30/1

Aidarskaia
16/>8

Vsesviatskoe
13/>7

Boguracharskii uezd

Roven'ki
45/4

Starobel'skii uezd

Figure 8.1 Numbers of applications vs. numbers of incidents of disorder in Ostrogozhskii uezd, 1851–1916.

Key: The figures on the map compare the number of peasant applications
to the zemstvo assemblies (first figure) to the number of incidents of
unrest (second figure). Thus, for example, in the southernmost volost,
Roven'ki, there were forty-five such applications and four incidents of
unrest.

the peasants reveal that the quality of the relations between them and the landlords varied significantly and that they continued to do so until the beginning of the twentieth century. Some peasants enjoyed paternalistic protection by their *pomeshchik*, while others did not.

In the north-east, one family of local landlord-magnates, the Teviashevs, appears to have treated its former serfs particularly well. Immediately after 1861, these landlords gave large amounts of land to the peasants on a long-term and reliable leasehold basis.[53] Even though most former serfs here were *darstvenniki*, who had opted for the so-called 'beggar's allotment',[54] they had sufficient amounts of leased land available for building up their own, stable economy.[55] Moreover, these peasants gained from the improving measures that the landlords undertook for them and for their own estates' economies. Evidence for this can be found in the zemstvo journals.[56]

One might be tempted to consider that bonds between these people, all of whom originally came to the area as free Cossacks – the Teviashevs as officers, the peasants as rank-and-file – would have helped to ameliorate and strengthen the relationship between landlord and peasants: among the peasants, there might have prevailed a sense of voluntary loyalty towards their former leaders, whereas the *pomeshchiki* might have felt a lasting sense of responsibility and obligation. But, while the Teviashevs, in the north-east, did provide for their former serfs, another *pomeshchik*, in the southern estate region of Ostrogozhsk, A. N. Kulikovskii, who was also a member of a family of former Cossack officers, provides an example of the contrary. Kulikovskii treated his peasants badly. Figuring prominently as 'one of the big debtors of the uezd',[57] instead of giving land to the peasants he exploited every means the Emancipation statute had put into his hands in order to gain as much from the peasants as he possibly could, without any parallel investments into his own estate in the volost of Evstratovka.[58] It seems more appropriate, therefore, to explain the differences in the relationships between former serfs and landlords not socially, but by differences in economic pre-conditions and to attribute the negligent behaviour of some landlords in the south to the prevailing unfavourable conditions for agriculture. Apparently, several local landlords, themselves often absent, for a long time displayed little interest in investments into their own economy and were even less inclined to invest in that of their former serfs. In the 1890s, some landlords did begin to modernize their economy; however, they did so in a non-paternalistic way. They engaged in sheep- and cattle-breeding and occupied much of the land that had previously been used by the peasants. A particular case in this context was the volost of Ol'khovatka, as was (in part) Mar'evka volost, where landowners ran a sugar factory[59] and were inclined to use more and more land for growing sugar-beet. This land, too, was thus lost to the peasants, who reacted with frequent upheavals.[60] In brief, the landlords, especially those in the south (who themselves were often zemstvo deputies), obviously violated the 'moral economy'[61] by the way in which they dealt with the peasants; and the peasants responded with levels of aggression that

Table 8.1 Incidents of disorder in total and of disorders in the period 1905 to 1907

Volosts	All incidents, 1861–1916	Incidents during 1905–07
Mar'evskaia	35	22
Rybensdorfskaia	0	0
Shaposhnikovskaia	11	10
Evstratovskaia	43	24
Vsesviatskaia	>7	>5
Karaiashnikovskaia	>7	>2
Lizinovskaia	>8	>4
Semeiskaia	8	6
Lushnikovskaia	1	0
Aidarskaia	8	3
Kolybel'skaia	>27	>11
Trostianskaia	>5	>2
Lysianskaia	1	1
Markovskaia	4	2
Podgorenskaia	6	2
Novosotenskaia	1	1
Starokalitvianskaia	2	1
Goncharovskaia	1	0
Dal'nepolubianskaia	13	6
Novokalitvianskaia	1	1
Ol'khovatskaia	>14	>13
Sagunovskaia	5	5
Rossoshanskaia	5	3
Belogorskaia	9	8
Rovenskaia	4	2
Karpenkovskaia	2	1
Total	>228	>135

were more severe than elsewhere and that began much earlier than 1905. Table 8.1 shows the numbers of incidents of disorder counted for the years 1905 to 1907, together with the total of those counted for the whole period under investigation. It indicates that those volosts heavily affected in 1905 to 1907 also experienced many disorders during the whole period of 1861 to 1916 (most of these, in fact, occurring between 1861 and 1904).

Apparently, the concept of the 'moral economy', as well as the fact that it was being violated by the *pomeshchiki*, was understood by the peasants, as it was by other contemporary observers. One of the most interesting sources, even with regard to the disorders of 1905 to 1907, is the lengthy report by the vice-governor of Voronezh, A. V. Chernov, of 1899.[62] According to his own testimony, Chernov felt obliged to write this report to the police department of the ministry of the interior after a series of severe riots in Evstratovskaia volost. He stated that, in view of those riots, many people overlooked how peaceful relations normally were. The peasants usually paid their dues and never claimed anything that was excessive. All they wanted was land at a fair price – namely, at the same price that they had paid the year before.[63] According to Chernov, the local landlords themselves were primarily responsible for the current disorders, and he went on to ascribe the landlords to two categories, both of which he blamed for endangering social peace by violating the traditional duties: some landlords, he argued, damaged the peasant economy out of neglect of their own estates' economies; others, he said, provoked peasant protest by their own, relentless eagerness for profit. Here, Chernov pointed in particular to a group of three landlords – a '*sindikat*', as he called them – who had come to a secret understanding, with the aim of keeping for themselves hay from the meadows that the peasants had previously cut and used.[64]

All the conflicts described by Chernov in his report occurred before 1899, and provide some examples to show that, especially in the southern estate region, long-standing conflicts frequently flared up. By 1905 to 1907, these had prepared the ground for disorders that were not only more numerous but also (as they included arson and serious theft and destruction) more violent than in other regions of the uezd. This greater degree of violence is also explained by the peasants' more difficult economic situation in the south and the lingering threat of poverty, which was further increased by the landlords' non-paternalistic modernizing efforts.[65] In the north-east, disorders also occurred, but there, where the peasants' situation and their relations with the landlords were better, rather than rioting, the peasants went on strike, or appeared in groups before the landlord in order to negotiate over certain claims, or they drove their cattle on estate fields. These forms of protest were probably less harmful for the future relationship between landlords and peasants than those that predominated in the south. Moreover, one may assume that, in the north, many disorders were encouraged by the general revolutionary crisis and, in particular, by disorders already going on elsewhere.[66]

Returning now to the zemstvo, how many applications for improvements were submitted by these former serf-inhabited volosts? And what does the differentiation made above between the former serf regions in the north-east and those in the south imply with regard to these applications?

Figure 8.2 shows the volosts sorted according to the numbers of applications submitted. The volosts mainly inhabited by former serfs (especially Kolybel'skaia, Markovskaia, Mar'evskaia, Shaposhnikovskaia, Evstratovskaia and Lizinovskaia)[67] predominate on the left, which means that fewer applications from them reached the zemstvo than from the state-peasant volosts. (Those latter were, in particular, the volosts of Rovenskaia, Novokalitvianskaia, Starokalitvianskaia, Belogorskaia and Sagunovskaia.)[68] The volosts Rossoshanskaia and Ol'khovatskaia constitute exceptions: their inhabitants were former serfs, but the villages were also central market places. Rossosh, a lively small town today, lay close to the railway station Mikhailovka.

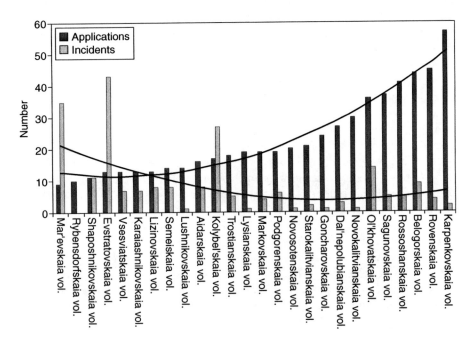

Figure 8.2 Numbers of applications vs. numbers of incidents of disorder, with trend lines.

This observation of former serf-inhabited volosts submitting fewer applications to the zemstvo can be explained in two ways, both of which relate to landlord paternalism and to the above-described differences in its quality. For the north-east, one might say that, because of the positive, paternalistic measures of their landlords, the peasants simply did not need to turn to the zemstvo, as long as they could rely on the *pomeshchik*. In the south, however, especially in Evstratovskaia volost, the picture was one of a very pressing situation for the peasants (with small land plots of bad quality, for which they had to pay redemption fees, lacked market access and – last but not least – had negligent landlords). If these peasants did not address the zemstvo, the reason was probably that zemstvo schools or medical aid would not have brought immediate relief, but would only have served to increase the peasants' expenses. In that respect, the fact that the peasants did not turn to the zemstvo can be regarded as energy-saving, rational behaviour. Nevertheless, neither they nor the former serfs in the north-east participated much in the learning process that the interaction with the zemstvo implied. In that respect, the state peasants, who had never enjoyed any landlord paternalism, were mentally ahead of the former serfs in dealing with the authorities (and with non-peasant society as a whole) on a new, institutionalized basis and in taking action for improvements on that basis. Except for the former serf inhabitants of Rossosh and Ol'khovatka, where there were big markets, the former serfs may, indeed, be regarded as comparatively more backward.

The most important and visibly striking conclusion to be drawn from Figure 8.2, with regard to the nature of the peasant disorders is, therefore, the inversely inclined trend lines of numbers of applications versus numbers of incidents of disorder. While the number of applications rises steeply from left to right (moving from the former serf-predominated volosts to those of the state peasants), the trend line for the numbers of incidents of disorder drops almost as significantly. This observation doesn't just confirm that the disorderly were mostly the former serfs; most importantly, the diverging trend lines also show that the disorderly were not the 'progressive' peasant communities. Those communities and volosts that eagerly took the initiative to modernize their economy – and that, since they were situated closer to the railway stations, were actually more exposed to revolutionary propaganda[69] – and that showed a greater interest in public participation at the zemstvo, were actually the peaceful ones. The disorderly in Ostrogozhsk were, primarily, the 'backward' peasants who, voluntarily or not, depended to a greater extent (and in more traditional modes) on the local landlords and their land.[70] They rose in protest, as the conditions that had long prevailed and secured them a living were changing around the turn of the century.

Notes

1 *Voronezhskoe slovo*, No. 46 (16 December 1906), p. 4.
2 For the social composition of the movement, see the questionnaire of the Imperial Free Economic Society (*Vol'noe Ekonomicheskoe Obshchestvo*) in *Rossiiskii Gosudarstvennyi Istoricheskii Arkhiv (RGIA)*, f. 91, *op.* 2, *d.* 786; and its evaluation in 'Agrarnoe dvizhenie v Rossii v 1905–1906gg.', *Ottisk iz 'Trudov I. V. E. Obshchestva'* (n.p. [St Petersburg], 1908). See also Maureen Perrie, 'The Russian Peasant Movement of 1905–1907: Its Social Composition and Revolutionary Significance', *Past and Present*, No. 57 (1972), pp. 12–55.
3 See P. Péchoux, 'L'Ombre de Pugačev', in R. Portal (ed.), *Le Statut des Paysans Libérés du Servage, 1861–1961* (Paris, 1963), pp. 128–66. The term *Pugachevshchina* refers to the Cossack rebellion of Emelian Pugachev, of 1773–75, that was commonly (and mistakenly) understood to be a 'peasant' rebellion.
4 An immediate effect of the riots was, for example, the manifesto of 6 November 1905, which abolished the peasants' redemption payments. Other positive results for the peasants were a significant drop in the lease prices of land and an increase in wages for agricultural workers. For example, in Ostrogozhsk, lease prices fell from fifteen to nine roubles per *desiatina* and wages rose from twenty-five to forty kopecks per day. See 'Agrarnoe dvizhenie', Vol. 1, p. 89. The subsequent Stolypin agrarian reforms were also, in many ways, a response to the agrarian disorders of 1905 to 1907. See, for a general overview, H. Gross, H. Haumann, H.-D. Löwe *et al.*, 'Über die Revolution zur Modernisierung im Zeichen der eingeschränkten Autokratie (1904–1914)', in G. Schramm (ed.), *Handbuch der Geschichte Russlands*, Vol. 3, Part I (Stuttgart, 1983), pp. 337–473 (especially pp. 364–70); David A. J. Macey, *Government and Peasant in Russia, 1861–1906: The Prehistory of the Stolypin Reforms* (DeKalb, 1987); and David A. J. Macey, 'The Peasantry, the Agrarian

Problem, and the Revolution of 1905–1907', in A. W. Cordier (ed.), *Columbia Essays in International Affairs*, Vol. 7 (New York, 1972), pp. 1–35.

5 See pp. 139–40 and notes 19 and 20, below, as well as the chapter by Beryl Williams in this book.

6 Franziska Schedewie, 'Selbstverwaltung und sozialer Wandel in der russischen Provinz. Bauern und Zemstvo in Voronež, 1864 –1914' (University of Heidelberg Ph.D. thesis, 2004). This thesis is yet to be published.

7 According to S. M. Dubrovskii, 30.6 per cent of all riots during the 1905 Revolution took place in the Central Black Earth Region. Significant turmoil also occurred in left- and right-bank Ukraine (11.8 and 13.7 per cent, respectively, of all riots) and in the region of the middle Volga (10.3 per cent of all riots). The new agricultural areas in the far south, as well as the Central Industrial Region around Moscow, remained relatively quiet and very few disorders occurred in the north. See S. M. Dubrovskii, *Krest'ianskoe dvizhenie v revoliutsii 1905–1907gg.* (Moscow, 1965), p. 60. P. N. Abramov names Voronezh as the province most heavily struck by disorders: P. N. Abramov, 'Iz istorii krest'ianskogo dvizheniia 1905–1906gg. v Tsentral'no-Chernozemnykh guberniiakh', *Istoricheskie zapiski*, Vol. 57 (1956), pp. 293–311 (here p. 293). Rural disorders took place in the peripheral areas of the Russian Empire too, but will not be discussed here since they must be considered in the light not only of socio-economic but also of nationality problems.

8 As Boris Veselovskii put it, 'the zemstvos have always served to a greater or lesser degree as a barometer for the mood of the population': Boris B. Veselovskii, *K voprosu o klassovykh interesakh v zemstve* (St Petersburg, 1905), p. 1.

9 Following Stefan Plaggenborg's summarized definition, 'modernization' is understood here in the sense of a steady process of transformation of social and economic structures that developed as capitalist relationships entered the agrarian order in rural Russia. See Stefan Plaggenborg, 'Bauernwelt und Modernisierung in der ausgehenden Zarenzeit', in Heiko Haumann and Stefan Plaggenborg (eds), *Aufbruch der Gesellschaft im verordneten Staat. Russland in der Spätphase des Zarenreiches* (Frankfurt am Main, 1994), pp. 138–64 (especially p. 138).

10 For example, *Zhurnaly Ostrogozhskago ocherednago uezdnago zemskago sobraniia. Sessii 1906 goda* (Ostrogozhsk, 1906). For descriptions in the historiography, see Boris B. Veselovskii, *Istoriia zemstva za sorok let*, 4 vols (St Petersburg, 1909–11; reprint Cambridge, 1973), especially Vol. 3, pp. 606–28 and Vol. 4, pp. 21–4; Scott J. Seregny, 'Peasants and Politics: Peasant Unions During the 1905 Revolution', in Esther Kingston-Mann and Timothy Mixter (eds), *Peasant Economy, Culture, and Politics of European Russia, 1800–1921* (Princeton, 1991), pp. 341–77 (here p. 351).

11 According to the data of V. A. Stepynin for four provinces of the Central Blackearth Region, of a total number of 1,862 incidents of upheaval counted between January 1905 and May 1907, 1,476 were directed against noble landowners (*pomeshchiki*), eighty-six against non-noble landowners or leaseholders, 158 actions were directed against representatives of the state and twenty-three against the Church. Of the 119 counted incidents remaining, sixty-eight were directed against better-off peasants (that is, the so-called 'kulaks'). See V. A. Stepynin, *Krest'ianstvo Chernozemnago Tsentra v revoliutsii 1905–1907 godov* (Voronezh, 1991), pp. 149–50.

12 It happened very often that those landlords who, at the zemstvo and elsewhere in public, were the most vociferous in their criticism of government policies and their defence of the peasantry were confronted with the most severe upheavals on their estates at home. An illustrative example is the case of the influential *tainyi sovetnik* and zemstvo deputy I. A. Zvegintsev, of Bobrovskii uezd in the province of Voronezh. Regarding the devastation on his estate, see *Zhurnaly*

Bobrovskago ocherednogo uezdnago zemskago sobraniia, sessii 1906 goda (Bobrov, 1907), p. 32. For the appeal to Sergei Iu. Witte (at the time head of the Council of Ministers) in which Zvegintsev asked for compensation for his losses, see S. M. Dubrovskii and B. Grave (eds), *1905. Agrarnoe dvizhenie v 1905–1907gg.*, Vol. 1 (Moscow and Leningrad, 1925), pp. 318–20. Zvegintsev's son, A. I. Zvegintsev, represented the interests of the 'Agricultural Centre' at the so-called Centre Commission of 1899 to 1901 and was also deputy to the uezd zemstvo assembly of Bobrov. See M. S. Simonova, 'Problema "oskudeniia" Tsentra i ee rol' v formirovanii agrarnoi politiki samoderzhaviia v 90kh godakh XIX – nachale XXv.', in *Problemy sotsial'no-ekonomicheskoi istorii Rossii. Sbornik statei k 85-letiiu so dnia rozhdeniia Akademika Nikolaia Mikhailovicha Druzhinina* (Moscow, 1971), pp. 236–63. Moreover, Ivan Zvegintsev's case shows that the peasants' memory of earlier protests apparently had a strong influence on the occurrence and the intensity of subsequent risings. Zvegintsev's estate, situated near the village of Maslovka, had once before provided the setting for a serious peasant insurrection, in 1855: then, the peasants had protested against their being prohibited from taking part in the Crimean War as volunteer soldiers. (Rumours had spread that this would have brought them their release from serfdom.) This protest, which was quashed by the army after a month, was expressed by means of a strike and by instances of illegal absenteeism from the estate, as well as by proclamations and petitions, in which the peasants tried to defend their views in front of the authorities. See David Moon, *Russian Peasants and Tsarist Legislation on the Eve of Reform: Interaction between Peasants and Official-dom, 1825–1855* (Birmingham, 1992), pp. 150–3.

13 See, for example, Oleg G. Bukhovets, 'K metodike izucheniia "prigovornogo" dvizheniia i ego roli v bor'be krest'ianstva v 1905–1907gg. (po materialam Samarskoi gubernii)', *Istoriia SSSR* (1979), No. 3, pp. 96–112; Andrew Verner, 'Discursive Strategies in the 1905 Revolution: Peasant Petitions from Vladimir Province', *Russian Review*, Vol. 54 (1995), No. 1, pp. 65–90; Andrew Verner, 'Pochemu krest'iane podavali prosheniia, i pochemu ne sleduet vosprinimat' ikh bukval'no (po materialam Iur'evskogo uezda Vladimirskoi gubernii vo vremia revoliutsii 1905)', in *Mentalitet i agrarnoe razvitie Rossii (XIX–XXvv.). Materialy mezhdunarodnoi konferentsii (Moskva 14–15 iiuniia 1994g.)* (Moscow, 1996), pp. 194–208.

14 Apparently, these petitions were afterwards used by the same people who had encouraged the peasants to write them as evidence for the sympathy of the population for the efforts of society, including the zemstvos. See, for example, Mikhail N. Surin, *Chto govoriat krest'iane o nuzhdakh derevni* (Moscow, 1906).

15 See, for example, *Zhurnaly Ostrogozhskago chrezvychainago i ocherednago uezdnago zemskago sobraniia {sessii 1894 goda}* (Ostrogozhsk, 1895), pp. 29–30.

16 Veselovskii, *Istoriia zemstva*, Vol. 3, pp. 606–30 (here p. 628). In analogy to the famous *khozhdenie v narod* ('movement to the people') of 1874, Veselovskii speaks of a '*zemskoe khozhdenie v narod*' (a 'move of the zemstvo to the people'): ibid., Vol. 3, p. 624.

17 'Zhurnal[y] zasedaniia sel'skokhoziaistvennoi kommissii pri Ostrogozhskoi zemskoi uprave', *Zhurnaly Ostrogozhskago ocherednago uezdnago zemskago sobraniia sessii 1905 goda* (Ostrogozhsk, 1906), pp. 352–81. Sessions of the commission are recorded for 24 June and 12–13 September 1905.

18 At Ostrogozhsk, however, almost none of these zemstvo deputies appeared. This was pointed out in the report of the zemstvo *uprava* (board): see 'Doklad po povodu zasedaniia sel'skokhoziaistvennoi kommissii', *Zhurnaly (Ostrogozhsk) sessii 1905 goda*, pp. 349–52 (here p. 349). The peasant representatives thus found themselves in a strange situation: apparently proud to be at the zemstvo, they nevertheless found themselves to be almost completely among their own

kind, as, except for the members of the *uprava*, the agronomist and one or two regular deputies, no other zemstvo members were present.

19 Elvira M. Wilbur, 'The Peasant Economy, Landlords, and Revolution in Voronezh: A Call for a Reappraisal of the Nature of the Russian Revolutionary Crisis at the Turn of the Century' (University of Michigan Ph.D. thesis, 1977); Elvira M. Wilbur, 'Peasant Poverty in Theory and Practice: A View from Russia's "Impoverished Center" at the End of the Nineteenth Century', in Kingston-Mann and Mixter (eds), *Peasant Economy*, pp. 101–27; Elvira M. Wilbur, 'Was Russian Peasant Agriculture Really That Impoverished? New Evidence from a Case Study from the "Impoverished Center" at the End of the 19th Century', *Journal of Economic History*, Vol. 43 (1983), No. 1, pp. 137–44.

20 See, for example, Heinz-Dietrich Löwe, *Die Lage der Bauern in Russland 1880–1905. Wirtschaftliche und soziale Veränderungen in der ländlichen Gesellschaft des Zarenreiches* (St Katharinen, 1987); Heinz-Dietrich Löwe, 'Differentiation in Russian Peasant Society: Causes and Trends, 1880–1905', in Roger Bartlett (ed.), *Land Commune and Peasant Community in Russia: Communal Forms in Imperial and Early Soviet Society* (London, 1990), pp. 165–95; and Heinz-Dietrich Löwe, 'Lenins Thesen über Kapitalismus und soziale Differenzierung in der vorrevolutionären Bauerngesellschaft', *Jahrbücher für Geschichte Osteuropas*, Vol. 32 (1984), pp. 72–113.

21 Fedor Shcherbina (1849–1936) was the chief zemstvo statistician in Voronezh. See M. D. Karpachev, 'F. A. Shcherbina – zemskii deiatel' Voronezhskogo kraia', *Voronezhskoe kraevedenie: opyt i perspektivy razvitiia. Materialy tret'ei oblastnoi nauchno-prakticheskoi konferentsii, 23–24 marta 1991 goda* (Voronezh, 1991), pp. 76–8. His major publications include the famous peasant household budget study employed by Elvira Wilbur (see note 19, above): Fedor A. Shcherbina, *Krest'ianskie biudzhety* (Voronezh, 1900). Particularly important for the present chapter is his statistical monograph on Ostrogozhskii uezd: Fedor A. Shcherbina (ed.), *Krest'ianskoe khoziaistvo po Ostrogozhskomu uezdu* (Voronezh, 1887). Equally important are the two compilations edited by the zemstvo of Voronezh province, with introductions by Shcherbina: *Naselennye mesta Voronezhskoi gubernii. Spravochnaia kniga* (Voronezh, 1900); and *Svodnyi sbornik po 12 uezdam Voronezhskoi gubernii. Statisticheskie materialy poddvornoi perepisei* (Voronezh, 1897).

22 Boris B. Veselovskii, *Krest'ianskii vopros i krest'ianskoe dvizhenie v Rossii (1902–1906gg.)* (St Petersburg, 1907), p. 93. For a comment on the peasant movement and pre-revolutionary conditions of land lease, see also, for example, A. V. Peshekhonov, *Agrarnaia problema v sviazi s krest'ianskom dvizheniem* (St Petersburg, 1906), p. 71.

23 The basic argument is that peasants preferred to pay in kind or labour instead of cash, as they preferred to employ their own workforce and tools (of which they usually had a surplus), instead of spending the little money they normally had. See Löwe, 'Lenins Thesen über Kapitalismus', pp. 82–3. On the theory of the peasant household economy, see the work of Chaianov: for example Alexander Tschajanov, *Die Lehre von der bäuerlichen Wirtschaft. Versuch einer Theorie der Familienwirtschaft im Landbau* (Berlin, 1923; reprint Frankfurt am Main and New York, 1987); and *A. V. Chayanov on the Theory of Peasant Economy*, eds Daniel Thorner, Basile Kerblay and R. E. F. Smith, with a foreword by Theodor Shanin (Manchester, 1966).

24 See Löwe, *Die Lage der Bauern*, pp. 95–110, 337–57.

25 See note 19, above.

26 Wilbur, 'The Peasant Economy', p. 5.

27 Ibid., p. 35.

28 Ibid., pp. 29, 36.

29 Ibid., p. 128.

30 See ibid., pp. 122–6, 227–38 (bibliography).

31 This study was based on the zemstvo statistical volumes compiled during the 1880s and 1890s: see (for examples) note 21 above.
32 Arson. The term is here meant to denote the most severe forms of upheaval, such as the various forms of physical violence against people, animals or property, or serious theft.
33 Trespass, intrusion; plundering or (partial) destruction of fields. The term is here meant to denote the less severe forms of upheaval, as well as the more modern forms (such as, in particular, the strike).
34 *Gosudarstvennyi Arkhiv Voronezhskoi Oblasti (GAVO), f.* I-1 ('Voronezhskoe gubernskoe zhandarmskoe upravlenie, 1867–1917'); and *f.* I-6 ('Kantseliariia Voronezhskogo gubernatora, 1886–1917'). The following published books and documentary collections have been used: G. V. Antiukhin and M. G. Chechuro (eds), *Revoliutsionnoe dvizhenie v Voronezhskoi gubernii 1905–1907gg. Sbornik dokumentov i materialov* (Voronezh, 1955); Dubrovskii and Grave (eds), *1905; Krest'ianka v agrarnom dvizhenii Voronezhskoi gubernii 1905–6 goda* (Voronezh, 1925); *Krest'ianskoe dvizhenie v Voronezhskoi gubernii (1861–1863gg.) Dokumenty i materialy* (Voronezh, 1961); *Krest'ianskoe dvizhenie v Voronezhskoi gubernii (1864–1904gg.) Sbornik dokumentov* (Voronezh, 1964); W. Markov (ed.), *Die Bauernbewegung des Jahres 1861 in Russland nach Aufhebung der Leibeigenschaft. Meldungen der Suitengeneräle und Flügeladjutanten, Berichte der Gouvernementsstaatsanwälte und Kreisfiskale,* parts 1 and 2 ([East] Berlin, 1958); T. M. Oleinikov, 'Iz istorii krest'ianskikh volnenii v 1905 godu v peredelakh Voronezhskoi gubernii', in Obshchestvo dlia izucheniia Voronezhskogo kraia (ed.), *Voronezhskii kraevedcheskii sbornik,* Vol. 1 (Voronezh, 1924), pp. 16–29; *Revoliutsiia 1905–1907gg. v Rossii. Dokumenty i materialy,* 15 vols (Moscow, 1955); 'Spisok agrarnogo dvizheniia krest'ian Voronezhskoi gubernii za 1905–1906gg. o vazhneishikh sobytiiakh', in *1905 god v Voronezhe. Ocherki krest'ianskago dvizheniia na Voronezhshchine,* Vol. 3 (Voronezh, 1925), pp. 59–95; and V. A. Stepynin, *Khronika revoliutsionnykh sobytii v derevne Voronezhskoi gubernii, 1861–1917gg.* (Voronezh, 1977).
35 Peasants also addressed the zemstvo individually, but these particular applications, for reasons of space, will not be considered here.
36 In less than 16 per cent of all the applications counted for Ostrogozhskii uezd from the zemstvo journals, the peasants merely asked for a postponement of due payments or the lowering of taxes and obligations: that is, they did not make any positive suggestions for improvements or ask for (financial) assistance for a specific purpose.
37 There were, on average, 12.7 applications per year before 1892, and 17.8 per year thereafter. See Schedewie, 'Selbstverwaltung', p. 216 (1892 was the first zemstvo election year after the promulgation of the new zemstvo statute in 1890).
38 The remaining twenty-seven applications, all of which were brought forward by peasant deputies at the zemstvo assemblies, concerned matters of a more general nature. As for the *prigovory,* the great majority of them came from the village level. Only a few (fifty-nine) originated at volost level – from the volost assembly *(skhod)* (fourteen applications) or the volost administration *(pravlenie)* (forty-five applications).
39 An additional thirty-two applications contained other requests concerning local fairs (the renaming of fairs, different opening times, different range of goods to be sold, etc.).
40 Ninety-two applications concerned schools in other respects. Some resolutions were about teachers, others asked for financial assistance. In only two applications did the peasants ask explicitly for the closing of a school.
41 This information can be gleaned from the zemstvo journals and the zemstvo

statistics, for Ostrogozhsk in particular (see Shcherbina, *Krest'ianskoe khoziaistvo*, pp. 16–87) as well as from other sources: for example, for Ostrogozhsk, Fedor Nikonov 'Byt' i khoziaistvo malorossov v Voronezhskoi gubernii', *Trudy Imp. VEO* (1864), No. 3, pp. 161–72; Grigorii M. Veselovskii, *Gorod Ostrogozhsk (Voronezhskaia guberniia) i ego uezd. Istoriko-statisticheskii i etnograficheskii ocherk* (Voronezh, 1867).

42 Schedewie, 'Selbstverwaltung, pp. 231–7.
43 Taradin, *Voronezhskaia derevnia. Sloboda Roven'ki* (Voronezh, 1926), p. 15.
44 The map is from Shcherbina, *Krest'ianskoe khoziaistvo*, p. 339. It has been digitally adapted to serve the purpose of this chapter.
45 Applications are for the period 1872 to 1914 (the period of available zemstvo journals); incidents of protest, for 1861 to 1916. On the map, the first figures denote the numbers of applications, followed by those of the incidents of protest. With regard to the latter, the methodological problems of distinguishing and counting are the same as have been described by Wilbur ('The Peasant Economy', pp. 43–8). In part, these problems, basically those of achieving consistency and keeping a proportional balance, have been countered by using the symbol '>' before some incident figures, to indicate that more incidents happened that, however, could not be clearly distinguished.
46 There were, in total, 153,012 state peasants, 56,714 *sobstvenniki* and 14,891 *darstvenniki* in 1885. See Shcherbina, *Krest'ianskoe khoziaistvo*, pp. 75–6. The two latter groups were both made up of former serfs, with the difference that the *sobstvenniki* had opted for the full land allotment (*nadel*), together with the concomitant redemption payments after 1861, whereas the *darstvenniki* had chosen the so-called 'beggar's allotment' (that is, one that was only a quarter of the size of the full *nadel* but without redemption payments). Land allotments were quite large, compared with other regions of the Agricultural Centre, with 13.4 *desiatinas* on average per state peasant household and 6.9 *desiatinas* per household of former serfs (here the average being for *darstvenniki* and *sobstvenniki* together) in 1905. See Stepynin, *Khronika*, p. 158. But one has to remember that, especially in the south, the soil quality was hardly excellent. According to Stepynin, the serfs of Ostrogozhsk lost 31.4 per cent of the land that they had previously used to the landlords in the course of the regulations after 1861. See ibid., p. 4. For the whole province of Voronezh, according to Zaionchkovskii, these so-called *otrezki* ('cut-offs') amounted to 21.6 per cent of the land previously used: P. A. Zaionchkovskii, *The Abolition of Serfdom in Russia* (Gulf Breeze, 1978), p. 158.
47 Estates were founded only after the beginning of the eighteenth century and many of them were large. Despite significant loss of land in the following century, landlords in Ostrogozhsk in 1893 still possessed 1,250 *desiatinas* on average, while landlords in Voronezhskii uezd of the same province owned, on average, only 435 *desiatinas* and those in Zemlianskii uezd just 310 *desiatinas*. See V. A. Beketov, *Voronezhskaia guberniia v sel'skokhoziaistvennom otnoshenii. Otchet po komandirovke v 1893g. ot Imp. Mosk. Obshch. Sel. Khoz.* (Moscow, 1894), p. 3. Six landlords in Ostrogozhsk owned estates larger than 10,000 *desiatinas*. See ibid., p. 4.
48 Shcherbina, *Krest'ianskoe khoziaistvo*, p. 29: 'Zdes narod vsiakii buv – odnogo pan kupiv, inogo pereviv iz drugogo mista, a inshii i sam prishov.'
49 Ibid., p. 29.
50 As the story went among the old people, the *stariki*, in the village of Karaiashnik, at the time 'when the steppe grass grew higher than man' and payable dues were still low, one of the peasant leaders had sold the land at a cheap price to a neighbouring *pomeshchik* and thereby cheated his fellow peasant settlers. These had even appealed to a court, but inevitably lost their case against the *pany*, 'who were the richer ones'. According to another legend, one peasant called

Lushchnikov protested against the unjust annexation of land by lying down on the ground where the border was supposed to be. Yet those who wanted to take the land demonstrated their cruelty so drastically that Lushchnikov was killed and buried on the spot. The local population worshipped his grave and declared that his action had not been for nothing, for, subsequently, they got back their lost land. See Veselovskii, *Gorod Ostrogozhsk*, pp. 174–6.

51 For example, at Rossosh, the peasants pointed out, according to Shcherbina, that the landlords had themselves 'seduced' the peasants onto their land ('samye pany zamanivali krest'ian') – Shcherbina, *Krest'ianskoe khoziaistvo*, p. 29 – which might connote the offering of false promises.

52 According to another source, serfs in Ostrogozhskii uezd used to refer to themselves as *'poddannye'*, meaning 'subjects', but which might denote 'subjects of the tsar' not the local landlord, their legal owner. See 'Istoricheskii ocherk postepennago zaseleniia Voronezhskago kraia', in *Voronezhskii iubileinyi sbornik na pamiat' trekhsotletiia g. Voronezha*, Vol. 2 (Voronezh, 1886), pp. 260–72 (here p. 270). Unlike state peasants, serfs did not take the oath to the tsar, as, according to the rules of serfdom, they were considered to be fully and exclusively subject to their noble owners.

53 Shcherbina, *Krest'ianskoe khoziaistvo*, p. 225; *Chastnovladel'cheskoe khoziaistvo i materialy dlia opredeleniia tsennosti i dokhodnosti zemel' po Ostrogozhskomu uezdu*, ed. by Voronezhskoe gubernskoe zemstvo (Voronezh, 1887), pp. 38–43.

54 See note 46, above.

55 See, for example, Shcherbina, *Krest'ianskoe khoziaistvo*, p. 225; and *Sel'skokhoziaistvennyi obzor po Voronezhskoi guberniia*, ed. by Voronezhskoe gubernskoe zemstvo (Voronezh, 1888), Vol. 2, p. 80.

56 One illustrative example of this is the establishment of an 'agricultural association' (*sel'skokhoziaistvennoe obshchestvo*), a type of co-operative, in the village of Kolybel'ki, which enjoyed the patronage of the landlord Teviashev. See *Zhurnaly (Ostrogozhsk) sessii 1904 goda*, p. 9. In that year, 1904, however, Teviashev's assistance and patronage appear to have been of no avail at the zemstvo assembly, as the co-operative was not granted the credit it had applied for.

57 *GAVO f.* I-6, *op.* 2, *d.* 39, *ll.* 66–84: Vitse-Gubernator A. M. Chernov, 'Ocherk poslednikh besporiadkov v slobodakh Evstratovke, Morozovke i khutore Kolbine Ostrogozhskago uezda, sostavlennyi na osnovanii konfidentsial'nogo soobshcheniia nachal'nika Voronezhskogo gubernskogozhandarmskogo upravleniia, raportov uezdnogo ispravnika i lichnykh moikh besed na meste s pomoshchikom nachal'nika Voronezhskogo gubernskogo zhandarmskogo upravleniia i i.d. Ostrogozhskogo prokurora'. This report was published, with an introduction by M. D. Karpachev and A. N. Akin'shin, as 'Vitse-gubernator A. M. Chernov o polozhenii derevni na iskhode XIX veka', in *Iz istorii Voronezhskago kraia. Sbornik statei*, Vol. 7 (Voronezh, 1998), pp. 185–225 (here p. 192).

58 As a temporary absentee landlord, who was resident at Khar'kov, Kulikovskii spent much of his time away from his estate. For an account of his conflict with the peasants of Evstratovka that escalated in 1899 when Kulikovskii and his watchmen denied the peasants access to water across his meadow and killed the peasants' poultry, see Chernov, 'Ocherk poslednykh besporiadkov', pp. 189–92.

59 A marginal, but important note is that the owners of the sugar factory around 1900 were non-nobles. Not only from the point of view of the noble *pomeshchiki* (who feared the competition of wealthy non-nobles and peasant-kulaks), non-noble landowners, who had never possessed and been responsible for serfs, could not be real 'paternalists'. Apparently, the peasants, too, had their own picture of a 'proper' landlord and traditional patron. Thus, more incidents of disorder affected estates owned by non-nobles, as well as those that were run by bailiffs, the owners being absent or women.

60 See Figure 8.1 and, for example, *GAVO f.* I-6, *op.* 1, *d.* 649, *l.* 88. Moreover, the traditional form of harvest division was impossible with sugar-beet. The peasants were thus severely threatened in their economic existence by losing altogether the land now used for beet-growing. Their protest was often expressed by their digging out the beets at night, thereby symbolically destroying the landlord's economic existence, just as he had destroyed theirs. See also Macey, 'The Peasantry', p. 27.

61 On the theory of the 'moral economy', see E. P. Thompson, 'Die "moralische Ökonomie" der englischen Unterschichten im 18. Jahrhundert', in E. P. Thompson, *Plebeische Kultur und moralische Ökonomie. Aufsätze zur englischen Sozialgeschichte des 18. und 19. Jahrhunderts* (Frankfurt, Berlin and Vienna, 1980), pp. 67–130; and J. C. Scott, *The Moral Economy of the Peasant: Rebellion and Subsistence in Southeast Asia* (New Haven, 1976).

62 Chernov, 'Ocherk poslednykh besporiadkov' (see note 57, above).

63 Ibid., p. 217.

64 Ibid., pp. 192–200. Moreover, they did not employ the local peasants for cutting the grass, but instead employed migrant workers from other provinces who would work for lower wages.

65 Here one may add, as a general remark, that also in the zemstvo assemblies' discussions (recorded in the zemstvo journals), the more paternalistic attitudes of landlords – as expressed in the frequent use of terms such as '*popechenie*' (care, solicitude) towards the peasant as a '*men'shii brat*' (an 'inferior brother') – gave way to an expressed ideology that instead placed increased emphasis on 'self-help and initiative' ('*initsiativa i samodeiatel'nost*'), on the part of the peasants. Yet, outside of the assemblies and *vis-à-vis* the government, the very same landlords still clung to the older, traditional notions of responsibility. Especially around 1901, as they proposed plans for the creation of zemstvos at sub-uezd level, noble *zemtsy* claimed that the villagers could not do without their assistance. The discrepancy between the voiced attitudes and the actual behaviour of the landlords may well have evoked among the peasants at that time an even stronger conviction than before that they had a substantial right to receive support (especially at times of bad harvest, as in 1901), but, alas, they did not receive it. This reinforced conviction may have been the background of a threat against the landlord V. I. Stankevich in 1905, for example, in which peasants announced that they would set fire to his estate because Stankevich had refused to grant them a credit of grain. See Dubrovskii and Grave (eds), *1905*, p. 289. (The neighbouring former serfs of Teviashev, by the way, had received such a credit.).

66 In the immediate vicinity of Kolybel'skaia volost, the most severe riots occurred in southern Bobrovskii uezd. See Wilbur, 'The Peasant Economy', p. 124.

67 Some volosts, like those of Aidar or Vsesviatskoe, were inhabited by former serfs and by state peasants. For the sake of clarity, they are neglected in this chapter. A close differentiation on village level, however, shows, too, that the state peasant villages submitted more applications per village. See Schedewie, 'Selbstverwaltung', pp. 241–4.

68 An exception that should not count for the analysis here is the German colony of Rybensdorf.

69 Propaganda leaflets by the revolutionary parties were often distributed at railway stations and along railway tracks.

70 It is no coincidence that the volosts that Shcherbina names as those volosts where the leasehold of land was most common and widespread in the 1880s (among them those of Mar'evskaia, Lizinovskaia, Kolybel'skaia and Evstratovskaia) were the most disorderly from 1905 to 1907. See Shcherbina, *Krest'ianskoe khoziaistvo*, p. 67.

9 Jews and revolution in Kharkiv

How one Ukrainian city escaped a pogrom in 1905

Michael F. Hamm

This chapter examines Jewish settlement in Kharkiv and Jewish participation in the city's revolutionary movement. It also re-examines Imperial Russia's 1905 pogroms in the light of recent research on ethnic riots in other cultures. How did Kharkiv avoid the pogrom violence that ravaged virtually all other sizeable Ukrainian communities in 1905? As revolutionary fervour reached its peak in October, Kharkiv's elected and appointed officials acted quickly and decisively against the mobs, while a militant core of labour leaders and socialist agitators took control of the streets, ensuring that revolution would not degenerate into massive ethnic violence.

On 17 October 1905, a humiliated Tsar Nicholas II issued a manifesto promising to guarantee basic civil liberties and to create a State Duma with an electorate consisting of all classes 'which at present are altogether deprived of the franchise'. Although the October Manifesto was the crowning achievement of the 1905 Revolution, it failed to appease many opponents of the regime and it triggered nearly 700 pogroms against the Russian Empire's Jewish communities, mostly in Ukraine. In Kyiv (Kiev), mobs attacked 1,800 homes and businesses and perhaps a hundred Jews were killed. In Odesa (Odessa), an estimated 10,000 families were victimized. As many as 800 died, and up to 2,500 were injured.[1] According to historian S. M. Dubnow, 'in hundreds of cities the carefully concealed army of counter-revolutionaries, evidently obeying a prearranged signal, crawled out from beneath the ground to engage in an orgy of blood'.[2] Many contemporaries shared this view; however, no evidence of such a signal being given has been found. Even so, 'almost without exception', John Klier has noted, scholars have continued to argue that 'tsarist authorities actively planned, encouraged or at least welcomed pogroms, in an effort to make the Jews the scapegoats for revolutionary violence, or to channel anti-tsarist protest in a less harmful direction'. These 'myths', he believes, have been effectively refuted.[3]

The truth of the matter may lie somewhere between the views of Dubnow and Klier. To be sure, it is unlikely that the 1905 pogroms were 'actively planned' or centrally directed. In fact, many high-ranking officials – Sergei Witte is one example – condemned pogroms for moral reasons, or because they feared that angry mobs could easily turn against authority itself. On the other hand, pogroms in Imperial Russia, like ethnic riots elsewhere, have tended to occur where they have been allowed to occur. 'The main culprit', wrote *Kievskoe slovo*, 'is the inactivity of the government, which simply winks its eye.'[4] Similarly, Justice Thurgood Marshall, while describing a Detroit race riot in 1943, observed that 'When disorder starts, it is either stopped quickly or permitted to spread into serious proportions, depending upon the actions of the local police.'[5]

Jews were prominent in the revolutionary movement in Kharkiv (Khar'kov), and the threat of pogroms persisted throughout much of 1905. Yet Kharkiv managed to avoid the pogrom violence that ravaged Kyiv, Odesa, and most other cities of the south. In Kharkiv, officials chose to confront the mobs, and, behind the barricades, socialist agitators and militant workers formed what may have been the best example of successful worker-led resistance to pogroms in the chaos of October 1905.

Jewish settlement in Kharkiv

Founded as a fortress in the mid-1650s, Kharkiv grew slowly as a trade centre, particularly after the 'Ukrainian Line' of fortifications, completed in the 1730s, diminished the threat from marauding Turks and Tartars. Until the mid-nineteenth century, Kharkiv's economy depended heavily on four annual fairs. Kreshchenskaia, which began on 6 January, accounted for half the fair trade and became the third largest fair in Imperial Russia.[6] By the eighteenth century, Kharkiv had a 'Jewish Street' and synagogue, a Jewish cemetery, and at least one Jewish-owned tavern. When the Pale of Settlement was created in 1794, Kharkiv was excluded, which effectively denied Jews residential rights in the city. A list of tavern-owners from 1799 mentions Ukrainians, Great Russians, Georgians and Greeks, but not Jews.[7] Nevertheless, some Jews continued to come and trade surreptitiously, often under assumed names, bringing goods that were valued by local craftsmen. Others accused Jews of unfair competition. In 1809, responding to one such complaint, Kharkiv's chief of police insisted that there were only three Jewish families in the city and that none was engaging in trade.[8]

A few Jews continued to live in Kharkiv, even in the 1840s when restrictions against them were strictly enforced. One was Iosif Nemirovskii, whose skill at embroidering gold filigree onto military uniforms made him indispensable. In the 1850s, Jews began to come openly to the fairs. At the Uspenskaia Fair (15 August to 1 September), for example, Jews purchased local farm produce for distribution in Russia, the Caucasus and Central Europe. In 1858, Alexander II granted first- and second-guild Jewish merchants access to Kharkiv's fairs and by the early 1860s some 18,000 to 20,000 Jews (including carters and freight handlers) were coming annually, providing substantial tax and rent income for the city and its residents. In 1855, the city sold its lucrative monopoly right to serve food to these arrivals to a Berdychiv (Berdichev) merchant, who in turn sold subsidiary feeding rights to others on the sly. When the contract was again put on offer in 1856 it went for twice the amount it had brought the previous year.[9]

By 1858, 149 Jews were officially living in Kharkiv, most of them students and soldiers. By 1867 that number had grown to 906; by 1873 to 2,397; and by 1881 to 5,600. Of that number, about half were craftsmen/artisans and their families. Approximately 1,000 were soldiers; 150 were students; 100 were merchants; and 100 were physicians, teachers and members of other free professions. By then, there were more than a dozen *heders* (Jewish schools) in Kharkiv and in 1867 a two-storey home on German Street was converted into a larger synagogue. From 1887 until 1914, the chief of police operated 'Table III' that granted Jewish residence permits, while the provincial administration also had its own 'Jewish Table'. By 1897, 9,848 Jews officially resided in Kharkiv; by 1913, 13,592. Both figures represented 5 to 6 per cent of the city's population. Of the cities outside the Pale, only St Petersburg and Kyiv had larger Jewish populations.[10]

Some Jews prospered in Kharkiv. In 1868, Roman Rubenshtein opened Kharkiv's first commercial bank, and his descendants continued to flourish commercially, founding the New Bavaria Brewery among other enterprises. Rubenshtein's grandson, Iosif, a patron of the arts, was the first Kharkivite to own an automobile. The composer-pianist Peter Tchaikovsky performed in his home in 1893.[11] Jews became prominent in the food, tobacco, paper and publishing trades and in law and medicine. Some of the attorneys and physicians were also professors. In the late 1870s, Elena Mikhailovna Gal'perina-Ginzburg, who had earned a law degree in Paris, became one of the first women to practise law in the Russian Empire. Later she moved to Kyiv, where she became a journalist.[12] Karaite Jews began to migrate into Kharkiv from the Crimea in the 1840s, numbering 525 in 1877. Karaites did not suffer the restrictions imposed on other Jews and were allowed open access to the schools. Thus, many Karaites joined the ranks of the professional classes. In the 1870s they also owned eight tobacco mills in the city.[13] In 1913, of the 9,200 individuals who owned taxable real estate in the city, 198 (2 per cent) were Jews. Of the 763 individuals in the top tax bracket – that is, those whose property produced at least 10,000 roubles of annual income – eighty-eight (or 12 per cent) were Jews.[14]

Jews and political opposition in Kharkiv

Quite by accident, while investigating the disappearance of a certain Madame Garshina, who had been accused by her husband of running off with another man, police discovered that a secret society had operated at Kharkiv University in 1856 and 1857. Although the society had disbanded, twenty of its members were arrested, including medical student Beniamin Portugal and five other Jews. In 1874, Portugal, who had become a published authority on alcoholism and public health, helped found Kharkiv's first *narodnik* circle. However, Jews were never as prominent in Kharkiv's *narodnik* movement as they were in Kyiv, and a recent study by S. G. Svatikov cautions against exaggerating Jewish oppositional involvement. Of 376 individuals brought to trial for political crimes between 1873 and 1879, he notes, only about 4 per cent (seventeen individuals) were Jews, the same percentage as that of Jews in the general population. When the People's Will formed its executive organ in 1879, only three of the thirty-eight members were Jews, and from 1879 until 1885, of forty-four individuals who served on this organ, only four were Jews.[15]

Although most Jewish activists were non-violent idealists, there were some exceptions. In 1879, Grigorii Gol'denberg, the son of a prosperous Berdychiv cloth merchant who had been schooled in Kyiv, shot and killed Kharkiv's governor-general, D. N. Kropotkin, as he passed by in his carriage. Gol'denberg, who also conspired to kill Alexander II, gave detailed testimony while in prison, implicating many of his associates before committing suicide.[16] In 1885, during a police roundup that was intended to liquidate the People's Will organization, Vinnytsia (Vinnitsia) native Saul Lisianskii killed a Kharkiv policeman. A number of those subsequently arrested were Jewish students. Such highly publicized incidents helped build the image of the Jew as a dangerous subversive and Jews were often punished more severely than Christians. For example, in 1880 the 17-year-old Kharkiv student I. I. Rogovskii was hanged simply for possessing a People's Will proclamation. The oddity of the Zionist movement further reinforced suspicions about Jewish loyalty. Kharkiv's first known Zionist organization emerged in January 1882, in the wake of the pogroms that followed the assassination of Alexander II. University student Izrail Belkind organized the group, and of the thirty students who initially joined it fourteen decided to emigrate to Palestine.[17]

From the 1870s, as Kharkiv began to grow as a railway and industrial centre, official concern developed that socialist ideas were 'undermining the state'. Evidence of this can be found in the reports of Kharkiv governors as early as 1877.[18] They had reason to be concerned: Kharkiv's 1900 *maevka* (May Day demonstration) brought out several thousand strikers and demonstrators – numbers that surprised even the city's socialist agitators. However, the police quickly regained the upper hand, and no major strikes occurred in Kharkiv during the next three years – not even in July 1903, when 'general strikes' gripped other southern cities. Likewise, in 1904, there was little open dissent until critics of the government began to organize the so-called 'banquet campaign' at the end of the year.

Although Kharkiv's fledgling labour movement struggled in 'an atmosphere saturated with anti-Semitism, alcohol, religious prejudice, and indifference to everything', according to Boris Lintser (who was, reportedly, the city's first Social Democratic convert),[19] Jewish agitators were now prominent in the city. According to one court record for October 1903, of sixty-four people convicted of Social Democratic activity, twenty-four were Jews. Many were young artisans, including tailors who had come from the Pale.[20] Tailors were the first artisanal group to strike in Kharkiv, in 1901, and they remained a prime target of Social Democratic agitation. In March 1905, some 260 tailors from thirty-three shops struck for eleven days, seeking wage and economic concessions.[21]

Jews were also prominent among Kharkiv's Socialist-Revolutionary (SR) agitators, although this movement had a much smaller following than the Social Democrats in the city. A police report dated 10 March 1904 lists sixteen Jews among the thirty-three SR activists who had been arrested over several months.[22] Those arrested included at least four university-level students and a number of women. Four of the women, all in their early twenties, were dental students.

Kharkiv's Jews had traditionally defended themselves by bribing police officials. In April 1904, as rumours of an Easter pogrom swirled about the city, the Social Democrat Aron Levitus and other socialist leaders formed Poale-Zion, mainly for the purpose of self-defence. Approximately 250 individuals formed units of about twenty-five men each, staving off the pogrom. Jewish youths aged 14–20 provided most of the manpower.[23] Apparently, Jews decided not to pay the traditional bribe in 1905,[24] indicating, perhaps, a newfound hope that self-defence could better ensure their safety. Self-defence could defend property – and it gave Jews a psychological lift – but it also provided an additional pretext for the Judaeophobic right to mobilize. For them, the existence of Jewish militias, even if defensive in nature, was another indication that political agendas would be won or lost on the streets, and pogroms could be justified as a legitimate political response to mob action from the left.

1905: politics redefined

On 9 January 1905, the Bloody Sunday massacre in St Petersburg opened a wave of ferment that would explode into revolution in October. On 14 January, police 'liquidated' Kharkiv's small SR organization, arresting Konstantin Lebedev and six others – all of them Jews, three of them women.[25] According to police, there were 'many Jews' at a Kharkiv Medical Society meeting on 6 April, where the government was excoriated for its general incompetence.[26] It is possible, of course, that police singled Jews out for arrest, but it is more likely that these bits of evidence underscore the fact that Jews were now prominent in the city's revolutionary movement. Of the eight or nine individuals given credit for organizing the Bolshevik *Vpered* faction in early 1905, four (and possibly five) were Jewish. One was 'Stepan' (Lev Isaakovich Epshtein), who had come to Kharkiv from Odesa with the Bolshevik 'Artem' (F. A. Sergeev), Kharkiv's most charismatic radical agitator in 1905.[27] Of eighteen Social Democratic activists known to police in May, about one-third were Jewish.[28]

Not surprisingly, the threat of pogroms surfaced periodically. In April, as large crowds of workers gathered to debate how to celebrate May Day, rumours circulated that a demonstration would be countered by a pogrom. During the summer, fears escalated again as right-wing agitators spread rumours that the well-known Jewish Ponizovskii commercial firm had aided the Japanese by providing gold.[29]

After eight months of sporadic strikes and unrest, prospects for real revolution began to emerge in September. With the university-level institutions reopened, large crowds of workers, students and others began to assemble, particularly at Kharkiv University, and the likelihood of violent confrontation grew accordingly. In October, as in other cities, a general strike shut down Kharkiv. Despite Nicholas II's issuing of the October Manifesto, conflict continued. In the capital itself, a workers' soviet, calling itself 'an organ of revolutionary self-government', continued to wield authority, championing popular causes such as the eight-hour day. In early November, 119,000 St Petersburg workers from 526 enterprises were still on strike.[30] In the countryside, the peasantry 'rose to join its urban brothers in the greatest, most destructive series of agrarian uprisings since the Pugachev Rebellion of the eighteenth century'.[31] And, within hours after news of the October Manifesto reached Russia's outlying cities, the horrific wave of pogroms began. Again, Kharkiv's Jews panicked. Many fled their apartments for the relative safety of hotels. 'Politics' had been redefined. The left had taken its agenda to the streets; the time for retaliation had arrived.

Parovozniki, the *Komitet bor'by* and self-defence

During the course of 1905, about 300 *parovozniki* (locomotive workers) took control of the Locomotive Assembly, Kharkiv's largest industrial enterprise, hiring and firing employees (at one point even hiring the Bolshevik 'Artem', the most notorious and effective agitator in the city). Working through Locomotive's *Otsenochnaia komissiia* (Review Committee), which had formed earlier to negotiate on piece-work rates and various other factory grievances, these militants also took command of the city's labour movement as a whole. Other Kharkiv workers relied on the *parovozniki* to help them organize their own strikes and win concessions. Workers also feared the *parovozniki* – and so did local police, who knew better than to try to enter the Assembly. As one memoirist put it, Locomotive became 'an autonomous republic in its own right'.[32]

During the October strike, *parovozniki* roamed about, 'convincing' reluctant shopkeepers to close down. Kharkiv's self-proclaimed 'patriots' reacted in kind. Led by a local merchant, a 'Black Hundred' mob began to beat Jews and students. When word that a student had been killed reached the university, barricades went up and, within hours, several hundred workers arrived from the Locomotive Assembly to support the students. The barricades had powerful symbolic significance, and behind them the Social Democrats quickly organized a *Komitet bor'by* (Battle Group), a precursor to the Kharkiv Federated Soviet, to co-ordinate the strike and defend workers, students and Jews against retaliatory assault. In the interest of revolutionary unity, Mensheviks, Bolsheviks and SRs each took three seats on the Battle Group. As police went from house to house, in an effort to find Jewish activists (and Jews who were in the city illegally), the *Komitet bor'by* mobilized its own militia, estimated at 600 to 900 men, which also went house to house, 'arresting thieves and plunderers' who were taken to Gelferikh-Sade (a farm machinery assembly), photographed and warned they would be shot if they were caught in a Black Hundred mob again. *Parovoznik* units also used the opportunity to extort money from the wealthy to aid the revolutionary cause.[33] Caught in the middle, liberals formed a Committee of Public Safety in order to mediate between the government and the barricades, but it was the *Komitet bor'by*, police acknowledged, that virtually overnight 'acquired general sympathy and well-known authority'.[34] Its militias, which almost certainly had a gentile worker majority, drove the pogrom mob from the city and brought order to the streets. Officials agreed to negotiate at a mass meeting and promised that troops would not be present 'as long as the *Komitet bor'by* maintained order'.[35]

Kharkiv suffered 156 casualties between 10 and 12 October, but only a few of them were Jews.[36] Thanks largely to the *Komitet bor'by* and its militias, Kharkiv had avoided the pogrom violence of this time that ravaged some 700 other communities, mostly in Ukraine.

Ethnic violence: some common patterns

Pogroms, Paul Brass tells us, are 'a warning to one's ethnic and political rivals'.[37] They attract political extremists, excitement-seekers, street thugs, vagabonds, drunks and looters, as well as 'religious illiterates' – individuals who reduce the complexities of religious faith to a handful of disparaging stereotypes and myths.[38] These myths often transcend political frontiers. For example, the blood libel, commonly accepted in the popular culture of Imperial Russia, found wide acceptance in the Ottoman Empire, although Christians there (mostly Greeks) were far more likely to commit pogroms against 'the murderers of the Savior' than were Muslims.[39]

Descriptions of pogroms and other forms of ethnic riot are uncannily similar from one culture to another. In 1905, witnesses in Kyiv observed that 'the pace of the looting was often leisurely'.[40] Likewise in East St Louis, Illinois, site of a July 1917 race riot that has been called America's worst pogrom, 'There was a visible coolness and premeditation about [the violence] . . . This was not the hectic and raving demonstration of men suddenly gone mad.'[41] The following passage describes an anti-Sikh riot in Delhi in 1984:

Local [officials] ... even in ministerial positions in the central government, provided direction, 'mobilized their local clients and thugs, provided them with liquor ... [and] ... distribute[d] the fuel for arson. They also provided information about the targets' ... Such information in turn was provided by 'informers and collaborators' within the residential colonies selected for attack.[42]

It is nearly identical to newspaper accounts of Imperial Russia's pogroms in 1905.

Rumour and racist journalism sparked riot everywhere. The newspaper *Bessarabets* paved the way for Kishinev's 1903 pogrom by accusing Jews of the ritual murder of a Christian boy. And the turmoil and insecurities of 1905 again ripened the environment for rumour. Kremenchuk's pogrom was preceded by a false report that police had confiscated 700 knives from Jews who had attended a rally. Kharkiv Jews were accused of spreading rumours that the tsar had fled Russia. In Zhytomyr (Zhitomir), *baby* (old women) ran through the fields swearing that Christians were being massacred, producing such terror that 'women and children one and all fled into the forests', while even left-leaning Kyiv newspapers carried reports that Jews were 'cutting up' Christians and sacking local monasteries.[43]

So too in Washington, DC: just prior to its 1919 race riot, the NAACP and the *Washington Post* exchanged accusations that 'inflammatory headlines and sensational articles' were stirring racial hatred.[44] East St Louis newspapers falsely asserted that 'thousands' of Negroes were being brought in to replace white workers and accused Negroes of murdering whites 'every other night or so'. The *St Louis Republic* boasted that the East St Louis pogrom had staved off a Negro plot to murder 25,000 whites, including women and children.[45] In Aligarh, near Delhi, one of India's most riot-prone cities, two of the largest-circulating Hindi newspapers published lurid rumours that Muslim doctors were killing Hindu patients in cold blood in a local hospital. Fabricated reports that Hindu temples had been attacked and that pigs had been thrown into mosques also helped spawn India's unprecedented wave of communal violence of 1989 to 1992.[46]

Defiance by those who are supposed to be servile can be particularly explosive in periods of perceived crisis. Race riots in Chicago, Washington and other American cities were triggered in part because the First World War and Wilsonian idealism had encouraged American blacks and civil rights activists to seek greater equality more aggressively. In Russia in 1905, peasants who challenged authority were seen as insubordinate and forced to remove their hats, kneel in the snow or mud, or bow in supine positions for long intervals while Cossack interrogators on horseback whipped them.[47] In October 1905, Jews were roundly accused of flaunting their extraordinary political triumph. The crowd that celebrated the October Manifesto in Kremenchuk was reported to be 'almost exclusively Jewish'.[48] In Katerynoslav (Ekaterinoslav), 'Jewish youths' had been especially defiant during the victory celebrations, and some apparently solicited donations 'for Nicholas II's coffin'.[49] Jews also predominated in huge demonstrations in September and October in Kyiv and at one point held an eight-hour rally in the auditorium at St Vladimir University, where their presence had been traditionally restricted.[50] Some witnesses would later testify that Jews comprised 85 per cent of the manifesto's celebrants in Kyiv. According to conservative professor and city council member Otto Eikhelman, the figure was closer to 'one in five', but even this figure underscores the fact that Jews were highly visible in the humiliation of the tsar.[51]

Ethnic riot tends to be concentrated in specific regions or towns. Nearly nine out of ten pogroms occurring in the Pale of Settlement in 1905 and 1906 took place in the Pale's seven southern provinces, accounting for 62 per cent of all Jewish fatalities.[52] Political scientist Ashutosh Varshney, who has studied Hindu–Muslim conflict in India, observes that significant communal violence has occurred in only four of India's twenty-eight states, and about half of all related deaths have occurred in only eight cities: Ahmedabad, Mumbai (Bombay), Aligarh, Hyderabad, Meerut, Baroda, Calcutta and Delhi. They account for only 18 per cent of India's urban population and only 5 per cent of its total population: 'Eighty-two per cent of the urban population (and 95 per cent of the total population) has not been "riot-prone".'[53]

Where ethnic riot does occur, apologists cast it as a spontaneous expression of popular emotion. However, in reality it is neither popular nor entirely spontaneous. Few people countenance rape or murder, while the wanton destruction of property frightens many. In 1905, Imperial Russia's pogrom mobs were usually small in size, and they lacked a powerful political or ideological base. *Pogromshchiki* shouted 'patriotic' slogans, but they defended the narrow interests of a repressive and discredited regime rather than a broader national cause. As Walker Connor has noted, 'despite the many advantages the state has for politically socializing its citizens in patriotic values, patriotism . . . cannot muster the level of emotional commitment that nationalism can'.[54]

The deafening silence of local authority

Most important of all, large-scale ethnic riot is usually provoked by the actions of what Paul Brass calls 'riot specialists', individuals who stand 'ready to be called out on such occasions'. In riot-prone communities, 'institutionalized riot-systems' have established themselves 'in which known actors specialize in the conversion of incidents between members of different communities into "communal riots" '.[55] These loosely organized networks of individuals 'maintain communal, racial or other ethnic relations in a state of tension, of readiness for riots . . . [T]here are regular fire-tenders who maintain the fuel at a combustible level, sometimes stoking it, sometimes letting it smolder. They are the conversion specialists, who know how to convert a moment of tension into a grander, riotous event.' Moreover, Brass observes, 'to start the riot and spread it, to provide noise, cover, and additional "spontaneous" recruits, further riot specialists also come into play: specially designated forces from the riot squads to act as "mobile gangs", persons designated to spread rumors, "shouters of slogans", and "instigators of violence among the public"'.[56]

Such 'riot specialists' are conspicuous in descriptions of Imperial Russia's 1905 pogroms. Odesa's pogrom 'was not a spontaneous riot', Weinberg tells us: 'Politically motivated pogrom-mongerers and rabble-rousers preyed upon the emotions and anxieties of gentile Odesans and sought to transform their anger into attacks on Jews and other perceived enemies of the state.' In Peresyp District, 'the pogrom started only after armed thugs from the city center arrived and began to incite local residents'.[57] Observers in Kishinev spoke of 'red-shirted men' among others who incited and directed the crowd,[58] while Kyiv's 'riot specialists' included 'the well-known local hooligan Vaska Grigor'ev' (son of a prominent boot-maker), D. I. Pikhno (editor of the anti-Semitic *Kievlianin*) and B. P. Vasilev (who managed the city's largest sugar refinery in outlying Demievka), as well as the police chief and a major-general.[59]

Pogrom mobs attacked rich and poor alike. Kyiv targets included lowly shopkeepers and peddlers, as well as the fashionable homes of the Brodskys, Ginzburgs, and Gal'perins in up-market Lypky. In character, pogroms resembled upheaval in the countryside, where wanton destruction also seemed an end in itself. There, entire villages or groups of villages ransacked estates. 'Everything the proprietor [of the estate] tried to rescue from the burning homes, the peasants cut into chips, trampled with their feet, demolished and tore to pieces', wrote Mariia von Bock, daughter of P. A. Stolypin.[60] Even estates of leftist political activists were destroyed, including the family estate of Vera Figner, the famous leader of the People's Will.

Neither pogroms nor rural rampages were directed centrally, but both had direction. Village assemblies discussed, planned and executed peasant rebellions: 'They usually set the time for the disorder and determined who was to participate and what tools, weapons, and equipment were needed.'[61] In the cities, newspapers from around the Empire exposed 'administrator-criminals' and 'police hooligans' who had assisted the mobs.[62] As *Voskhod*, a Jewish newspaper, reported: 'One thing is clear as day. Governors, *gradonachal'niki* [town governers] and police captains openly, cynically, organized the pogroms, dispatched troops to shoot at self-defence [units], provided leadership for the mobs, while refusing to protect those who were violated.'[63] In Odesa, if civil and military officials did not plan the 1905 pogroms, their 'encouragement and connivance' is clear.[64] Violence spread where it was allowed to spread. Even where local officials opposed pogroms, many declined to resist the mobs, recognizing that they were a permissible form of political retaliation, given the extraordinary circumstances of October 1905. Thus, as Kyiv's pogrom began, its mayor, V. N. Protsenko, simply left his city. The man in charge of troops on the streets, General Bez-sonov, reported this exchange with an onlooker: 'Sir: A pogrom is underway and nothing is being done. Do you understand?' 'What pogrom', came the response: 'I really don't understand. They are indeed plundering shops. But this is not a pogrom. It is a demonstration!'[65]

Police and pogroms

Police were the first line of defence against mobs, but in Kyiv pogroms spread from neighbourhood to neighbourhood 'under their watchful eyes'. Individual Kyiv policemen directed small bands of *pogromshchiki*, sometimes distributing lists of Jewish homes and businesses and occasionally even par-ticipating in the plunder of shops.[66] After the pogrom in the city's Solomenka district, irate residents petitioned for the removal of the entire police force because it had refused to protect life or property.[67] In Kharkiv, the Social Democrats accused police of trying to 'arrange' pogroms.[68]

'Pre-revolutionary Russia was notoriously under-policed', John Klier cor-rectly notes, 'and the authorities often had little choice or flexibility in dealing with street disorders.'[69] Such arguments do not tell the entire story, however, for pogrom mobs were usually small, poorly armed and (poten-tially) easily dispersed. In Kyiv they carried only 'crowbars, pickaxes, hammers, rocks, and knives'. A mere handful of patrolmen dispersed the rioters in that city's Lukianivka (Lukian'ovka) Bazaar because they feared for the security of a nearby prison.[70] Where authorities declined to show force, they reinforced the belief, often trumpeted by the mob, that it was permiss-ible for pogroms to last for three days. When officials intervened – often on the third day – the disturbances quickly ended. Likewise, in India, a single courageous police chief brought peace to Bhiwandi, a city 'whose capacity for rioting had become legendary', and maintained peace, even during the riots of 1988 to 1991 that followed the Hindu nationalist destruction of the Baburi mosque.[71] Where ethnic riot succeeded – whether it be in Ukraine, India or America – police tended to disappear as mobs formed and were accused of trying harder to disarm the targets of the mobs, allegedly for their own safety, than the mobs themselves. Corruption and prejudice are more responsible for police inactivity than understaffing, Brass contends,[72] and I believe this to be true of Russia in 1905.

Troops were often called in as a second line of defence against mobs, but they took their cues from local police. Where police remained inactive, sol-diers often followed suit. 'Until five o'clock [East St Louis] might have been saved if the soldiers had behaved differently. Instead the mobs became emboldened by their indifference.' Troops 'were laughing and joking, as if it were a picnic rather than a riot', according to local residents. When officials decided to quell the violence, they did so with relative ease: 'When guards-men approached with drawn weapons, resistance crumbled.' Mobs dispersed, regrouped, dispersed again 'until it became clear to the whites that further violence would not be tolerated'.[73] Meanwhile, in Kyiv, one apartment owner protected his five-storey building by paying off a single soldier. In Odesa, Weinberg writes:

> The evidence indicates that policemen behaved with the knowledge and tacit approval of their superiors. Neither [city governor Dmitrii] Neidhardt nor [commander of the Odesa Military District Baron Aleksandr] Kaul'bars took any decisive action to suppress the pogrom when disorders erupted. Consequently, full responsibility for the savagery of the pogrom must ultimately be placed on them as the two officials responsible for maintaining law and order. As the head of the Odessa gendarmes reported, the military did not apply sufficient energy to end the pogrom. In fact, pogromists greeted soldiers and policemen with shouts of 'Hurrah' and then continued their rampage and pillage free from interference.[74]

It is worth noting, finally, that other elements of the authorities may also contribute to ethnic riot. In October 1905, responding to a letter published in a Kyiv newspaper accusing the Cave Monastery of printing an inflammatory 'Black Hundred' pamphlet that had encouraged the pogrom mob to mobilize, a Monastery spokesman denied that his institution had printed the pamphlet; he called it 'nothing more than a sincere, Christian patriotic publication' and conspicuously chose not to use the opportunity to condemn the pogrom itself. Thus, one of the Empire's most revered centres of Christian spirituality declined to publicly concern itself with the fact that local mobs had killed dozens of people.[75] Whether Church officials typically agreed with the Judaeophobic *Kievlianin*'s assertion that Kyiv's *pogromshchiki* had 'acted with God in their heart'[76] is impossible to know, but when those charged with upholding moral authority refuse to speak out publicly and forcefully against violence they too bear some responsibility for it.

Inter-ethnic association and the prevention of violence

Ashutosh Varshney believes that interaction between rival communities may also deter mob violence. Where Gandhi's disciples and India's Congress Party created strong trade and labour associations that integrated Hindus and Muslims, partition riots were averted in 1947 and 1948. As the Congress Party declined, the integrative network declined as well, and hundreds subsequently died in riots in communities that had previously been peaceful. Calicut, in Kerala State, remained peaceful, even during India's violent disorders of 1989–92. According to Varshney, 'Calicut is a place of "joiners". Associations of all kinds – business, labor, professional, social, theater, film, sports, art, reading – abound ... [W]hat is distinctive is the extent of inter-religious interaction in nondenominational organizations.'[77] More than 80 per cent of Calicut's Hindus and Muslims eat together, while

90 per cent of its Hindu and Muslim children play together. Kerala has the highest rate of literacy of any state in India, and Calicut's reading rooms, 'a unique Kerala institution', give young people a chance to read and discuss contentious issues. Even Calicut's 10,000 'headloaders' (bazaar porters), about 60 per cent of whom are Hindu and 40 per cent Muslim, have an unusually strong union in Calicut. Spread across the city's smaller shops and enterprises, this inter-ethnic union has helped stave off conflict.[78] Significantly, Calicut's peace committees are inter-communal. They provide links for communal interaction 'all the way down to the neighborhood level'. By contrast, in riot-prone towns such as Aligarh, interaction – both formal and informal – has been far less common, and organizations tend to be intra-communal rather than inter-communal.[79]

We know little about associational patterns between Jews and gentiles in Imperial Russia, so it is difficult to speculate about the extent to which inter-ethnic association helped prevent pogroms. Varshney believes that even if large integrative organizations such as India's independence movement are absent, smaller local organizations can serve as important mechanisms for integrating adversarial groups. Political parties can serve in this capacity – indeed, Indian inquiry commissions' studies of communal riot have emphasized that purely communal parties should be banned, or at least regulated.[80] Arguably, in Kharkiv, it was the socialist movement, and particularly the Social Democrats, that played an important integrationist role in 1905.

Kharkiv's socialists: leadership on the streets

Kharkiv's Social Democrats, by far the city's most important revolutionary organization, had campaigned forcefully against pogroms, particularly after the Kishinev massacre in 1903. They also sought to prevent the socialist movement from fragmenting into ethnic factions. In their call 'To All Men and Women Workers of Khar'kov', which was published a few weeks after Bloody Sunday, and in their other leaflets, the Social Democrats emphasized that only a broad-based 'Russian proletarian *family*' that embraced *all* faiths and nationalities could protect against pogroms and win political equality and economic opportunity for all.[81] The logic of this appeal was compelling – not least for those specifically Jewish socialist organizations that had found it difficult to recruit followers in the city. Kharkiv's Poale-Zion was unable (or unwilling) to hold demonstrations on its own in 1905: its members took to the streets only within the broader demonstrations organized by the Social Democrats.[82] The Bund was active in Kharkiv – in March 1904 police seized a variety of Bund leaflets published in London and a partial list of thirty-two Jewish families who presumably were to be the recipients[83] – but its influence was modest. When Mirna Karasin, who had returned to Kharkiv for the first time since participating in a 1901 demonstration, tried to hand out Bund leaflets to Jewish workers in July 1905, she found few takers.[84]

Although Social Democratic activists organized the *Komitet bor'by*, who led and who followed during the stormy October days is not entirely clear. Agitators from all the revolutionary parties had access to Locomotive's *Otsenochnaia komissiia*, while both Artem and the SR activist Zabelin were said to have special influence there. On the other hand, *parovoznik* militants clearly understood the exceptional influence they had won among local workers, and they were not reluctant to take action on their own. The socialist message certainly did not resonate with all Kharkiv workers, but — unlike in Moscow, where even workers who were sympathetic to the strike movements were said to be hostile to intelligentsia activists who brought political messages[85] – it did inspire the militant and it did elicit a powerful symbiosis between socialist agitators and militant *parovozniki*. As the pogrom mobs began to attack, the Social Democrats and the *parovozniki* responded jointly, providing the critical leadership and organizational structure for those who were willing to battle the Black Hundreds for control of the streets. Recognizing this symbiosis, one *okhrana* agent wrote that arresting fifty *parovozniki* and a few *intelligenty* would end rebellion in Kharkiv.[86]

The commitment to defend against pogroms continued after the barricades came down. On 29 October, *Khar'kovskii listok* published a letter 'with thousands of signatures' promising to take whatever measures necessary to prevent additional pogroms.[87] Worker militias continued to patrol the city until the revolutionary movement was finally quashed in mid-December. Thus, Kharkiv presents an interesting contrast to the industrial towns of the Donbass–Dnepr Bend, where 'a huge number of workers joined other members of the lower classes in the drunken looting, battery, rape and murder characteristic of the pogroms'.[88] According to Charters Wynn, the 'pogromist proclivity' of the Donbass–Dnepr workers followed 'frustration and anger over the outcome of general strikes . . . that inflamed long-standing ethnic hostility in a region where violent behavior was central to working-class culture'.[89] Self-defence squads, manned by Social Democrats, radical Jewish artisans and skilled Russian workers, did form in Katerynoslav, preventing pogrom mobs from entering the central districts of the city. But, overall, Donbass workers 'were at best only superficially influenced by revolutionary propaganda' and the revolutionary parties, in fact, 'were caught off guard by the reactionary violence that erupted so quickly on the heels of their [October] triumph'.[90] Kharkiv workers also felt victimized by repeated strikes, and many regarded Jews with suspicion or hostility. But because Kharkiv had a bold core of authoritative labour and socialist leaders who were determined to make use of the solidarity of the moment to combat pogroms, the city's 'Days of Freedom' did not degenerate into the savagery that unfolded elsewhere in Ukraine.

Taking their cue from labour resistance, on 23 November 1905 some soldiers also took a public stance against Black Hundred violence. Behind two military bands, members of three regiments came out of their Kharkiv barracks, without their officers, to demonstrate on behalf of a variety of demands, one of which was assurance that soldiers would not be asked to fire on civilian demonstrators. As pogrom mobs again began to form, the soldiers promised to 'protect the peaceful population' from Black Hundred activists.[91] Workers and soldiers acted quickly to dispel the mobs, arresting seventy 'hooligans', searching the apartments of known pogromists and removing the merchandise taken from two plundered trade wagons.[92]

No riot-system here: Kharkiv officials also hold their ground

Kharkiv's elected and appointed officials also acted quickly and decisively to prevent a pogrom. City officials had already displayed some sensitivity to Jewish concerns, opening a special 'Hebraic-Judaica' section at the public library in 1903, for example,[93] but overall Kharkiv did not seem particularly distinguished in its civic culture by 1905. Only 24 per cent of its small propertied electorate had bothered to vote in the city duma election in 1902, and the same percentage voted in the following election in 1906.[94] Merchants dominated the city duma until 1910, when professional people took control. Over the next four years, Kharkiv came to be regarded as a model of civic leadership and developmental accomplishment.[95]

But in 1905, when it mattered most, Kharkiv's elected and appointed leaders rose to the occasion. A. K. Pogorelko, a chemistry professor and liberal activist who served four consecutive terms as mayor between 1900 and his death in 1912, stood firmly against mob violence and, in October 1905, helped organize the Committee of Public Safety to mediate between radicals and government troops.[96] Pogorelko also supported the idea of a people's defence militia and used city funds to pay for the funerals of those killed in October. Meanwhile, K. S. Starynkevich, Kharkiv's governor-general, refused to allow troops to position themselves near the student barricades in order to minimize the likelihood of confrontation. After negotiating with the *Komitet bor'by*'s leaders, he agreed to allow individuals to leave the barricades without arrest, as long as they surrendered their weapons. At least sixty weapons were surrendered but, more importantly, Starynkevich had defused an explosive situation by allowing his adversaries to back down while saving face. This cool-headed, common-sense tactic cost Starynkevich his job and he was summarily relieved of his duties on 13 October. However, his successor, Lieutenant-General V. V. Sennitskii, wasted no time in making his zero-tolerance policy towards violence clear. Owners were made *personally* responsible for any shots fired from their buildings and unauthorized gatherings were broken up with buckshot.[97]

During the pogrom wave of 1881, the leadership of Governor-General E. I. Totleben had helped stave off violence in the north-western provinces of the Pale, while in 1905 the Iaroslavl' authorities also stopped a pogrom within an hour of railway workers (apparently gentiles) threatening to strike and vandalize the railroad.[98] Such leadership was rare in 1905, however, especially in Ukraine, where Kharkiv was very much the exception. Co-operation – however temporary – between local officials and socialist-inspired militants in a common defence of order was even rarer. More typically, officials looked the other way (or even vacated their posts) as pogrom mobs began to form. Later, these officials would blame one another for the violence, arguing lamely over who had been responsible. The same pattern can be found elsewhere, and explanations sometimes bordered on the bizarre. Illinois Guardsmen commander Colonel S. O. Tripp sat idly in his East St Louis office as racial violence escalated on the streets outside. Finally, at 3.00 p.m., an underling, acting on his own initiative, called in reinforcements. Tripp would later defend himself before a Congressional committee by noting that 'the President never goes out of his office'.[99]

Conclusion

Jews had been prominent in Kharkiv's revolutionary movement from its inception and in 1905 were highly visible in the Social Democratic movement, by far the city's most important revolutionary organization. The threat of pogroms surfaced periodically during that year, but especially during the tense days of October. During the general strike, a Black Hundred mob began to beat Jews and students. When word that a student had been killed reached the university, barricades went up and violent confrontation seemed imminent. Behind the barricades, however, an authoritative group of socialist and labour leaders, many of them militant *parovozniki*, joined forces to confront the mobs. The militias of the *Komitet bor'by* took control of the streets, ensuring that a pogrom would not envelop the city.

Imperial Russia's 1905 pogroms bear many similarities with ethnic violence elsewhere, and press descriptions of pogroms are at times almost interchangeable with newspaper accounts of ethnic riot in the United States and India, among other countries. In riot-prone cities everywhere, riot specialists stood ready to attack 'enemy' communities, but they could succeed only where local officials and police allowed them to do so. In the charged atmosphere of October 1905, Kharkiv's elected and appointed officials refused to allow a pogrom, joining forces, temporarily, with the radical workers and socialists to maintain order. In this regard, events in Kharkiv in late 1905 differ significantly from those in Odesa, Kyiv and the towns of the Donbass.

On 12 December 1905, artillery fire tore through the factory walls at Gelferikh-Sade, killing twenty-seven, injuring more than a hundred and effectively ending the revolution in Kharkiv.[100] Some of the same Kharkivites who had fought the pogrom mobs died pursuing radical socialist agendas. Even then, bursts of retaliation against pogromists and their kind continued. On 13 December, a 'court' (headed by Artem and fellow Bolshevik agitator Aleksei Korytin), representing the militant *parovozniki*, tried and convicted five members of the Black Hundred, sentencing them to death.[101]

Notes

1 For Kyiv, see *Voskhod* (30 December 1905); and Michael F. Hamm, *Kiev: A Portrait: 1800–1917* (Princeton, 1993), Chapter 8. For Odesa, see Robert Weinberg, *The 1905 Revolution in Odessa: Blood on the Steps* (Bloomington, 1993), p. 164. Shlomo Lambroza, 'The Pogroms of 1903–1906', in John D. Klier and Shlomo Lambroza (eds), *Pogroms: Anti-Jewish Violence in Modern Russian History* (Cambridge, 1992), pp. 226–31, surveys the geography of the pogroms and the various means of estimating the number of victims.

2 S. M. Dubnow, *History of the Jews in Russia and Poland*, Vol. 3 (Philadelphia, 1920), p. 127.

3 John D. Klier, 'Preface', in Klier and Lambroza (eds), *Pogroms*, p. xv.

4 *Kievskoe slovo* (23 October 1905), editorial.

5 Cited in Hans Rogger, 'Conclusion and Overview', in Klier and Lambroza (eds), *Pogroms*, p. 360. In 1943, Marshall was the director of the The National Association for the Advancement of Colored People (NAACP).

6 D. I. Bagalei and D. I. Miller, *Istoriia Khar'kova za 250 let ego sushchestvovaniia s 1655 do 1905g.*, Vol. 2 (Khar'kov, 1912), p. 497. The other fairs were called Troitskaia, Uspenskaia and Pokrovskaia. The Ukrainian Line of fortifications stretched from the Dnepr to the Don river.

7 Naum Freiman, 'Iz istorii evreev Khar'kova', *Istoki*, Vol. 3 (July–December 1998), p. 133.

8 Bagalei and Miller, *Istoriia Khar'kova*, Vol. 2, p. 135. One was a boot-maker, one was a lace-maker and one was an eye doctor.

9 Freiman, *Ocherki iz istorii evreev Khar'kova* (Khar'kov, 1999), pp. 25–6; Bagalei and Miller, *Istoriia Khar'kova*, Vol. 2, p. 136. At this time, Governor Sivers sought to eliminate the practice of allowing Jews to rent an apartment only after procuring the proper permit from the police.

10 Freiman, *Ocherki*, p. 23; Bagalei and Miller, *Istoriia Khar'kova*, Vol. 2, pp. 134–7. For 1913, see *Rossiiskii Gosudarstvennyi Istoricheskii Arkhiv* (hereafter *RGIA*), f. 1288, op. 95, d. 77 (1913), l. 83. In 1913, Kharkiv had about 235,000 residents.

11 Freiman, *Ocherki*, p. 31.

12 Ibid., p. 41.

13 Freiman, 'Iz istorii', pp. 146–7. In the eighth century Judaism was split by a religious schism into the Karaites, who upheld the teaching of the Old Testament only as emanating from divine provenance, and the Rabbanites, who regarded the later interpretations recorded in the *Mishna* and the *Talmud* as equally sacred.

14 *RGIA*, f. 1284, op. 25, d. 77, l. 71. Taxes were based on *dokhodnost'*, the income-producing potential of real estate. Assessment methods differed widely from city to city. Much larger Kyiv, for example, had the same number of tax-payers as Kharkiv (*RGIA*, op. 5, d. 170, l. 130). Rates were often three to five times below bank assessments – sometimes more so – and they were often out-dated. See *Kievskaia mysl'* (5 September 1910). Kharkiv reassessed real estate in 1911, having last done so in 1895. The Ministry of Finance permitted property to be valued at rates 35 to 50 per cent lower than bank assessments. See *Gorodskoe delo*, Vol. 21 (1 November 1911), pp. 1510–11.

15 S. G. Svatikov, 'Evrei v russkom osvoboditel'nem dvizhenii', in Oleg Budnit-skii, *Evrei i russkaia revoliutsiia* (Moscow, 1999), pp. 93–5. For Portugal and the 1850s, see Freiman, 'Iz istorii', pp. 144–9.

16 Svatikov, 'Evrei', pp. 95–102.

17 Freiman, *Ocherki*, pp. 57, 59.

18 *Rabochii klass Rossii ot zarozhdeniia do nachala XX v.* (Moscow, 1989), p. 381.

19 L. Feinberg, 'V riadakh Khar'kovskoi sots.-dem organizatsii (1893–1900gg.)', *Letopis' revoliutsii*, Vol. 3 (May–June 1925), No. 12, p. 133.
20 *Gosudarstvennyi Arkhiv Rossiiskoi Federatsii* (hereafter *GARF*), *f.* 124, 43, *d.* 491 (1905), *ll.* 44–61.
21 *Khronika revoliutsionnogo rabochego dvizheniia na Ukraine (1900–1917)* (Kiev, 1987), p. 66. The strike ended in compromise.
22 *GARF*, *f.* 124, *op.* 11, *d.* 710, *ll.* 75–80.
23 *Tsentral'nyy Derzhavnyy Istorichnyy Arkiv Ukrainy u m. Kyevi* (hereafter *TsDIAU*), *f.* 304, *op.* 2, *d.* 18 (1905), p. 194; *op.* 1, *d.* 63 (1904), *l.* 2. Aron Shapiro and Iosif Mal'kenzon were other Social Democrat activists who were specifically mentioned as self-defence organizers. Apparently, only three Jews were arrested for their efforts at self-defence – allegedly because they were Social Democrats.
24 'Kak podgotovlialsia Kremenchugskii pogrom', *Voskhod* (11 November 1905), p. 30, states that in Kremenchuk and Kharkiv the bribe was not paid in 1905.
25 *TsDIAU*, *f.* 304, *op.* 1, *d.* 45, *l.* 279. Anatoly Sazonov, who had organized the local SR committee, had been arrested on 28 December 1904.
26 *TsDIAU*, *f.* 304, *op.* 1, *d.* 77, *l.* 22.
27 Kh. Fradkin, 'O Khar'kovskom bol'shevistskom komitete', in S. Kramer (ed.), *1905 v Khar'kove* (Khar'kov, 1925), p. 153.
28 *TsDIAU*, *f.* 304, *op.* 1, *d.* 75, *ll.* 150–2.
29 Bushev, 'Oktiabr'skie dni', in Kramer (ed.), *1905 v Khar'kove*, p. 167.
30 Gerald D. Surh, *1905 in St Petersburg: Labor, Society, and Revolution* (Stanford, 1989), pp. 329, 357.
31 Roberta T. Manning, *The Crisis of the Old Order in Russia* (Princeton, 1982), pp. 140–1.
32 V. Kozhemiakin, 'O KhPZ i ob Artem', in Kramer, *1905 v Khar'kove*, p. 143; *TsDIAU*, *f.* 304, *op.* 1, *d.* 50-a, *l.* 72. Founded in 1895, Locomotive had about 2,500 employees in 1905. Later the plant produced bulldozers, farm machinery and other equipment to compensate for fluctuating demand for railway stock. During the First World War, demand for workers rose, and Locomotive employed more than 6,200 men by 1916.
33 One memoirist – L. Basalygo, 'Revoliutsionnoe dvizhenie v Khar'kove v 1905–06gg.', *Letopis' revoliutsii*, Vol. 1 (1924), pp. 122–4 – argues that Bolsheviks led the self-defence units. See also S. Brainin ('Andrei'), 'Oktiabr'–dekabr' 1905 v Khar'kove', *Letopis' revoliutsii*, Vols 5–6 (1925), pp. 122–3; and *TsDIAU*, *f.* 304, *op.* 1, *d.* 77 (1905), *ll.* 215–16.
34 *TsDIAU*, *f.* 838, *op.* 3, *d.* 22, *l.* 1; *f* 304, *op.* 1, *d.* 77, *l.* 217. The Committee of Public Safety also apparently tried to organize a defence militia, but this effort quickly gave way to that of the *Komitet bor'by*.
35 *TsDIAU*, *f.* 304, *op.* 1, *d.* 77 (1905), *ll.* 194, 199–200, 217; *f.* 304, *op.* 1, *d.* 63 (1904), *ll.* 1–3; *f.* 304, *op.* 2, *d.* 18 (1905), *l.* 194; f. 838, *op.* 3, *d.* 20, *l.* 1; see also *Pravo* (20 November 1905), p. 22. Police reports do not indicate the exact composition of the *Komitet bor'by*'s militias.
36 *Iuzhnyi krai* (20 October 1905); *Russkie vedomosti* (27 October 1905). Only about thirty-two of the casualties were injured by the pogrom mobs. One specific attack on Jewish residences at No. 7 Voznesenskaia ploshchad' is mentioned by P. Belokonskii, 'Kogda zh vse eto okonchitsiia', *Russkie vedomosti* (28 October 1905).
37 Paul R. Brass, *Theft of an Idol: Text and Context in the Representation of Collective Violence* (Princeton, 1997), p. 14.
38 R. Scott Appleby, *The Ambivalence of the Sacred* (Lanham, Md., 2000), pp. 69–70, 282.

39 Paul Dumont, 'Jewish Communities in Turkey during the Last Decades of the Nineteenth Century in the Light of the Archives of the Alliance Israèlite Universelle', in Benjamin Braude and Bernard Lewis (eds), *Christians and Jews in the Ottoman Empire*, Vol. 1 (New York, 1982), p. 224. Ottoman officials generally tried to prevent pogroms, sometimes calling on the Orthodox Metropolitan to re-establish peace. Muslim violence against Jews was comparatively rare except in eastern Anatolia, where Kurds had a long tradition of violence against Jews.

40 See the descriptions from various newspapers in Hamm, *Kiev: A Portrait*, p. 197.

41 From a reporter in the *East St Louis Daily Journal* (5 July 1917), cited in Elliott M. Rudwick, *Race Riot at East St Louis, July 2, 1917* (Carbondale, 1964), p. 46.

42 Brass, *Theft of an Idol*, p. 15.

43 *Volyn* (30 April 1905). For Kremenchuk, see *Voskhod* (11 November 1905), p. 36. For reports from Kyiv's newspapers, see Hamm, *Kiev: A Portrait*, pp. 196–7.

44 Constance McLaughlin Green, *The Secret City: A History of Race Relations in the Nation's Capital* (Princeton, 1967), pp. 190–1.

45 Rudwick, *Race Riot*, pp. 71–2. East St Louis, 'the Pittsburgh of the West', had about 85,000 residents. Like Kharkiv, it was a rail centre (twenty-seven rail lines radiated from it). As in Kharkiv, most workers lived in wooden shacks near their place of employment. Eight whites and thirty-nine blacks were killed in the East St Louis pogrom.

46 Ashutosh Varshney, *Ethnic Conflict and Civic Life: Hindus and Muslims in India* (New Haven, 2002), pp. 123–4.

47 Manning, *Crisis*, p. 171.

48 'Opisanie pogroma v Kremenchuge', *Voskhod* (11 November 1905), p. 34.

49 Charters Wynn, *Workers, Strikes and Pogroms: The Donbass–Dnepr Bend in Late Imperial Russia, 1870–1905* (Princeton, 1992), p. 212.

50 GARF, f. 124, op. 43, d. 1424 (report dated 12 October 1905); *Voskhod* (13 October 1905).

51 *Kievskie vesti* (15 January 1908). Interestingly, there is no mention of large crowds turning out to greet the news of the October Manifesto in Kharkiv.

52 Lambroza, 'The Pogroms of 1903–1906', p. 230. The provinces were Chernigov, Poltava, Ekaterinoslav, Kherson, Podolia, Kiev and Bessarabia.

53 Varshney, *Ethnic Conflict*, pp. 6–7.

54 Walker Connor, *Ethnonationalism: The Quest for Understanding* (Princeton, 1994), p. 208.

55 Brass, *Theft of an Idol*, p. 9. Brass studies India's communal riots but he believes that riot-systems enabled ethnic riot in Imperial Russia, America and elsewhere as well.

56 Ibid., p. 16.

57 Weinberg, *The 1905 Revolution in Odessa*, pp. 167, 174.

58 Lambroza, 'The Pogroms of 1903–06', p. 201.

59 Hamm, *Kiev: A Portrait*, pp. 194–5. Vasilev's refinery workers were encouraged to participate in pogroms and did not suffer loss of pay for their absence from work.

60 Manning, *Crisis*, p. 142.

61 Ibid., pp. 150–1.

62 See, for example, the editorials in *Kievskie otkliki*, *Kievskie novosti* and *Kievskoe slovo* for 23 October 1905. These moderate and leftist papers had closed down during the general strike. In my view, local newspapers offer the best available blow-by-blow accounts of the 1905 pogroms.

63 'Sud', *Voskhod* (11 November 1905), p. 3.

64 Weinberg, *The 1905 Revolution in Odessa*, p. 174. I offered similar conclusions elsewhere for Kyiv: see Hamm, *Kiev: A Portrait*, pp. 197–200.

65 Reported in S. A. Stepanov, *Chernaia sotniia v Rossii (1905–1914gg.)* (Moscow, 1992), p. 71.

66 Letters to *Kievskie otkliki* (27 October 1905) and *Kievskoe slovo* (3 November 1905) are particularly revealing about police participation in Kyiv's pogrom. See Hamm, *Kiev: A Portrait*, pp. 197–203.

67 *Kievskie otkliki* (26 October 1905).

68 See, for example, their appeal to Kharkiv's tailors in *TsDIAU, f.* 838, *op.* 1, *d.* 964 (1905).

69 John D. Klier, 'The Pogrom Paradigm in Russian History', in Klier and Lambroza (eds), *Pogroms*, p. 23.

70 'Korrespondentsii i soobshcheniia o pogromakh. Kiev', *Voskhod* (11 November 1905); *Kievskie otkliki* (24 October 1905). Lukianivka prison held a number of political prisoners.

71 Varshney, *Ethnic Conflict*, pp. 293–5.

72 Brass, *Theft of an Idol*, pp. 55–7, 201.

73 Rudwick, *Race Riot*, pp. 32, 79.

74 Weinberg, *The 1905 Revolution in Odessa*, pp. 172–3.

75 See the exchange of letters in *Kievskie otkliki* (3 and 5 November 1905).

76 *Kievlianin* (20 October editorial and 27 October 1905).

77 Varshney, *Ethnic Conflict*, pp. 8–15, 127.

78 Ibid., pp. 126–30. By contrast, in riot-prone Aligarh, social interaction was much less common, especially in the poorer neighbourhoods where the violence occurred. Hindus and Muslims got most of their information from their own communal elders. While Calicut's press investigated and neutralized rumours, Aligarh's press spread misinformation. See also Radha Kumar, 'India's House Divided: Understanding Communal Violence', *Foreign Affairs*, Vol. 81 (July–August 2002), No. 4, p. 174.

79 Varshney, *Ethnic Conflict*, p. 124.

80 Ibid., pp. 287–93.

81 *TsDIAU, f.* 838, *op.* 1, *d.* 960 and 964.

82 *TsDIAU, f.* 304, *op.* 2, *d.* 18 (1905), *l.* 194; *op.* 1, *d.* 110. Poale-Zion literature tried to echo the Social Democrat appeal by emphasizing the potential breadth of a 'worldwide, all-Jewish organization'.

83 *GARF, f.* 124, *op.* 43, *d.* 492 (1905), *l.* 9.

84 *TsDIAU, f.* 304, *op.* 1, *d.* 110, *ll.* 87–9. N. A. Bukhbinder, 'Evreiskoe rabochee dvizhenie v 1905 godu', *Krasnaia letopis'*, Vol. 7 (1923), pp. 7–11, makes no mention of Kharkiv in his survey of Bund activity. However, the Bund grew stronger as the Mensheviks grew weaker after 1905 in Kharkiv. By 1915, only the Bolsheviks had a stronger organization than the Bund, according to A. Baltun, 'Khar'kovskaia organizatsiia RS-DRP Bol'shevikov vo vremia voiny', *Letopis' revoliutsii*, Vol. 5 (1923), p. 14.

85 Laura Engelstein, *Moscow, 1905: Working-Class Organization and Political Conflict* (Stanford, 1982), p. 161.

86 *Istoriia Khar'kovskogo parovozostroitel'nogo zavoda* (Khar'kov, 1955), pp. 153–4. This report is dated 3 October 1905.

87 This letter was noted by *Voskhod* (11 November 1905). The recollections of K. Basalygo, 'Revoliutsionnoe dvizhenie', pp. 124–7 also note the role of workers' militias in maintaining ethnic peace in Kharkiv.

88 Wynn, *Workers, Strikes and Pogroms*, p. 211.

89 Ibid., p. 226. More recently, Gerald Surh has argued that 'Charters Wynn's notion that frustrated workers were the main force behind the Ekaterinoslav pogrom is not borne out by a close examination of its origins and composition.'

See Gerald Surh, 'Ekaterinoslav City in 1905: Workers, Jews, and Violence', *International Labor and Working-Class History*, No. 64 (Fall 2003), pp. 144–52.

90 Wynn, *Workers, Strikes and Pogroms*, pp. 206, 214, 225. The number of self-defence units in the Donbass multiplied greatly in November (p. 235).

91 Kramer, *1905 v Khar'kove*, pp. 81–4.

92 *Russkie vedomosti* (6 December 1905).

93 *Voskhod* (1 September 1905), p. 27. During 1904 and 1905, it purchased 590 books specifically for Jewish readers.

94 *RGIA, f.* 1288, *op.* 95, *d.* 77 (1913), *l.* 82. Of 2,291 eligible voters in 1902, 538 voted. Of 3,097 eligible in 1906, 722 voted. The number of eligible voters declined slightly in 1910, but 35 per cent turned out to vote. Kyiv's turnout was higher – 45 per cent in 1902 and 1906, 59 per cent in 1910 – possibly because Kyiv's Nationalist Club injected Polonophobia and Judaeophobia into the elections. Baltic towns such as Riga had much higher participation rates. Voting data for nineteen representative towns can be found in Michael F. Hamm, 'Khar'kov's Progressive Duma, 1910–1914: A Study in Russian Municipal Reform', *Slavic Review*, Vol. 40 (1981), No. 1, pp. 34–5.

95 Gorod Khar'kov, *Spravochnik po gorodskomu obshchestvennomu upravleniiu* (Khar'kov, 1913). Kharkiv's 1901 duma had thirty-eight merchants, by far the most common occupation among its elected members. In 1906, thirty-five merchants were elected, as were fourteen professors. In 1910, only twenty-three merchants were elected, giving greater weight to the elected cadre of professional people that included nine physicians, ten engineers, ten attorneys and seven professors. See Hamm, 'Khar'kov's Progressive Duma', for the 1910 duma's accomplishments and the progressive municipal movement in general.

96 Pogorelko briefly resigned as mayor during October 1905, probably because city government was barely functioning during the chaos. He led the so-called municipal 'Progressives', who favoured developing revenue-producing utilities and services. At the time of his death in 1912, Kharkiv had amassed the fourth largest municipal budget in Russia (about 6 million roubles), behind only Moscow (48 million), St Petersburg (47 million) and Riga (8 million). See *Gorodskoi vestnik* (Samara) (18 September 1913).

97 *GARF, f.* 124, *op.* 44, *d.* 1784 (1906), *ll.* 16ff. For Sennitskii's proclamation, see *l.* 31a. See also *Istoriia Khar'kovskogo parovozstroitel'nogo zavoda*, pp. 178–9 for Sennitskii's firm stance against the Kharkiv Federated Soviet.

98 For Totleben, see Rogger, 'Conclusion and Overview', p. 316. For Iaroslavl', see 'Administratsiia i pogromy', *Voskhod* (27 October 1905), p. 6. In Odesa, students, workers and Jews organized a Coalition Council that fought the pogrom mobs, but with little success.

99 Rudwick, *Race Riot*, p. 85.

100 See Michael Hamm, 'On the Perimeter of Revolution: Kharkiv's Academic Community, 1905', *Revolutionary Russia*, Vol. 15 (June 2002), No. 1, pp. 54–60 for a discussion of the showdown at Gelferikh-Sade.

101 *TsDIAU, f.* 304, *op.* 1, *d.* 78, *l.* 321.

10 Socialists, liberals and the Union of Unions in Kyiv during the 1905 Revolution

An engineer's perspective

Anthony Heywood

This chapter analyses the emergence, collapse and political significance of the Kyiv branch of the Union of Unions in October 1905. It endorses the general argument that the political obstacles to a liberal–socialist alliance – especially divisions over longer-term aims and tactics – outweighed the shared aim of over-throwing autocracy. But it also argues that, in Kyiv, these two elements of the opposition camp had effectively rejected each other even before the authorities – in an attempt to achieve that very end – published the October Manifesto. For Kyiv's professionals, the Union of Unions was too radical; for the revolutionary left, the Union of Unions was not radical enough.

Kyiv (Kiev) was a prime candidate for serious popular unrest when revolution gripped the Russian Empire during 1905. As the Empire's third city, after St Petersburg and Moscow, it was a major centre of regional governance, industry, commerce, communications, higher education and culture. Its population, numbering nearly 600,000, included large contingents of skilled and unskilled workers, while the existence of its university and recently opened polytechnical institute ensured the presence of several thousand students, whom the regime traditionally viewed as a volatile radical element. The city had a long tradition of radical activism and, by 1905, its political scene included a wide variety of illegal, anti-tsarist organizations, notably the liberal Union of Liberation, the Party of Socialists-Revolutionaries (PSR), Russian Social Democrats (of both Bolshevik and Menshevik persuasions), the Ukrainian Social Democratic Union (the 'Spilka') and the Jewish Bund. Also, large amounts of proscribed subversive literature were able to reach the city, as a consequence of the proximity of the Empire's western border. In short, there seemed good reason for the head of the Kyiv gendarmerie to report in 1902 that the city had become the centre of revolutionary and socialist activity of all factions in the south of the Empire.[1]

Unrest did, indeed, occur in 1905. Although it was sporadic during the spring and summer, it threatened to become overwhelming by the early autumn, as a revolutionary upsurge engulfed the whole country. As happened elsewhere, the university and polytechnical institute (after reopening in September) quickly became locations for numerous large rallies of students and workers. From about 9 October, many local railway workers joined what became an Empire-wide railway strike and, ultimately, a general political strike. After the publication of the tsar's October Manifesto, Kyiv, like many other cities, experienced vicious right-wing violence in the form of an horrific pogrom, which the city authorities did little to stop for three days and in which some 500 people were killed or maimed. Despite martial law, the creation of a local Soviet of Workers' Deputies in late October was followed by a wave of strikes and the appearance of a so-called 'workers' republic' in the Shuliavka district, on the city's western edge. On 18 November, at least 800 officers and men of the Kyiv garrison's Third Sapper Brigade mutinied and paraded through the city before being attacked by troops still loyal to the regime; at least thirty people were killed and total casualties may have exceeded 200. Not until December did the authorities regain control, notably through the repression of the Shuliavka 'republic' and the arrest of most members of the Kyiv Soviet.[2]

A key factor in the autumn's events, both across the Empire and in Kyiv, was the relationship between the liberal camp and the radical left: the possibility of a liberal–radical alliance represented one of the regime's greatest fears and the October Manifesto was specifically intended to allay it. In the historiography, Soviet accounts generally treat the question critically. They tend to argue that liberals were trying to distract the working class from revolution and were ultimately collaborating with the regime against the masses, especially after the manifesto's publication. The Mensheviks and the PSR, for Soviet historians, were petty bourgeois organizations that betrayed workers' interests by preaching co-operation with the liberals, while only the Bolshevik party consistently represented workers' true interests by rejecting the 'timid bourgeois' position. Thus, for instance, it is argued that Kyiv's Mensheviks tried to steer the Soviet into formal co-operation with the liberal-dominated Union of Unions in early November, but failed thanks to resistance by Bolshevik deputies; similarly, the refusal of the city's Menshevik-dominated Social Democratic party committee to prepare for an armed workers' uprising and its failure to liaise with supporters in the army garrison explain why the Social Democratic organization was caught napping by the sappers' mutiny.[3] Western analyses, by contrast, have stressed that the unprecedented degree of liberal–socialist unity was a fundamental reason for the success of the October strike, not least thanks to the efforts of the Union of Unions as an organization dedicated to enhancing liberal–socialist co-operation. However, this unity was undermined by chronic tension over aims and tactics both between and within the two camps, and by the realization that liberals and radicals were competing for the workers' support. Playing on these strains, according to Western historians, the regime managed to regain the political initiative by using the October Manifesto to open a gulf between the two camps.[4]

Such issues are notoriously difficult to analyse because of the inevitable paucity of reliable sources about 'illegal' political activity. Indeed – and, doubtless, partly for this reason – little has been written on the liberal–socialist relationship and the Union of Unions in Kyiv.[5] The purpose of this chapter, then, is to introduce and analyse data from a good, previously unused archival source concerning the relationship between liberal and socialist organizations in Kyiv during 1905, and especially the role of the Union of Unions. The chapter provides more support for the general argument that the political obstacles to a liberal–socialist alliance – especially divisions over longer-term aims and tactics – outweighed the shared sense of purpose in opposition to the tsarist regime. But it argues also that, in Kyiv, the two camps had effectively rejected each other *before* the authorities published the October Manifesto. Furthermore, the chapter contests the prevailing view of the role of the Kyiv Bolsheviks *vis-à-vis* the liberals. It shows that, far from resisting collaboration with liberal-dominated groups, the principal Bolshevik leader, A. G. Shlikhter, may have played the most important role in promoting such collaboration, through the Union of Unions, in October 1905. By contrast, much greater caution was displayed by the coalition committee (formed at about the beginning of October 1905) to co-ordinate the activities of all the revolutionary parties in Kyiv.

The unpublished memoirs of Iurii Vladimirovich Lomonosov (1876–1952) are the principal source of data for this chapter. In 1905, Lomonosov was a young professor of engineering at the Kyiv Polytechnical Institute (KPI). He acted as an intermediary between the city's revolutionaries and the professional unions during the October events and was an underground Social Democratic activist for some 18 months thereafter. He would later hold high office on the tsarist and Soviet railways and would earn an international reputation as a locomotive expert, before going into foreign exile, in 1927, for the rest of his life. His memoirs, which cover the period 1876 to 1930 in some 15,500 (mostly handwritten) pages, were penned in exile and are, essentially, a personal story rather than a political tract: they generally lack the political polemics usual both in Soviet memoir literature and in its anti-Soviet counterpart. Needless to say, this source must be used with caution. Indeed, Lomonosov himself warns that, when writing Volume 3 (which covers the years 1901–07), he lacked documents and could not properly remember many details. Yet, as memoirs go, this source is remarkably good. It contains a vast amount of detailed factual information, which numerous corroborative checks indicate has a high degree of accuracy. Lomonosov's description of his illegal political activity is inevitably difficult to check, but several sources have been found which confirm his involvement and certain points of detail. Provided that discrepancies and errors are noted, there appears to be no reason for treating this source with any more caution than is usual with memoirs. Indeed, there are good reasons for accepting the factual essence of Lomonosov's account.[6]

Shlikhter and Lomonosov

At the beginning of 1905, the situation of Kyiv's Social Democrats was fairly difficult. Some of the problems were common for the movement throughout the Empire. The number of members was small, at about 500, not least because most workers still preferred not to join any political party.[7] Intense police surveillance hindered movement, meetings and agitation. Also, the party had split into Bolshevik and Menshevik factions, the latter being much the larger group in Kyiv. Although the extent of this rift may have been less severe in Kyiv than it was elsewhere, it seems clear that the two factions in the city did function separately by early 1905; indeed, the Bolsheviks formed a separate local branch of *Vpered* at that time. Problems more specific to Kyiv were the lack of a party printing press and competition from a range of leftist organizations, which included not just the PSR but also Ukrainian nationalist groups, Ukrainian and Polish Social Democrats and the Bund.[8]

That said, Kyiv's Bolsheviks had the advantage of an experienced and persistent leader in Aleksandr Grigorevich Shlikhter (1868–1940). Described by Hamm as the 'dominant personality and most notorious symbol of the "heroic days" of Kyiv's labour movement', Shlikhter was the son of a skilled worker from Poltava. He participated in Populist circles during the 1880s, but joined the Social Democratic movement at the end of that decade. After several years in emigration in Switzerland, he returned to Ukraine in 1892, but was arrested the following year for conducting Social Democratic propaganda and was imprisoned for two years before being required to spend five years in internal exile (latterly in Samara). In 1902, Shlikhter moved to Kyiv, where he became a member of the local Social Democratic committee, and in 1903 he helped to organize a general strike. Thereafter, he continued his party work in Kyiv, living legally as an office worker in the headquarters of the South Western Railways until his dismissal in the spring of 1905 for involvement in the All-Russian Union of Railway Workers and Employees. Shlikhter was a founding member of the *Vpered* group in Kyiv, where his close associates included the lawyer V. Vakar (V. Pravdin) and the engineer G. M. Krzhizhanovskii, a fellow veteran of exile in Samara and future chairman of the all-union Gosplan. These men would duly play important roles in Kyiv's October Days in 1905.[9]

The portrayal of Shlikhter as a courageous and uncompromising Leninist is central to Soviet accounts of the 1905 Revolution in Kyiv. Therein, the heroic figure of a principled Bolshevik leader emphasizes the contrast being drawn with the 'class treachery' of the Mensheviks. Shlikhter himself endorsed this image in his various memoir-type publications and was always keen to highlight his later work with Lenin (in the Petersburg area and in Finland) during the winter of 1905–06.[10] But Lomonosov's memoir evidence suggests a more complex picture. He reports that he heard Shlikhter address functions with predominantly liberal audiences in November 1904 and early October 1905. Furthermore, Lomonosov states that on 12 October 1905, at their first meeting, Shlikhter advocated an alliance between the liberal-dominated professional unions and the revolutionary parties through the founding of a local branch of the Union of Unions.

The first occasion on which Lomonosov claims to have heard Shlikhter speak was during the famous 'banquet campaign' of autumn 1904, which was launched by the Union of Liberation to promote the cause of reform and, especially, to push demands for a constitution.[11] Lomonosov reports that he attended the banquet held in Kyiv on 20 November to mark, ostensibly, the fortieth anniversary of the 1864 legal reform. According to the professor, some 300 people gathered at the Hotel Continental. The first speeches were made by men who would later become Constitutional Democrats (Kadets), on the moderate left of the liberal spectrum. After an interval, further speeches included a call for a constituent assembly by 'the Social Democrat Shlikhter' and a call for press freedom by Prince E. N. Trubetskoi, who would figure in the new Kadet party's leadership a year later.[12]

How reliable and significant is this description? It does warrant caution because of discrepancies with other sources – specifically, with the reports of two agents of the *Okhrannoe Otdelenie*, the political police.[13] Two of the differences are minor at worst: one of the agents notes the location as the Literary-Artistic Society, and both reports note some 200 students and workers present in addition to about 360 members of various social organizations.[14] Potentially more significant is the fact that neither police report mentions Shlikhter. However, this is not conclusive. It may be that Lomonosov's memory was at fault, but equally plausible is that Shlikhter was not recognized as a Social Democrat by the police, or that Shlikhter subsumed his contribution among the others made by the onlooking workers and students. In Lomonosov's favour is the fact that the radical onlookers did play a clear role in shaping the Kyiv banquet's resolution, which (according to Terence Emmons) was one of only six in the country to call for a constituent assembly elected by four-tailed suffrage.[15] On balance, one is inclined to believe that Shlikhter did speak, as Lomonosov reports. If accurate, the account reveals for the first time that Shlikhter tried to woo support from liberals during late 1904, and it contradicts the assertion in at least one Soviet source that Shlikhter, unlike the Mensheviks, had no faith in banquets or the liberal bourgeoisie as agents of political change.[16]

The second occasion on which Lomonosov reportedly heard Shlikhter address a mainly liberal audience was in early October 1905. It was connected with the spread of the railway strike from Moscow, where the protest had begun on 6 October, to the railway companies serving Kyiv (including the South Western Railways). Meetings were convened of the local branches of professional unions, such as the All-Russian Union of Engineers and Technicians and the All-Russian Academic Union, to discuss the strike, and, according to Lomonosov, Shlikhter addressed a gathering of the KPI branch of the Academic Union on 9 October. That day, Lomonosov went first to the engineers' meeting, where he found little sympathy for the strike, even though certain members (like Krzhizhanovskii) were involved in it. This attitude, though disappointing for the more radical members, was hardly a surprise for Lomonosov, since he believed that most Kyiv members of the professional unions shared an unspoken preference to battle against autocracy without the help of workers, peasants and soldiers.[17] The KPI meeting also reflected that general caution, but was more supportive of the strike. From the chair, the chemist Professor M. M. Tikhvinskii proposed (and the meeting agreed) that the Kyiv coalition committee of revolutionary parties should be invited to send a representative to speak. The invitation was accepted and Shlikhter was the committee member who appeared. His aim was clearly to get their support and he succeeded in at least obtaining expressions of sympathy with the strikers' general aims. However, the professors were divided over the method. For instance, the KPI's recently elected director, Professor N. P. Chirvinskii, rejected the strike tactic, whereas the engineer N. A. Artem'ev strongly endorsed it. Eventually the meeting agreed to go a certain way beyond mere moral support: it decided to send a telegram to the presidium of an important, liberal-dominated congress on railway pensions, which was then being held in St Petersburg, and to accept Lomonosov's offer to convey strike information surreptitiously to A. M. Arkhangelskii, an acquaintance who was among the more radical congress delegates.[18]

Unfortunately, no alternative source of information about this professorial meeting has been found. Generally the *Okhrannoe Otdelenie* appears to have had little detailed information about the Academic Union's activities in Kyiv and Soviet accounts pay it scant attention. Nevertheless, Lomonosov's description rings true. Since the coalition committee used to meet at the KPI, it is conceivable that a representative could appear quickly. Tikhvinskii's reported role is certainly plausible, for although he was listed by the political police in 1905 as a suspected Socialist Revolutionary, he was actually the most important Bolshevik in the KPI staff: known in the underground as 'Comrade Ellips', he was using his chemical expertise to assist the Central Committee in bomb-making. Other sources confirm the political views attributed to Chirvinskii and Artem'ev. Finally, Arkhangelskii had studied with Lomonosov in St Petersburg in the 1890s; the two had holidayed together on a couple of occasions and had met as recently as early August. There seems no reason, therefore, to doubt Lomonosov's assertion that the two men agreed a simple personal code at that time.[19]

If accepted, Lomonosov's account of the union meetings suggests, first, that in early October the political moods of the engineers' and professors' unions in Kyiv differed markedly from the stances of their colleagues in St Petersburg. The engineers' apparent lack of sympathy for the strike contrasts with the militancy of their union at the national level during 1905: the central organization joined with the railway workers' union at the end of

April to try to organize a general political strike and it also played an important role in organizing the October general strike. Meanwhile, the KPI professors seem somewhat bolder than the Academic Union at the centre, which was always amongst the most moderate unions there and, indeed, was effectively the first to withdraw from the umbrella organization of the professional unions, the Union of Unions, as the latter became more radical during the summer.[20] Second, the description implies that Shlikhter had little chance of winning much liberal support for the strike with his own rhetoric. As in the capital, perhaps the key reason for the failure of the professional unions to cultivate worker support in Kyiv was not simply a lack of organizational support and resources but, primarily, a lack of desire.[21]

It was the railway strike that finally brought Lomonosov into direct contact with Shlikhter a few days later on 12 October 1905. The professor was taking a close interest in the protest for several reasons. He was radically minded, he had worked on the railways from 1897 to 1901 (his academic specialism being railway engineering and operations), he was a consultant to the South Eastern Railway Company and he was still formally registered as an employee of the Ministry of Ways of Communication (thanks to his education as an engineer of ways of communication). He became involved in the strike following the arrest of several engineers of the South Western Railways, including A. P. Ruzskii (brother of the KPI professor D. P. Ruzskii). On 12 October Professor Ruzskii and Krzhizhanovskii invited Lomonosov to participate in a Union of Engineers' protest delegation to the head of the railway. This *démarche* was apparently successful, whereupon Lomonosov and the local chair of the Union of Engineers were taken – possibly by Krzhizhanovskii – to address a meeting at the university that was being chaired by Shlikhter.[22]

What, then, were Lomonosov's politics?[23] His memoirs indicate that he saw himself as not simply an *intelligent* but also as 'a non-party Marxist'.[24] He had been brought up in a liberal-minded, minor gentry family in the countryside of Smolensk province, but had moved towards the right during his schooling at the prestigious First Moscow Cadet Corps, a bastion of monarchism. In 1891, however, he had witnessed a fellow cadet being run over and killed by the tsar's carriage and he appears to have regarded this event as an indication that the tsar and his regime were at war with society. His politics began to move leftwards and by 1900 he had reached a position that he described as 'Marxism'.

Essentially, this journey was intellectual and was not based on contact with workers. The primary influence was apparently G. D. Dubelir, a fellow student and close friend at the elite Institute of Ways of Communication in St Petersburg. Lomonosov had contact with railway navvies during summer work-placements in 1895 and 1896, but appears not to have discussed politics with them. His encounters with industrial workers at this time were limited to conversations during a short placement at the Nevskii shipyard in the capital in 1897, supervisory work on locomotive testing with workers of the Kharkiv locomotive building factory in 1898, and more supervisory work in 1900 with employees of the Poltava railway workshops. These contacts did include some frank political conversations at Nevskii and Poltava, but their results he regarded as disappointing. Of the Nevskii workers he wrote:

> The horizon of my interlocutors did not extend beyond the factory or even the workshop. The interests of the working class as a whole were completely foreign to them. But they had heard something of the fact that such interests exist. It was very difficult for me to make them understand that freedom of speech and assembly and also a parliament were necessary for workers too, and that they would not obtain their rights without them.[25]

Similarly, despite the presence of genuine revolutionary agitators, most of the Poltava workers seemed to respect the works manager, to be uninterested in politics and to be concerned only about wage rates and a co-operative; they cursed the police and landowners, but still expected truth and justice from the tsar.[26]

These discussions evidently helped to move Lomonosov to a somewhat idiosyncratic and revisionist understanding of the term 'Marxism'. Essentially, he saw it as a materialist philosophy, which he counterpoised to religion. He identified with its advocacy of social justice, of ending the material poverty of the masses and of reorganizing the economy on a scientific basis. He accepted its fundamental analysis of class war and revolution and also the necessity of war against the regime for control of the state. But at the same time he strongly supported the liberal emphasis on freedom of conscience, freedom of the press and the parliamentary struggle. The crucial issue, in Lomonosov's view, was timing. He wanted an early improvement in the material conditions of the masses, yet he saw no sign of mass political consciousness among industrial workers. He reportedly concluded that world revolution was unlikely for 500 years and that, by focusing on revolution, the radical left was condemning the masses to long-term poverty; better, he thought, to accept a constitutional monarchy now – as a way to improve the conditions of the masses sooner rather than later.[27] In these circumstances, he further concluded that he should adopt 'a compromise formula' *vis-à-vis* the question of political activism:

> To struggle with autocracy is the duty of every honest person. But I never had any intention of being a professional revolutionary. I set myself a different task: to become an educated railwayman. For this I needed to study, not march in demonstrations. But if a real revolution began, I would have to drop everything and if necessary lay down my life.[28]

In many respects, then, one could argue that Lomonosov was intellectually located in the 'interstitial left', between the positions of the future Kadets and the Social Democrats.[29] Indeed, he comments that he regarded himself, during the spring of 1905, as vacillating between these two party positions.[30] That said, Lomonosov makes no reference to either of the two groups that would occupy that political space in 1906: the *Bez zaglaviia* group and the Popular Socialist Party. Moreover, other evidence indicates that he disagreed fundamentally with the *Bez zaglaviia* Marxists' rejection of 'Jacobin tactics', on the one hand, and with the Populist tradition of the Popular Socialist Party, on the other.[31]

How Lomonosov's contemporaries assessed his politics is a separate matter. Naturally, he discussed such issues only with a very few trusted friends, leaving others to form their own opinions of him. These varied widely prior to 1905. Among students, he seems quickly to have been defined as a rightist – to the extent that one student approached him for advice about whether to join the *Okhrannoe Otdelenie*. Lomonosov explained this reputation by stating that, although he voted with 'radical' colleagues on political matters in the KPI Council, he sided with the so-called 'rightist' professors on academic matters such as discipline – a stance that would hardly endear him to agitated students. Among colleagues, he was probably seen as a dark horse. Despite the fact that his main friendships were with three 'radicals' (Tikhvinskii, Artem'ev and A. A. Radtsig), and despite his claims about voting in Council, he was firmly rebuffed when he tried to contact the revolutionary movement via Tikhvinskii's partner, V. A. Solomon, in 1903, after the horrific Kishinev pogrom. Apparently there were concerns that he might be an agent of the political police.[32] The *Okhrannoe Otdelenie*, for its part, suspected hostile inclinations: a report of February 1904 noted that a KPI employee had been sacked as 'a gendarme spy' on Lomonosov's insistence and advice.[33]

During 1905, Lomonosov's public conduct indicated that his political position was at least reformist, and he managed to gain sufficient trust for Solomon to offer him a revolutionary's role in the autumn. Chancing to be in St Petersburg in early January, Lomonosov signed the famous declaration of professors about reforming higher education.[34] A few days later, when the Kyiv chief of police went to the KPI with some 200 Cossacks and an infantry contingent, Lomonosov was reportedly the source of the idea to repel them with fire hoses – a spectacular event which drenched the police chief and persuaded the local authorities to close the institute.[35] By spring 1905, Lomonosov was active in the engineers' and professors' unions in Kyiv and he made a report about the Kyiv situation to the Academic Union in St Petersburg in early April.[36] And when he complained to Solomon (in late September) of frustration at not being involved in helping the revolution, she invited him (on 1 October) to help collect money for political prisoners.[37] When Shlikhter and Lomonosov were introduced on 12 October, Shlikhter duly presented him to the meeting as a representative of 'the honest intelligentsia'.[38]

Although there is no detailed corroboration of this political picture in other contemporary sources, its essential veracity is suggested by some circumstantial evidence. First, several authoritative Soviet sources confirm that Lomonosov did participate in underground activities of the Social Democratic Party in 1905 and 1906. For example, Shlikhter notes that Lomonosov organized his evacuation from Kyiv after the October pogrom and Krzhizhanovskii names Lomonosov as an associate of the *Vpered* activists.[39] Second, the city authorities concluded that he was politically unreliable: in 1906, the city governor recommended him for dismissal, as one of the more politically active KPI professors; and, in 1907, the *Okhrannoe Otdelenie* reported that during 1905 Lomonosov had 'covered up criminal activity by students' and had commanded a detachment of the Kyiv organization for Jewish self-defence.[40] At the very least, therefore, one can state that Lomonosov was certainly active in the radical left by the end of 1905.

The Union of Unions

At the time, Lomonosov felt, according to his memoirs, that he was burning his boats by attending the university gathering on 12 October so conspicuously.[41] In fact, his appearance evidently went unnoticed by the police. Assuming that he correctly remembered the date and place, one suspects that this omission occurred because he seemed (or was assumed simply to be) a liberal.[42] Whatever the reason, the result was that events of the following evening proved to be far more important for Lomonosov's involvement with revolutionary politics. A Menshevik engineer named E. M. Ianovskii invited him to a secret rendezvous with Shlikhter and at least two other 'professional' revolutionaries, including one member of the revolutionary coalition committee. The initiative in the conversation was taken by Shlikhter, who suggested that if the 'intelligentsia unions' also wanted to battle with autocracy they should form a Union of Unions, like the one in St Petersburg. The new union should then make contact with the coalition committee, which would be able to allocate it two or three seats on the committee.[43]

This development was potentially very dangerous for the Kyiv authorities. One of the regime's greatest fears was a revolutionary alliance of the liberal intelligentsia with the workers' and peasants' movements. Precisely this objective lay behind the creation of the Union of Unions in St Petersburg in spring 1905, as a 'roof organization' for the new liberal-dominated professional unions: to quote its first chair, P. N. Miliukov, the Union of Unions would serve as the 'connecting link' between liberals and revolutionaries. Initially its strategy was the fusion of 'liberal tactics with the threat of revolution' but, as the summer progressed without real concessions from the regime, the Union of Unions became much more radical, to the point of losing the support of moderate liberal constitutionalists (and, indeed, of Miliukov himself). By the early autumn, the Union was taking over the leadership of the left-liberal intelligentsia in the capital and was set to play an important role in the impending general strike.[44] If a local branch appeared in Kyiv and aligned itself with the radical left, the authorities would be confronted by a very potent alliance.

There is no doubt that the Kyiv authorities were already very concerned about this possibility during the summer. Among papers seized during a police search of Tikhvinskii's apartment on the night of 22–23 June was one entitled 'Manifesto Note concerning a Union of Unions'. This was a general document, not specific to Kyiv, which defined the union's main aim as 'the co-ordination of its activities with the activities of the democratic parties'. The extent of police concern in Kyiv, though, is shown by the consequent resolution of the assistant chief of police, dated 13 August. He accused Tikhvinskii of being an activist of 'the secret anti-government organization called the Union of Unions' and of having drafted the manifesto document. Though the professor was already under suspicion, as part of an investigation into the 'Kyiv Fighting Group' of the PSR, a separate investigation into his political reliability was now held to be urgently needed, as a matter of state security.[45]

In the absence of any other sources (and assuming that Lomonosov's account is reliable), one can suggest several possible motives for Shlikhter's proposal. A local branch of the Union of Unions could potentially have helped the radical parties not just with general support but also with professional expertise, such as medical aid. It is possible, too, that the proposal was intended to test Lomonosov's revolutionary commitment and resolve; whether Shlikhter saw the professor as anything more than just a possible left-liberal ally at this juncture seems unlikely. Furthermore, police investigations of Tikhvinskii – a significant member of the Bolshevik Central Committee's military–technical group – might be deflected, if someone like Lomonosov took the leading role in organizing the Union of Unions locally.

For his part, Lomonosov accepted Shlikhter's invitation with gusto and successfully stimulated sufficient interest for an inaugural meeting. Colleagues at the KPI were his first, natural port of call. Surprisingly, he reports that Tikhvinskii was sceptical; no reason is given. But others were enthusiastic, including Artem'ev and a former chair of the KPI group of the Academic Union, G.A. Arnol'd. One of the most active KPI liberals, Professor S. A. Ivanov, helped, in his capacity as chair of the Kyiv Literary-Artistic Society, by arranging for the meeting to be held under the society's auspices. Tikhvinskii's partner, Solomon, began mobilizing colleagues in the medics' union. Lawyers were approached by Vakar and an SR named Slutskii. As for a delegation from the Union of Engineers, Lomonsov tried unsuccessfully to contact Krzhizhanovskii.[46] Surprisingly, the professor makes no reference to other important professional unions, such as the railway workers' union and the printers' union; whether approaches were made to them remains unclear.

Held on 15 October 1905, the inaugural meeting of the Kyiv Union of Unions was clearly a success in its organizer's terms. The audience was respectably large, with about sixty people present; outside, monitoring the proceedings for the coalition committee, was an SD party member known to Lomonosov as 'Mikhail'. As the first speaker, Lomonosov stressed the obligations of the intelligentsia towards the people and also spoke cautiously about the coalition committee. The outcome, after minimal discussion, was a resolution that supported the creation of a local Union of Unions organization for participation in the battle against the autocracy. A three-man organizational committee was created, which Lomonosov describes as a 'presidium'; its members were confirmed as the socialist lawyer M. B. Ratner, a university professor named V. A. Zheleznov and Lomonosov (with three named deputies, including Artem'ev, in case of arrests).[47]

The course of the Presidium's first meeting, which was convened immediately as a continuation of the inaugural meeting, emphasizes the point that the project's focus was co-operation with the left. The first issue to be discussed was the allocation of the key portfolios, including Lomonosov's appointment as secretary. Thereafter, organizational matters were put to one side for the time being, so that the meeting could concentrate on the question of relations with the coalition committee. There was apparently little dispute about whether the Presidium should contact the committee; the contentious issue was whether this mandate should have conditions attached. Eventually, only one was specified: the Presidium was to ensure that its representatives joined the committee on the same terms as its existing members. It was also decided that he Union's committee representatives were to be elected and that the Presidium members were to serve as acting representatives pending those elections.[48]

For all this sympathy and harmony, the implementation of these decisions was problematic from the outset. Three difficulties arose during the next 24 hours that, together, threatened to derail the project. One was completely outside the union's control – the arrest of Ratner that night – but the other two derived from mutual distrust between liberals and radicals. On the liberal side, Zheleznov opposed Lomonosov's proposal to mobilize Artem'ev and meet the coalition committee representatives; he instead wanted there first to be a wider discussion of Ratner's arrest. Eventually Zheleznov gave way and Artem'ev was invited to the new Presidium's next session. But at this meeting, held during the evening of 16 October, Zheleznov again refused to attend the first formal exploratory meeting with coalition committee representatives, which was scheduled for that night. Hence, only Artem'ev and Lomonosov went. Now, however, the radical side's distrust for the moderates manifested itself. Although Shlikhter had personally reassured Lomonosov that afternoon that the Union of Unions could have two places on the coalition committee, the two committee representatives indicated that seats would not be allocated to such an 'alien element'. All that was agreed was that the Union of Unions would issue a proclamation about its existence and its solidarity with the coalition committee; the printing of this document would be done by one of the revolutionaries' presses.[49]

Events during the next day, 17 October, showed that these tensions were insuperable. The putative Union of Unions organization split over the fundamental question of protest tactics. Zheleznov, literally and metaphorically, distanced himself from the union: Lomonosov was told that Zheleznov had 'gone away to his dacha' and that the proclamation text, drafted by Lomonosov, which talked of a revolutionary battle with autocracy, was too radical for other Union members. According to Lomonosov's memoirs, five or six colleagues whom he consulted at the KPI demanded that the emphasis should be on peaceful protest and said that Lomonosov had abused their trust. Nonetheless Lomonosov and Artem'ev decided, as the only available Presidium members, to send the text for printing. However, this text did not impress the coalition committee, which confirmed its refusal to admit representatives from the Union of Unions. 'Mikhail' commented to Lomonosov that the proclamation was really the main value of the Union of Unions for the committee. Appalled at this 'treachery' (*verolomstvo*), Lomonosov retrieved the text from the underground printer shortly after midnight and secured a promise that the printing would not be done.[50] The Shlikhter–Lomonosov project was defunct.

As yet, no other sources about this episode have been located.[51] But, again, the circumstantial evidence suggests the veracity of Lomonosov's account. First, to repeat the point made above, the mass of data confirming hundreds of other episodes which Lomonosov relates makes it overwhelmingly likely that some such events did occur. Second, the existence of a Kyiv branch of the Union of Unions is certain because several sources describe how two of its representatives addressed the Kyiv Soviet on 6 November. Third, the argument that the branch was formed just before 18 October – a point crucial for any assessment of its broader political significance – is given credence by the fact that Shlikhter was in hiding from 18 October until his evacuation from Kyiv on 1–2 November, and by the fact that Lomonosov accounts in reasonable detail for his time throughout the autumn period.[52]

Assuming, then, that this episode is related accurately, one can suggest that the Shlikhter–Lomonosov project failed for several underlying reasons. One was the role played by Shlikhter as initiator. It seems likely that Shlikhter regarded an alliance with liberal unions as a question of tactical convenience, in precisely the same way that he later described Bolshevik participation in the coalition committee as a 'tactical step'.[53] In taking this approach, Shlikhter, it could be argued, was in tune with the mood of most workers, who were basically uninterested in ideological arguments between the revolutionary parties.[54] But clearly he raised unrealistic expectations by assuring and reassuring Lomonosov about representation on the coalition committee. In fact, contrary to appearances, Shlikhter could not speak for the committee. Moreover, the committee as a whole was more concerned to avoid admitting an 'alien element', just as Bolshevik delegates would demand in the Soviet on 6 November. In other words, even before the

October Manifesto was published in Kyiv, on the organized left the ideology of class rivalry prevailed over considerations of the tactical advantages of inter-class co-operation, despite the fundamental common ground of opposition to the autocracy.

With regard to the liberal camp, several issues were problematic. The episode suggests that there was not much support in Kyiv for the Union of Unions, especially as a radical entity. Not only was there no initiative to create a local branch until October, but the initial stimulus had to come from outside – indeed, it had to come from the most unlikely source: Shlikhter. Moreover, it is evident that those involved from the professional unions by no means all agreed with the radical position being taken by the Union of Unions in St Petersburg. The key issue here was probably that of violence. Although at a national level the Union of Unions supported 'the most radical measures' to topple the regime, most of Kyiv's professional union activists were clearly opposed to this. Quite what they were thinking, then, when they resolved to seek membership of the radical coalition committee on 16 October is uncertain; perhaps they hoped to link with the Mensheviks, as a moderating influence. Whatever the reason, one can see now that their aspirations did not match the coalition committee's emphasis on revolutionary struggle. A secondary issue may have been the professional union members' general preference (mentioned on p. 183) not to enlist the help of workers, peasants and soldiers in the struggle against autocracy.

Some active interest and support for liberal–radical collaboration via the Union of Unions did remain in Kyiv after the October Manifesto was published there on 18 October. A local branch of the Union continued to exist, to judge by the fact that two engineers representing the Union of Unions addressed the Kyiv Soviet, on 6 November, with a call for co-operation. And that call did find support among a significant minority of the Soviet delegates.[55] Two weeks later, on 20 November, the question of organizing a Union of Unions branch in Kyiv was the first item on the agenda of a meeting of the KPI Academic Union group.[56] But such initiatives were unlikely to succeed because of dramatic changes in the local political landscape within only a few days of 18 October. The October Manifesto could only increase – as the regime intended – the prevailing unease among Kyiv's liberals about co-operation with radicals. Indeed, Lomonosov describes how his fund-raising mission among doctors, lawyers and other professionals in early October was very successful, whereas on 24 October most of the same people declined to give money.[57] The nascent Union of Unions branch lost its most energetic activist, for Lomonosov played no further part after 17 October: rather, he volunteered for involvement in the Social Democratic underground and organized Shlikhter's escape from Kyiv on 1–2 November.[58] Moreover, Shlikhter's hurried departure deprived the radical camp not just of its most prominent leader but also of its main proponent of co-operation with the liberals; the way was then open for an ideologically uncompromising stance to prevail, as would be evident when the Soviet heeded the Bolshevik voices of hostility towards the Union of Unions.

Conclusions

This affair confirms that in Kyiv, as in many other major cities of the Russian Empire in 1905, the obstacles to a liberal–radical alliance were far more significant than any shared sense of purpose. Shlikhter evidently tried to focus minds on the battle against autocracy – the issue on which the two camps had most in common. But there was no real chance of broad agreement between liberal and radical groups and parties because majorities in both camps continued to dwell on questions of longer-term aims and of tactics, where disagreement and antipathy prevailed. Moreover, there was, if anything, less support among Kyiv's professionals for the pro-strike stance being taken nationally by the Union of Unions in October 1905 than was the case in the capital. And so, in the event, the Kyiv authorities did not need the October Manifesto to drive a wedge between the two opposition camps. Rather, the liberals and radicals of Kyiv had rejected each other beforehand.

The episode also helps to clarify the role of the Bolshevik group in Kyiv during the autumn. Ironically, given Lenin's enduring dislike of such class compromise, the most important advocate of a liberal–radical alliance here was the local Bolshevik leader, Shlikhter. Moreover, the main reason why the radical camp backed away from the idea was the greater degree of intransigence among the other, non-Bolshevik leftist parties about dealings with 'alien' class elements. In short, this affair undermines the notion propagated in Soviet sources that the Bolsheviks formed a principled and decisive bulwark against an alleged Menshevik sell-out mentality in Kyiv during 1905. The well-documented exchanges in the Soviet on 6 November, when Bolshevik delegates opposed Mensheviks over co-operation with the Union of Unions, have obscured a more nuanced picture. Not only was the relationship between Bolsheviks and Mensheviks somewhat closer than has been suggested previously, but the Bolshevik group's leader played a much more flexible and tactically adventurous role – unless, of course, we simply interpret the new evidence in polemical Soviet fashion as showing that Shlikhter was a Menshevik.

Acknowledgements

For assistance and encouragement in the preparation of this chapter, I am grateful to M. Baker, G. M. Browning, E. P. Consey, R. D. Davies, B. P. Kurinnyi, M. F. Hamm, O. I. Mikhailova, A. Prusin, O. M. Redko, A. A. Strutinsky, G. D. Surh, G. Tan and R. Thurston. I am grateful also to the Royal Society for funding my research in Kyiv.

Notes

1 On the city's revolutionary tradition see, for example, Michael F. Hamm, *Kiev: A Portrait, 1800–1917* (Princeton, 1993), pp. 173–5. The police chief is quoted in V. A. Golobutskii *et al.* (eds), *Istoriia Kieva v dvukh tomakh*, Vol. 1 (Kiev, 1963), pp. 496–7.

2 On these events see, for instance, F. E. Los *et al.* (eds), *Revoliutsiia 1905–1907gg. na Ukraine: Sbornik dokumentov i materialov v dvukh tomakh, tom 2, chast 1: Revoliutsionnaia bor'ba na Ukraine v period pervoi russkoi revoliutsii (1905g.)* (Kiev, 1955), pp. 456–62; Golobutskii *et al.* (eds), *Istoriia Kieva*, pp. 511–33; V. Manilov, *Kievskii Sovet rabochikh deputatov v 1905g.* (Kiev, 1926); V. Manilov, 'Kievskaia voennaia organizatsiia RSDRP i vosstanie saper v noiabre 1905 goda', *Letopis revoliutsii* (1925), No. 5–6, pp. 212–13, 218; I. N. Bondarenko, *Bolsheviki Kieva v pervoi russkoi revoliutsii (1905–1907gg.)* (Kiev, 1960), pp. 228–9; and Hamm, *Kiev: A Portrait*, pp. 173–219.

3 Examples are: T. Stepanenko, 'Kievskaia sotsial-demokraticheskaia organizatsiia nakanune pervoi russkoi revoliutsii 1905–1907 gg.', in P. N. Troitskii (ed.), *Kievskii Politekhnicheskii Institut: Uchenye zapiski: Trudy kafedry Marksizma–Leninizma* (Kiev, 1956), p. 109; Bondarenko, *Bolsheviki Kieva*, pp. 192, 194–7, 215–16, 228–9; T. V. Glavak *et al.* (eds), *Ocherki istorii kievskoi gorodskoi i oblastnoi partiinykh organizatsii* (Kiev, 1981), pp. 61–2, 67.

4 For instance, Shmuel Galai, *The Liberation Movement in Russia, 1900–1905* (Cambridge, 1973), pp. 244–5, 254–9; Gerald D. Surh, *1905 in St Petersburg: Labor, Society and Revolution* (Stanford, 1989), pp. 51–2, 257, 325, 381; Abraham Ascher, *The Revolution of 1905: Russia in Disarray* (Stanford, 1988), pp. 35, 61, 236–7, 285–6, 343; and Jonathan E. Sanders, 'The Union of Unions: Economic, Political, and Human Rights Organizations in the 1905 Russian Revolution' (Columbia University Ph.D. thesis, 1985), *passim*.

5 It is noteworthy that Sanders has very little on the Union of Unions in the provinces in general and nothing at all about it in Kyiv: see Sanders, 'Union of Unions', pp. 915, 925, 1208–9. Also, the surviving files of the Union's central organization contain no correspondence with the Kyiv branch: see especially *Gosudarstvennyi Arkhiv Rossiiskoi Federatsii (GARF)*, f. 518, *op.* 1, *dd.* 16, 18.

6 University of Leeds, Leeds Russian Archive, G. V. Lomonossoff Collection, MSS 716.2.1.1–716.2.1.10: Iu. V. Lomonosov, 'Vospominaniia', Vols 1–10. (The main source for the present chapter is Vol. 3.) I have developed this chapter from work in progress on the biography of engineer Iurii Vladimirovich Lomonosov. The best available account of Lomonosov's life is Hugh A. Aplin, 'Iurii Vladimirovich Lomonosov (1876–1952)', in his *Catalogue of the G. V. Lomonossoff, R. N. Lomonossoff and George Lomonossoff Collections* (Leeds, 1988), pp. vii–xx. For a more involved assessment of these memoirs as an historical source and for a discussion of Lomonosov's politics to 1917, see A. J. Heywood, 'Liberalism, Socialism and "Bourgeois Specialists": the Political Identity of Iu. V. Lomonosov to 1917', in *Revolutionary Russia*, Vol. 17 (2004), No. 1, pp. 1–30.

7 Ascher, *The Revolution of 1905*, p. 184; Hamm, *Kiev: A Portrait*, pp. 179, 184. Estimates given by Ascher for SD party membership and 'organized workers' in other cities include: St Petersburg (1,200 Mensheviks and several hundred Bolsheviks); Ivanovo-Voznesensk (600 Bolsheviks); Kharkov (300); Ekaterinoslav (1,000).

8 See, for instance, Stepanenko, 'Kievskaia sotsial-demokraticheskaia organizatsiia', p. 109; M. Maiorov, *Bolsheviki i revoliutsiia 1905g. na Ukraine* (Tashkent, 1934), p. 67; Hamm, *Kiev: A Portrait*, pp. 178–80.

9 Hamm, *Kiev: A Portrait*, p. 178; A. T. Lane (ed.), *Biographical Dictionary of European Labour Leaders*, Vol. 2 (Westport, Conn., 1995), pp. 888–9; O. S. Rovner

and R. Ia. Korolik, *Oleksandr Grigorovich Shlikhter, 1868–1940: Bibliografichnyi pokazhchik* (Kyiv, 1958), pp. 6–11; D. F. Virnyk, *Aleksandr Grigorevich Shlikhter* (Kiev, 1979), pp. 7–9, 26; H. Reichman, *Railwaymen and Revolution: Russia, 1905* (Berkeley, 1987), p. 176. Some police sources describe Shlikhter as 'petty bourgeois' (*meshchanin*), though this may be due to his occupation as an office manager. See *Tsentralnyi Derzhavnyi Istorichnyi Arkhiv Ukrainy* (*TsDIAU*), *f.* 442, *op.* 855, *spr.* 342, *fol.* 5 and verso: Head of Kyiv Gendarmerie to Manager of Kyiv Governor-General's Chancellery (7 November 1905); and 'Oktiabrskie sobytiia 1905 goda v Kieve v izobrazhenii okhrannogo otdeleniia', *Letopis revoliutsii* (1925), No. 2, p. 114.

10 See, in particular, A. Shlikhter, *Ilich, kakim ia ego znal: Koe-chto iz vstrech i vospominanii* (Moscow, 1970).

11 On the banquet campaign, see Terence Emmons, 'Russia's Banquet Campaign', *California Slavic Studies*, Vol. 10 (1977), pp. 45–86.

12 Lomonosov, 'Vospominaniia', Vol. 3, pp. 964–5.

13 *TsDIAU, f.* 275, *op.* 1, *spr.* 552, *fol.* 12 and verso: Report about a banquet on 20 November 1904; also *fos.* 43–7: [Report about banquet of 20 November 1904], by Spiridovich.

14 Workers, students and Social Democratic 'professionals' were present at banquets in several cities: Emmons, 'Russia's Banquet Campaign', pp. 58–63.

15 Ibid., p. 61. The demand for a 'four-tailed Constituent Assembly' – that is, one elected by universal, direct, equal and secret ballot – was a Social Democratic slogan from the second party congress of 1903. See ibid., pp. 53, 59.

16 See S. Kokoshko, *Bilshovyky u Kyievi naperedodni i za revoliutsii 1905–1907rr.* (Kharkiv and Kyiv, 1930), pp. 57–8.

17 Lomonosov, 'Vospominaniia', Vol. 3, pp. 997–8.

18 Ibid., pp. 997–8, 1210–22. According to Lomonosov, the coalition committee held its meetings in the KPI Physics Auditorium; a brief description is given in V. Pravdin, 'Epokha "neslykhannoi smuty" na Kievshchine (Nabroski)', *Letopis revoliutsii* (1925), No. 2, pp. 100–4. On the cautious stance of the pension congress and Arkhangelskii's leading role, see Reichman, *Railwaymen and Revolution*, pp. 186–223.

19 On the professors see, for example, *TsDIAU, f.* 275, *op.* 1, *spr.* 152, *fol.* 17: 'Information' [about M. M. Tikhvinskii], [1905]; *f.* 275, *op.* 1, *spr.* 1250, *fol.* 75a: 'Kyiv Polytechnical Institute' [political views of staff], [circa March 1908?]; S. M. Pozner (comp.), *1905: Boevaia gruppa pri TsK RSDRP(b) (1905–1907gg.): Stati i vospominaniia* (Moscow and Leningrad, 1927), pp. 44, 46, 48–50, 52, 54, 151–3; *TsDIAU, f.* 274, *op.* 1, *spr.* 888, *fol.* 34: 'Kyiv Polytechnical Institute' (16 February 1904); Z. Kushch and M. Glovatskii, 'Kievskii Politekhnicheskii Institut nakanune i v period pervoi russkoi revoliutsii', in Troitskii, *Kievskii Politekhnicheskii Institut*, pp. 135, 138; *TsDIAU, f.* 275, *op.* 1, *spr.* 734, *fos.* 108–10: [Report of popular meeting at the KPI on 5 October 1905] (8 Oct. 1905); and *Derzhavnyi Arkhiv m. Kyieva* (*DAK*), *f.* 18, *op.* 2, *spr.* 8, *fol.* 112 and verso: 'Attestat [N. A. Artem'eva]'. Lomonosov's comments about Arkhangelskii are in 'Vospominaniia', Vol. 3, pp. 1123, 1126–7, 1215–16.

20 Galai, *Liberation Movement*, pp. 234, 248; Ascher, *The Revolution of 1905*, p. 143; Sanders, 'Union of Unions', pp. 970–89.

21 Lomonosov, 'Vospominaniia', Vol. 3, pp. 997–8; Surh, *1905 in St Petersburg*, pp. 243–9, 257–8, 411–12.

22 Lomonosov, 'Vospominaniia', Vol. 3, pp. 1217–22. For confirmation that the Okhrana regarded A. P. Ruzskii as a revolutionary see 'Oktiabrskie sobytiia 1905 goda v Kieve', p. 114. The same source (on p. 115) also describes the meeting at the university.

23 For a fuller discussion of Lomonosov's politics see Heywood, 'Liberalism'.

24 This phrase is at Lomonosov, 'Vospominaniia', Vol. 3, p. 1279.

25 Ibid., Vol. 2, pp. 222–3.

26 Ibid., Vol. 2, pp. 615–17. He attributed the workers' frankness to his impending departure to an academic post and to the fact that he spent long periods with them away from the works while testing locomotives: ibid., p. 616.

27 For a fuller discussion of this issue see Heywood, 'Liberalism'. Lomonosov's desire for mass prosperity was partly a moral judgement, but it arose also from an awareness that, as a fairly affluent professional, he might himself become a target for worker or peasant retribution.

28 Lomonosov, 'Vospominaniia', Vol. 2, p. 199.

29 On this term see Terence Emmons, *The Formation of Political Parties and the First National Elections in Russia* (Cambridge, Mass., 1983), p. 78.

30 Lomonosov, 'Vospominaniia', Vol. 3, p. 997.

31 On these two groups see Emmons, *Formation of Political Parties*, pp. 78–88.

32 See, for instance, Lomonosov, 'Vospominaniia', Vol. 3, pp. 157–8, 160–2, 168–9, 661, 869–70. In reporting votes, the minutes of the KPI Council usually indicate only the total number of votes for each viewpoint and do not detail who voted for what. See, for example, the minutes for 1905 in *DAK*, *f.* 18, *op.* 1, *spr.* 557. To judge by the same sources, Lomonosov rarely intervened in Council debates throughout his time at the KPI.

33 *TsDIAU*, *f.* 274, *op.* 1, *spr.* 888, *fol.* 34: 'Kyiv Polytechnical Institute' (16 February 1904).

34 Lomonosov, 'Vospominaniia', Vol. 3, p. 973.

35 Ibid., pp. 985–8. The incident is mentioned in many sources: for example, M. I. Mebel (ed.), *1905 god na Ukraine: Khronika i materialy, t. 1: ianvar–sentiabr* (Kharkov, 1926), pp. 296–7. The police chief described his drenching in a report of 16 January to the city governor: *Derzhavnyi Arkhiv Kyievsko Oblasty* (*DAKO*), *f.* 2, *op.* 221, *spr.* 55, *fos.* 4–5.

36 Lomonosov, 'Vospominaniia', Vol. 3, pp. 997–9. The *Okhrannoe Otdelenie* recorded Lomonosov as a member of the professors' union: *TsDIAU*, *f.* 274, *op.* 1, *spr.* 1,113, *fol.* 141 verso. However, police lists of academic and engineers' union members in Kyiv did not include Lomonosov: *TsDIAU*, *f.* 275, *op.* 1, *spr.* 1,122, *fos.* 22–23 verso.

37 Lomonosov, 'Vospominaniia', Vol. 3, pp. 1206–7.

38 Ibid., p. 1222.

39 M. K., 'Bolsheviki v 1905g. v Kieve (Po materialam vechera vospominanii)', *Letopis revoliutsii* (1925), No. 4, p. 53; and Kushch and Glovatskii, 'Kievskii Politekhnicheskii Institut', pp. 134–5. See also, for instance, V. Manilov and G. Marenko (eds), *1905 rik u Kyivi ta na Kyivshchini: zbirnik stattiv ta spogadiv* (Kyiv, 1926), p. 310.

40 *TsDIAU*, *f.* 442, *op.* 855, *spr.* 322, *fol.* 204: Kyiv City Governor to Kyiv Governor-General (18 April 1906); *DAKO*, *f.* 2, *op.* 44, *spr.* 171, *fol.* 4: Head of Kyiv *Okhrannoe Otdelenie* to Kyiv City Governor (16 May 1907).

41 Lomonosov, 'Vospominaniia', Vol. 3, pp. 1222–3.

42 That the authorities lacked detailed information about this meeting is suggested by the text of a report of 16 October 1905 by the city governor to the governor-general: *TsDIAU*, *f.* 442, *op.* 855, *spr.* 322, *fos.* 112–13. See also 'Oktiabrskie sobytiia 1905 goda v Kieve', p. 115.

43 Lomonosov, 'Vospominaniia', Vol. 3, pp. 1223–8.

44 The principal source on the Union of Unions in 1905 is Sanders, 'Union of Unions'. Other works include D. Sverchkov, 'Soiuz soiuzov', *Krasnaia letopis* (1925), No. 3, pp. 149–62; Shmuel Galai, 'The Role of the Union of Unions in the Revolution of 1905', *Jahrbücher für Geschichte Osteuropas*, Vol. 24 (1976), No.

4, pp. 512–25; Galai, *Liberation Movement, passim*; and Ascher, *The Revolution of 1905*, p. 143.

45 *TsDIAU, f.* 274, *op.* 1, *spr.* 1,113, *fos.* 255–6: 'Manifesto Note concerning a Union of Unions', [n.d.]; *TsDIAU, f.* 274, *op.* 1, *spr.* 1,113, *fol.* 249 and verso: 'Resolution No. 1' [13 August 1905]. It seems unlikely that, as the police alleged, Tikhvinskii wrote the note, since he was not even a member of the Union's Central Bureau: Sanders, 'Union of Unions', pp. 956–7.

46 Lomonosov, 'Vospominaniia', Vol. 3, pp. 1228–31.

47 Ibid., pp. 1232–3. Ratner was an SR and 'Kiev's most influential Jewish radical': Hamm, *Kiev: A Portrait*, p. 183. Zheleznov had been one of the speakers at the banquet of 20 November 1904: *TsDIAU, f.* 275, *op.* 1, *spr.* 552, *fos.* 43–7: [Report about banquet of 20 Nov. 1904], by Spiridovich.

48 Lomonosov, 'Vospominaniia', Vol. 3, pp. 1233–4.

49 Ibid., pp. 1234–8, 1240–1. The two committee representatives were the SD 'Mikhail' and one unnamed leader of the Spilka.

50 Ibid., pp. 1239–43.

51 In particular, nothing has been found in the collections of the Kyiv gendarmerie and *Okhrannoe Otdelenie*.

52 Some Soviet accounts appear to imply that Shlikhter did not leave Kyiv until December, or that he left after the pogrom, returned, and then left again in December. See, for example, Golobutskii *et al.* (eds), *Istoriia Kieva*, p. 533. Shlikhter himself refers to only one departure, organized by Lomonosov: M. K., 'Bolsheviki v 1905g. v Kieve', p. 53. Since Lomonosov makes no reference to Shlikhter being in Kyiv after 2 November, but did meet him in the St Petersburg area in early 1906, one is inclined to conclude that Shlikhter was not in Kyiv after 2 November.

53 See Golobutskii *et al.* (eds), *Istoriia Kieva*, p. 522.

54 On this worker attitude see Hamm, *Kiev: A Portrait*, pp. 185–6.

55 For examples of accounts by contemporaries see Manilov, *Kievskii Sovet*, pp. 17–20; F. Iastrebov, *1905 rik u Kyievi* (Kharkiv and Kyiv, 1930), pp. 76–8; Maiorov, *Bolsheviki i revoliutsiia*, pp. 78–9; and the report of *Kievskaia gazeta* (8 November 1905), reprinted in Los *et al.*, *Revoliutsiia 1905–1907gg. na Ukraine, tom 2, chast 1*, pp. 626–30.

56 *TsDIAU, f.* 274, *op.* 1, *spr.* 1,113, *fol.* 228: [Notice of meeting of KPI group of Academic Union].

57 Lomonosov, 'Vospominaniia', Vol. 3, pp. 1206–10, 1261–2. He states that his (targeted) collections netted some 8,000 roubles in early October but less than 3,000 roubles on 24 October.

58 Ibid., pp. 1260–1, 1269–81.

11 Kadet domination of the First Duma and its limits

Shmuel Galai

This chapter discusses the extent to which, if at all, the Kadets were responsible for the failure of the 'Constitutional Experiment' – that is, for the failure to establish a government acceptable to the Duma. On the basis of a fresh look at existing secondary and primary sources and an examination of new material (the draft notes of the protocols of the last two sessions of the First State Duma and the condensed minutes of Goremykin's government), it concludes that the chances that Nicholas II would have agreed to the establishment of such a government were very slim and became even slimmer when it transpired that the Kadets were unable to muster a solid majority in the Duma.

Russia's First State Duma, elected in spring 1906, reflected the voters' craving for an end to the revolutionary turmoil and for rapid improvement in their conditions, as well as their deep hatred of the tsarist regime. Overwhelmingly oppositional in its composition, it was immediately nicknamed the 'Duma of the People's Wrath' (*Duma narodnogo gneva*). Its lifespan was brief: it opened on 27 April 1906 and was dissolved on 9 July 1906.[1]

The elections to the Duma were multi-stage and, since balloting was not conducted simultaneously throughout the Empire, slightly less then 450 deputies were present at its opening. The number grew to about 500 on the eve of dissolution, but this was still short of the statutory complement of 524 members.[2]

The great victors of the elections, the Kadets, became the dominant faction in the House, first and foremost because they formed the largest caucus in the House. All the available sources agree that about a third of the deputies belonged to the Kadet caucus.[3] At the opening session, it had 153 members (34.1 per cent of the total at that time) and on the eve of dissolution 161 (32.3 per cent of the total). Second place was held by the Trudoviks, with 107 deputies (23.8 per cent of the total) at the beginning of the session. But as a result of differentiation inside that caucus (in particular after the arrival of the Social Democratic deputies from the Caucasus), the number of Trudoviks dropped to ninety-seven (19.4 per cent of the total) on the eve of dissolution. Moreover, the Trudovik caucus was far from being homogeneous. Replying to questions about their party affiliation and/or ideological inclinations, two of its members identified themselves as Social-ists-Revolutionaries, nine as members of the Peasant Union, seven as non-party socialists, one as a radical and two as Free Thinkers, while eighteen described themselves as left of the Kadets, eight were Autonomists and twenty-one 'non-party'. The ideological inclinations of twenty-five were unknown and four were unaccounted for.

On the eve of dissolution, the remainder of the Duma deputies were affili-ated to several other groups. The Autonomists were a loose coalition of seventy representatives of national minorities, who did not belong to all-Russian parties. Thirty-five of them belonged to the Polish *Kolo*, while the others were Ukrainian, Lithuanian, Latvian and Muslim. The Party of Peace-ful Renewal caucus (an affiliate of the Octobrists) had some twenty-five deputies, the Party of Democratic Reforms caucus had fourteen, and the Social Democrats had seventeen. Twelve deputies defined themselves as 'Pro-gressives' (or 'Moderate Progressives') and a group of 105 independent deputies were labelled 'non-party'.

On major issues, the Kadets could usually count on the support of the fourteen deputies of the Democratic Reforms group (who were very close to them ideologically) and the twenty-one non-party deputies. Together, they formed a bloc of about 200 deputies, or 40 per cent of the total, and were thus about sixty deputies short of an absolute majority. In order to assure a majority for their initiatives, they needed, therefore, to come to understand-ings with other groups, in particular the Trudoviks. This they managed to do for most of the Duma sessions, without paying an excessive price, because, in addition to size, they were better organized than almost all the other groups and their members accepted party discipline more than any other Duma deputies excepting, perhaps, the Social Democrats.

The Kadet deputies were also better educated and more experienced in conducting parliamentary business than most, if not all, other deputies (except for some of the members and leaders of the Party of Democratic Reforms and the Party of Peaceful Renewal). The Kadet leaders in the Duma and outside it (the latter included Pavel Nikolaevich Miliukov, Prince Pavel Dmitrievich Dolgorukov and Petr Berngardovich Struve) were well-known public figures, with considerable influence in educated society. Last, but not least, the Kadets entered the Duma with a very impressive legislative agenda.[4]

The election of the speaker of the Duma and his two deputies attests to the high esteem in which the Kadet leaders were held in the House by other political groups – in particular the Trudoviks – at least at this early stage. The Kadets were the only political caucus to submit a candidate for the position of speaker – Sergei Andreevich Muromtsev – who was elected almost unanimously at the first meeting (gaining 426 of 436 votes cast in the first round). It was therefore decided not to hold a second round, and Muromtsev was elected unanimously by acclamation.[5]

The election of two deputy speakers, the Duma clerk and five deputy clerks was scheduled for the next meeting. This time, however, the elections were contested by candidates from other parties and the Kadets were obliged to recruit support, particularly from the Trudoviks. The latter held a meeting at which the issue of the election of the two deputy speakers was on the agenda, the Kadets having informed them that their candidates were Prince Petr Dmitrievich Dolgorukov and Vladimir Dmitrievich Nabokov. Some of the Trudoviks wanted to submit a candidate of their own for one of the posts, but the majority opposed this, arguing that none of their deputies possessed the necessary qualifications or stature. The meeting decided, therefore, to support the Kadet candidates, but on condition that Professor Nikolai Andreevich Gredeskul replace Nabokov as candidate. They preferred him due to his record as a martyr for the cause of liberation (he had been released from prison just before the opening of the Duma). This proposal was discussed at a joint meeting of the Kadets, the Trudoviks and some other deputies. Nabokov immediately agreed to step down and the meeting agreed to support the Kadet candidates.[6]

Consequently, the Kadet candidates won by an overwhelming majority in the first round of the 29 April elections. From the votes of 429 deputies, Gredeskul won the support of 361 and Dolgorukov 351, while Count Petr Aleksandrovich Geiden (the leader of the soon-to-be-formed Party of Peaceful Renewal) received seventy-four votes and Vladimir Dmitrievich Kuzmin-Karavaev (leader of the Party of Democratic Reforms) only twenty-seven. In the second round, Dolgorukov was elected by a majority of 382 against forty-seven and Gredeskul by a majority of 372 against fifty-six.[7]

In the elections for the positions of clerk and five deputy clerks, Prince Dmitrii Ivanovich Shakhovskoi, the Kadet candidate, gained an overwhelming majority in the first round (362 votes out of 431), while Kuzmin-Karavaev, his closest rival, won only fifty-four votes.[8] Meanwhile, of the five deputy clerks elected, two were Kadets (Fedor Fedorovich Kokoshkin and Gavriil Feliksovich Shershenevich), two were Trudoviks (Grigorii Nikitich Shaposhnikov and Semen Martynovich Ryshkov) and the fifth was an independent candidate from Volynia (Shchensnyi Adamovich Poniatowski), who later joined the Autonomists.[9] His election was, undoubtedly, part of a deal with groups and deputies representing ethnic minorities.

After achieving control of the presidium, the Kadets succeeded in dominating the various committees established by the House. Before electing the committees, the Duma had to verify the credentials of its members. To do this, the deputies were divided by lot into eleven sections, with no section to have more than fifty members.[10] Ten of the sections had Kadets as their leaders.[11] Although the process was protracted, by 12 May the credentials of 262 deputies had been verified, sufficient to ensure the legality of the Duma proceedings. By the time the Chamber was dissolved, the credentials of 500 deputies had been verified. The Duma only annulled the election of eleven (out of twelve) deputies from Tambov.[12]

Simultaneously with this process, the Duma began to form committees, seven of them permanent and ten *ad hoc*.[13] The Kadets completely dominated three of the permanent committees and shared power to various degrees with the Trudoviks and the Party of Democratic Reforms in the remaining four. They also fully dominated two of the *ad hoc* committees and were co-leaders of the remaining eight. (Only one of the *ad hoc* committees had no Kadet officers. However, together with members of the Party of Democratic Reforms, the Kadets formed a majority on its board.)

The Kadets' controlling position on all internal administrative matters did not necessarily ensure a smooth passage for their proposals. As the session progressed, there was increasing opposition to their plans on the part of those they denoted 'their neighbours on the left' – that is, mainly, the Trudoviks.[14]

The growing friction between the Kadets and the Trudoviks stemmed from a number of factors. Among these were the dynamics of parliamentary work, the political dynamics within the Trudovik caucus and Kadet attempts to moderate the Duma's anti-government stance (in order to avoid a violent clash with the authorities and to prevent the House from engaging in unlawful activities).[15] However, one of the most important causes of friction before the arrival of the Social Democrat deputies from the Caucasus was the intervention in Trudovik affairs of radical leftists from the *Bez zaglaviia* group and from the Populists (most of whom were later among the founders of the Party of Popular Socialists).[16] They were particularly closely involved in the formulation of the Trudovik agrarian programme.

The *Bez zaglaviia* and the future Popular Socialists did everything in their power to put an end to what they saw as the capitulation of the Trudoviks to Kadet dictates. These people, who until the summer of 1905 had belonged to the Union of Liberation and had been close allies of the future Kadets, became their bitter rivals after the Kadet Party was formed. Like the revolutionaries, they had campaigned actively for a boycott of the elections to the Duma. After their failure and the Kadets' electoral success, they then exploited, from outside the Duma Chamber, every means at their disposal to undermine the authority of their former allies in the Chamber and thereby to shorten the life of the Duma.[17]

One of the first radical 'outsiders' to participate in a meeting of the Trudovik caucus was Vasilii Vasil'evich Vodovozov, of the *Bez zaglaviia* group. He had been a founding father of the Union of Liberation,[18] but was now a bitter critic of the Kadets. He urged the Trudoviks to use every means at their disposal to replace the Kadets as the dominant faction in the Chamber.[19] Vodovozov was later joined by the Populists Ivan Sergeevich Bunakov, Benedikt Aleksandrovich Miakotin, Aleksei Vasil'evich Peshekhonov and one of the SR leaders, Viktor Mikhailovich Chernov. At a meeting of the Trudovik caucus on 7 May they were invited to participate in the formulation of their agrarian programme.[20] It was the differences of opinion on the formulation of that programme, as well as on such issues as the death penalty, political amnesty, the Kadet draft bill on freedom of assembly and their refusal to ignore the legal restraints imposed on the Duma by the Fundamental Laws, which eventually put an end to the co-operation between the Trudoviks and the Kadets.

When the Duma first began to debate the agrarian question, the Tru-dovik proposals did not differ greatly from those of the Kadets. In the Duma's reply to the Speech from the Throne, which contained an outline of its legislative agenda, the Kadets deferred to the Trudoviks and omitted from the final version the provision that private (that is, non-institutional) owners of confiscated land would be compensated.[21] Three days later, however, the Kadets introduced their own agrarian proposal ('The Proposal of the 42'), which included the compensation clause.[22]

The ultimate aim of their agrarian policy, they now declared, was to transfer all the land to those who cultivated it with their own labour. Until that happened, the main aim was to increase the size of the peasant plots to an amount which an average peasant household would be able to cultivate by its own labour (the 'working norm') so that it would generate enough income to enable it to cover its basic expenses on food, clothing, dwelling and taxes (the 'consumption norm'). Land, the Kadets said, would be acquired for this purpose by the compulsory transfer into a state land fund of all the land holdings of the state, the Imperial family (both that land held in trust and that held as private property by the Romanovs – *udel'nye i kabinet-nye zemli*), the Church and the monasteries, as well as by the confiscation of required amounts of privately owned land, with the state then compensating the present owners at equitable (that is, not market) prices. All the land thereby accumulated was to constitute a specially created state land fund. It was specified, however, that privately owned estates which were of excep-tional value to the community (and/or on which factories existed) should be exempt from confiscation. The lands constituting the state land fund would then be distributed to those peasants who were entitled to increase their plots (that is, peasants whose landholdings were below the size defined by the above-named norms, or those who had lost their land and had become agricultural or industrial labourers but desired to return to agriculture). This would be done in accordance with local customs of land tenure and usage, but although the peasants would be required to pay a fee for the land it would not become their private property and would be non-transferable.

A few days later, the Trudoviks introduced an agrarian plan of their own ('The Proposal of the 104'). With the exception of demands for partial nationalization of the mineral wealth of the state and for the establishment of local committees elected on the basis of the 'four-tail formula' (that is, universal suffrage and direct, equal and secret ballot) to oversee the imple-mentation of the agrarian reform, the Trudovik proposal was similar to that of the Kadets. It even included a provision for compensating private owners of confiscated land.[23]

The introduction of these proposals launched the lengthy and often fierce Duma debate on the agrarian question.[24] But until the second Trudovik project was presented on 8 June ('The Proposal of the 33'),[25] the exchanges and disputes did not, on the whole, create unbridgeable rifts and only led to marginal realignments in the political composition of the Duma. Perhaps the most famous case was that of Nikolai Nikolaevich L'vov, one of the Kadet leaders, who sharply disagreed with their agrarian proposal and criticized it very severely in the Chamber.[26] A few days earlier, during the debate on the reply to the Speech from the Throne, he had broken ranks with his party colleagues and voted with the future Peaceful Renewal group on the issue of revolutionary terror[27] – so his days in the Kadet caucus were numbered. He left it shortly afterwards and joined Peaceful Renewal.[28]

The relative cohesion of the opposition on the agrarian issue was apparently influenced by two factors. First, the all-Russian political groups in the Chamber (including Peaceful Renewal and its parent organization, the Union of 17 October) concurred on the need to increase the amount of land available to the peasants and their programmes included a demand for confiscation of part or all of the privately owned land stock for that purpose.[29] Second, the authorities' refusal, in the name of the sanctity of private property, to contemplate any kind of forceful confiscation of privately owned land (even with full compensation for the owners) united almost the entire Duma against the government. The Chairman of the Council of Ministers, Ivan Loginovich Goremykin, clarified the government's position on this issue in replying to the Duma's response to the Speech from the Throne. Speaking on 13 May, he rejected most of the legislative proposals in the Duma reply, in particular the proposal to confiscate private lands.[30] Since he offered no concrete proposals of his own, even the future Peaceful Renewal adherents turned against him and the Duma passed a vote of no-confidence in his government.[31]

The Duma vote had no practical consequences, apart from further exacerbating the already strained relations between the government and the Chamber. The government's adamant opposition to the confiscation of privately owned land was demonstrated again several days later when Aleksandr Semenovich Stishinskii (the acting minister of agriculture) and Vladimir Iosipovich Gurko (the deputy minister of the interior) intervened in the Duma debate. Their appearances before the House on 19 May and, in particular, on 23 May, transformed the debate into an anti-government demonstration, galvanizing the deputies and uniting them against the authorities.

Stishinskii addressed the Duma first. Since only the Kadet proposal was officially on the agenda, he reiterated (in milder terms) Goremykin's previous statement that confiscation of privately owned land ran counter to the spirit and the letter of the law and, hence, was inadmissible. He also criticized the proposal on practical and economic grounds, citing an argument that was also being made in some opposition circles. This was that even if all the land held by the state, the Imperial family, the Church and monasteries and private owners was to be transferred to the peasants, it would not solve the agrarian problem in the long run. The only effective solution was to introduce more intensive cultivation methods into Russian agriculture, by increasing peasant landholdings through land purchases (with the help of the Peasant Bank) and by encouraging emigration to less populated parts of the Empire. His department, Stishinskii said in conclusion, was preparing legislation to introduce such measures. He did not refer to the need to raise the standard of peasant education as a prerequisite for introducing intensive modes of cultivation. Nor did he mention the need to increase the pace of industrialization and urbanization as a method of reducing overpopulation in the countryside. Still, the Duma heard him out in silence and without interruption. The fact that he spoke soberly and made no provocative remarks was undoubtedly to his advantage.[32]

Gurko, who followed Stishinskii to the rostrum,[33] cited the same arguments, but in a manner that bordered on open demagoguery. Thus, in order to prove his (and, by implication, the government's) 'impartiality' in defence of the 'sanctity' of private property, he declared, without foundation, that the landlords were not frightened by the Kadet project. The reverse was true: they were all anxious to sell their estates and the proposal, if implemented, would provide the machinery and the money for achieving this aim. To this Mikhail Iakovlevich Gertsenshtein commented that everything came down to the question of money: the landowners wanted to sell but at an exorbitant price.[34]

Gurko also tried to influence the peasant deputies by scaring them off. He claimed that if the project was implemented, the peasants would suffer most, since the same 'working norm' would apply throughout the Empire and the upper limit for their plots would be fixed at four *desiatinas* per (male) capita. Hence, those peasants whose plots were larger than the norm, either as private property or as allotment land, would lose part of their land. Due to this and other examples of demagoguery, his speech was interrupted and the uproar ceased only after intervention from the chair.[35]

Gurko concluded by repeating a passage in Goremykin's declaration of 13 May (which had apparently been drafted by Gurko),[36] which was scarcely noticed by his audience at the time but was to acquire great significance soon afterwards: 'Not by abolishing private property in land but by transforming all allotment land into peasant private property will the Duma gain the gratitude of the people', he declared.[37]

Stishinskii and Gurko addressed the Duma again on 23 May. This time Gurko spoke first. By the time he was called to the rostrum, the mood of the assembly was already very tense. It had just discussed two proposals – one presented by the Kadets and the other by the Trudoviks – to establish a 'committee of inquiry into unlawful activity of officials'.[38] It had then dealt with the arraignment of thirty-five civilians before the Riga military court and the possibility that some of them might be sentenced to death.[39] Only then did it return to the agrarian problem.

The moment Gurko mounted the podium, pandemonium broke loose. Amid deafening noise and calls for his resignation from all sides, Gurko tried vainly to reply to Gertsenshtein's criticism of his previous address. Calls for his resignation continued well after he ended his relatively brief speech.[40] Stishinskii fared not much better. He tried to defend the government's proposals but his words were drowned out in the general uproar and in calls for his resignation. When he promised that his department would shortly lay before the Duma a bill concerning the government's proposed solution to the agrarian question, he was greeted with jeers.[41]

The Duma then resumed the agrarian debate on a much calmer note, but not for long. It culminated, on 6 June 1906, in the election of an *ad hoc* agrarian committee that was to prepare a draft bill, using the Kadet and Trudovik proposals as the basis for its deliberations.[42] However, two days later a group of Trudoviks headed by Aleksei Fedorovich Aladin submitted another proposal on the agrarian question. Aladin demanded that the proposal be submitted, without discussion, to the *ad hoc* committee as additional material for the preparation of the draft bill. This proposal, known as 'The Project of the 33', was much more radical than the original Trudovik 'Proposal of the 104'. It advocated total abolition of private property in the agricultural and mineral sectors of the economy throughout the Empire. It also specified that only 'People's Power' (*Narodnaia vlast'*) — meaning, presumably, a government answerable to a national assembly elected on the basis of the 'four-tail formula' — could be entrusted with the implementation of the project.[43]

The proposal and the demand for its submission, without discussion, to the *ad hoc* committee were vehemently opposed by the Kadets. Ivan Ilich Petrunkevich suggested that the Duma either dismiss the proposal outright or debate it before transferring it to the committee. Otherwise, he said, it might appear that the Chamber agreed with its principles.[44] After a short but heated discussion, the demand for its transfer to the committee without discussion was rejected by 140 votes to seventy-eight.[45]

This was not the first time that the Kadets and the Trudoviks had voted against one another. On 26 May, for example, they voted differently on an issue relating to capital punishment. Almost all the deputies demanded an immediate halt to executions, and the Kadets and the Trudoviks differed only in regard to the wording of the resolution. The Kadet proposal was milder than the two Trudovik versions and was approved by a majority vote.[46] Also, two days later, the Trudoviks (supported by members of the caucus of Democratic Reforms and other deputies) defeated the Kadets on a procedural issue by a vote of 142 to eighty-nine.[47] However, the vote on the agrarian issue was the most significant division of opinion between the Kadets and the Trudoviks so far.

Opposition to the Kadet dominance in the Duma intensified after the establishment of the Social Democrat caucus on 12 June.[48] The Social Democrats' radical, confrontational style influenced the conduct of many of the Trudoviks. This was particularly evident in the debate over the Kadets' draft bill on freedom of assembly.[49] But these efforts did not succeed in wresting the leadership of the Duma away from the Kadets, who continued to dominate the Chamber almost to the bitter end (in fact, until the penultimate session on 6 July). It was government policies and attitudes that were, to a large extent, responsible for this situation.

Thus, for example, Goremykin's refusal to reply to repeated Duma interpellations on the publication of Black Hundred cables in the *Pravitel'stvennyi vestnik*, the official gazette, infuriated the deputies. Apart from containing vicious attacks on ethnic minorities (especially Jews) and on 'undesirable elements' in general, these cables also called the Duma a 'revolutionary assembly' and claimed that it was serving the interests of foreign powers and working for the dismemberment of the Russian Empire. The publication of these cables in *Pravitel'stvennyi vestnik* was a more accurate reflection of the authorities' true feelings than the soothing statements of tsarist officials, wrote the British second in command in St Petersburg to the Foreign Office in London,[50] while Goremykin's refusal to deal with the matter impelled the Duma to condemn his conduct as a grave abuse of power.[51]

Another issue that exacerbated the conflict and rallied the opposition against the government was the Duma debates on the Jewish question. It had become an urgent issue as a result of the Bialystok pogrom of 1–3 June 1906.[52] And, indeed, from the beginning of June until its dissolution, the Duma devoted more time to the Jewish question than to any other topic, including the agrarian issue.[53]

Its debates on this issue, which were widely reported in the press at home and abroad, infuriated the authorities – and the right in general – for several reasons. The debates highlighted a degree of legal discrimination against Jews that made Russia unique among the European great powers. They also exposed the role of the authorities, including people close to the throne, in unleashing (or at least tolerating) widespread violence against Jews. This exposure not only damaged the image of the Russian government at home and abroad but also threatened the state's finances which only two months earlier had been stabilized by a huge foreign loan. The Bialystok pogrom was perceived by many in the West as the harbinger of a new cycle of violence that might again plunge Russia into anarchy. The financial markets reacted accordingly and the price of Russian securities fell dramatically on the leading stock exchanges.[54]

Finally, on 2 June, the Duma decided on the immediate dispatch of a commission of enquiry to Bialystok, mostly in order to ascertain to what extent the authorities had been involved. It was also hoped that, if the pogrom was still raging, the commission's arrival would check the violence.[55] However, by dispatching the commission, the Duma was overstepping its authority.[56] The tone of the debates and the fact that the decision was approved unanimously, suggest that the deputies were not fully aware of the dire consequences of their action for the future of the Chamber.[57]

The debates over the Jewish question, the agrarian problem, the issue of capital punishment and related topics stemming from the authorities' repressive policies, brought relations between the government and the Duma to breaking point. By early June, it was apparent that one of the sides would have to give way. Either the Council of Ministers would be replaced by a government acceptable to the House, or the Duma would be dissolved.

Goremykin's cabinet discussed these options at lengthy meetings on 7 and 8 June,[58] which were attended by all the ministers (except for the acting head of the Ministry of Commerce and Industry, Aleksandr Aleksandrovich Shtof). The majority – Goremykin, the minister of court Baron Vladimir Borisovich Frederiks, the war minister Aleksandr Fedorovich Rediger, the minister of the navy Aleksei Alekseevich Birilev, the procurator of the Holy Synod Prince Aleksei Aleksandrovich Shirinskii-Shikhmatov, the state comptroller Petr Khristianovich Shvanebakh, the head of the Ministry of Agriculture Stishinskii, the minister of ways of communications Nikolai Konstantinovich Shaufus, the minister of the interior Petr Arkadevich Stolypin, and the justice minister Ivan Grigorevich Shcheglovitov – pressed for dissolution at the first favourable opportunity. They claimed that it was too late to achieve a compromise with the Duma, since its members would only agree to the establishment of a Kadet ministry or a government of public activists. In either case, the result would be the same: the new government would be unable to stem the revolutionary tide. Meanwhile, the House was becoming the nerve centre of the revolutionary movement; hence, the sooner it was dissolved, the better. Two examples were cited to buttress this claim: first, the dispatch of the delegation to Bialystok proved that the Chamber was already usurping executive powers; and second, the House was trying, contrary to the letter and the spirit of the law, to win total immunity for its members. It is interesting that the condensed minutes contain no reference to the agrarian question.

The assertion that the Duma had impinged on the Crown's executive prerogatives was repeated in the manifesto of 9 July 1906, which gave the official explanation for action against the Duma. It was one of the three cited examples of the Chamber's transgressions, which, according to Nicholas II, justified its dissolution. (In the words of the manifesto, the Duma 'dared to investigate the actions of local authorities appointed by Us'.) The other two were the Duma's attempts to change the Fundamental Laws without the tsar's consent and its (debatable) approval of the 'Appeal to the People',[59] issued in response to the government communiqué on the agrarian issue.[60]

Only three members of Goremykin's government – Finance Minister Vladimir Nikolaevich Kokovtsov, Minister of Foreign Affairs Aleksandr Petrovich Izvol'skii and Minister of Education Petr Mikhailovich fon Kaufman – expressed different views. It was too early to despair of the prospect of co-operation with the Duma, they claimed. But in order to achieve it, the current Council of Ministers should be replaced by a cabinet composed of enlightened bureaucrats and public activists, who might be acceptable to the Duma.

In view of the impossibility of reaching a unanimous decision and the importance of the topic under discussion, the participants accepted Kokovtsov's proposal that the issue be discussed and decided by a special conference, under the chairmanship of the tsar, with the participation of the ministers and others.

While the majority of the Council of Ministers favoured immediate dissolution, those members of the ruling elite who feared that this would lead to a new revolutionary outbreak and/or genuinely favoured implementing the October Manifesto's promises, started negotiations with Duma leaders. The aim was to replace Goremykin's government by a cabinet acceptable to the majority of the Chamber. This majority, as they well knew, was led by the Kadets.[61]

The attempts to form a cabinet acceptable to the Duma began almost simultaneously in government circles and at Court. Though these efforts were apparently unco-ordinated, Nicholas II was undoubtedly kept informed. Furthermore, he met with the moderate liberal and Octobrist leader Dmitrii Nikolaevich Shipov and discussed with him the possibility of establishing such a ministry.

There were various attempts at contact between the ruling circles and the leaders of the Kadets, Peaceful Renewal and the Party of Democratic Reforms in the Duma, in the State Council and outside the legislature. As early as 22 May 1906, an attempt was made to sound out the leader of Peaceful Renewal, Count Geiden, about the possibility of official co-operation with the Kadets. It was initiated by his relative, A. F. Geiden, who held an important position at Court.[62] By mid-June, when the struggle between the Duma and the government had resulted in a complete stalemate, the contacts became more intensive. The former governor-general of St Petersburg (now court commandant), Dmitrii Fedorovich Trepov, met with Miliukov and they continued their exchanges in the press. Izvol'skii and Stolypin also conducted negotiations with Miliukov, Shipov, Geiden and others. (Shipov and Miliukov apparently sensed that Stolypin had ulterior motives for participating.)[63] And Aleksei Sergeevich Ermolov, the former liberal minister of agriculture, then one of the leaders of the Centrist group in the reformed State Council,[64] met with Muromtsev, Miliukov and others.[65] And this is only a partial list.

The meeting between Trepov and Miliukov is still considered the most crucial, for obvious reasons. First, since Trepov was believed to be omnipotent at court, the negotiations were assumed to have the blessing of Nicholas II. Second, while all other negotiators on the part of the authorities advocated a coalition government to include not only Kadets but also more moderate liberals and some enlightened bureaucrats, Trepov alone was prepared to contemplate a Kadet administration, and he did so publicly. Given his position at Court and his notoriety, Trepov's pronouncement created a sensation and was widely reported in the press. Though his meeting with Miliukov was kept secret, his contemporaries had no doubt that he had met with Kadet leaders before expressing his views.

Trepov's readiness to consider a Kadet cabinet naturally appealed greatly to the leaders of the party in general and to Miliukov in particular. The latter believed that their negotiations opened up the prospect of transferring power in all internal matters to the Kadets and thus changing the course of Russian history. The later treatment of these negotiations by Miliukov and his colleagues undoubtedly influenced others, including historians, in their discussion of this episode in the annals of the First Russian Revolution. However, it would be erroneous to attribute excessive importance to these negotiations, since this assessment is based on an exaggerated view of Trepov's influence at Court – especially at the time of his meeting with Miliukov. He had undoubtedly been highly influential at Court during Witte's premiership.[66] However, the published excerpts from Nicholas II's diary for the first eight months of 1906 suggest that the tsar was not on very intimate terms with Trepov, even when the latter was at the height of his influence.[67] While other members of his close entourage were quite often invited to his table for lunch or supper (among them the minister of court Baron Frederiks, A. F. Geiden, and others),[68] Nicholas never mentioned Trepov as one of his dining companions – not even when they met very frequently, and more than once a day, for very long sessions, from February to mid-May 1906. (Trepov was not always the only participant in these meetings apart from the tsar.) Subsequently, Trepov's influence seemed to have waned rapidly.

From mid-May to the eve of the Duma's dissolution, the tsar's diary mentions only one meeting with Trepov, on 12 June.[69] Presumably, it was then that he gave him permission to negotiate with the Kadets. We also know for certain that Nicholas received Trepov three times on the eve of dissolution: on 3, 5 and 8 July. All three meetings were very brief (the first two lasted about fifteen minutes each) and were part of the series of consultations which the tsar held with many ministers and high-ranking officials – including Goremykin, Rediger, Stolypin, Izvol'skii, Shvanebach, the Grand Duke Nikolai Nikolaevich, Baron Frederiks and many others – before finally deciding on dissolution.[70]

So much for Trepov's 'omnipotence'. But what were the tsar's intentions? Did he ever contemplate the formation of a government responsible to the Duma, not to mention a Kadet cabinet? It seems unlikely: would the man who refused, under the hazardous conditions of 1916, to consider a government acceptable to the Duma have agreed, in the less-threatening situation in 1906, to a more unacceptable version of the same solution?

The tsar's real feelings on the matter can be ascertained from a note he wrote to Stolypin shortly after the dissolution of the Duma, while the negotiations for a coalition government were still going on: 'I was against the inclusion of a whole group of people in the government on the basis of some programme or other', wrote Nicholas.[71] Still, one should not forget that these words were written when it was obvious that no revolutionary outbreak would occur after dissolution.

By then, the most the tsar seemed prepared to concede was the appointment as ministers of some moderate liberals, such as Shipov and, perhaps, Aleksandr Ivanovich Guchkov. This was on condition that they received no important portfolios, that they joined the government as individuals and not as representatives of a party, and that they were few in number.[72] However, before the dissolution, when many of the people who had access to Nicholas II feared the worst and advised him to adopt a cautious approach and arrive at accommodation with the Chamber,[73] he may have considered briefly the possibility of a coalition government acceptable to the Duma but responsible to himself.

The Kadet leaders were well aware of the tsar's opposition to any further limits on his prerogatives, beyond those he had granted under duress in the October Manifesto. They harboured no illusions, therefore, as to the prospect that he would appoint a Kadet cabinet of his own free will. Hence, when approached by Trepov,[74] they apparently regarded this as an indication that Nicholas had realized the danger of dissolution and was prepared to accept the inevitable and come to an understanding with the dominant party.

Miliukov met Trepov in the Kiuba Restaurant in St Petersburg not later than 15 June.[75] According to Miliukov's own account, Trepov accepted his three basic conditions for participation in the efforts to form a new government: first, that what mattered (and hence should be discussed) was the programme of the proposed administration and not its personal composition; second, that the new government should be formed on the basis of the Kadet platform; and third, as a corollary to that, that it should be not a coalition government but a cabinet composed of people supported by the Duma majority. To Miliukov's surprise, Trepov accepted all his conditions. He raised no objections even to two of the three tricky points on the Kadet agenda: the granting of universal suffrage and the confiscation of privately owned land. The only point unacceptable to Trepov was the demand for full political amnesty, because he believed that the tsar would never agree to that.[76]

Though Miliukov met Trepov 'on his own responsibility', he was not censured by his colleagues for so doing, as some modern historians claim.[77] Miliukov did not keep his colleagues in the dark as regards the meeting. He must have immediately disclosed to them the content of the conversation (although perhaps without revealing Trepov's name) because on 15 June the Kadet caucus in the Duma discussed the issue of amnesty in relation to the distinct possibility that their leaders would be called on to form a government.

The question put to the deputies was what to do if the Trudoviks introduced a bill granting full political amnesty. The Kadet caucus decided unanimously not to support such a motion, in view of the fact that it was impractical and unduly provocative at that time, since the issue pertained to the sphere of the tsar's prerogatives. Furthermore, they stated, since a government responsible to the Duma was about to replace the cabinet of Goremykin, Stolypin and Shcheglovitov, an amnesty would shortly be announced, since 'no administration responsible to the Duma will agree to take power unless an amnesty is granted'.[78]

A day later, Miliukov published a very revealing piece in the Kadet newspaper, *Rech'*, entitled 'The Impossibility of a Coalition Government'.[79] Its tone, no less than its content, indicates that its author was apparently convinced that he and the Kadets were about to assume power in the state. The days of Goremykin's government were numbered, he wrote, and the authorities would not dare to dissolve the Duma. Hence, they had no choice but to appoint an administration that could co-operate with the Chamber. However, the court was still toying with the idea of achieving this aim by replacing the current ministers with people of a better reputation who might be more acceptable to the Duma. But, Miliukov warned, such an approach would be futile and its only result would be a waste of very valuable time.

He then repeated in writing what he later claimed to have said to Trepov face to face. What was needed was a change of direction and not just a change of personnel. The court should stop looking for the 'right' personalities for appointment as ministers and focus on the right movement – that is, a movement which, on the basis of its programme and past activities, had gained the support of the population. It should entrust it with forming the cabinet and choosing the ministers. That was the only possible solution to the crisis. All other combinations were doomed to failure.

Two days later, on 18 June, Miliukov returned to the theme of the transfer of power to his party in another article in *Rech'* entitled, appropriately enough, 'Is there Enough Support in the Duma for a Kadet Ministry?'[80] He was responding to an article in *Nasha zhizn'* by one 'G.A.L.' The latter had expressed doubt as to the possibility that the Crown might ask the Kadets to form a government. And, even in the unlikely event that the tsar did approach them, he wrote, the Kadets would be unable to form a government of their own and would have to establish a coalition with the Duma left, in particular the Trudoviks.

Miliukov dismissed the first point out of hand, claiming that it amounted to mere sophistry, and focused on the second. He wrote that the Trudoviks were unfit to enter the government for two reasons: they lacked people of ministerial stature; and none of their leaders was ready to exchange their oppositional status for the more onerous task of governing. However, Miliukov wrote, luckily for the Kadets, their dominant position in the Duma was not dependent on the goodwill of the Trudovik caucus and the more radical left: his party could muster a majority by relying on the support of twenty-five independents (non-party), twenty-six members who were only nominally affiliated to the Trudoviks and eighteen followers of the Party of Democratic Reforms. Together with the 177 members of their own caucus, the Kadets would then enjoy an absolute majority of 246 deputies (although

Miliukov erroneously gave the number as 240). Furthermore, he argued, the Kadets could also count, in most cases, on the support of the thirty-four members of the Moslem caucus and the thirty-one deputies from the Polish *Kolo*.

In conclusion, Miliukov claimed that he had shown that a Kadet ministry would enjoy the support of a solid majority in the Duma. It would also be very durable, since, it being entirely dependent on the Duma, the Chamber would not dare to pass a no-confidence motion against it for fear that it might be replaced by a reactionary bureaucratic cabinet. Hence, there was no need for a coalition government (although, like the tsar – but for contrary reasons – he did not preclude the admission into the Kadet government of a few persons who were not party members, as individuals and not as representatives of a political movement).

A week later Miliukov received what he must have regarded as proof of the seriousness of the Court's intentions in regard to the formation of a Kadet cabinet. In an interview with Reuters on 24 June, extracts from which appeared in the Russian press a day later,[81] Trepov publicly acknowledged his support for the establishment of a Kadet ministry. After blaming the Jews for starting and directing the revolution, and after directing some veiled threats at the revolutionaries and the radicals, he declared that the best way to restore law and order in Russia without a bloodbath was to nominate a Kadet cabinet. Such a move, Trepov said, would isolate and marginalize the radicals and enable the Duma to fulfil the task (of legislation) for which it had been called into existence. But in order to assume power, the Kadets would have to modify their programme. There could be no general amnesty nor confiscation of privately owned land. Although the formation of a Kadet cabinet was risky, he admitted, it also held out great promise of restoring law and order and of introducing the necessary reforms by peaceful means. Only if this experiment failed would the authorities be justified in resorting to other means in order to put down the revolution.

Miliukov replied immediately in an article in *Rech'* on 27 June,[82] addressed to two main audiences: the Kadet supporters and the tsar and his advisers (chief among whom, Miliukov believed, was Trepov). To the former group he explained that:

> [N]o large political party can afford the luxury of refusing to assume power if the conditions are right. The Kadets already envisioned the possibility of taking power in January of this year. For them to assume the burden of power entails a huge sacrifice. But they are prepared to make this sacrifice as long as it serves the aims they proclaimed during the election campaign.

For the benefit of the tsar, he implied that the Kadets were as interested as Nicholas was in ending the revolution and restoring law and order. However, he explained, a Kadet government would employ different and much more successful means of achieving this aim than those used by the current (and all previous) administrations, with such abysmal results for the country. The Kadets believed that the only way to disarm the revolution was to convert the revolutionaries into supporters of the new status quo. This they hoped to achieve by introducing radical political and social reforms that would undercut the propensity to employ violent means in order to achieve political aims. Therefore, Miliukov concluded, the Kadets must insist on acceptance of their full programme. In particular, they could not afford to omit the demands for confiscation of privately owned land and for a full amnesty. They would refuse to accept power if these two points were omitted from the government's programme.

Miliukov's rejection of Trepov's two demands – in particular regarding amnesty (which he must have realized after the meeting in the Kiuba Restaurant was unacceptable to the tsar) – was to some extent a result of his misunderstanding of Trepov's role at Court. Convinced of the latter's omnipotence, he assumed that Trepov's interview indicated the weakness of the tsar's position. He therefore concluded that Nicholas was aware that only one option remained – to form a Kadet cabinet – and had raised his stakes accordingly. The Kadet leader could not have been more mistaken.

But Miliukov also miscalculated the Kadets' ability to muster a solid majority in the House without the support of the Trudoviks and other leftists. Less than three weeks after making this claim, the Kadets found themselves in the unenviable position of isolation in the Chamber. This was to some extent a result of their mishandling of the debate over the reply to the government communiqué on the agrarian question. But to a much larger extent it reflected the disintegration of the united opposition front, as a result of the appearance on the scene of the Social Democrat caucus and the growing frustration of many deputies, in particular on the left, at their inability to change government policy. This led them to advocate abandoning the legal constraints of parliamentary work. Finally, the demands of the representatives of ethnic minorities, in particular the Polish *Kolo*, contributed to the disarray in the opposition ranks.

The government communiqué (*soobshchenie*) on the agrarian issue, of 20 June 1906,[83] was neither new in form – a day later a similar document was published on the Bialystok pogrom, which caused a stir only because of the distortions it contained[84] – nor innovative in content. It reiterated the absolute opposition of the authorities to forcible confiscation of privately owned land and it reiterated Gurko and Stishinskii's statements in the Duma about official plans for solving the agricultural crisis. The only new note appeared in the concluding sentences. Without mentioning the Duma by name, it warned the peasants not to believe rumours about imminent partition of the landowners' land and urged them to await calmly the solution of their problems by the tsar and his emissaries.

The Duma, which was then preoccupied with the Jewish question, was slow to react to the publication of this document. It was almost a week before it appeared on the agenda. (It was not mentioned at all during the first three sessions which followed its publication – sessions 30, 31 and 32, of 20, 22 and 23 June – and was discussed for the first time only at session 33, on 26 June.) After a relatively short debate, the Duma charged the *ad hoc* 'committee for inquiry into unlawful activities of officials' (the 'Committee of 33') with the task of composing an urgent interpellation on this subject, addressed to Goremykin, and ordered the agrarian committee to prepare a detailed reply to the government communiqué, to be distributed to the people.[85]

The interpellation was approved at the next meeting on 27 June. In essence it demanded that Goremykin withdraw the communiqué from circulation and explain to the readers of the papers where it had appeared that the government proposals on agriculture would be null and void if they were not approved by the Duma. Finally, it was requested that the prime minister must guarantee not to publish such documents in the future.[86]

The Duma returned to this issue on 4 July, when the agricultural committee, as requested, submitted a draft of the detailed reply to the government communiqué. It emphasized the Duma's commitment to forcible confiscation of private land, but concluded by appealing to the peasants to await the results of Duma legislation on this matter. The lengthy and heated debate that followed occupied most of the 4 July session,[87] as well as almost all of the next session on 6 July.[88] In the end, the main differences between the Kadets and their 'neighbours on the left' related not to the content of the reply but to its conclusion. The Trudoviks refused to support the call for calm. Instead, they favoured calling on the peasants to support the Duma in its struggle with the government. Since the Kadets refused to accept their demand, the Trudoviks declared that they would abstain from the vote on the proposal.

The Polish *Kolo* also decided to abstain, because the Kadets had refused to agree to the reply containing the promise of full autonomy to the Polish lands in implementing the planned agricultural reform. As a result, when the final draft was put to the vote it was approved by a narrow margin: 124 in favour (almost all of them Kadets),[89] fifty-three against, and 101 abstentions. Since, according to Muromtsev's ruling, abstainers were not counted as present during the vote, the number of votes cast was calculated as 177 – only thirteen votes more than the required quorum of 164.[90] And, in fact, two further proposals regarding the reply – where to publish it and the need to translate it for the benefit of peasants from ethnic minorities – were not passed because of the lack of a quorum.[91]

Thus, the Kadets found themselves in an unenviable position. For the first time since the opening of the Duma they were almost totally isolated and unable to muster a majority for their proposals. It is true that, at the (final) 7 July session of the Duma, they again won a majority for their resolution on the Bialystok debate.[92] Equally, they dominated the debates on the interpellations for the rest of the session.[93] But what had happened on 6 July could not be undone. If there was ever a prospect (and this is doubtful) of the tsar appointing a cabinet responsible to the Duma, or – what is even more unlikely – a Kadet ministry, it depended on that party's ability to muster a solid majority in the Chamber. It now appeared the Kadets were unable to do that. As one of their top leaders admitted at the time, 'the idea of forming a Duma government received a deadly blow on that day'.[94]

Acknowledgement

The author would like to thank Professor Bela Davidovna Galperina for assistance in locating important material in the *Rossiiskii Gosudarstvennyi Istoricheskii Arkhiv (RGIA)*.

Notes

1 The First Duma held forty sessions between 27 April and 7 July. The minutes of the first thirty-eight sessions were published at the time by the State Publishing House as *Gosudarstvennaia Duma. Stenograficheskiie Otchety. Pervyi Sozyv. Sessiia Pervaia. 27.4–4.7, 1906* (St Petersburg, 1906) (hereafter *GDSO.*) For the first use of the term 'Duma of the People's Wrath', see ibid., p. 95. The minutes of the last two sessions of the Duma – Nos. 39 and 40 (6 and 7 July) – were not published at the time, apparently because of the dissolution of the House on 9 July. An unedited draft of their proceedings is in *RGIA, f.* 1,278, *op.* 1, *d.* 204 and *d.* 205 (hereafter referred to as *Draft Proceedings* 39 and 40 respectively).

2 On this see, *inter alia,* V. A. Kozbanenko, *Partiinye fraktsii v I i II Gosudarstvennykh Dumakh Rossii, 1906–1907* (Moscow, 1996), p. 41; S. M. Sidel'nikov, *Obrazovanie i deiatel'nost' Pervoi Gosudarstvennoi Dumy* (Moscow, 1962), pp. 189–90; and Terence Emmons *The Formation of Political Parties and the First National Elections in Russia* (Cambridge, Mass., 1983), pp. 355–6.

3 Unlike the minutes of the Third and Fourth Dumas, those of the First and Second Dumas do not contain official information on party composition. Information on the political affiliation of the First Duma deputies is derived, therefore, from estimates in various contemporary publications. In my opinion, the most complete information on the subject can be found in M. M. Boiovich (comp.), *Chleny Gosudarstvennoi Dumy. Pervyi Sozyv.* (Moscow, 1906). See also *Dumskii Sbornik. Gos. Duma Pervago Sozyva (27 Aprelia–8 Iiulia 1906g.) Besplatnoe Prilozhenie k gazete 'Tovarishch'* (St Petersburg, 1906), pp. 9–10; N. A. Borodin, *Gosudarstvennaia Duma v Tsifrach* (St Petersburg, 1906); and N. A. Borodin, 'Lichnyi sostav Pervoi Gosudarstvennoi Dumy', in N. A. Mukhanov and V. D. Nabokov (eds), *Pervaia Gosudarstvennaia Duma* (St Petersburg, 1907), pp. 1–39 (especially pp. 23–8). For a partial list of Kadet Duma deputies see the roster in P. N. Miliukov's archive in *Gosudarstvennyi Arkhiv Rossiiskoi Federatsii (GARF), f.* 579, *op.* 1, *d.* 887, *ll.* 3–6. See also *Partiia demokraticheskich reform. Rechy chlenov partii v I Dume* (St Petersburg, 1907), pp. iii–iv; *Partiia Mirnogo obnovleniia. Ee obrazovanie i deiatel'nost' v Pervoi Gosudarstvennoi Dume* (St Petersburg, 1907), pp. 3–5; and *Trudovaia gruppa v Gosudarstvennoi Dume* (n.p., n.d.), pp. 2–3. Cf. Emmons, *The Formation*, pp. 355–9, 366, 500 (n. 217).

4 On this see N. Astrov *et al.* (eds), *Zakonodatel'nye proekty i predlozheniia Partii narodnoi svobody, 1905–1907* (St Petersburg, 1907).

5 *GDSO*, pp. 2–3.

6 See *Vestnik Partii narodnoi svobody* (hereafter *Vestnik*), No. 9 (4 May 1906), cols 616–18; and *Novoe vremia*, No. 10,819 (29 April 1906), p. 4, col. 5.

7 *GDSO*, pp. 17–18.

8 Ibid., p. 19.

9 Ibid.; and Borodin, 'Lichnyi sostav', p. 2.

10 For the names of the Duma deputies in each section, see *GDSO*, pp. 279–84.

11 Borodin, 'Lichnyi sostav', pp. 2–3, gives a detailed list of the elected officers of the various sections and of their party affiliation. The list, however, suffers from many factual errors, which I have corrected by consulting Duma minutes and other contemporary sources. See ibid.; Boiovich, *Chleny*; *GDSO*, pp. 254–5, 279–92, 1093–6, 1155, 1214–15, 1397–8, 1760, 1859, 1896; and *Gosudarstvennaia Duma. Ukazatel k stenograficheskim otchetam. Pervyi Sozyv* (St Petersburg, 1907) (hereafter *GDU*), pp. 21–139 (names index).

12 See *GDSO*, pp. 1507, 1555–64 (*Prilozhenie* [Supplement]).

13 For information on the various committees, their dates of establishment, jurisdiction, tasks, etc., and on the party affiliation of their elected officers, see Borodin, 'Lichnyi sostav', pp. 3–5; V. A. Demin, *Gosudarstvennaia Duma Rossii (1906–1917). Mekhanizm funktsinirovaniia* (Moscow, 1996), pp. 105–15; *GDSO*, pp. 374, 408, 749–50, 767–90, 970, 1088–9, 1121, 1152, 1157, 1196, 1213–14, 1372, 1391, 1422–3, 1440, 1468, 1505; and *GDU*, pp. 23–237 (name and subject indexes).

14 See M. Vinaver, *Konflikty v Pervoi Dume* (St Petersburg, 1907).

15 See, for example, the 10 May decision of the Kadet central committee on the necessary means of preventing deputies aiming verbal abuse at the government on the occasion of the imminent appearance before the house of Prime Minister Goremykin: in Shmuel Galai and D. B. Pavlov *et al.* (eds), *Protokoly Tsentral'nogo komiteta Konstitutsionno-demokraticheskoi partii. Tom I: 1905–1911* (Moscow, 1994), p. 76.

16 'The Interstitial Left' was the apt term applied to this grouping by one historian. See Emmons, *The Formation*, pp. 78–88.

17 For a vivid description of this campaign by a Kadet witness, written shortly after the dissolution of the First Duma, see Vinaver, *Konflikty*, pp. 47–59 and *passim*.

18 Shmuel Galai, *The Liberation Movement in Russia, 1900–1905* (London, 1973), p. 177.

19 See *Rech'*, No. 63 (3 May 1906), p. 4, col. 1; and No. 70 (11 May 1906), p. 4, cols 6–7.

20 *Rech'*, No. 68 (9 May 1906), p. 5, col. 6.

21 On the lengthy debate over the Reply and its final, approved version, see *GDSO*, pp. 73–243 (p. 241 for the relevant passage here).

22 Ibid., pp. 248–9 (first referred to mistakenly as 'The Proposal of the 38').

23 Ibid., pp. 560–2.

24 Ibid., pp. 381–7, 451–72, 477–95, 496–530, 560–84, 811–62, 867–87, 977–1006, 1049, 1074–5.

25 Ibid., pp. 1142–50; and *Prilozhenie*, pp. 1153–6.

26 *GDSO*, pp. 477–80.

27 Ibid., p. 237.

28 On L'vov's joining the caucus of Peaceful Renewal, see *Partiia Mirnogo obnovleniia*, p. 3.

29 On the (ambivalent) Octobrist attitude to the question of confiscation of privately owned land, as included in their programme, see D. B. Pavlov and V. V. Shelokhaev (eds), *Partiia 'Soiuz 17 Oktiabria'. Protokoly s''ezdov i zasedanii TsK.*

Tom I, 1906–1907 (Moscow, 1996), pp. 148–51, 235, 329–31. The agrarian programme of Peaceful Renewal is found in V. Petrovo-Solovovo, *Lichnaia zemel'naia sobstvennost' po agrarnoi programme partii 'Mirnago obnovleniia'* (Tambov, 1906), *Prilozhenie*, pp. 37–40. For the agrarian programme of the Party of Democratic Reforms, see *Partiia demokraticheskich reform*, pp. 183–6.

30 *GDSO*, pp. 321–4 (here p. 322).

31 Ibid., pp. 352–4. Only eleven deputies voted against, about half of them from the future caucus of Peaceful Renewal. They did so not because they approved of Goremykin's statement but mainly because they claimed – justifiably – that the vote implied that the government was answerable to the Duma and not to the tsar, a proposition that they rejected.

32 Ibid., pp. 509–17.

33 Ibid., pp. 517–23.

34 Ibid., p. 524.

35 Ibid., p. 519.

36 See V. I. Gurko, *Features and Figures of the Past: Government and Opinion in the Reign of Nicholas II* (Stanford, 1939), pp. 472–3.

37 *GDSO*, p. 523.

38 Ibid., pp. 536–53.

39 Ibid., pp. 557–60.

40 Ibid., pp. 566–7.

41 Ibid., pp. 568–9.

42 Ibid., pp. 1142–3.

43 Ibid., pp. 1153–6 (*Prilozhenie*).

44 Ibid., p. 1142.

45 Ibid., pp. 1142–50.

46 Ibid., pp. 660–2.

47 Ibid., pp. 795–801.

48 See Kozbanenko, *Partiinye fraktsii*, p. 67.

49 *GDSO*, pp. 809, 1400–40, 1452–68, 1523–49, 1707, 1723.

50 PRO FO 371/122 [18151], No. 324: Spring-Rice to Sir Edward Grey (23 May 1906, n.s.).

51 *GDSO*, pp. 389, 639–40, 969, 1704, 1868–9.

52 On the Bialystok pogrom and the Duma debates, the impact of these debates on public opinion at home and abroad and on relations between the Chamber and the government, see Shmuel Galai, 'The Jewish Question as a Russian Problem: The Debates in the First State Duma', *Revolutionary Russia*, Vol. 17 (2004), No. 1, pp. 31–68.

53 *GDSO*, pp. 952–71, 1006–22, 1049–74, 1097–141, 1157–97, 1213, 1343, 1577–605, 1623–45, 1723–47, 1775–91, 1806–44; and *Draft Proceedings*, 40, pp. 1–16.

54 On this see, *inter alia*, *The Times* (16 June 1906), p. 7, cols 1–2; and *The Times* (18 June 1906), p. 5, cols 1–3.

55 *GDSO*, pp. 952–61.

56 See Marc Szeftel, *The Russian Constitution of April 23, 1906: Political Institutions of the Duma Monarchy* (Bruxelles, 1976), p. 286.

57 See p. 205.

58 See *Osobie zhurnaly Soveta ministrov tsarskoi Rossii. 1906 god* (Moscow, 1982; restricted edition), Vol. 1, No. 4, pp. 30–43.

59 The text of the manifesto appears, *inter alia*, in *Pravo*, No. 28 (16 July 1906), cols 2370–1.

60 The text of the communiqué appears, *inter alia*, in *Novoe vremia*, No. 10,871 (20 June 1906), p. 2, cols 2–4.

61 The extensive literature on these negotiations mostly consists of contemporary press accounts and of memoirs written and published much later. For treatment of the negotiations in historical literature see: Abraham Ascher, *The Revolution of 1905: Authority Restored* (Stanford, 1992), pp. 180–97; V. V. Shelokhaev, *Kadety – glavnaia partiia liberal'noi burzhuazii v bor'be s revoliutsiei 1905–1907gg.* (Moscow, 1983), pp. 214–22; Sidel'nikov, *Obrazovanie*, pp. 329–45; and V. I. Startsev, *Russkaia burzhuaziia i samoderzhaviie v 1905–1917gg.* (Leningrad, 1977), pp. 52–130. Though the last of these is the most detailed account, it is the least accurate. In fact, Startsev shows a cavalier attitude towards facts. Thus, for example, he refers to V. N. Kokovtsov as minister of finance in Witte's cabinet (p. 66), while in reality this post was held by I. P. Shipov. For a partial list of the contemporary published sources and later reminiscences, see Shmuel Galai, 'The Tragic Dilemma of Russian Liberalism as Reflected in Ivan Il'ic Petrunkevich's Letters to his Son', *Jahrbücher für Geschichte Osteuropas*, Vol. 29 (1981), Part 1, pp. 16–17 (nn. 85–7).

62 Startsev, *Russkaia burzhuaziia*, p. 67.

63 See D. N. Shipov, *Vospominaniia i dumy o perezhitom* (Moscow, 1918), pp. 445–59; and P. N. Miliukov, *Tri popytki. K istorie russkogo lzhe-konstitutsionalizma* (Paris, 1921), p. 27.

64 See *Vestnik*, No. 16 (1906), cols 1086–8.

65 Startsev, *Russkaia burzhuaziia*, p. 76.

66 See Andrew M. Verner, *The Crisis of Russian Autocracy: Nicholas II and the 1905 Revolution* (Princeton, 1990), pp. 253–6.

67 *Dnevnik Imperatora Nikolaia II* (Berlin, 1923), pp. 231–52.

68 Ibid., pp. 238, 243.

69 Ibid., p. 242.

70 See Startsev, *Russkaia burzhuaziia*, pp. 101–4.

71 'Perepiska Vil'gel'ma II i Nikolaia II, 1904–1907', *Byloe*, Vol. 1 (1917), pp. 103–43 (here p. 143).

72 On this see Galai, 'The Tragic Dilemma', pp. 16–17.

73 See *Ascher, The Revolution of 1905*, pp. 195–6; and Startsev, *Russkaia burzhuaziia*, pp. 105–6. Among those who advised Nicholas II to come to an accommodation with the Duma was Kaiser Wilhelm II. See 'Perepiska Vil'gel'ma II', p. 133. See also the tsar's description of the gloomy expressions of many of his luncheon guests on 9 July, after they learned of the dissolution of the Duma, in *Dnevnik*, p. 244.

74 The court commandant first made overtures to Petrunkevich and Muromtsev, and only after they refused to negotiate without prior permission from the Kadet central committee did he approach Miliukov, who was prepared to act, in this matter, 'on [his] own responsibility'. See Startsev, *Russkaia burzhuaziia*, p. 72.

75 See p. 206.

76 Miliukov's memoirs are the sole source for the proceedings of this meeting. However, his exchanges with Trepov in the contemporary press in late June 1906, the abbreviated minutes of the discussions in the Kadet central committee (on such questions as the formation of a Kadet cabinet and its programme, and the attitude to a coalition government) – on which see Galai and Pavlov (eds), *Protokoly*, pp. 84–6 – largely corroborate Miliukov's version. For the treatment of the meeting in the historical literature, see Ascher, *The Revolution of 1905*, pp. 181–3; Shelokhaev, *Kadety*, pp. 214–17; and Startsev, *Russkaia burzhuaziia*, pp. 72–4.

77 See, for example, Ascher, *The Revolution of 1905*, p. 194.

78 *Vestnik*, No. 16 (22 June 1906), cols 1043–4 (here col. 1044).

79 P. N. Miliukov, *God Bor'by. Publitsisticheskaia khronika 1905–1907* (St Petersburg, 1907), pp. 490–2.
80 Ibid., pp. 492–5.
81 See, for example, *Novoe vremia*, No. 10,876 (25 June 1906), p. 2, cols 2–3. For the full text of the interview see the *Daily Telegraph* (9 July 1906, n.s.), p. 12, cols 2–3. For a summary in English see Ascher, *The Revolution of 1905*, pp. 184–6. See also Startsev, *Russkaia burzhuaziia*, pp. 80–1.
82 Reprinted in Miliukov, *God bor'by*, pp. 495–9.
83 For the text of the communiqué see, for example, *Novoe vremia*, No. 10,871 (20 June 1906), p. 2, cols 2–4.
84 See, for example, the complaint of a Kadet deputy (V. P. Obninskii) on this score: *GDSO*, pp. 1749–50. The text of the government communiqué on Bialystok can be found in *Novoe vremia*, No. 10,872 (21 June 1906), p. 1, cols 7–8, and p. 2, col. 1.
85 *GDSO*, pp. 1747–53; and *Prilozhenie*, pp. 1754–6.
86 *Prilozhenie*, pp. 1792–3.
87 Ibid., pp. 1953–76, 1982–2002.
88 *Draft Proceedings*, 39, pp. 9–135.
89 See Vinaver, *Konflikty*, p. 175.
90 *Draft Proceedings*, 39, pp. 130–1.
91 Ibid.
92 Ibid., 40, pp. 2–15.
93 Ibid., pp. 16–137.
94 Vinaver, *Konflikty*, p. 176.

12 Lenin and the 1905 Revolution

Christopher Read

The period between 1902 and 1907 was vital to the emergence of Lenin. In those years he turned from leading acolyte to Plekhanov into a challenger for his leadership. He also developed ideas about the stages of revolution and the role of Social Democracy in a future revolution – notably the question of that party's participation in a provisional revolutionary government and the inevitability of armed uprising – which corresponded with positions he later took in 1917. Finally, his actions of the period open up questions about the nature of the split in the Social Democratic Party. Despite polemics that reached peaks of bitterness, there was no complete break.

Have we got Lenin wrong? His reputation has suffered, above all, at the hands of two groups of people: his supporters and his detractors. The former turned him into an idol; the latter into a monster. Lenin was neither. For all but the last five years of his life he was an anonymous, little-known member of a tiny sect of squabbling émigrés. On his party questionnaires, filled in during the 1920s, he described himself as a 'writer' or 'journalist' more frequently than anything else – and that is exactly what he was: a revolutionary writer, theorist and teacher. It was only by chance that he became an important revolutionary practitioner. Before October 1917, writing and arguing were his practice: *they* were the means by which he was, in the phrase he made famous, a 'professional revolutionary'. Within this framework, he was an ordinary (albeit extremely gifted) person. He had a close, loving family – although he had no children, much as he loved having them around – and loyal, supportive friends and colleagues.

The present chapter is devoted to looking at some of the connected aspects that we may, indeed, have got wrong: notably, when 'Lenin', as opposed to Vladimir Ilich Ulianov, was born; and his role in provoking the split in the Russian Social Democratic Party.

When was Lenin born? Obviously, we know when Vladimir Ulianov was born (it was in 1870), but the process of creating 'Lenin' was not so simple. The portentous phrase attributed to him by his sister Maria, on the occasion of his brother Alexander's execution – 'We will not go that way' – was used, in Soviet times, to imply that Lenin the Bolshevik was almost miraculously generated by the time of his seventeenth birthday. This is clearly nonsense. Trotsky is not much better. He argued that Lenin's 'fundamental features' were 'fully formed' by 1894.[1] More plausibly, most (though not all) commentators once suggested that Lenin was born in 1902, with his pamphlet *What is to be Done?* In fact, this pamphlet was greeted at the time as a declaration of orthodoxy, not as a declaration of war within the party. The Second Party Congress, of 1903, would appear to be the latest moment that one could select as marking the birth of Lenin and the birth of Bolshevism.[2] However, closer observation of the tangled polemics of these and the next few years shows that things are not so simple and that certain questions still need further elucidation.

One of the least well understood of these questions is about Lenin personally. Up to 1902 Lenin had been content – indeed proud – to be a devoted acolyte to the luminaries of Russian Marxism, notably Plekhanov and Aksel'rod. He, along with his inseparable friend and ally, Martov, represented a rising generation that could be critical but was not yet challenging for leadership. The majority of Lenin's writings had, up to that point, been extensions and defences of Plekhanov's seminal ideas on the inadequacies of Populism that he presented in *Our Differences* (1885). Lenin had added glosses and, in the case of *The Development of Capitalism in Russia* (1899), had made an important contribution of his own, arguing, in effect, that the debate about whether Russia might avoid capitalism was no longer a live issue because the country was already caught up in its tentacles.

Contrast this with Lenin in early 1905. Martov was his enemy. Plekhanov had been mortally offended. Lenin had been refused space by Kautsky to respond to a swingeing attack in *Neue Zeit* by Rosa Luxemburg. No Social Democrat of the first magnitude supported Lenin. With the partial exception of A. A. Bogdanov, Lenin had argued with all the major intellects of the Russian and European movements. According to many commentators, he had also split the party by this time. No longer the devoted acolyte, he appeared to be a contemptuous and isolated heretic.

These were extraordinary developments to have taken place in such a short period of time and many of the received opinions about why they happened are wrong. The present chapter is devoted to re-examining aspects of what happened in these years. They represent the crux of Lenin's own life and career and were crucial in shaping the whole of twentieth-century socialism. Had they turned out differently, Russian and world history in the twentieth century might well also have been very different.

Disputes in the party (1902–03)

In order to prepare the way for understanding this period of Lenin's life, it is necessary to go over familiar ground. In particular, it is necessary to make some reference to the context and to reopen some ancient arguments.

The phase of Lenin's life here under review really started around 1902 with the publication of one of his best-known works, *What is to be Done? Burning Questions of Our Movement,* and continued into the formal 'split' in the party conventionally dated from its Second Congress in Brussels and London in 1903. Although lacking the time or space to go into these moments in detail, it is necessary to make one or two comments. First, it has been shown convincingly by Neil Harding and others that *What is to be Done?* is best understood as a restatement of orthodoxy in Russian Social Democracy rather than as a challenge to it. Its targets were so-called Economism and Bernsteinian revisionism rather than an as-yet non-existent Menshevism. It was broadly welcomed as such at the time by the major figures in Social Democracy. It was only later that the book was reinterpreted as a blueprint for Leninism. Nonetheless, the idea is still widespread that it was a heretical document. It was not. So this is another false birthday for Lenin and Leninism.

Surely, then, the Second Party Congress must be the moment of the birth of Lenin? According to much conventional wisdom, Lenin determined to split the party and ruthlessly did so, resisting all attempts at reconciliation, camouflaging his actions with a false veneer of attempted reunification up to and even beyond the Fifth Congress in 1907. Once again, however, the issues are not so clear-cut. At the Second Congress, as everyone knows, Lenin's proposal on defining party membership was actually defeated. His 'majority' emerged over elections to the editorial board of the party newspaper, *Iskra.* The 'split' did not occur overnight and it took years to solidify.

These well-known developments set the scene, but for what? Various powerful mythologies about the direction of Lenin's life and career at this time have emerged among his admirers and detractors. Both sides tend to share certain key foundations of interpretation, notably Lenin's strong and determined character. One side sees it as admirable, the other as a source of evil. For both, Lenin emerges as a strong, ruthless, determined splitter of the existing party and builder of a renovated party and movement devoted to Lenin and the emerging principles of Leninism. Further tropes purport to explain why Lenin was as he was. These include the Machiavellian power-hungry, control freak driven by the embryonic dictator within. Others see an obsessive-compulsive personality given to intrigue and treachery in the name of asserting his ideas. He is also seen to have been deeply affected by his brother's execution and determined to exact revenge for it from the system that killed him. Admirers, of course, see a far-sighted genius moving inexorably through his moves towards victory like a chess grandmaster. However, looking at the next few years of Lenin's life (that is, up to his return to Russia and eventual retreat to Western Europe in December 1907), there is much to contradict the notion of a single-minded party-builder and splitter. Indeed, it is the argument of the present study that Bolshevism and Leninism were only really born in the years 1905 to 1906. It is also contended that Lenin, in these years, is best understood as a tactical improviser and strategic conviction politician who did what he did in order to promote what he considered to be the essential policies for the party and the movement. Party structure and party discipline were not the end but the means. The 'split' was secondary, not primary. In order to support this it would be helpful to look at Lenin's views on the party and the split at this time and to look at his revolutionary tactics as they evolved in the revolutionary crisis.

It cannot be doubted that Lenin's behaviour at the Second Congress was boorish in the extreme. His intensity led him into almost frenzied interventions. Indeed, he later admitted as much in a letter to A. N. Potresov of 13 September 1903. He had, he wrote, 'often behaved and acted in a state of frightful irritation, frenziedly' and was even prepared to admit to 'this *fault of mine*'.[3] He was, not, however, prepared to accept that any of the decisions he had forced through the congress were wrong. The congress had seen a new side of Lenin, the ruthless, stop-at-nothing side. It also showed that he was prepared to sacrifice anything – in this case his close friendship with Martov – if political necessity demanded it.

Lenin appeared to be riding high as the congress broke up. He had established himself as second in the party pecking order to the venerable Plekhanov and, in practice, as the most active party member. Plekhanov was almost a symbolic chairman, Lenin a hands-on chief executive: he was, it seemed, the *de facto* leader of the party. In fact, however, appearances were deceptive. Plekhanov was no extinct volcano and he was at pains to try to reverse the split that had taken place. After all, the party did not have resources to squander. In Plekhanov's eyes, the Martovites were first-rate Marxists and revolutionaries who had to be brought back into the fold.

Tangled polemics (1903–04)

Almost all the main protagonists seemed to feel that the acrimonious falling-out at the congress was really just an incident that could be patched up. For a year or so afterwards, an elaborate game of political relationships was conducted. In September and October 1903, Lenin and Plekhanov tried to reach agreement with Martov. However, in late October and November, when progress was being made, it was Lenin who dug his heels in. He complained to Plekhanov, resigned from the Party Council and urged Plekhanov to 'not give everything away to the Martovites'.[4] In his resignation letter he stated: 'I by no means refuse to support the new central Party institutions by my work to the best of my ability.'[5] On 4 November he complained to a friend that Plekhanov had 'cruelly and shamefully let me down' and that 'the situation is desperate'.[6] On 6 November Lenin also resigned from the editorial board of *Iskra*, a painful wrench for him after he had done so much for the newspaper. From that point on, Plekhanov sided with the Mensheviks. Lenin, for the time being, led the Central Committee, but the Mensheviks controlled the newspaper, the key to the party. A bitter struggle between the factions in the party continued.

The hardening of Lenin's position after the Second Congress first became apparent, as far as his published writings were concerned, in his *Letter to a Comrade on Our Organizational Tasks*. In it, Lenin's key phrase was that a 'disciplined party of struggle' was needed. The *Letter*, originally drafted in 1902, had circulated widely in Russia in a sort of *samizdat* form and was published as a pamphlet with a new preface and postscript in both Russia and Geneva in January 1904. However, the main declaration of his new principles came in the more extensive *One Step Forward, Two Steps Back – The Crisis in Our Party*, which appeared in March 1904. It is actually longer than the much-better-known *What is to be Done?* and could be said to contain many of the propositions which are harder to find in the latter.

One Step Forward, Two Steps Back is an odd piece of work. It is a detailed commentary, from Lenin's perspective, on the minutes of the Second Congress. It goes, issue by issue, through the debates and resolutions. It maintains a high level of vitriolic energy towards Lenin's growing band of opponents. The excruciating detail, the childishly sustained heavy sarcasm and the difficulty of reviving the context in which it was produced make it a very difficult and unprepossessing item to read today. Lenin's worry that it would only be the occasional reader who would have 'had the patience to read' the whole of some of his opponents' writings could apply to readers of Lenin's pamphlet also.[7] Its importance lies in the fact that it appears to tighten up the looser concepts of *What is to be Done?*

In *One Step Forward* Lenin complained that 'Shells rained on my head',[8] and sought to return fire. Three words, above all, characterize his views on party organization: authority, centralism and discipline. The key concepts he was attacking were autonomy, reformism, anarchism and even (in a particular sense) democracy. Together, for Lenin, they made up the ever-expanding category of 'opportunism'. In his view, the demands from certain quarters for 'autonomy' (that is, decentralization) were inappropriate. For Lenin, the moment was one of transition. 'Previously, our Party was not a formally organized whole, but merely a sum of separate groups', was a point he reiterated several times. The looser relations this imposed were no longer applicable: '*Now* we have become an organized Party, and this implies the establishment of authority . . . the subordination of lower Party bodies to higher ones.'[9] Lenin supported 'top downward'[10] organization and, in a phrase that resounds today, defended bureaucracy over democracy in that 'Bureaucracy *versus* democracy is in fact centralism *versus* autonomism; it is the organizational principle of revolutionary Social Democracy as opposed to the organizational principle of opportunist Social Democracy.'[11] The crucial question here is: what did Lenin mean by 'bureaucracy'? Earlier he had argued that bureaucracy (in the sense of careerism, place-seeking and wrangling over co-option rather than ideas) was unquestionably 'undesirable and detrimental to the Party'.[12] So, do we have in *One Step*

Forward the blueprint for Bolshevism that is actually somewhat elusive in *What is to be Done?*

At one level, as the extracts above indicate, Lenin was being more forthright about the need for a strongly led party where the organizational principle was, in his expression, from the 'top downward'. In addition, the rhetoric indicated an increasingly unbridgeable gulf between the participants. Actual manoeuvrings and deep squabbles had become endemic. Lenin's determination and his lone battle had, indeed, brought shells raining down on him from all directions. Plekhanov had written an article pointedly entitled 'What Should Not Be Done', and Martov had complained of 'A State of Siege' in the party in a pamphlet containing that phrase in its title.[13] Discussions to bring unity led only to deeper divisions. In October Lenin wrote: 'You can't imagine even a tenth of the outrages to which the Martovites have sunk ... War has been declared.'[14] Party bodies voted in favour of one side and then for the other, as the search for compromise continued. Plekhanov said he could not bear to 'fire on his comrades' and that 'rather than have a split it is better to put a bullet in one's brain'.[15] Lenin himself was so preoccupied with his thoughts that he once walked into the back of a tram and, according to Krupskaia 'very nearly had his eye knocked out'.[16] He resigned from central party bodies, including the *Iskra* editorial board, in November, and wrote harshly about Plekhanov who, he said, had 'cruelly and shamefully' let him down by reopening discussion with the Martovites.[17] By late November he was co-opted onto the party Central Committee. The bewildering array of attacks and counter-attacks continued and one might conclude that, as Lenin wrote later, 'Bolshevism exists as a political movement and as a political party since 1903.'[18]

However, some of the ambiguities present in *What is to be Done?* continue into *One Step Forward*. Kautsky, the archetype of orthodoxy, was presented as an example of the kind of centralizer Lenin had in mind. A contemporary dispute in the German Social Democratic Party, about the right of the centre to intervene in the affairs of constituencies, was held up as an analogy to what Lenin was writing about. He also claimed that he stood for 'Social Democratic European' practices against his opponents who were 'Social Democratic Asiatics'.[19] There were occasional tones of conciliation. The day after writing that 'war has been declared', Lenin joined Plekhanov in offering to co-opt Martov onto the *Iskra* editorial board! On several occasions he stated that he recognized that his opponents were honourable, although sometimes he did so in such a patronizing way one might doubt the sincerity involved. For example, Lenin said 'it would be unwise to attribute to sordid motives even the most sordid manifestations of the squabbling that is so habitual in the atmosphere of émigré and exile colonies. It is a sort of epidemic disease engendered by abnormal conditions of life, disordered nerves, and so on.'[20] He used the same concept much more crudely towards the end of the pamphlet, where he talked about a 'sordid story brought about by [Martov's] morbid imagination' and also made reference to 'a number of *incorrect statements* (evidently due to his over-wrought condition)'.[21] It was in mid-September that Lenin wrote the letter for Potresov in which he admitted his 'fault' of 'frightful irritation' and frenzy.[22] However, there is no doubt that the only way Lenin would join with the transgressors would be if they capitulated to his principles.

One Step Forward, Two Steps Back also merits consideration beyond its detailed contents. Overall, Lenin was seeking a new level of party organization that corresponded to a new situation. His demand for a unified and disciplined party, with a strong central executive (and this is clearly what he meant by 'the bureaucratic principle' of organization) was not unreasonable in itself. Other parties were evolving in much the same way, notably the liberals, who emerged as the Constitutional Democratic (Kadet) Party, and the Populists, who formed the Party of Socialists-Revolutionaries (PSR). In fact, the degree to which his conception of party organization was fundamentally different from theirs is open to dispute. Many will also sympathize with his complaint that one of the roots of the problem lay in 'intellectual individualism'[23] which accepted only 'purely Platonic and verbal' acceptance of organizational relations.[24] At heart, Lenin could be seen to be trying to instil some necessary discipline into a chronically individualist body of people. He said as much: 'Sneering at discipline – autonomism – anarchism – there you have the ladder which our opportunism in matters of organization now climbs and now descends, skipping from rung to rung and skillfully dodging any definite statement of its principles.'[25] This also reflected the greater anti-intellectualism of *One Step*, emphasizing that he was urging the party to abandon its *kruzhok* ('study group') mentality.[26]

In contrast to his opponents, Lenin's extraordinary insistence on following rules and minutes showed a mind desperate for a fixed point in an ever-shifting universe. He was looking for a solid foundation from which to build a disciplined party devoted to the undiluted goal of revolution and eluding the siren grasp of opportunism. However, few saw it in that light. Rosa Luxemburg attacked his views in summer 1904, accusing him of 'ultra-centralism' and of being 'full of the spirit of the overseer'. His principles threatened to 'bind' the movement rather than develop it. His concern, she argued, was 'not so much to make the activity of the party more fruitful as to control the party'.[27] Kautsky, in turn, refused to print Lenin's reply. No major figures in the European or Russian movements came to Lenin's defence. He was alone with his own mini-group. As we shall see, his stance attracted a rising generation, including A. A. Bogdanov and A. V. Lunacharskii (not to mention the crucial support of Maxim Gorky, who was a major source of finance), but for the time being Lenin had alienated all the major figures of European Marxism. While one might argue about the exact meaning of Lenin's written text, his actions seemed less ambiguous: he was building a centralized, revolutionary party around himself, formed of members who accepted his priorities. For the moment, however, it was only a small acorn.

The language of *One Step Forward* is also interesting from the point of view of nomenclature. The term 'Bolshevik' does not appear at all, although the regular Russian word *bol'shinstvo* (majority), from which it is derived, is used constantly by Lenin to describe the group to which he claimed to belong. The word 'Menshevik' appears only once, in inverted commas,[28] as does the term 'Leninism' in the phrase 'revolt against Leninism' that Lenin says was coined by Martov.[29] Clearly, the terminology had not been defined any more than the party differences themselves.

Organizationally, a decisive turning point was reached in summer 1904. Since February of that year, a group of Lenin's supporters had urged conciliation. By July and August they completely dominated the Central Committee. Lenin had lost control of his last institutional redoubt. He was being edged out into the wilderness. Heavy blows from the international socialist community followed. It was in September that Rosa Luxemburg's article had appeared. Lenin was desperate. Loss of influence also left him without funds and without an outlet for his writings. The leading figures of Russian and German Social Democracy – Plekhanov, Pavel Aksel'rod, Vera Zasulich, Martov, Kautsky and Luxemburg – were all opposed to him. His own supporters – F. V. Lengnik, M. M. Essen and R. S. Zemliachka – were comparative nonentities. Former stalwarts like V. A. Noskov, L. B. Krasin and G. M. Krzhizhanovskii had gone over to the 'conciliators'. But, even at this point, Lenin refused to compromise. For him, the split was essential and had to be maintained despite the odds against him. Why had he become so implacable, and how was he to dig himself out?

The answer to the first question seems to be that Lenin, now 33 years old, had reached a decisive and maturing point in his development. His ideas and principles had become sacred to him. His interpretation of what they meant was his guiding light. He was no longer prepared to learn from and defer to the older generation. At the heart of his writings on the party was the deep conviction that it should be small, advanced and secret. To see his beloved party adopting what he considered suicidal principles of broad membership was too much for him to accept. He would fight the process all the way. We might surmise here that Lenin's background of prison and exile had convinced him of the need for conspiracy, while many of his opponents had spent long years in Western Europe and had been more deeply imbued with the spirit of liberal democracy and wanted to adapt it. Lenin had a different vision, which the struggle was hardening rather than softening. He was becoming a fundamentalist, unwilling to compromise what he considered to be the essence of his faith. He had always been self-confident, and it was a virtue that stood him in good stead. At this conjuncture, however, one could say that it was, like other of his virtues at various times, threatening to turn into a vice. It was becoming a basis for dogmatism, narrowness and intolerance. Lenin knew what he wanted and had stopped listening even to his close friends if they tried to tell him any different. For his supporters, this was admirable determination and clear-sightedness. His opponents could only shake their heads in sorrow and disbelief.

The confidence and determination were, however, what pulled him through. Without money, resources or influence, he was forced to remake his career and to build, in Bolshevism, a personally loyal instrument that would never let him down. A new mouthpiece was imperative and Lenin set out to build one, the newspaper called *Vpered* (Forwards!). It looked like being an uphill struggle, but the situation was about to change radically. On 9 January 1905, Cossacks fired on a peacefully demonstrating crowd in St Petersburg. The sporadic rebellions of 1899 to 1904 now turned into potential revolution.

Perhaps the most ironic aspect of *One Step Forward*, the dispute and the whole two-year obsession with organization was that it diverted the émigré leadership from keeping a proper watch on Russian politics, so that when the revolution of 1905 exploded out of the rumblings of the previous four or so years, many of the leaders of Russian Social Democracy, including Lenin, were caught by surprise.

The revolution seen from Geneva (1905)

Despite the multitude of extraordinary events taking place in Russia in the years before 1905 – the general strikes, peasant disturbances and spectacular assassinations – there was no doubt among the émigrés that Bloody Sunday had raised the situation to a whole new dimension: that of potential revolution.

For Lenin, the new situation did not so much stimulate new initiatives (though there were some) as reinforce the importance of the themes with which he was already dealing. His major concerns – breaking with the 'study group' mentality and developing a proper Social Democratic party and analysing what form a revolution could take in Russia's peculiar conditions – became increasingly important and dominated his writings and actions in the first phase of the revolution. Unlike in 1917, when the abdication occurred at the beginning of the revolution and conditions of relative freedom emerged rapidly, in 1905 it was only after the October Manifesto that Lenin felt the situation had changed sufficiently for him to venture back to Russia. For the first ten months of 1905, Lenin remained in Western Europe and, despite a growing number of articles analysing events in Russia, the old themes of the party dispute continued to be uppermost in his thoughts.

A central focus of the dispute (and the centrepiece of Lenin's strategy for ending it) was the idea of convening a new party congress to thrash the issues out. Lenin, at this period of his life, was almost obsessed with the notion of the party congress. As we have seen, one of the most extraordinary features of *One Step Forward* was its assumption that resolutions were almost like concrete building materials. Like an engineer assembling structural girders, Lenin's mind revolved around designing, making and utilizing binding resolutions to construct a solid edifice held together not by the forces of physics but by those of discipline. He clung determinedly to such notions as the only way to bring order out of chaos.

At one level, such a concern for collective decision-making fits poorly with some of the more hostile interpretations of Lenin's life and activities. If he were a ruthless, self-centred potential dictator, why would he urge the convening of congresses that might not agree with him? To say he ignored decisions that went against him is not true at this time. Several major party meetings were held during the period 1905 to 1907. As we shall see, they by no means adopted a tame, submissive attitude to Lenin, but Lenin went along with them nonetheless. It is also the case that at no point did the party split become a complete break and at no point could the factions be considered to be completely separate, independent parties. This also suggests that the birth of Lenin and Leninism was less simple than the traditional admirers and detractors suggested. A form of dialogue continued within what participants still perceived as a single (though clearly faction-ridden) movement. In the French political sense, the warring groups continued to be part of the same *famille* and acknowledged their special relationship (though, like the family in the everyday sense, the very closeness added substantially to the heat that quarrels could generate).

Nevertheless, many aspects of the relationship between the party factions remained baffling to outsiders and to later observers. In some respects, the differences are best interpreted as a consequence of the conventions of political discourse – notably that, if my opponent takes a position, I must disagree with it. In part, this is what got the supposed champions of broad party democracy, the *men'shinstvo* (minority), to oppose what appeared the most democratic outcome to the dispute – a party congress. However, there was more to it than that. They feared that Lenin would dominate such a congress but, whether he did or not, they were afraid it would create deeper party divisions, not heal them. The minority had adopted boycott tactics towards party bodies on and off since 1903, and continued to do so with respect to the congress. It was therefore not entirely Lenin's fault that, when the Third Congress convened in London on 25 April 1905, all the delegates were Leninists. Not surprisingly, the key themes were the division in the party and the appropriate tactics to adopt in the revolution. We will now examine each in turn.

Lenin and the party in 1905

Although his detractors would claim he was being insincere, Lenin appealed time and time again for the Third Congress to be representative of the whole party. He did this in part because of his belief that the split was largely an émigré issue which had little resonance within the real party in Russia – a concept in which he was encouraged by his closest ally at this moment, Aleksandr Bogdanov, who was himself mainly a Russian resident (thanks to prison and exile) rather than a permanent émigré. Bringing the leadership together with the membership would, Lenin hoped, provide grounds for getting the whole party back to reality and focused on the issue of the developing revolution. In the last issue of *Vpered* to appear before Lenin's departure from Geneva for the congress in London appeared his 'Open Letter' to Plekhanov, who was addressed as the chairman of the RSDLP Council, imploring him one more time to submit 'the entire conflict to the judgment of the Party itself'.[30] Even though this appeal was rhetorical and the earlier ones may have been a bluff, they were a bluff that should have been called. Through them, Lenin was able to command at least a substantial proportion of the moral high ground in the eyes of party members. They, too, were largely baffled by the vehemence and obstinacy of the leadership factions, particularly in the eye of an increasing revolutionary storm.

Lenin used the Third Congress, which lasted until 12 May, to establish a Leninist grip on key party institutions. The existing newspapers (*Iskra* and *Vpered*) were declared disbanded and a new paper, *Proletarii*, was established as the official party newspaper (under Lenin's editorship), while an all-Leninist Central Committee was elected composed of Lenin, Bogdanov, Krasin, D. Postalovskii and A. I. Rykov.

For the first months after the Third Congress, Lenin tried to establish his group as the entire official party. He wrote to the International Socialist Bureau in Brussels in June, demanding it recognize *Proletarii* as the only official Russian Social Democratic newspaper and de-recognize *Iskra*. Calls for unity became muted in the face of this new tactic. It was at this point that the split looked at its deepest and most irreconcilable. Lenin wrote as though the whole party was now in the hands of the Leninist CC.

However, appearances were still deceptive. The International Socialist Bureau and, especially, the most prestigious members of the German SDP (with Kautsky at the forefront) were not prepared to grant Lenin his victory. A weakening of Lenin's tone can be found in his letter to the CC of 28 July 1905, in which he said, in response to efforts by August Bebel and others to bring pressure on the Leninists, that their 'mediation should be agreed with thanks'. He also returned to an old theme: binding arbitration should be refused, he said, because only a Fourth Party Congress could legitimately decide the issue.[31] Once again, detractors might say the apparent willingness to compromise was tactical and insincere – but such a claim can only be speculative and is not necessarily correct. Lenin's stunning letter to Plekhanov of late October underlined the complexity. In it he said the 'need for social democratic unity can no longer be put off'. In a sentence that could only be heartily endorsed by any baffled observer trying to thread a way through this labyrinth, Lenin continued: 'We are in agreement with you on over nine-tenths of the questions of theory and tactics, and to quarrel over one-tenth is not worthwhile.'[32] Disingenuously, he went on to add that he had never attempted to impose his views on any other Social Democrat and that none of the editors of *Proletarii* had entered into an agreement to be a 'Leninist'.

Nevertheless, the new sense of urgency over reconciliation was clear, as was its prime motivation. The October Manifesto had changed the situation, making revolutionary unity more imperative than ever – not least because there was agreement that there should be a united front to get real democratic concessions out of the autocracy. The manifesto also opened the way for exiles to return, and the further development of party unity was to take place in the very different context of a return to Russia, where we will pick it up after looking at the other theme preoccupying Lenin in his last months of exile: revolutionary tactics and strategy.

Lenin's views on revolutionary tactics and strategy in 1905

One thing the party factions did agree on was that the upcoming revolution in Russia would be bourgeois. Sadly, however, that did not mean that they agreed on what was meant, in practice, by a 'bourgeois revolution'. Lenin's own version evolved as the revolutionary year unfolded. He considered three aspects of tactics to be especially important. These were: the definition of which classes would be dominant; the question of an armed uprising as an essential element in the seizure of power; and the issue of relations to a provisional revolutionary government. All these issues emerged again in Lenin's mind in 1917, and are worth investigating in their 1905 context, not least because of the light thrown on Lenin's later ideas. Many commentators have argued that Lenin changed his line radically in 1917: some of his own party members thought that to be the case; and historians have talked of Lenin's 'doctrinal revolution' of April 1917.[33] Notwithstanding such interpretations, there were actually strong elements of continuity between Lenin's tactical views of 1905 and those of 1917, even though they were not identical.

As far as class was concerned, the problem for any Russian Marxist was the specific class make-up of Russia. As a largely rural country, in the early stages of transition between feudalism and capitalism, it could not, of course, exemplify the classic Marxist conditions for bourgeois (let alone socialist) revolution. The middle class was underdeveloped and was more dependent on the state than the self-confident, developed capitalist classes of America, Britain and France, for example. Second, there was a vast petite bourgeoisie, in the form of the peasantry, which comprised at least four-fifths of the Russian population. Third, the working class was small and underdeveloped. The full ramifications of these peculiarities are beyond our present scope, but what is important is how Lenin addressed them, given the general expectation that a bourgeois revolution was emerging.

Notwithstanding the caricatural views common in much subsequent historical writing, no socialist group in 1905 (with the possible exception of the Economists) was prepared to sit back and let the bourgeois revolution run its pre-ordained course. For Leninists and Plekhanovites alike, it was necessary to aid the weak Russian bourgeoisie to attain its destiny. Lenin was not the only one inspired by the ringing phrase in the original 1898 party manifesto, drafted by Petr Struve, that:

> The further east in Europe one proceeds, the weaker, more cowardly, and baser in the political sense becomes the bourgeoisie and the greater are the cultural and political tasks that devolve on the proletariat. The Russian working class must and will carry on its powerful shoulders the cause of political liberation.[34]

Nonetheless, the logic of political discourse, as we have already commented, more or less required each group to refine a distinctive position of its own. In March 1905, in an article in *Vpered*, Lenin launched his concept of a 'democratic dictatorship of the proletariat and peasantry'. A further article, in April, elaborated his views and was published as a separate pamphlet. The formulation had already changed and was now, as the title proclaimed, *The Revolutionary-Democratic Dictatorship of the Proletariat and Peasantry*. It became the basis for much of Lenin's contribution to the Third Congress, which convened two weeks later. It achieved its most developed exposition in Lenin's main pamphlet of 1905, *Two Tactics of Social Democracy in the Democratic Revolution*, which he worked on in June and July and which was published in August. Here it interacted with the theme of the party's attitude to a provisional revolutionary government and to the theme of armed uprising.

Although they sometimes appear to be contradictory, Lenin's views expressed in this pamphlet help clarify a great deal about his tactics and strategy in 1905 and in 1917. For those who doubted that he believed in the importance of the bourgeois revolution, he stated clearly and unequivocally that 'A bourgeois revolution is *absolutely* necessary in the interests of the proletariat.'[35] However, the complications begin from there. An issue that arose immediately from that assumption was that of what role the Social Democrats would play in such a revolution. Lenin's formula was perhaps evasive, but it was not unreasonable. Echoing the decision of the Third Party Congress on the issue, he said that participation in a provisional revolutionary government was possible but was 'subject to the alignment of forces and other factors which cannot be exactly predetermined'.[36] It was, he said, 'impossible at present to speak of concrete conditions' under which the decision to join or not join should be made.[37] For example, should the wavering bourgeoisie ultimately turn to tsarism for protection the result would be disastrous for the left: 'Social Democracy will find its hands actually tied in the struggle against the inconsistent bourgeoisie. Social Democracy will find itself "dissolved" in bourgeois democracy in the sense that the proletariat will not succeed in placing its clear imprint on the revolution.'[38]

Lenin's fear that the distinctive proletarian imprint would 'dissolve' in the thick porridge of bourgeois democracy was, of course, related to his view of the fate of revolutionary socialism in the bourgeois democratic countries of the West. Lenin was determined to keep the distinctive proletarian imprint, and remembering this helps us to see a consistency between his ideas in 1905 and 1917.

He picked the implications up elsewhere in the pamphlet and in other of his writings of this time. In particular, he wrote, the proletarian should remember that the bourgeois revolution was a means and not an end: 'A Social Democrat must never for a moment forget that the proletariat will inevitably have to wage a class struggle for socialism even against the most democratic and republican bourgeoisie and petty-bourgeoisie. This is beyond doubt.'[39] In a comment that almost exactly fitted his attitude to the provisional government in 1917, he said there needed to be a separate class party to keep as strict a watch 'over our ally as over an enemy'.[40]

He also invoked the distinction made by most major Russian parties between a minimum programme and a maximum programme. Referring once more to the Third Congress's resolution, Lenin said that 'the resolution, by making implementation of the minimum programme the provisional government's revolutionary task, eliminates the absurd and semi-anarchist ideas of giving immediate effect to the maximum programme and the conquest of power for a socialist revolution'. The minimum programme – meaning, essentially, the establishment of a democratic republic – would only open up the road to socialism at a point in the future. Again, in a tone that was to re-emerge in 1917, Lenin cautioned:

> The degree of Russia's economic development (an objective condition), and the degree of class-consciousness and organization of the broad masses of the proletariat (a subjective condition inseparably bound up with the objective condition) make the immediate and complete emancipation of the working class impossible. Only the most ignorant people can close their eyes to the bourgeois nature of the democratic revolution which is now taking place; only the most naïve optimists can forget how little as yet the masses of the workers are informed about the aims of socialism and the methods of achieving it.[41]

One is tempted to say: 'Spoken like a true Menshevik!'

The parallels with 1917 do not end there. The issue of armed uprising had also raised its head and the deeper into the revolutionary year he went, the more anxious Lenin became that the issue of armed uprising should be clearly addressed. Once again arguing more sensibly than some of his opponents on this uncomfortable issue, Lenin started out from the assumption that 'Major questions in the life of nations are solved only by force. The reactionary class themselves are usually the first to resort to violence ... as the Russian autocracy has systematically and unswervingly been doing everywhere ever since 9 January.'[42] However, far from being carried away with the prospect of violence, Lenin's views, though based on realism, seem naive in the extreme. In late October, in a much-quoted passage, he made one of his most sustained analyses of the use of force, but it is one that appears more naive than penetrating. Giving instructions on setting up revolutionary army contingents, he said:

> The contingents may be of any strength, beginning with two or three people. They must arm themselves as best they can (rifles, revolvers, knives, knuckledusters, sticks, rags coated in kerosene for starting fires, ropes or rope-ladders, shovels for building barricades, pyroxilin cartridges, barbed wire, nails [for use against cavalry], etc. etc.) Under no circumstances should they wait for help from other sources, from above, from the outside; they must procure everything themselves.[43]

The idea that such raggle-taggle bands could fight their way into power was truly ludicrous.

What did these various formulations add up to? In brief, Lenin was saying that Russia's revolution would be bourgeois, but it would have its own special characteristics. Clearly, Lenin did not believe the socialist revolution was just around the corner. As in 1917, he pointed to the backwardness of the workers and the need to raise their consciousness as a process that would take some time. Exactly how much time, Lenin was not prepared to say and throughout 1905 (as in 1917) the question remained ambiguous. He was concerned that the Social Democratic movement should not confuse the two phases of the revolution. Although alliance with liberals was necessary, too close an association with the bourgeoisie would blunt the prospects for socialism, and it was here that he was suspicious of the Mensheviks. Once the democratic revolution had occurred it was the task of socialists to use the new conditions to prepare for the socialist revolution. It is surprising that, in April 1917, some of Lenin's closest followers (let alone his opponents) seem to have forgotten these aspects of Lenin's earlier ideas.

Be that as it may, the October Manifesto had changed the situation sufficiently to allow Lenin and other, but not all, leading revolutionary émigrés to consider returning to Russia. Lenin made up his mind and arrived in St Petersburg on 21 November 1905.

Lenin in Russia (December 1905 to December 1907)

Lenin spent the next two years based in Russia and Finland. In the early weeks he had to report to the police and lived apart from Krupskaia, who had arrived separately, ten days after Lenin. Because of irksome restrictions and police surveillance, Lenin went underground on 17 December. Using a false passport, he took a trip to Finland, returning on 30 December. From the middle of March 1906 he was mainly based in Finland, at Kuokkala and later at Styrs Udde. He travelled frequently to St Petersburg and Moscow, as well as to overseas party and associated meetings in Stockholm, Copenhagen, London, Stuttgart and elsewhere. He finally left in December 1907, making a perilous journey over thin ice that almost gave way beneath him. Thus, for two full years Lenin was closer to the heart of events than he had ever been or was to be again until 1917 itself. What do his writings and actions of this period tell us about him?

On the crucial question of the party, the signs remained confused. At times Lenin seemed as determined as ever to plough his own furrow. At others, he worked comfortably even with Menshevik majorities. In part, the complexity was the result of his new perspective as an insider rather than an émigré. It had been part of his view of the split that it was generated by the intensity and artificiality of émigré life and that it did not affect the party in Russia to anything like the same degree. This contributed to his insistence on solving problems by calling full party congresses in order that the healthy elements of the party in Russia could counterbalance the shaky nervousness of the exiles.

The new perspective also brought the two major aspects of his discourse closer together. Once in Russia, the issue of solving the split in the party became closely linked to the question of revolutionary tactics. Reuniting Social Democracy was, even more forcefully, the first step in any revolutionary strategy.

In terms of these two interrelated issues, there were no significant alterations in Lenin's positions in 1906 or 1907. The principles he had already worked out – party unity through congresses; armed uprising; hostility towards 'constitutional illusions'; the belief that only the proletariat and peasantry could enforce the completion of the 'bourgeois' revolution in the form of the democratic dictatorship of workers and peasants – remained his guiding stars. However, there were some unexpected twists and turns. In November 1905, Lenin contributed an article on 'The Reorganization of the Party' to Gorky's newspaper, *Novaia zhizn'*, in which he called for the party's democratization.[44] It was, of course, consistent with his views before and after 1905 that underground and conspiratorial tactics were not ideal, they were simply the necessary response to oppressive conditions. Once those conditions changed, such tactics were no longer obligatory. More conventional open and democratic party relations could be embarked upon – in this case, in the form of what was becoming known as 'democratic centralism'. Lenin had already outlined this in *One Step Forward* and *Two Tactics*. He was determined that the centre would remain the decisive element of the party, but local bodies would have the right to approach it and fight for changes in its outlook without having the right to go their own way on any significant policy issues.

Also at this time, as part of an initial drive to clarify the role and tasks of the party, Lenin wrote two more articles destined to have an important impact later on. In 'Party Organization and Party Literature' (13 November) he expressed the view that all party publications should be approved from the centre.[45] Without going into the complexities here, it is clear that Lenin was making the eminently sensible point that anything published in the party's name should be officially approved by it. It is also clear that what

Lenin meant by 'party literature' was political pamphlets. This article came to haunt Soviet literature in the Stalin era when its strictures were applied not only to political pamphlets but to all kinds of written material – including even artistic literature. It also came to apply not only to official party publications but (since, in Stalin's day, there was little scope for publishing anything independently of the party) to everything published. In fact, it remained a guiding light of Soviet publishing and censorship policy almost until the end.

A second article that came to have baleful consequences was devoted to 'Socialism and Religion'. It was published in mid-December 1905, in the last issue of *Novaia zhizn'*, before its closure by the police.[46] In it Lenin condemned all forms of religion and expressed the view that they should not be tolerated in the party. He quoted Marx's dictum that religion was 'the opium of the people', although without reference to Marx's further elaboration that it was 'the sigh of the oppressed creature; the heart of a heartless world; just as it is the spirit of a spiritless situation: it is the opium of the people'.[47] For Marx, religion was more subtly understood as a comfort in the alienating world of capitalism, while Lenin saw it solely as an agent of stupefaction and corruption. It marked a significant turn away from Marx in the direction of Bakunin, who also put hostility to religion in the front rank of the revolutionary's outlook. Together with an article of 1909 entitled 'The Attitude of the Workers' Party Towards Religion' (in which Lenin disagreed with wider European practice that religious belief was a private matter for each party member and instead insisted that the party should be actively opposed to religion at all levels),[48] this laid down guidelines for party policy on religion for much of the Soviet era.

The fact that Lenin occupied his first weeks back in revolutionary Russia writing organizational articles is, in itself, rather extraordinary, even though the pattern was to be repeated in 1917. Lenin had arrived in the middle of the most tumultuous upheaval Russia had so far endured. And yet he played little practical role in it. He was not an active member of the Petrograd Soviet and visited it on only a few occasions. He advocated armed uprising and fully supported the Moscow workers when they embarked on one, but his contribution to it was minimal. Ironically, for a movement that later came to pride itself on its revolutionary praxis (that is, the active combination of theory and practice), Lenin eschewed direct activism. Theory *was* his practice. Where an active revolutionary like Bakunin was often to be found on the streets or in the countryside encouraging and organizing rebellion (as he did in 1848, for example), Lenin preferred the committee room, the study and the print shop. He focused his activities in 1906 and 1907 on attending important party policy-making meetings, including a variety of conferences and congresses.

As has been mentioned, the new perspectives of being in Russia and in a revolution brought the key elements of party unity and revolutionary tactics closer together. The party was too small and the situation too acute for anything else. If Social Democracy were to have any influence, it would have to stand together. In fact, Lenin's position was a *tour de force* of either duplicity or party loyalty. While he fought constantly for his vision of the armed uprising, democratic dictatorship and, eventually, Duma boycott, he did it within the context of both Menshevik- and Bolshevik-dominated party institutions.

The ambiguity began from the first meetings. In late November, Lenin was a guest at the Second All-Russian Menshevik Conference held in St Petersburg. In December 1905, at Tampere, a Bolshevik conference supported Lenin's positions. No surprise there – except that one of Lenin's positions was a call for unity with the Mensheviks on a basis of full equality.[49] In February 1906, he contributed to a joint party newspaper, *Partiinye izvestiia*, and then spent the next months working towards the Reunification Congress to be held in Stockholm in late April and early May. Despite being in the minority, Lenin played an active part throughout, ironically getting his version of party membership accepted. Despite all this, the judgement that the congress had no impact is almost universal. For example, in their invaluable chronology of Lenin's life, Gerda and Herman Weber describe the situation thus: 'The unity is only formal, the split remains and Lenin is, as before, the leader of the Bolsheviks.' In the next entry (for 8 and 9 May), they quote from Lenin's own 'Appeal to the Party by Delegates to the Unity Congress who Belonged to the Former "Bolshevik" Group' that 'there is a split no longer'.[50] Note also the reference to the 'former "Bolshevik" group'. The evidence suggests that Lenin hoped and believed the split could be overcome.

As the revolutionary years unfolded, the situation became no clearer. At first the split seemed to narrow. For the rest of 1906 and during early 1907, Lenin worked alongside Mensheviks. For instance, he and the Menshevik Feodor Dan were co-speakers at a St Petersburg Party Conference held at Terijoki in June 1906. At a nationwide party conference at Tampere, Mensheviks were in the majority but the Bolsheviks attended and worked within it. Defeat for Lenin's position on electoral agreements with the Kadets led him, predictably, to call for a Fifth Congress to decide the issues. This particular question became so hot that in February 1907 Lenin was back in full polemical flood in his article 'The St Petersburg Elections and the Hypocrisy of the Thirty-one Mensheviks',[51] accusing his opponents of 'selling' votes to the Kadets. This set off an apparent collapse of the façade of unity and the Menshevik majority in the Central Committee called him before a tribunal, which met in April. Lenin, again predictably, defended himself by claiming it was the Mensheviks in question who had disregarded party discipline, while he, Lenin, hated splits. Splits, he said, he considered to be 'a great crime against the Party', adding that he was unforgiving in his pursuit of those who provoked them, hence the sharp tone of his article.[52]

Nevertheless, joint meetings and conferences continued (for instance, at

Terijoki, once more, in April 1907) and, in May 1907, the Fifth Congress itself opened in London, with 303 delegates representing a claimed 150,000 members. Of these delegates, 106 were Bolsheviks and ninety-seven were Mensheviks. Both groups worked within the framework of the party, Lenin taking his turn to chair sessions, motions coming and going in a normal way and a Central Committee being elected with thirteen full members (including six Bolsheviks and four Mensheviks) and eighteen candidate members (twelve of whom were Bolsheviks, including Lenin). In July, Lenin was elected as CC representative to the International Socialist Bureau. All of this looked like unified party activity within the somewhat federal structure it had had since the beginning – that is, as an alliance of factions gathered round shared principles of Social Democracy. All sides had their own news-papers and party meetings as well, but – however one approaches it – at this moment there was only one party, not two. No faction claimed the whole of party legitimacy for itself.

In any case, the issues dividing the factions were also in a state of evolu-tion. In 1906 and 1907 no one was arguing about party membership and professional revolutionaries. Democratic centralism, Lenin claimed with some justification, was 'now universally recognized'.[53] The central issues were armed uprising and (particularly for Lenin, who is our concern here) the convoluted tactics opposing constitutional illusions and electoral pacts, but also boycotting and then opposing the boycott of the various State Dumas.

Despite its failure, the Moscow armed uprising remained Lenin's ideal pretty well throughout 1906. He continued to write about the growing prospects for a successful repetition of it, criticized Plekhanov for his opposi-tion to the rising in February 1906, and was heartened by the Kronstadt and Sveaborg insurrections which were sparked off in July 1906 by the dissolu-tion of the First Duma. Even in September, he drew the 'Lessons of the Moscow Uprising', which he continued to see as a peak of revolutionary effort and a model for the future, since, he wrote, 'A great mass struggle is approaching. It will be an armed uprising.'[54]

In reality, however, the revolutionary wave was subsiding and the issue of attitudes to the Duma was more pressing. Lenin, having at first called for a boycott of the First Duma, changed his position *vis-à-vis* the Second. In Lenin's view, as was made clear in his denunciation of the thirty-one Men-sheviks, the party should stand alone, without making any deals with anyone. As we have seen, he had already warned against mistaking support for (or at least an expectation of) the bourgeois revolution with a policy of getting too involved in it. In March 1907, he continued to argue that the revolution was bourgeois but could only be brought to fruition through the joint action of the proletariat and the peasants.[55] As ever, the distinctions were very fine, but they were nonetheless real to Lenin. The class principle had to be remembered and any blurring of it by over-enthusiastic relation-ships with class enemies was to be avoided. The main barbs were directed at

Plekhanov, whose plans to return to Russia had been thwarted by illness. He had not only opposed the Moscow armed uprising but had also promoted a policy of the Social Democrats making electoral pacts with other parties (notably the Kadets) in the Second Duma elections.[56] In July, Lenin continued to argue that, despite the changes in the electoral system, the correct position for the party was to participate in the elections to the Third Duma, as a separate, distinct group. The ebbing of the revolutionary tide meant that instead of promoting armed uprising (about which he was now silent) Lenin was prepared to settle for using the Social Democrat caucus in the Duma as a publicity mouthpiece for the movement.

Lenin now spent less and less of his time and energy on Russia and, in the summer of 1907, spent more and more time liaising with the International Socialist Bureau (not least in his never-ending quest for party funds). In August, he attended the International Socialist Conference in Stuttgart. The excitement of Russia was beginning to pall, the revolutionary opportunity clearly over for the time being, though Lenin did not overtly acknowledge this fact. Back in Finland, Lenin wrote one of his best-known descriptions of émigré life in a letter to Grigorii Aleksinskii:

> Over there, you are frightfully out of touch with Russia, and idleness and the state of mind which goes with it, a nervous, hysterical, hissing and spitting mentality, predominate ... there is no *live* work or an environment of live work to speak of.[57]

Perhaps Lenin had a premonition, because he was almost disengaging from Russian politics as the summer turned to autumn. Reaction was back in control. In early December, the first volume of a selection of his major works, including *One Step Forward* and *Two Tactics* was seized by the police. Lenin needed no further hint. He went into hiding, moving from Kuokkala to Helsinki. Krupskaia recounts Lenin's tale of how he then left the Russian Empire. Despite having a false identity (as 'Professor Muller', a German geologist), police surveillance caused him to take the almost fatal decision to avoid joining the steamer to Sweden at Åbo (Turku), since there had been arrests of revolutionaries escaping via that route. Instead, he decided to walk across the treacherous ice to a neighbouring island and pick the boat up there. It was too dangerous for any sensible guide to lead him. He had to entrust himself, instead, to the care of 'two rather tipsy Finnish peasants':

> In crossing the ice at night they and Il'ich very nearly perished. In one place the ice began to move beneath their feet. They only just managed to extricate themselves ... Il'ich told me that when the ice began to slide from beneath his feet, he thought, 'Oh! What a silly way to have to die'.[58]

Lenin had left Russia behind and was only to return, via the Finland Station, in April 1917. From intense polemic and the intoxication of the nearness of revolution, Lenin returned to the nerve-jangling world of exile. The pangs of exile were softened by an immersion in philosophy, sojourns in Capri and the establishment of rival party schools in Capri and Paris. For the time being, however, revolution gave way, once again, to preparation for some renewed future upsurge. Lenin did not know what was to come. Indeed, had he not escaped the ice the Lenin story would have ended there and then. Had it done so, how would Lenin be remembered today, especially with regard to his role in the turbulent revolutionary years of 1905 to 1907?

Conclusion

The most obvious conclusion to make about Lenin's activity in this period is that the events of the 1905 Revolution had more influence on Lenin than he did on them. He delayed his return to Russia for so long that, when he did eventually arrive in St Petersburg, he was forced underground almost immediately. From that restricted position he occupied himself largely with party matters (including newspaper publication), rather than with public institutions such as the Soviet or trade unions or rallies and demonstrations, which he visited rarely. Nonetheless, this period (if we extend it backwards somewhat to include 1902) was vital to the emergence of 'Lenin'. Between 1902 and 1904–05, Lenin turned from leading acolyte to Plekhanov and the older generation of Social Democratic leaders into a challenger for their leadership. This seems to have been provoked less by the power lust detected in many versions of the Lenin story than by a determination to defend and apply principles of organization that he believed to be essential for the adaptation of the party. Too much of the spirit of the intellectual discussion circle remained, for Lenin. Instead, he wanted the party to be more professional, more dedicated and more active than it had hitherto been. He wanted it to break out from its tiny foothold in Russian politics and challenge the larger radical parties, the Kadets and the PSR, on their own ground and in their own way. He also developed ideas about the stages of revolution and the role of Social Democracy in a future revolution that corresponded with positions he later took in 1917. Notably, he was wary of participation in a provisional revolutionary government, though he did not rule it out. He also believed a period of 'democratic dictatorship of workers and peasants' would be a necessary prelude to the transition to socialism. This last, he argued, would ultimately only be achieved by force, as the elite would not surrender its property in any other way. Nonetheless, his views on preparing for such an 'armed uprising' to contribute to the 1905 Revolution were extraordinarily naive. Finally, his actions of the period open up questions about the nature of the split in the party. At no stage, despite polemics that reached peaks of bitterness, was there a complete break. There were also long intervals of co-operation between the factions and a general sense that both sides belonged to the same party. They were fighting for the soul of that party, but were doing so from within – as though it were a quarrelling political family – not as two separate parties.

Notes

1 Leon Trotsky, *The Young Lenin* (Harmondsworth, 1974), p. 232.
2 Exceptionally, but by no means implausibly, Neil Harding has argued that 'Unambiguously, it was the war [of 1914–18] that led Lenin to Leninism': Neil Harding, *Leninism* (London, 1996), p. 78.
3 V. I. Lenin, *Collected Works* (Moscow, 1960–70), Vol. 34, p. 164 (hereafter *CW*). All emphases are from the original, unless stated as being otherwise.
4 Ibid., Vol. 34, p. 185.
5 Ibid., Vol. 7, p. 91.
6 Ibid., Vol. 34, p. 186.
7 V. I. Lenin, *Selected Works* (Moscow, 1967), Vol. 1, p. 298 (hereafter *SW*).
8 Ibid., Vol. 1, p. 409.
9 Ibid., Vol. 1, pp. 398–9. See also p. 420.
10 Ibid., Vol. 1, p. 424.
11 Ibid., Vol. 1, p. 424.
12 Ibid., Vol. 1, p. 396.
13 Iu. O. Martov, *Bor'ba s 'osadnym polozheniem' v RSDRP (otvet na pis'ma N. Lenina)* (Geneva, 1904).
14 Lenin, *CW*, Vol. 36, p. 128; Gerda Weber and Hermann Weber, *Lenin: Life and Works* (London, 1980), p. 35.
15 Quoted in Lenin, *SW*, Vol. 1, p. 400.
16 Nadezhda Krupskaya, *Memories of Lenin* (London, 1979), p. 94.
17 Lenin, *CW*, Vol. 34, p. 186; Weber and Weber, *Lenin*, p. 35.
18 Weber and Weber, *Lenin*, p. 34.
19 Lenin, *SW*, Vol. 1, p. 424.
20 Ibid., Vol. 1, p. 392ff.
21 Ibid., Vol. 1, pp. 447–8.
22 Lenin, *CW*, Vol. 34, p. 164.
23 Lenin, *SW*, Vol. 1, p. 398.
24 Ibid., Vol. 1, p. 399.
25 Ibid., Vol. 1, p. 431.
26 It has been plausibly argued by Jimmy White that Bogdanov's influence can be detected in this: see James D. White, *Lenin: The Practice and Theory of Revolution* (London, 2001), p. 70.
27 Rosa Luxemburg, 'The Organizational Question of Russian Social Democracy'. There is an English translation in Mary-Alice Waters (ed.), *Rosa Luxemburg Speaks* (New York, 1970), pp. 114–30. The quotation is on p. 122.
28 Lenin, *SW*, Vol. 1, p. 398.
29 Ibid., Vol. 1, p. 433.
30 Lenin, *CW*, Vol. 8, pp. 335–43.
31 Ibid., Vol. 34, pp. 320–2.
32 Ibid., Vol. 34, pp. 363–4.
33 Jonathan Frankel, 'Lenin's Doctrinal Revolution of April 1917', *Journal of Contemporary History*, Vol. 4 (1969), No. 2, pp. 117–42.
34 Quoted in Richard Pipes, *Struve: Liberal on the Left* (Cambridge, Mass., 1970), p. 195.
35 Lenin, *CW*, Vol. 9, p. 50.
36 Ibid., Vol. 9, p. 24.
37 Ibid., Vol. 9, p. 32.

38 Ibid., Vol. 9, p. 58.
39 Ibid., Vol. 9, p. 85.
40 Ibid.
41 Ibid., Vol. 9, pp. 28–9.
42 Ibid., Vol. 9, p. 132.
43 Ibid., Vol. 9, p. 420.
44 Ibid., Vol. 10, pp. 29–43.
45 Ibid., Vol. 10, pp. 44–9.
46 Ibid., Vol. 10, pp. 83–7.
47 Karl Marx, *Contribution to the Critique of Hegel's Philosophy of Right: Introduction* (1844), in Karl Marx and Friedrich Engels, *Collected Works*, Vol. 3 (London, 1975), p. 175.
48 Lenin, *CW*, Vol. 15, pp. 402–13.
49 Incidentally, the terms 'Bolshevik' and 'Menshevik' were by now in wide circulation and the transitional terms *'bol'shinstvo'* and *'men'shinstvo'* were largely superseded.
50 Weber and Weber, *Lenin*, p. 49.
51 Lenin, *CW*, Vol. 12, pp. 33–44.
52 Ibid., Vol. 12, pp. 421–32.
53 Ibid., Vol. 10, pp. 147–63.
54 Ibid., Vol. 11, pp. 61–8.
55 Ibid., Vol. 43, p. 175.
56 See Weber and Weber, *Lenin*, p. 52 (entry for 26–27 January), but also elsewhere.
57 Lenin, *CW*, Vol. 43, p. 176.
58 Krupskaya, *Memories*, p. 146.

13 Leon Trotsky and 1905

Ian D. Thatcher

Leon Trotsky is associated with the Revolution of 1905 as one of the leaders of the St Petersburg Soviet of Workers' Deputies, as the theoretician of the revolution and as its historian. This chapter examines these three aspects of Trotsky's relationship with 1905 and argues that the 1905 Revolution may have had more of an impact upon Trotsky than he had upon it. Certainly Trotsky's autobiography, My Life *(1930), is an unreliable guide to its hero's role in 1905.*

Not only was 1905 a momentous year for late-imperial Russia, it also marked an important turning point in Leon Trotsky's biography. It was precisely in 1905 that, as Trotsky himself stated, he first advanced the theory of 'permanent revolution' – a doctrine that was to be associated with him until his death and beyond.[1] If this were not enough, 1905 was a notable event in Trotsky's life for other reasons, in that it offered him a first opportunity of participating in an actual revolutionary situation. In 1905, he acted as a revolutionary journalist and orator, joined the St Petersburg Soviet of Workers' Deputies and, briefly (for one week), became one of three co-chairman of the Soviet's Executive Committee. He was then arrested, tried and convicted. During the trial of the Soviet's leaders, Trotsky made a characteristically flamboyant denouncement of tsarism from the witness stand. He did not meekly accept his punishment of internal exile, but soon affected a successful escape, which he later described in true *Boy's Own* adventure fashion in the essay 'There and Back'.

Trotsky emerged from 1905, if only in his own writings, with a reputation as a man of action and as a revolutionary of great courage and daring. Finally, it was in the post-1905 period that Trotsky established himself as a historian of the Russian revolution, most notably in the book *1905* (1909). It was an interest that would characterize Trotsky for the rest of his life. He would return to the themes of *1905* in works such as his magnum opus of the early 1930s, *The History of the Russian Revolution*. If we are to seek the origins of Trotsky's subsequent reputation, not only as a revolutionary but also as theoretician and historian, we must therefore turn to 1905. This chapter will examine each of these aspects of Trotsky's activities.

1905: Trotsky as revolutionary

Trotsky returned to Russia from European exile in February 1905. He went first to Kiev and then, after several weeks, travelled to St Petersburg, the centre and initial spark of the revolution, following the events of Bloody Sunday. But Trotsky soon considered St Petersburg to be too dangerous. Fearing arrest, he spent the summer and early autumn in Finland, returning to the capital after the strike movement of October had taken off. It was in this relatively short period – from mid-October to early December, at which point he was arrested – that Trotsky was to gain invaluable experience of revolution, working primarily as an orator and journalist in the fire of events.

His first port of call was the recently founded Soviet of Workers' Deputies, which had been established on the initiative of the (Menshevik) Petersburg Group. It had summoned a body of elected workers' representatives, with one deputy for each 500 workers, in order to provide an organization for workers to co-ordinate their efforts and action. The first meeting of the Soviet took place on 13 October 1905 in the Technological Institute. The 30–40 delegates in attendance approved the principle of election of one deputy per 500 workers, called for a general strike of all St Petersburg workers and approved a basic programme, the chief features of which were demands for an eight-hour working day and a constituent assembly.[2] From these modest beginnings, the Soviet grew into a body of some 562 delegates, representing 147 factories, thirty-four workshops and sixteen trade unions. It was overwhelmingly male in composition (only six of its delegates were women), with the largest proportion of deputies coming from the capital's metal workshops and factories. The Soviet acquired a certain prominence, especially in October and November 1905, before it was crushed by the arrest of its leading figures in early December.

At its second meeting, on 14 October, the Soviet elected a deputy from the Union of Printing Workers, Georgii Stepanovich Nosar (P. A. Khrustalev), as chairman. Nosar served in this post until his arrest on 26 November. He subsequently outlined the various campaigns that the Soviet led and the tasks it undertook under his chairmanship:

> The Soviet of Workers' Deputies led three strikes (October, November and the post-telegraph [strike]); ... it issued up to 500,000 proclamations and news-sheets to the workers, soldiers and other groups; ... it declared freedom of the press and implemented this during October in St Petersburg; ... it attempted to introduce the 8-hour working day; ... it formed self-defence units and armed the workers; ... it organized help for the unemployed; ... it united all St Petersburg workers; ... it tried to unite the whole working class of Russia in local Soviets and in an All-Russian Congress; ... it joined forces with all fighting organizations for joint efforts; ... it aided the coming together of the revolutionary proletariat with the revolutionary army...[3]

It was in the Soviet that Trotsky would seek practical experience of revolution and genuine contact with actual workers. His journalism throughout 1905 had outlined how the revolution should progress in general terms. In the pre-October period he penned articles for the Menshevik journal *Iskra* (The Spark) and for internal party bodies, and in the heady days of press freedom of October to December he was a frequent contributor to several socialist newspapers – most notably the Soviet's bulletin (ten issues of which were published), the Menshevik *Nachalo* (The Beginning) and the *Russkaia gazeta* (Russian Gazette), which he co-edited with Alexander Parvus (Helphand).

In a clear and aggressive style, written from a Marxist perspective, Trotsky's journalism demolished any hope of meaningful reform coming from the tsarist regime. Particularly galling for Trotsky was the notion that, in promising a consultative assembly in the manifesto of 17 October, Nicholas II had consented to the main demands of the revolution. Such assemblies might satisfy the propertied classes that would dominate them, he said, but they in no sense answered the needs of the working class. In an open letter to the leading liberal Professor P. N. Miliukov, for example, Trotsky explained that a real political change occurs only when 'the material means of armed supremacy pass from the hands of absolutism into the hands of the people'.[4] By 'the people', of course, Trotsky meant ordinary workers and peasants.

As he was an urban-based activist, it is understandable that Trotsky considered the proletariat to be his most immediate and important target audience. He did, nevertheless, on several occasions address specifically peasant concerns. In these articles he tried to convince the peasants that they were still, in all essentials, in a state of serfdom. The so-called Emancipation of the 1860s had done little to free them. Indeed, he argued, one could claim that the peasants had experienced further impoverishment: the keywords of their life were 'grief and suffering'. To overcome this state of affairs, Trotsky urged the peasants to take several actions. First, they had to stop believing in the goodness of the tsar. Was it not clear to them that their 'gracious lord' was on the side of the landowners? Second, they should become aware of the slogans and actions of the urban proletariat and follow them, their true brothers, in demanding an end to oppression and the beginnings of genuine popular democracy in the form of a constituent assembly. Third, the peasants should educate themselves in the advantages of socialism by involving themselves with the Social Democrats. The Socialists-Revolutionaries were mistaken in thinking that a redistribution of land within capitalism could solve the peasants' land-hunger. Finally, each village should contact its conscripts in the army and encourage the peasant-soldiers to abandon the war with Japan and to ignore orders to shoot strikers. Only a worker–peasant alliance in this form, he maintained, could guarantee the revolution's victory.

Acting amongst the workers, Trotsky not only propagated the

programme and slogans of revolutionary Social Democracy, he also became more intimately involved in the strike movement. In this instance his main efforts were exerted as a member of the St Petersburg Soviet's Executive Committee. The Executive Committee was formed at the Soviet's fourth gathering, on 17 October. It consisted of thirty-one delegates: twenty-two worker deputies from the Soviet were joined by nine party representatives (three Bolsheviks, three Mensheviks and three Socialists-Revolutionaries). The party representatives were to enjoy a consultative voice only, in keeping with the determination of the Soviet to be a non-party body elected by and for – and answerable to – the workers.

It is most likely that Trotsky was included in the Executive Committee as one of the Mensheviks. Despite having a consultative voice only, Trotsky worked for the Soviet with energy and passion, delivering speeches at its meetings and writing numerous proclamations. He urged the workers to develop the strike as a weapon to win not only economic demands (chiefly the eight-hour working day): it should also be used for political purposes – for example, to protest against the imposition of martial law in Poland, or the passing of excessively repressive sentences on mutinous sailors. In both instances, however, Trotsky was keen for the workers to know the limits of what could be achieved through strikes, especially if they were limited to one industrial sector or to the capital. The biggest mistake, for Trotsky, was to expect too much of strike activity, when all the odds were still stacked in the factory owners' favour. He was never afraid of calling off a strike when he thought that this was in the workers' best interests. Trotsky was well aware of how lacking the workers still were in organization and arms, but he reasoned that time was on the workers' side. They could only become stronger. In the meantime, they should take heart from what concessions they had already achieved through disruption of production and through withdrawing their labour. The tsar, for example, would not have granted a consultative Duma, he said, had it not been for the workers' strikes. The workers should also prepare for the decisive battles of the future by joining the RSDLP, by seeking a wider union of forces with brother soldiers and peasants and by demanding the formation of a people's militia.

It is difficult to gauge the exact influence that Trotsky had upon the course of the 1905 Revolution. One approach is to examine the most favourable view of a powerful and active Trotsky: the case that was made by none other than Trotsky himself. Looking back at 1905, in his autobiography of the late 1920s, Trotsky made several claims on his own behalf. First, he held that the papers he edited were far more interesting in content and had a much greater circulation than any rival publication:

> With Parvus I took over the tiny *Russian Gazette* and transformed it into a fighting organ for the masses. Within a few days the circulation rose from thirty thousand to one hundred thousand. A month later it had reached the half million mark. But our technical resources could not

keep up with the growth of the paper. We were finally extricated from our difficulties by the government raid.

On 13 November, in alliance with the Mensheviks, we had started a big political organ, *Beginning*. The paper's circulation was jumping by leaps and bounds. Without Lenin, the Bolshevik *New Life* was rather drab. The *Beginning*, on the other hand, had a tremendous success. I think this paper, more than any other publication of the past half-century, resembled its classic prototype, the *New Rheinland News*, which was published by Marx in 1848. Kamenev, one of the editors of the *New Life*, told me afterwards how he watched the sale of newspapers at the stations when he was passing through by train. The St Petersburg train was awaited by endless lines. The demand was only for revolutionary papers. 'Beginning, Beginning, Beginning', came the cry of the waiting crowds. 'New Life', and then again, 'Beginning, Beginning, Beginning'.[5]

We have, of course, no way of knowing how many people were affected by Trotsky's journalism. It is unlikely that his words reached many peasants. He simply lacked connections with the villages and there was not a mass distribution of his appeals to the peasantry. Even in the capital, his main stomping-ground, the impression made by his journalist endeavours may have been limited. After all, the period in which the revolutionary press appeared was very short, lasting only from mid-November to early December. Only sixteen issues of *Beginning* were published, from 13 November to 2 December. It was not until 15 November that the *Russian Gazette* fell into the hands of Trotsky and Parvus. Furthermore, the claim of a circulation of a 'half million' seems somewhat exaggerated. The editors of Trotsky's collected works cite a circulation figure of 100,000.[6] This was still impressive, but not so far ahead of *New Life*'s 80,000.[7] Even these figures have to be qualified. The number printed says nothing about the numbers actually read, while the police would seize newspapers without warning: over half of *New Life*'s twenty-seven issues were confiscated, for example. Furthermore, since these newspapers were collective endeavours, there is no way of knowing which author's articles the readership most preferred out of those that reached the public domain. Indeed, despite differences in emphasis and outlook, the contemporary reader may have been struck by the similarity of viewpoint across the revolutionary press. Comparing *Beginning* and *New Life* Lenin noted that there were

> arguments only over matters of detail in the appraisal of events: for example, *Beginning* regarded the Soviet of Workers' Deputies as organs of revolutionary local self-government, while *New Life* regarded them as embryonic organs of revolutionary state power that united the proletariat with the revolutionary democrats. *Beginning* inclined towards the dictatorship of the proletariat. *New Life* advocated the democratic dictatorship of the proletariat and the peasantry. But have not disagreements

of this kind been observed at every stage of development of every socialist party in Europe?[8]

In this context, it is worth remarking that Lenin participated in the production of New Life following his arrival in St Petersburg on 8 November. In
total, fourteen of Lenin's articles were published in New Life from 10
November to the paper's closure on 3 December. Indeed, contradicting his
earlier remarks, later in the autobiography Trotsky says of Beginning and
New Life that:

> the papers defended each other against bourgeois criticism. The New
> Life, even after the arrival of Lenin, came out with a defence of my art-
> icles on the permanent revolution. Both newspapers, as well as the two
> factions, followed the line of party unity. The central committee of the
> Bolsheviks, with Lenin participating, passed a unanimous resolution to
> the effect that the split was merely the result of the conditions of foreign
> exile, and the events of the revolution had deprived the factional
> struggle of any reasonable grounds. I defended the same line in Begin-
> ning.[9]

The second – and perhaps more important – representation of Trotsky in
My Life is not that of an effective propagandist but as the real leader of the
revolution in general and of the Soviet of Workers' Deputies in particular.
Trotsky portrays himself as having stood head and shoulders above his comrades. The leading Mensheviks were caught 'unawares' and thrown 'into
confusion' by the pace of events. The Bolsheviks were sidelined by their
negative attitude towards the Soviet, which they perceived as a rival to the
party. Lenin had to overturn this attitude when he arrived in November, but
by then the reversal in Bolshevik thinking was too late for the faction to
gain 'a leading position in the events of the first revolution'. As for Trotsky
himself:

> there was not one from whom I could learn anything. On the contrary, I
> had to assume the position of teacher myself . . . In October I plunged
> headlong into the gigantic whirlpool, which, in a personal sense, was
> the greatest test for my powers. Decisions had to be made under fire. I
> can't help noting that these decisions came to me quite obviously . . .
> The events of 1905 revealed in me a revolutionary intuition . . . I
> cannot, in the appreciation of the political situation as a whole and of its
> revolutionary perspectives, accuse myself of any serious errors of judge-
> ment.[10]

In this picture, Trotsky becomes the natural leader of the Soviet of
Workers' Deputies. Its chairman, Nosar, is dismissed as an 'intermediate
stage between Gapon and the Social Democracy'. The only figure that

Trotsky allows to have any influence over the decisions of the Soviet is Lenin. Yet even Lenin, absent in Trotsky's account from its sessions, had to appear through intermediaries. It is clear, states Trotsky, that 'all the decisions of the Soviet, with the exception perhaps of a few that were accidental and unimportant were shaped by me; I submitted them first to the Executive Committee, and then, in its name, I placed them before the Soviet'.[11] Indeed, given Trotsky's belief that the workers backed the Soviet 'to a man' – based perhaps on his self-proclaimed ability to see the effects of events 'on the minds of the workers' for today and tomorrow – one could argue that Trotsky was the main actor of 1905.[12] He was the revolution and the revolution was he.

There is, indeed, evidence that suggests that Trotsky's role in the Soviet was far from minor and that he may have been one of the most prominent members of the RSDLP within the Soviet's ranks. One participant records, for example, that Trotsky was 'the unchallenged leader of the Mensheviks in the Petersburg Soviet'.[13] Another member of the Soviet (and Trotsky's close ally) recalled in his memoirs that Trotsky was the Soviet's 'intellectual leader'.[14] His performances in the meetings of the Soviet showed off his oratorical talents, and in resolving issues of whether to continue, extend or call a halt to strikes, Trotsky's recommendations carried some weight.[15] Trotsky became proud of a passage in Anatolii Lunacharskii's memoirs, in which Lenin is reported to have approved of Trotsky's 'rising star' in the Soviet, a boost he deserved for his 'brilliant and unflagging work'.[16] Some other socialists came to identify Trotsky with the Soviet and blamed him personally for the Soviet's 'excessive' radicalism that, in their estimation, served only to push the authorities into arrests and closure.[17]

Each of these remarks is in some sense justified, although they need to be qualified. Trotsky's status as the Soviet's 'intellectual leader' can rest upon the resolutions he penned for the Soviet and the fact that when a volume of reminiscences of the Soviet was published in 1906, it was precisely Trotsky who was called upon to address the theme of 'The Soviet and the Revolution'. Therein the Soviet's significance is analysed largely in terms of its attempt to become an 'organ of power'. For Trotsky, power was the revolution's key aim and the Soviet provided a model of proletarian 'self-government'. Isolated in the capital, the St Petersburg Soviet was unable to seize power on an all-Russian scale, although for a while it did take over part of the postal service and the railways. The tasks for the future were to organize Soviets in all urban centres, to replace town councils, and to establish a Soviet of Peasants to lead the agrarian revolution.[18] Trotsky's remarks are interesting, even though they were penned after the Soviet had fallen. One cannot say that Trotsky developed an elaborate and sophisticated theory of the Soviets and their role in the revolution. For example, it was unclear what relationship he thought that the Soviets would have with a constituent assembly, which remained one of his other key demands. And later in his life Trotsky made only passing reference to the Soviets. They were used as evidence of how advanced forms of proletarian political struggle had appeared first of all in backward Russia, but the Soviets did not become a central part of Trotsky's outlook and thinking. However, it is natural that the task of explaining the relationship between the Soviet and the revolution more broadly, if only in a rudimentary form, should have been delegated to one of the Soviet's prominent politicals.

It is far more problematic to substantiate the claim that Trotsky was responsible for the numerous practical decisions taken by the Soviet. The editorial notes to his collected works, produced in the early 1920s, state that Trotsky had a particular influence over two of the Soviet's many resolutions. For example, on 22 October 1905, the Soviet met to discuss its previously declared intention to hold (on the following day) commemorative meetings and demonstrations to accompany the funerals of colleagues who had recently fallen in struggle. Earlier, a Soviet delegation had paid a visit to the prime minister, Count Witte, seeking permission for the processions to go ahead, but with the Soviet assuming responsibility for security. The Soviet did not want any of the government's gendarmes in attendance, but the governor of St Petersburg, D. F. Trepov, had made clear his intention to police the streets. Fearing a confrontation with the authorities, Trotsky urged the Soviet to cancel the call for mass demonstrations. After a lengthy debate, the editors note that 'an overwhelming majority voted for Trotsky's resolution'. Also, in early November, the Soviet resolved that the St Petersburg workers should enforce an eight-hour working day. This met with fierce resistance from the factory management. Again, it was precisely Trotsky, the editors claim, who proposed that the Soviet recommend the workers to return to work under the old conditions. And, again, Trotsky's stance held the day.

This account of Trotsky's specific influence over key decisions of the Soviet is far removed from that of *My Life*, in which untold numbers of Executive Committee and Soviet resolutions were mere rubber stamps of Trotsky's views. In the two instances cited (and certainly also on other occasions), however, Trotsky's role in the Soviet has probably been exaggerated. Several memoirs recall that the Soviet was mindful of its independence. It did not desire politicals to speak for the workers and it was precisely for this reason that the politicals were given a consultative voice only. The Soviet guarded its independence not only from party men but also from its own Executive Committee, in which workers also predominated. The Executive Committee could not issue resolutions in the Soviet's name but had to take them to the Soviet for approval. The workers were quite capable of forming their own demands and resolving their own dilemmas and, in fact, it was often local trade unions or factories that took initiatives,[19] the Soviet then reacting to events by offering its support. In this process, trade unions and factories could retain the right to disagree with the Soviet and maintain an independent stance.[20] Not only were there disagreements on the floor of the Soviet, there were also conflicting assessments between factories and trade unions, not to mention arguments amongst the workers themselves. Not all of the capital's workers were happy, for example, with the Soviet's decision for workers to implement an eight-hour working day across St Petersburg.[21] Some workers thought that the Soviet was overestimating the proletariat's influence and expected a retreat. After all, the workers knew better than anyone about their lack of rights. There was little, if any, genuine tenure of appointment in the factories and, in the absence of strike funds, few could afford lengthy work stoppages. The workers could feel even more vulnerable when they lacked broader social support or sympathy, as may have been the case after the tsar promised some type of elected assembly in the October Manifesto. When Trotsky worried lest the Soviet had been too adventurous in decreeing the eight-hour working day, he shared a general concern and was not articulating a view that did not exist before his intervention. He might even have been reacting to views first expressed by workers. Indeed, in 1906 Trotsky presented a far more modest, and probably more accurate, account of the role of politicals in the Soviet:

> On all the important questions – strikes, the struggle for the 8-hour working day, the arming of the workers – the initiative came not from the Soviet, but from the more advanced factories. Meetings of worker-electors passed resolutions that were then taken by deputies to the Soviet. In this way the organization of the Soviet was, factually and formally, an organization of the overwhelming majority of St Petersburg's workers ... [R]epresentatives of the party did not enjoy, either in the Soviet or in the Executive Committee, a deciding vote; they participated in debates but not in the voting. The Soviet was organized by the principle of representation of workers according to factory and profession, not according to party groups. Party representatives could serve the Soviet by their political experience and knowledge, but they could not have a deciding vote breaking the principle of the workers' self-representation.[22]

In the autobiography Trotsky is also too dismissive of the part played by politicals other than himself. One cannot deny that Trotsky was a prominent political: he was, after all, one of only nine party figures on the Executive Committee. However, it is unfair to represent other members of the RSDLP as being sidelined by their dismissive attitude to the Soviet (the Bolsheviks) or as being simply confused (the Mensheviks). It is true that there were members of the Bolshevik St Petersburg Committee who thought that the Soviet should subordinate itself to the party and, before his arrival in St Petersburg, Lenin was moved to send a letter to comrades in the capital in which he questioned a view expounded in *New Life* of 'Soviet or Party' (although he admitted that this criticism was formed in exile and that he might change his views once in St Petersburg). In the event, any attempt by the party to take control over the Soviet would most likely have failed, given the workers' oft-quoted impatience with factional politics.[23] And, if some

Bolsheviks were unhappy with the Soviet's dominance, it did not prevent them (including Lenin) from addressing the Soviet or serving in it. Indeed, in a letter of 1922 to the Institute of Party History, Trotsky claimed that the joint activity of all factions in the Soviet generated a real sense of party unity. In this context, he reveals that resolutions produced in the heat of the moment and presented to the Executive Committee were elaborated beforehand by a group of leading Bolsheviks and Mensheviks.[24] Resolutions he subsequently claimed as his own, therefore, could actually have been jointly authored. Even in the autobiography, for example, Trotsky admits that it was the Mensheviks – not he – who first implemented the idea of calling for a Soviet. Yes, we are told, it was a close run thing, and Trotsky was robbed of the distinction of being the Soviet's founder only by a whisker: he had headed for the capital with the intention of forming a Soviet, only to discover one already in existence. But, even so, the Mensheviks were obviously far from 'confused'. This could be the only instance in which Trotsky admitted that he developed an idea simultaneously and independently of anybody other than Lenin. But, to reiterate, in the Soviet Trotsky worked as part of a team. It was thus fitting that, following the arrest of the first chairman, Trotsky was elected as co-chair along with two other representatives. This arrangement was to last for just seven days and it occurred when the Soviet's influence was on the wane. There were to be only two meetings of the Executive Committee in that week and none of the full Soviet. It was at the second of these gatherings of the Executive Committee that Trotsky, along with others, was arrested as a member, not leader, of the Soviet.[25]

In fact, if the Soviet had any public face in 1905 it was that of Georgii Nosar (Khrustalev). In the memoirs of the prime minister of the day, Count Witte, Trotsky does not merit a mention. Witte could only call to mind Nosar, as first elected leader of the Soviet.[26] His name probably stuck in Witte's memory because of two meetings in which Nosar led a delegation to the prime minister.[27] Witte's memory may have altered, of course, had he lived to write his memoirs after the Bolshevik revolution, instead of completing them in 1912, but this only confirms the limited public impression Trotsky made at the time. Following Nosar's arrest, at the end of November, the factories abounded with resolutions calling for his release.[28] It was therefore most unfair of Trotsky subsequently to belittle Nosar's role. In 1906, Nosar wrote an extensive and useful essay on the history of the Soviet.[29] Moreover, in 1909 Trotsky was happy to write about the Soviet's chairman in a much more balanced fashion. He was

> a man of practical ability and resourcefulness, an energetic and skilful chairman although only a mediocre orator . . . Khrustalev's lack of political allegiance facilitated the Soviet's relations with the non-proletarian world and especially with the organizations of the intelligentsia, from which it received considerable material assistance.[30]

The problem with *My Life* is that it was produced after a public spat between Trotsky and Nosar in 1913;[31] indeed, it was produced after Nosar had been shot for counter-Soviet activities in 1918. This merely helped Trotsky focus on the polemical purpose of *My Life*, rather than present an honest evaluation of 1905.

Still, even if Trotsky did not have as great an impact upon 1905 as his autobiography subsequently claimed, 1905 certainly did have a great impact upon him. In 1905 he was able to witness the workers acting spontaneously and independently. He also saw Bolsheviks and Mensheviks working together under the pressure of the workers and of the revolution. This may have boosted his hopes for unity within the RSDLP and helped to vindicate his non-factional stance. Although the workers did not attain victory in 1905, and although the unity in the RSDLP was short-lived, Trotsky had hope for the future; 1905 also cemented Trotsky's reputation as a revolutionary, even if to a limited audience. But, whatever criticisms were laid at his door, and however his role may have been exaggerated, henceforth Trotsky could be guaranteed a hearing amongst Social Democrats, even if he was not sufficiently powerful to be an acknowledged general leader. He certainly emerged from 1905 with an identity of his own and a proven capacity for independent action.

1905: Trotsky as theoretician and historian

Following the revolution's defeat, Trotsky had time to reflect upon the broader meaning of 1905. In several books, including *Our Revolution* (1906) and *1905* (1909), Trotsky discussed the significance of 1905 in theoretical and semi-historical terms. To questions that had long troubled Russian socialists – What form will a Russian revolution take? Would tsarism be replaced by a bourgeois-capitalist or a socialist regime? – Trotsky answered with 'permanent revolution'. Although many books and articles have been written probing the meaning and profundity of this concept, its basic propositions, which Trotsky developed from late 1904 onwards, can be summarized quite easily.

According to Trotsky, the course of Russian history and the structure of its current class relations meant that the key actor in the coming Russian revolution would be the proletariat. In a long history of struggle for survival against the more powerful economies of the West, the Russian state had been forced to grow and defend itself partly through excessive exploitation of the country's scattered population and resources and partly through securing foreign loans on the international money markets. This process had produced a state that stood above society and that was opposed to it. But the forces of opposition were weak. An impoverished peasantry was incapable of playing an independent political role, while the underdeveloped indigenous bourgeoisie was timid and cowardly. However, Russian industrialization of the recent decades had brought into existence a small but powerful working class. Concentrated in large factories that utilized the latest technology, the workers had forged the most up-to-date methods of class struggle, as they battled against poor working conditions and political oppression. Having a strategic importance that far outweighed their percentage of the country's population, the workers were the only truly revolutionary class able to overthrow tsarism. Once in power, however, Trotsky emphasized that a workers' government would introduce socialism, including state control of the national economy. Such measures would be increasingly opposed by Russia's peasants, with their petit-bourgeois prejudices regarding private property, and would also bring forth the hostility of the international bourgeoisie, anxious, amongst other things, to protect the interest payable on loans made to the tsarist regime. In this context, a workers' regime in Russia could survive only if socialist revolutions (and, hence, sympathetic regimes) developed in advanced Western Europe. Fortunately, in Trotsky's conception, the workers of Russia could be optimistic about the prospects of European-wide revolution. This would be a strong possibility, partly because of an already evident heightening of class tensions in Western Europe, but also because West European workers would take the side of Russian comrades should the international bourgeoisie seek to crush a Russian revolution.

A Russian revolution was therefore 'permanent' in two senses for Trotsky. First, there would be no lengthy period or historical stage separating tsarist Russia from socialism. Second, a socialist revolution in Russia would not seek to confine itself to its national borders but would try to extend itself internationally. Only when socialism was established across the globe would the 'permanent' revolution be achieved.

There are several ways in which we can evaluate Trotsky's political programme of permanent revolution. We can ask, for example, how original it was in conception. Certainly several of its elements were in common circulation. Apart from the co-operation with Parvus, who edited and introduced some of Trotsky's writings of the time, Trotsky also mentioned several instances in which his ideas – even if only in embryonic form – could be found in Karl Kautsky's earlier works. Furthermore, the weakness and cowardice of the Russian bourgeoisie had been noted by, amongst others, Peter Struve (at the First Congress of the RSDLP). The separation of the Russian state from society, so that the two stood opposed to one another in a hostile relationship, was already a feature of Miliukov's writings on contemporary Russia. The notion that the revolution would pass quickly, or 'in permanence', from its bourgeois stage to socialism could also be read in the publications of the peasant-based Socialists-Revolutionaries.[32] Finally, the dependence of a Russian revolution for its success upon socialist revolution in the more advanced Western Europe was also a condition that had been set by Marx and Engels in the 1882 Preface to the second Russian edition of the *Communist Manifesto*. However, there was undoubted originality in the way in which Trotsky synthesized these various currents to form a unique outlook. Previous propositions were transformed beyond recognition. For example, Marx and Engels had assumed that the social relations contained in the village commune offered Russia a chance to bypass capitalism. Trotsky, on the other hand, saw nothing in the countryside as a model for progressive change. Indeed, he assumed that, after an initial period of gratitude to the workers for the overthrow of feudalism, there would be serious peasant resistance to socialism.

We can credit Trotsky, then, with a fertile and original mind. His analysis provides a fruitful starting point for discussion about the nature of Russian history and the prospects for revolution. Certainly, Trotsky himself did not subsequently feel the need to renounce or significantly modify the main tenets of 'permanent revolution': the propositions associated with it, from the view of the peculiarities of Russian historical development to the class analysis of the driving forces of the Russian and international revolutions, were to remain with Trotsky (despite future additions, reformulations and even the odd retreat) for the rest of his life.

A second point of interest is how Trotsky's contemporaries responded to the notion of 'permanent revolution'. Did the idea create theoretical allies or enemies for Trotsky? At the high points of the revolution, it is true that several Marxists seemed to become infected with aspects of permanent revolution. In the first half of 1905, for example, not only Karl Kautsky but also Rosa Luxemburg specifically referred to the need for 'permanent revolution' in analyses of Russian events;[33] while in September 1905, Lenin wrote that 'from the democratic revolution we shall at once . . . begin to pass to the socialist revolution. We stand for uninterrupted revolution. We shall not stop halfway.'[34] Even the Mensheviks A. S. Martynov and Iu. O. Martov, in separate articles, admitted that the Russian proletariat might be forced to seize power because of the weakness of Russian liberals. In this event, they said, a workers' government in Russia, which could not survive in isolation, would do its utmost to spread revolution to the West. From abroad, Pavel Aksel'rod, who placed much more emphasis upon the leading role of the bourgeoisie in a bourgeois revolution and who advocated alliances between workers and professionals in opposition to tsarism, worried that Martov and others were allowing themselves to fall under the spell of permanent revolution.[35] However, when the 'conditions of revolutionary madness', as Trotsky called them,[36] had died down, most of the above returned to their previously negative evaluations of the idea of permanent revolution. Several comrades, including Rosa Luxemburg, for example, agreed with the German socialist Franz Mehring's arguments that the Russian workers could not leap from tsarist oppression to socialism. In a revolution that would remain bourgeois, he predicted, the most that could be achieved were the very important rights of suffrage, association, freedom of speech and publication, and better working conditions – all of which would help the movement to build for the eventual goal of socialism. Martov returned to the general Menshevik fold and to his earlier viewpoint that an immediate seizure of power by the working class was not possible. For him, the immediate goal, in which the workers would remain in revolutionary opposition helping the bourgeoisie where appropriate, was the establishment of a bourgeois-democratic republic. Lenin's concession to 'permanent revolution' also proved to be a very fleeting aberration. A more typical response of Lenin on the nature of current events is the rebuff to Parvus and Trotsky contained in an essay of April 1905. Therein Lenin rejected the 'be more revolutionary than anyone else' approach of the 'windbag Trotsky': a sober assessment of the current situation revealed, he said, that there could be no workers' government until the workers were a conscious majority of Russia's population, and that 'the objective logic of historical development' made a democratic – not socialist – revolution the task of the day.[37] 'Permanent revolution', therefore, not only marked a new stage in Trotsky's thinking, it also set him apart – increasing his sense of uniqueness and isolation – from other currents in Russian Social Democracy.

A final method of evaluating Trotsky's formulation of permanent revolution is to ask how its prognoses stand up against the mass of research which historians have carried out into late-imperial Russia. Did Trotsky have a sensible estimation of the class forces and the general march of history, notwithstanding the objections of his contemporary critics? To begin with, we can note the substantial overlap between Trotsky's analysis of the late-tsarist economy and the recent findings of economic historians. Both highlight, for example, the coexistence of the most modern and most outdated forms of production in late-tsarist Russia. In this picture, the advanced sectors of the economy are concentrated in foreign-owned and state-supported capital industries (railway building, defence, etc.), while the more backward elements predominate in the agricultural sector, where most producers aimed at little more than self-sufficiency.[38] Much historical research would also concur with Trotsky's view that tsarism was heading for a revolutionary crisis. Robert B. McKean, a distinguished historian who has devoted much of his career to the question of 'whither imperial Russia?', for example, doubts whether tsarism could have evolved into a stable, constitutional monarchy. The reasons for this pessimism fit well into Trotsky's analysis of Russia's social instability. McKean also identifies a bourgeoisie that, despite the undoubted growth of a professional middle class, remained relatively small and divided between sectional interests – factors that fatally undermined its political weight. Furthermore, the tsar did not adequately address the undoubted difficulties faced by peasants and workers, both of whom were alienated from the regime. The government's great power ambitions also promised to undermine its stability, not least because of the shortcomings of the armed forces.[39]

If Trotsky's broad analysis of late-imperial Russia's future fate has much to commend itself, what of his narrower account of 1905? Here, again, one can find several themes that Trotsky's works of the time share with subsequent histories. Let us take, for instance, the issue of why tsarism survived the onslaught of 1905. In answer, both Trotsky and one of the most recent and detailed investigations of 1905 highlight the facts that the armed forces remained loyal to Nicholas II and that protest in urban and rural settings did not unify into one, coherent opposition.[40] Trotsky's awareness of opposition taking different forms in varying regional and occupational settings is also reflected in subsequent scholarly studies. This is true above all of case studies of urban and rural unrest. Here, Trotsky's point that factory and plant workers (especially metalworkers and printers) were in the vanguard of labour protest is echoed in the works of several labour historians.[41] Similarly, the forms of peasant protest identified by Trotsky – from evicting landlords to the seizure of land and grain, from a refusal to pay land rents to ignoring the military draft – are still to be found in modern textbook accounts.[42] Furthermore, Trotsky's suggestion that peasant uprisings took on features peculiar to the local environment, with Saratov being a centre of particularly violent outbursts and radical politics, has been confirmed by regional studies of peasant behaviour in 1905.[43] Trotsky was also a keen observer of the Russian bourgeoisie, including its intra-class tensions. He noted, for example, the differences between the Moscow textile owners and the St Petersburg metallurgists. The former, he contends, were more independent of the state and therefore more overtly critical of the tsar. The topic of the pre-revolutionary Russian bourgeoisie remains under-researched, although some historians have supported, if unconsciously, Trotsky's interesting asides.[44] As well as offering insights into the class and occupational bases of protest, Trotsky also concerned himself with ethnic tensions, in particular violence against the Jews in pogroms. Here the role of alcohol, rumour, encouragement from the anti-Semitic press and other nationalist organizations, as well as tacit approval from the police and army, feature both in Trotsky's and in more recent accounts.[45]

The largest flaw in Trotsky's conception of 1905 may well be in his understanding of peasant behaviour. However nuanced his analysis of peasant protests, and however much he emphasized the importance of peasant opposition if tsarism was to be dealt a mortal blow, Trotsky appreciated the peasants only to the extent that they displayed 'proletarian characteristics'. Thus, according to Trotsky, peasant conscripts could not possibly have led rebellions in the army – that had to be the responsibility of advanced worker recruits. Furthermore, for Trotsky, uprisings in villages remained 'confused and chaotic' until they adopted urban-based political forms of councils, executive committees and general (preferably socialist) political slogans, exemplified above all in the formation of the so-called Peasant Unions.[46] While such statements are understandable, given Trotsky's Marxist prejudices against Russian backwardness, they do run counter to recent work that has taken a more sympathetic view of peasant life. Such studies present the Russian peasants as being far from dull and stupid. David Moon, for example, argues that peasants were rational and creative and that the peasants' way of life – and their strategies in its defence – makes perfect sense once one understands their circumstances.[47] It is because

Trotsky lacked such an understanding, one could claim, that he underestimated the extent of peasant opposition to his planned post-revolutionary modernization and enlightenment campaigns and overestimated what a workers' government could achieve in the countryside by controlling the state. However, this dilemma, in its extreme form, was not evident to Trotsky in 1905. In general, it is impressive that Trotsky's theoretical and semi-historical analyses of 1905 have been largely confirmed by more recent scholarship.

Conclusion

It is tempting to examine 1905 for the precedent it set for the future, most notably the revolution of 1917. This is precisely what Trotsky attempted in his autobiography. Here 1905 is presented as a dress rehearsal for 1917, which was, indeed, to repeat 1905 in many instances. The confusion and failure of the Mensheviks, the wavering of the Bolsheviks without Lenin and the fact that only Lenin and Trotsky were capable of the truest and most decisive revolutionary leadership were already apparent from Russia's first revolution. It may be true that the experience of 1905 was remembered by Trotsky in 1917. He may have felt on familiar ground and had a sense of *déjà vu*. The task of seizing power would relegate previous differences to insignificance. Such thoughts may have aided his joining the Bolsheviks after only so recently engaging in long and bitter polemics with that very faction. But none of this was evident in 1905. From reading the sources produced at the time, in and around 1905, it emerges that Trotsky worked as a revolutionary socialist within organizations over which he had no clear control. He was happy to serve the cause and made his own valuable contributions, chiefly as an orator and propagandist. However, what is more interesting than the fate of one man is how the revolution's goals were driven not so much by socialist intellectuals but by workers fighting for their economic and political rights. In this struggle, the workers developed their own agendas and decisions and they guarded their independence carefully. Trotsky may have celebrated the workers' radicalism as confirmation of 'permanent revolution' and his belief that a revolution in Russia would be led by the workers and would be for socialism. For the most part, though, he seems to have articulated concerns common to both workers and intellectuals at the time. The fifty days of the Soviet's existence coincided with Trotsky's presence in St Petersburg. He neither founded nor led the Soviet, but he did what he could. It would be a great disservice to the workers and to the Soviet to overemphasize Trotsky's role, just as it would be unfair to Trotsky to write him out of the history of 1905.

On balance, then, the 1905 Revolution may have had more of an influence on Trotsky than Trotsky had on the revolution. It was under the impact of 1905 that Trotsky developed the theory of 'permanent revolution' – a concept he developed and defended in numerous publications for the rest of his life. It was in 1905 that Trotsky established a reputation as a revolutionary man of action. Finally, it was 1905 that Trotsky was to portray and embellish in his famous history of that year. One can claim that the Trotsky that so impresses audiences to this day – as a political actor, thinker and historian – was a product of 1905.

Notes

1 Leon Trotsky, *1905* (Moscow, 1922), p. 4.
2 Kuzovlev, 'Kak voznik Sovet', in *Istoriia Soveta Rabochikh Deputatov* (St Petersburg, 1906), pp. 42–3.
3 G. Khrustalev-Nosar, 'Istoriia Soveta Rabochikh Deputatov (do 26-Noiabria 1905)', in *Istoriia Soveta*, p. 148.
4 L. D. Trotsky, 'Open Letter to Professor P. N. Miliukov' (transl. and ed. by Ian D. Thatcher), *Revolutionary Russia*, Vol. 3 (1990), No. 2, p. 226.
5 Leon Trotsky, *My Life: An Attempt at an Autobiography* (Harmondsworth, 1975), pp. 182–3.
6 L. D. Trotsky, *Sochineniia*, Vol. 2, Part 1, *Nasha pervaia revoliutsiia* (Moscow, 1925), pp. 517, 610–11.
7 V. I. Lenin, *Polnoe sobranie sochinenii*, Vol. 12 (Moscow, 1979), pp. 441–2. The editors of this volume give a very different account of the impression *New Life* made at the time. Highlighting a very talented pool of journalists, it is stated that 'the paper enjoyed a great popularity amongst the workers. Letters were sent from across the country from workers, peasants, servants, the military and students'.
8 V. I. Lenin, *Collected Works* (Moscow, 1960–70), Vol. 10, p. 252.
9 Trotsky, *My Life*, pp. 187–8.
10 Ibid., pp. 189–91.
11 Ibid., pp. 181, 186–7, 189–90.
12 Ibid., pp. 184, 189.
13 Solomon M. Schwarz, *The Russian Revolution of 1905 and the Formation of Bolshevism and Menshevism* (Chicago, 1967), p. 179.
14 D. F. Sverchkov, *Na zare revoliutsii* (cited in Trotsky, *My Life*, p. 187).
15 For an appreciation of Trotsky's leading role in the Soviet see, for example, Gerald D. Surh, *1905 in St Petersburg: Labor, Society and Revolution* (Stanford, 1989), pp. 338–9, 398–401.
16 V. Lunacharsky, *Revolutionary Silhouettes* (Harmondsworth, 1967), p. 60. See also Trotsky, *My Life*, p. 187.
17 For these criticisms see, for example, J. L. H. Keep, *The Rise of Social Democracy in Russia* (Oxford, 1963), pp. 241–2.
18 N. Trotsky, 'Sovet i revoliutsiia', in *Istoriia Soveta*, pp. 9–21.
19 See, for example, S. Vvedenskii, 'Noiabr'skaia zabastovka', in *Istoriia Soveta*, pp. 201–16; and B. Petrov-Radin, 'Bor'ba za vos'michasovoi rabochii den'', in ibid., pp. 242–64.
20 M. Kiselevich, 'Soiuz rabochikh pechatnago dela', in ibid., pp. 292–310.
21 N. Nemtsov, 'Na metallicheskom zavode Rasteriaeva', in ibid., pp. 271–80.
22 N. Trotsky, 'Sovet i prokuratura', in ibid., pp. 312–13, 317.
23 See, for example, the comments made by Kuzovlev, 'Kak voznik Sovet', in ibid., pp. 31–2.
24 The letter to Istpart is reproduced in Trotsky, *Sochineniia*, Vol. 2, Part 1, pp. 515–18.
25 V. Svezdin, 'Poslednie dni Soveta (26 noiabria–3 dekabria)', in *Istoriia Soveta*, pp. 170–200.

26 S. Iu. Vitte, *The Memoirs of Count Witte* (London, 1921), pp. 270–7.

27 P. Zlydnev, 'U grafa S. Iu. Vitte', in *Istoriia Soveta*, pp. 265–70.

28 See, for example, the comments made by various contributors to *Istoriia Soveta*, pp. 170, 280, 305.

29 G. Khrustalev-Nosar, 'Istoriia Soveta', in ibid., pp. 45–169.

30 Trotsky, *1905*, pp. 218–19.

31 Trotsky published two articles critical of Nosar in 1913. These are reproduced in Trotsky, *Sochineniia*, Vol. 2, Part 1, pp. 508–14.

32 For more on this see Maureen Perrie, 'The Socialist Revolutionaries on "Permanent Revolution"', *Soviet Studies*, Vol. 24 (1972–73), No. 3, pp. 411–13, and the interesting subsequent correspondence that this article inspired in *Soviet Studies*, Vol. 25 (1973–74), No. 1, pp. 153–5, and Vol. 26 (1974–75), No. 1, pp. 145–7.

33 For Luxemburg's views on 1905 see, for example, Ia. S. Drabkin (ed.), *Roza Liuksemburg o sotsializme i russkoi revoliutsii* (Moscow, 1991).

34 Lenin, *Collected Works*, Vol. 9, pp. 236–7.

35 For Menshevik views on permanent revolution see, for example, Israel Getzler, *Martov: A Political Biography* (Melbourne, 1967) and Abraham Ascher, *Pavel Axelrod and the Development of Menshevism* (Cambridge, Mass., 1972).

36 Trotsky, *1905*, p. 185.

37 Lenin, *Collected Works*, Vol. 8, pp. 288–92.

38 See, for example, the excellent summary of modern research into the general structure of the tsarist economy in R. W. Davies, Mark Harrison and S. G. Wheatcroft (eds), *The Economic Transformation of the Soviet Union, 1913–1945* (Cambridge, 1994), pp. 1–4.

39 McKean has studied the issue of 'whither imperial Russia' from his Ph.D. at the University of East Anglia (1971) to the present day. For a summary of his latest thoughts on this issue, see Robert B. McKean, 'The Constitutional Monarchy in Russia, 1906–17', in I. D. Thatcher (ed.), *Regime and Society in Twentieth Century Russia: Selected Papers from the Fifth World Congress of Central and East European Studies, Warsaw, 1995* (Basingstoke, 1999), pp. 44–67. Some of McKean's research has been inspired by the work of Leopold Haimson. For Haimson's most recent reconfirmation of his view that tsarism was heading for a revolutionary crisis, see Leopold Haimson, ' "The Problem of Political and Social Stability in Urban Russia on the Eve and War and Revolution" Revisited', *Slavic Review*, Vol. 59 (2000), No. 4, pp. 848–75.

40 Compare, for example, Trotsky, *1905*, pp. 55, 98–9, 235, 255, 263 and Abraham Ascher, *The Revolution of 1905: Russia in Disarray* (Stanford, 1988), pp. 341, 343. Trotsky (pp. 197–8) and Ascher also agree that the awakening of the Russian people to political action was one of the most important consequences of 1905.

41 Compare, for example, Trotsky, *1905*, pp. 106, 250, 254 with Surh, *1905 in St Petersburg*, pp. 311–12; and with Victoria E. Bonnell, *Roots of Rebellion: Workers' Politics and Organizations in St Petersburg and Moscow, 1900–1914* (Berkeley, 1983), pp. 442–3.

42 Compare, for example, Trotsky, *1905*, p. 188 with Vladimir Andrle, *A Social History of Twentieth-Century Russia* (London, 1994), pp. 64–5.

43 Compare, for example, Trotsky, *1905*, pp. 187–90 with Maureen Perrie, 'The Russian Peasant Movement of 1905–1907: Its Social Composition and Revolutionary Significance', in Ben Eklof and Stephen Frank (eds), *The World of the Russian Peasant: Post-Emancipation Culture and Society* (Boston, 1990), pp. 193–218. For more on Saratov see, for example, T. Fallows, 'Governor Stolypin and the Revolution of 1905 in Saratov', in Rex A. Wade and Scott J. Seregny (eds), *Politics and Society in Provincial Russia: Saratov, 1590–1917* (Columbus, O.,

1989), pp. 139–59; and T. R. Mixter, 'Peasant Collective Action in Saratov Province, 1902–1906', in ibid., pp. 191–232.

44 Compare, for example, Trotsky, *1905*, p. 40 with James D. White, 'Moscow, Petersburg and the Russian Industrialists. In Reply to Ruth Amende Rossa', *Soviet Studies*, Vol. 24 (1972–73), No. 3, pp. 416–20.

45 Compare, for example, Trotsky, *1905*, pp. 132–9 with the essays on the period in John D. Klier and Shlomo Lambroza (eds), *Pogroms: Anti-Jewish Violence in Modern Russian History* (Cambridge, 1992).

46 Some recent research shares Trotsky's interest in peasant political activity as a reflection of a modernizing process. See, for example, Scott J. Seregny, 'A Different Type of Peasant Movement: The Peasant Unions in the Russian Revolution of 1905', *Slavic Review*, Vol. 47 (1988), No. 1, pp. 51–67.

47 David Moon, *The Russian Peasantry 1600–1930: The World the Peasants Made* (London, 1999). Some of Moon's themes can also be found in the articles on Saratov cited in note 43 above.

14 The 1905 Revolution on Tyneside

David Saunders

Most responses to the 1905 Revolution in the vicinity of the River Tyne in north-east England (and, broadly speaking, in Britain as a whole) were either liberal (as exemplified by Robert Spence Watson and his 'Society of Friends of Russian Freedom') or socialist (as exemplified by the manual workers Charles Flynn and Heinrich Matthäus Fischer). At a remove, it can be seen that the differences among them mirrored differences of opinion in Russia. An examination of these differences may also support the contention that, in the early twentieth century, political consensus was breaking down at the western end of Europe no less than in the east.

Ten days before 'Bloody Sunday' in St Petersburg, Dr Robert Spence Watson drew up an appeal in his capacity as president of Britain's 'Society of Friends of Russian Freedom'. Writing at his home in Bensham, a district of Gateshead on the south side of the River Tyne in north-east England, he declared: 'There has never been a time ... when it was more necessary, in the direct interests of our work, that we should be furnished with funds sufficient to carry it on with the greatest vigour.'[1] Four days after 'Bloody Sunday', on the opposite side of the River Tyne, in a western district of the city of Newcastle, 'A meeting of Elswick workmen was held during the dinner hour at the Water Street entrance to the works ... to protest against the massacre in St Petersburg. There was only one speaker, Mr Flynn, who, in vigorous language, denounced the sham Russian Government which had committed those unspeakable atrocities upon workmen and peaceable citizens.'[2] Thus, both sides of the Tyne, and representatives of both the privileged and the unprivileged parts of the Tyneside population, seemed to agree on the need to further the Russian Revolution of 1905. North-east England looked as if it was about to provide one more instance of that enthusiasm for foreign liberation movements which the British had evinced during the Greeks' struggle for independence in the 1820s, the Hungarians' battles with Vienna in 1848 and 1849, the Italians' quest for unity in the 1850s and 1860s and the Serb and Bulgarian conflict with the Turks in the mid-1870s.

Appearances, however, can be deceptive. It is misleading to say of British people in general, and of Tynesiders in particular, that they were unanimous in their attitude towards Russia at the time of the revolution of 1905. Robert Spence Watson was a lifelong Liberal, Charles Flynn an adherent of the Independent Labour Party. Both men sought the collapse of the tsarist regime, but they disagreed about what should replace it. To the left of Flynn, furthermore, a German-Russian revolutionary named Heinrich Matthäus Fischer, who had been living in the Benwell district of Newcastle since 1901, was willing, in the pursuit of change in Russia, to countenance more forthright methods than almost all the people around him. He would demonstrate, in 1906 and 1907, that a commitment to socialism did not preclude a 'direct action' approach to the maintenance of the revolutionary momentum in the Russian Empire. Discussing the differences among these people may illustrate the notion that the 'mid-Victorian consensus' in British politics (if, indeed, there had ever been one) was breaking down and may support the idea that one of the reasons why the Russian Revolution of 1905 enjoyed only partial success was that the people who were trying to further it did not agree on their objectives or on how they should go about achieving them.

In the nineteenth century, British antipathy to the tsarist regime ran very deep. Not many books on Russian matters were as judicious as Mackenzie Wallace's *Russia* of 1877.[3] Two considerations underpinned Britain's hostility: her material rivalry with the Russian Empire and the ideological incompatibility of the British and Russian political systems. The material rivalry dated back at least as far as Catherine the Great's 'Armed Neutrality' of 1780. Although Britain and Russia fought on the same side in the Napoleonic Wars, they did so only in the earlier and later stages, and after 1815 the two states were almost always at loggerheads. Their rivalry showed up especially in the Balkans and Central Asia. Although after Germany and Austria went into alliance in 1879 it was always likely that London and St Petersburg were going to resolve their differences over the Balkans in order to block future Germanic advances in that direction, discord in Central Asia remained. New differences, meanwhile, arose over China and Britain formed an alliance with Japan in 1902, partly in order to give herself a bulwark against Russian encroachment on her eastern interests. When war broke out between Russia and Japan at the beginning of 1904, Anglo-Russian relations deteriorated. When the Russian fleet fired on British trawlers off the Dogger Bank in the North Sea on 21 October 1904, they plummeted.[4]

Geopolitical friction between the two countries exacerbated their ideological antipathy. Nineteenth-century British commentators made much of the fundamental irreconcilability of the Russian and British political systems, holding the former to be interventionist but the latter permissive and facultative. Escapees from the lands of the tsar tended to confirm their analysis.[5] British officials held that the right of the inhabitants of the British Isles to freedom of speech extended even to non-Britons. More than one foreign country sought clarification of this aspect of British policy. Uruguay, for example, enquired of the British Foreign Office in January 1897 what view it took of 'anarchist' activity within the frontiers of Britain. A clerk in the Home Office replied that 'to be an Anarchist is not in itself any offence against English law, any more than it is to hold any other theory with regard to social or political questions'.[6]

At a time when revolutionary movements seemed to be gaining ground not only within the Russian Empire but also in many parts of Europe, the tsarist regime found the British attitude to the rights of foreigners on British soil difficult to accept. Along with various other continental European countries, Russia tried in the years before 1905 to put in place international agreements on the control of revolutionaries. When it sought British adhesion to them, however, the British would not play ball. Lord Salisbury, Britain's prime minister between 1895 and 1902, expressed his country's position on revolutionary movements at the time of the Rome Anti Anarchist Conference of 1898: 'In this country,' he wrote, 'and possibly in others, great objection would be felt to any attempt to meet the dangers of the anarchist conspiracy by restraining or encroaching upon the liberty of the rest of the community.'[7] Two years later, after the assassination of King Umberto of Italy, a clerk in the British Foreign Office noted that the Russian government was trying to persuade other governments to 'make it penal to advocate anarchist doctrines even where no crime is directly recommended ... Such legislation', he went on, 'would in Lord Salisbury's opinion be quite impossible in England.'[8] When Britain was invited by Germany and Russia in May 1904 to sign up to an international 'Secret Protocol' on Anarchist Crimes, her commissioner of police raised multiple objections. Britain's police systems, he said, were too decentralized to allow the establishment of the sort of Central Bureau envisaged by the Protocol; Britain was unable to engage in the sort of political surveillance which was to be found on the continent because it lacked an internal passport system; the British police had no power to make 'domiciliary visits'; and they could find out about revolutionaries only by making use of informers, who would not help them if they thought that the information they supplied was to be communicated to foreigners. The foreign secretary pointed all this out to the Russian ambassador.[9] Finally, in November 1906, Britain turned down a request from the St Petersburg Department of Police to be allowed to communicate with its London equivalent directly (rather than through the Russian Embassy in London), with the comment: 'An imprudent policeman might land us in a most awkward political situation.'[10]

Tynesiders reflected the general British hostility towards Russia from at least the 1840s.[11] The Russia-related activities of local opinion-formers such as Joseph Cowen and Robert Spence Watson reached the wider community, for when Heinrich Fischer took up residence in the Newcastle area in 1901 he found that, 'one way or another', his fellow workers 'were not badly informed about the condition of things in Russia'; they gave him to understand that the source of their knowledge was 'the agitation which in his own day Peter Kropotkin conducted throughout England' – agitation in which the 'anarchist prince' had been assisted by a wealthy Newcastle radical and newspaper owner called 'Robert Cowen'. By prefacing Cowen's surname with Spence Watson's first name, Fischer inadvertently recognized that, between them, these leaders of Tyneside society had arranged at least five speeches by Kropotkin in Newcastle in the 1880s and 1890s.[12]

On the face of it, then, the readiness of all sorts of British people to express opposition to tsarist despotism seemed to be unqualified at the beginning of the twentieth century. In fact, however, the coin was two-sided. British concern about the extent of immigration from the Russian Empire had been growing since the 1880s.[13] Although Britain's political police (the 'Special Branch') had come into being in the late nineteenth century in order to monitor subversion on the part of the Irish, it soon began to take an interest in other sorts of political activist. In 1897 and 1898, for example, it played a key part in the incrimination and trial in London of Vladimir Burtsev.[14] Although, officially, Britain continued to maintain that people could not be prosecuted in British courts merely for the opinions they held, behind the scenes some people in responsible positions were prepared to enunciate modified versions of the country's libertarian position. In 1898, a month after Lord Salisbury had said that it was impossible to curtail the liberty of British people in order to 'meet the dangers of the anarchist conspiracy', a clerk in the Home Office referred to the recent prosecution of Burtsev in terms which made it clear that he did not think the trial had been a unique event: 'might it not be well to remind FO [the Foreign Office]', the clerk noted, 'that English law allows of the punishment of prisoners who conspire or incite to murder abroad whether their motives are political or not, that there is no hesitation about putting this law into force and that a Russian extremist has recently been convicted and sentenced to imprisonment for a breach of it in respect of a newspaper intended for circulation abroad'.[15] Moreover, despite the fact that in 1904 Britain's commissioner of police objected to the idea of British adhesion to the international 'Secret Protocol' on Anarchist Crimes, 'At the same time H.M. Govt intimated that they would assist as far as possible in the proposed arrangements and that the Metropolitan Police undertook to notify known departures abroad of dangerous anarchists, and would do all possible to get credible information as to plots to commit crimes abroad and would communicate such information to the foreign authorities concerned.'[16] Clearly, then, 'official' Britain was by no means wholehearted in its opposition to the Russian Empire; and London, rather than St Petersburg, appears to have been the prime mover in the long series of exchanges that eventually gave rise to the Anglo-Russian Entente of 1907.[17]

Signs of British sympathy for the tsarist regime around the time of the 1905 Revolution were not confined to the ranks of British officialdom. Although most British journalists who specialized on Russia – Harold Williams, Bernard Pares, Robert Wilton – tended to back the reform movement, Sir Donald Mackenzie Wallace, who was more distinguished than any of them, 'considered that throughout the revolutionary period of 1905–07, the tsarist regime's actions had been justified'.[18] A second British journalist, W. T. Stead (a Tynesider, though he had moved to London in the 1880s), made an extended visit to Russia between late August and late October 1905, the principal purpose of which was to reconcile the emergent political parties with the forces of order. It came to nothing, but Stead did not draw the conclusion that 'official' Russia had to give more ground. On the contrary, he was still supportive of the tsar in November 1907, when he wrote to Robert Spence Watson to complain about the latter's objection to Russia's chairmanship of the second Hague peace conference. 'The Russians', he wrote, 'have used their influence at the Conference uniformly as that of moderators with a strong bias in favour of progressive proposals.'[19]

Robert Spence Watson, however, continued to seek fundamental change in Russia. After Burtsev's arrest in London in 1897, he wrote to the Tory Home Secretary to point out what might happen 'if papers which have been taken possession of by the English police should be communicated by them to the Russian police'.[20] In 1898, he asked the Liberal grandee Earl Grey to use his good offices with the Tory home secretary to ameliorate Burtsev's prison conditions.[21] Six years later, he still found it remarkable that the British authorities had 'actually prosecuted [Burtsev] upon the charge of inciting Russians to kill the Tzar'.[22] By then, his attention had turned to 'the extraordinary Aliens Bill which had been introduced in the House of Commons', which 'gave almost an absolute power to the Secretary of State over the liberties, and practically the lives, of political refugees'. 'No man', he believed, 'should be entrusted with such a power.'[23] By this time, 1904, Spence Watson was angry. A 'great causes' politician,[24] he had found in Russian affairs, not for the first time, an issue that he considered to be worthy of his full attention. The pericarditis from which he suffered in the last part of his life made concentration on one issue at a time even more natural for him than it had been formerly; and, in the young David Soskice, he had just acquired a new and vigorous editor of *Free Russia*, the journal of the 'Society of Friends of Russian Freedom' of which he was president.[25]

Immediately after 'Bloody Sunday', Spence Watson permitted Soskice to use his name 'for a Fund to assist the strikers'. 'I can and will do anything in my power', he said, 'to relieve the necessities of those who are being so shockingly treated and whose needs must be very great.'[26] Later in the revolutionary year he cast doubt on the Russian regime's hesitant moves in the direction of political change: 'As for the so called constitution,' he wrote, 'from the first it seemed to me to be simply a dodge.'[27] In September 1905, he did not doubt that 'The autocracy must give way very much further than it has done if it is to avoid the fate which ultimately awaits all one-man governments founded upon the woes of the people who are misgoverned.'[28] In late October he wrote Soskice a long letter about the massacres at Baku.[29] In early November, he described himself as 'thankful that the Tzar and Witte are not trusted', and lamented 'What a mockery of good intentions are the massacres of the Jews!' '[T]he one crumb of solid comfort' he perceived at that time was 'that the old rogue Pobiedonostseff is gone – if indeed that be true.'[30] When, in the middle of November, he learned that Soskice intended to take advantage of Nicholas II's recent amnesty and go back to Russia, he confessed that 'although I am sure that these matters are much better left to the people of the country, I have had a most intolerable craving for the last 3 months to go over and see and hear for myself'.[31] In mid-December, when Soskice was on the point of actually leaving, Spence Watson wished him good luck, expressed the hope that he 'may be of signal service there', and confessed that he was 'only afraid of matters getting prolonged and of some autocrat coming forward who has ability to work himself into a position of power'.[32] After Soskice had gone, he returned to the hostility he felt towards Britain's Aliens Act, a measure which he was certain made it harder for political refugees to base themselves in England.[33]

Although Spence Watson was probably Tyneside's most vocal liberal on Russian matters in 1905, he was by no means the only one. The principal Newcastle daily newspaper, the *Chronicle*, maintained a very public commitment to the idea of liberal change in Russia throughout the year.[34] The highpoint of the liberal Tyneside response to the Russian Revolution of 1905 was perhaps a public meeting on behalf of Russia's Jews that took place at the Lovaine Hall in central Newcastle on 22 November. The Jewish population of Newcastle was well established. The synagogue on Leazes Park Road in the town centre celebrated its twenty-fifth anniversary in 1905.[35] Many local Jews were of east European provenance. The Newcastle Jewish Board of Guardians received 344 applications for financial support in 1904 on behalf of 158 people, 'of whom 120 were Russians'.[36] One of the Newcastle daily newspapers pointed out, in a long leader of 2 May 1905, that the political changes which had been taking place in Russia did not yet include relief for Jews.[37] Shortly afterwards it reported the murder of Jews in Zhitomir and a gathering of 'Newcastle Zionists'.[38] A new young rabbi, B. N. Michaelson (or Michelson), was inducted at the Leazes Park Road synagogue on 9 September.[39] Preaching on 11 November, he announced the forthcoming public protest meeting and pointed out that 'As yet those who denounced the Bulgarian atrocities [of 1876] so vigorously have had little to say about the barbarities committed by those who, at the time of the Russo-Turkish war were looked to as the interpreters of the will of Holy Russia, the saviour of mankind.'[40] The meeting itself was a major event. There was a 'large attendance'.[41] Although Spence Watson was too ill to attend, the rabbi read out a letter from him in which he wrote, amongst other things, 'It has been carefully computed in late years that, in the reign of Terror of the French Revolution at the end of the 18th century, from 1,400 to 2,000 persons perished. I see that it is stated in Kischineff alone and in Odessa many more of your co-religionists have been shamefully put to death. It is appalling that in this twentieth century such atrocities can be perpetrated in

Europe.' From the chair, Thomas Burt, the MP for Morpeth, went so far as to say that 'there could not be a shadow of a doubt . . . that the authorities of the [Russian] Government . . . had connived at these atrocities'. A local councillor pointed out that 'a more orderly set of people, a more sober, law-abiding people [than Newcastle's Jews] could not be found anywhere'. Seconding one of the meeting's protest motions, a certain John Havelock argued that if the British 'should close their doors to these poor refugees from Russian despotism, then they would go a long way to deserve that charge that they had done something to shut the gates of mercy'. Rabbi Michelson claimed at the end of the meeting that 'the atrocities had been so fiendish that they could find no parallel even in the most barbarous annals of the most barbarous peoples'. The speaker who seconded the vote of thanks for Burt's chairmanship recalled the days when Joseph Cowen had led Newcastle in its championship of oppressed continental Europeans. The liberal tradition of the city appeared to be in fine shape.

Public meetings of this kind were not unusual in England in 1905,[42] but the one in Newcastle differed from the others in that a politically active German-Russian émigré, Heinrich Matthäus Fischer, took exception to it. Fischer thought that Thomas Burt 'said nothing but liberal pap (*razmaznia*)'; he urged the assembled company 'to address yourself not to the Russian government but to the Jews themselves, whom you should call upon to fight the Russian government and summon to organized and armed resistance, whilst placing all the blame for these pogroms on the money-bag owners, the Lords Rothschild'.[43] In Fischer's opinion, liberal disquiet was an inadequate response to the events of 1905 in Russia.

Up to a point, Fischer was right to say that the response of 'liberal' Newcastle to the pogroms in Russia left something to be desired. Spence Watson, for example, took the view that 'men holding authority' had 'clearly . . . instigated' the pogroms in Russia, but he specifically exempted Witte and his circle from these strictures.[44] Thomas Burt not only held that the Conservative British foreign secretary, Lord Lansdowne, 'had acted with great promptness in making representations to the Russian Government', but also doubted whether it was time for Russian Jews to emigrate *en masse* 'to some colony by themselves' and believed that 'The principle of brotherhood would solve this matter.' Another MP at the Lovaine Hall meeting claimed that 'the Tsar must have had good thoughts towards his people when the [October] manifesto was issued'. In view of these bland sentiments, it was perhaps not surprising that at least one person in the audience wanted to take a stronger line.

Greater outspokenness would not have been enough, however, to render the politics of Newcastle's liberals acceptable to Heinrich Fischer, for his objectives were socialist rather than liberal and the methods he was prepared to employ included 'organized and armed resistance'. Socialism was beginning to make a mark on Tyneside. 'The first socialist candidate to fight a parliamentary election in Newcastle was Fred Hammill in 1895.'[45] The city returned its first Labour MP at the general election of 1906, while Edward Hartley sought unavailingly to capture Newcastle's other parliamentary seat for socialism in an exciting by-election of 1908.[46] Although the north-east of England did not become a Labour stronghold until after the First World War,[47] the wind of change was blowing. Indeed, there were already enough socialists in the region for differences to have appeared among them. Fischer was to the left, for example, of Charles Flynn, the speaker at the meeting of Elswick shipyard workers who made an appearance at the beginning of this chapter. He gives the impression in his memoirs that he attended Flynn's meeting.[48] Whether or not he did, the two men were certainly acquainted. Early in February 1905, Fischer expressed an intention to write to a body called the North-East Coast Federation of Socialist Societies to ask whether it would organize meetings about the Russian movement at which he could be the speaker.[49] On 9 May 1905, Flynn wrote to Fischer in his capacity as honorary secretary of this federation. It is probable, therefore, that Fischer and Flynn were in touch throughout 1905, and it is clear from what Fischer did with the letter that he received from Flynn that he thought of him as a man whose socialism differed from his own. Flynn was writing to enquire about the best place to send funds collected on Tyneside for the Russian revolutionary movement. Fischer copied the letter to Lenin in Geneva, adding that its author had nothing to do with Britain's Social Democratic Federation but was an adherent of the more moderate Independent Labour Party.[50] Fischer, therefore, was already in the business not just of socialism but of a socialism of a particular kind. He was probably about as left wing as it was possible to be in the England of 1905.

I have attempted a full account of Fischer's life elsewhere.[51] Here, it need only be said that 'Bloody Sunday' in St Petersburg appears to have galvanized him. Apart from speaking at Flynn's Elswick meeting (if he did), he collected money for Russian strikers with the help of a Newcastle councillor for Benwell and the members of a free-standing club called the Newcastle Socialist Institute.[52] He bought envelopes and stamps in order to post Lenin's journals *Vpered* and *Proletarii* to Russia. In connection with his money-raising endeavours, he spoke frequently at branch meetings of his trade union, the Amalgamated Society of Engineers. He also hosted other Russian émigrés who came to Newcastle and he spoke at a branch meeting of the Social Democratic Federation in South Shields. He was delighted to learn that the Bolsheviks were to hold a congress in London. With a handful of like-minded fellow Russians in Newcastle, he founded an official cell of the Bolshevik fraction of the RSDLP. He organized his own meeting on behalf of Russian Jews at the Newcastle Socialist Institute and arranged for Lenin's London lieutenant, Nikolai Alekseev, to come up from the capital to speak to it. He canvassed among the Russian crews of the *Ermak* and the *Smolensk* when they were in dock on the Tyne for repair, enjoying more success, by his own account, with the latter than the former.[53]

Although some of these activities sound not dissimilar to those of Spence

Watson, Fischer was prepared to countenance a wider range of methods. He did not devote himself solely to speech-making, meetings, collecting money and disseminating literature. In fact, in mid-1906 he became personally involved in the transportation of weapons and ammunition to the Russian Empire.

Spence Watson, a Quaker, rejected military methods on principle. When writing to David Soskice immediately after 'Bloody Sunday', he pointed out: 'I am President of the Peace Society and I cannot subscribe to buy ammunition and the like.' Three days later he wrote: 'It may be that you ... mean to start a fund for the purpose of supplying what I might call "war material". I very much doubt if a fund of that kind would receive any considerable support. It may be that there are rich men who would support it, taking quite a different view from that which I entertain on the matter, but they would have to be found out individually, and I do not know any such.'[54]

To judge by the way Fischer behaved in 1906 and 1907, he disagreed strongly with this sort of quietism. He was not, of course, the only person in Britain in 1905 who thought that it was time to use force against the tsarist regime. Nor were like-minded people to be found only among the ranks of Russian exiles, for in 'the late winter of 1904' a businessman called S. G. Hobson began sending revolvers to Riga in barrels of lard on behalf of the Socialist Revolutionary Nikolai Chaikovskii. When the contact man in Riga fell silent, Hobson even travelled to the Baltic provinces, on Chaikovskii's behalf, to find out what had gone wrong. On his return, he was warned by 'a detective from Scotland Yard' that Lord Lansdowne, the British foreign secretary, had received a letter about him from the Russian consul-general. 'Obviously,' he related, 'my wild and whirling career as a hardware merchant and lard exporter had reached an inglorious end.'[55]

Gun-running as a whole, however, did not come to an end. Much ink has been spilt on the voyage of the *John Grafton* from Britain's Channel Islands via Hull or Newcastle or Edinburgh to the coast of Finland in the late summer of 1905.[56] Even after the very public fiasco in which that voyage ended, Britain remained a suitable place from which to despatch weapons, for the reason that, ultimately, the British authorities set greater store by the profits of British arms dealers than they did by the internal security of the Russian Empire. They seem to have warned off Hobson, but they did not accede to requests from Russian diplomats for more systematic intervention in Russia-related aspects of the British arms trade. In late January 1906, ambassador Sergei Sazonov wrote from Russia's London Embassy to Sir Edward Grey, Britain's new Liberal foreign secretary, to point out that Denmark was collaborating with St Petersburg in the latter's attempt to enforce a ban on the importation of firearms into the Polish, Baltic and Finnish parts of the tsar's domains. But Grey was less co-operative than the Danes had been. He would do no more than place a note about the Russian ban in the *London Gazette*. In his opinion, 'the circumstances of the case would not warrant His Majesty's government in prohibiting the export of arms and munitions of war from this country'. When Sazonov wrote a second time, the British authorities went to greater lengths to justify their attitude. The Foreign Office wrote to the Home Office, the Home Office to the Customs. Customs pointed out that British exporters who were banned from consigning arms to Russia would simply send their goods to intermediate ports. Moreover, a civil servant in the Home Office recorded Britain's economic grounds for objecting to the Russian request: 'It is difficult', he wrote, 'to forecast the influence on the explosives trade of a measure of this kind [that is, the ban sought by St Petersburg]. I can however if called on quote a somewhat analogous case in which a very considerable trade in explosives was entirely sacrificed in deference to the representations of a foreign government – such trade being at once absorbed and *retained* by another European Power which had declined to be influenced by such representations.' Later in 1906 a clerk in the Foreign Office pointed out (in response to yet another Russian request for action on the arms trade) that 'HMG refrained from interfering a few years ago with the trade in arms etc clandestinely introduced from Trinidad into Venezuela to assist in the Revolution there.'[57] Adding insult to injury, at the end of 1906 and in 1907 Britain further refused to comply with Russian requests that misuse of explosives be made an extraditable offence under the Anglo-Russian Extradition Treaty of 1886.[58] Thus, Britain never went beyond the note about the Russian ban on the importation of weapons that it had placed in the *London Gazette* after Sazonov wrote for the first time.

To judge by a querulous response to that note from a member of the 'North of England Protecting and Indemnity Association' (whose office was in central Newcastle),[59] Tyneside was likely to have been a particularly good part of the United Kingdom from which to attempt the covert despatch of weapons to the Russian Empire. The region certainly had a strong interest in the arms trade, for its most famous nineteenth-century manufacturer, Lord Armstrong (founder of the Elswick Works where Charles Flynn had spoken), was a sort of 'English Krupp'.[60] Ordinary people in the region were used to explosives, which were employed extensively in the local coalmines. To these reasons why Tyneside was a good place for a Russian revolutionary to contemplate gun-running, two more may be added: the natural orientation of much of the region's trade meant that ships sailed constantly from its many ports to places on the Baltic; and local surveillance by the police, finally, was minimal. Although one of the reasons why the British government chose not to monitor the activities of 'anarchists' outside London had to do with its commitment to the principle of civil liberty, another was that it thought that most of the people at issue 'reside[d] within the Metropolitan area'; 'with few exceptions,' a British official said, 'they are aliens, and they find in the Metropolis facilities as regards their native language and communication with friends and countrymen which are not available elsewhere'.[61]

For all these reasons Heinrich Fischer was well placed, on Tyneside, to turn his attention to gun-running. In a letter to Spence Watson at the beginning of 1906, Feliks Volkhovskii asserted 'that the centre of gravity of all Russian political activity has been fully and entirely transferred to Russia. There is nothing to be done here [that is, in western Europe] to help the movement, new possibilities having sprung up within the rebellious Empire.'[62] But the gun-running in which Fischer engaged in 1906 and 1907 was to cast doubt on this declaration.

Fischer's two accounts of his gun-running may be summarized, roughly, as follows. At the request of a Latvian by the name of Al'fred Nagel', who had located him through the newspaper of Britain's Social Democratic Federation, he agreed to receive, store and despatch weapons and ammunition to the Russian Empire. British socialists helped him. Latvian stokers on ships between north-east England and the Baltic undertook the delivery of the material. The conspiracy worked well for some months, but fell apart when the British police lit upon a cache of weapons in Sunderland and then a letter from Nagel' which led them to Fischer in Newcastle. Trials ensued in Sunderland, Newcastle, Edinburgh and Glasgow – though Fischer himself was not prosecuted because no weapons were found at his home, while Nagel' disappeared from view.[63]

Many of these details can be verified. The key book on the 'first Bolshevik fighting organization' points out that it was reinforced in 1906 by Latvians who left their homeland in the wake of the tsarist regime's 'punitive expeditions' of that year.[64] It was not surprising that there were people whom Fischer calls 'Latvian comrades' on 'Russian steamers', for the Latvian maritime tradition dates back at least to the seventeenth century.[65] To judge by the fact that a mid-nineteenth-century Latvian intellectual 'suggested that Russian Imperial power and the interest of the Latvian peasantry coincided in the area of seapower and maritime trade', Latvians in the late Russian Empire may have been actively encouraged to go to sea.[66] In 1905 and 1906 Fischer's name appeared as that of the secretary of the Newcastle branch of Britain's Social Democratic Federation in the latter's weekly newspaper.[67] The 'English comrade' whom Fischer refers to as the manager of his store of arms in Newcastle turns out to have been a certain Thomas Dugger Keast, whom the investigating authorities initially thought to be a Russian or Polish Jew but later decided was a Cornishman from Launceston.[68] The 'space in the business part of town' which Fischer says that he hired in Newcastle was a room at 42 Leazes Park Road, in the centre of the city, a terraced house about fifty yards up the hill from the synagogue where Michelson had announced his concern for Russian Jews in November 1905. Fischer's statement that 'steamers came from Hamburg' to Newcastle with weapons is implied by a letter in Latvian from Newcastle to Hamburg which fell into the hands of the Russian consul in Newcastle in early September 1906; for, apart from giving clear indication that the illegible author was moving between Newcastle and Edinburgh, and apart from asking 'how do you like the bomb explosion in St Petersburg?' (a reference to the attack on Stolypin at his dacha on Aptekarskii Island in St Petersburg on 12 [25] August

1907), this document employed conspiratorial language to tell the prospective recipient to 'forward to Newcastle another parcel like the last one'.[69] The 'English comrade in Sunderland' whose arms dump the British police lighted upon was called Daniel Currie; the 'bachelor lad' to whom Fischer says that Currie entrusted part of his stock was a certain Robert Hutchinson; Al'fred Nagel' seems to have worked for the Second International in Brussels; Fischer's address in Newcastle which Nagel' inadvertently gave away when he wrote to Currie in Sunderland was 113 Hampstead Road, Benwell; the trials which took place in Sunderland, Newcastle, Edinburgh and Glasgow between April and July 1907 resulted in fines for various people (but no east Europeans) for storing explosives illegally under the Explosives Act of 1875; and, luckily for the gun-runners, the English authorities decided not to prosecute and the Scottish authorities failed to achieve convictions under the more severe Explosive Substances Act of 1883, which threatened custodial sentences rather than fines for the more serious offence of possessing explosives for illicit purposes.[70]

Above all, the contemporary British archival and newspaper sources make clearer than Fischer's memoirs that, by 1906 to 1907, he had associates in north-east England and Scotland with whom he could take much more vigorous steps to modify the tsarist regime than those contemplated by Robert Spence Watson. Clearly, the gamut of opinion about Russia in north-east England (and Scotland) was very far from being confined to the politically correct liberal centre. It may be the case, indeed, that the British people who were involved in the Tyneside gun-running of 1906–07 provide additional support for Graham Johnson's recent attempt to rehabilitate the idea that Britain's Social Democratic Federation was a genuinely revolutionary organization.[71] Since, furthermore, the Englishmen who went to trial in Sunderland and Newcastle as a result of Fischer's gun-running were represented by a lawyer named Edward Clark, who was obviously acting for them because he shared their belief in the value of what they were doing, and since a second Newcastle lawyer gave evidence at the Glasgow trial to the effect that, as the official British agent for the Hamburg armaments manufacturer who supplied the circle's goods, he saw nothing reprehensible in the circle's activities, it looks as if support for the notion of direct action against Russia was to be found in more than one layer of Tyneside society.[72] Thus, the left-leaning end of the spectrum of Tyneside opinions about Russia in 1906 and 1907 appears not to have been wholly confined to the unprivileged elements of the local community.

Aspects of Fischer's gun-running about which one would like to know more include the means employed by the authorities to unravel the affair after their initial strokes of luck in Sunderland; the true identities of some of the people in the case; the question of whether north-east England or Scotland was the British heart of the operation; and the particular sub-section of the Russian revolutionary movement to which Fischer's activities related. When the police raided Fischer's home, did he tell them about the arms store at 42 Leazes Park Road? If he did not, it is hard to see what put them on to it. Although it is certain that Al'fred Nagel' employed the pseudonym 'Stronmer' and variants thereof (because that was the name contemporary sources gave for the person who wrote from Fischer's flat in Benwell to Donald Currie in Sunderland), it is possible that he also employed the name 'Thomas Denvers' and variants, under which name an article about the gun-running appeared in 'the organ of Tyneside socialism' at the time the Newcastle trials were going on.[73] It is imaginable, furthermore, that Thomas Dugger Keast, keeper of the arms store in Leazes Park Road, was the pseudonym of a person whose real name has never been identified – not least because a previous investigator of the 'north British' gun-running of 1906 to 1907 failed in extensive attempts to locate a person with this name in any other appropriate context.[74]

Answers to these questions of identity would permit fuller definition of the ramifications of the gun-runners' circle. Perhaps they would help also in resolving whether the epicentre of the 1906–07 gun-running was in Scotland rather than on the Tyne. One of the earliest printed accounts in English of the gun-running of those years (the authors of which had some personal knowledge of the affair) is almost entirely Scottish in its coverage (and incidentally puts a certain 'Alf' at the heart of the matter, thus confirming the importance of Nagel').[75] Since, in the early twentieth century, Glaswegians often took their holidays at Whitley Bay, near the mouth of the Tyne, and since Tyneside was in a position to raise a brigade of 4,000 Scottish infantry in the early days of the First World War,[76] it is not difficult to imagine that Scottish gun-runners got in touch with comrades on Tyneside rather than the other way round. The Scottish socialist John Leslie wrote in 1918 that he had twice been 'actively engaged in the smuggling of arms and ammunition into Russia': on the first occasion 'immediately prior to the outbreak of 1905–07', on the second, 'immediately subsequent to and during the height of the reactionary terror'.[77] Since he then made the second rather than the first occasion sound like the operation in which Fischer was engaged, his account strengthens the notion that Scots were sending arms to Russia before people started doing so in north-east England.

The most important unresolved question relating to Fischer's gun-running, however, is that of whether it was a Latvian operation, an aspect of the Bolshevik gun-running operations of Maksim Litvinov (and Leonid Krasin), or the work of some other sub-division of the Russian revolutionary movement. Fischer himself wondered in his memoirs whether, at a remove, the Socialist Revolutionary and police agent Evno Azef had been behind it all.[78] Since Litvinov was a member of the Riga Bolshevik Committee in 1904 and 1905 and represented it at the Third Congress of the RSDLP in London in 1905,[79] it may not be sensible to try drawing distinctions between the gun-running operations he set up and others run by Latvians. After the 'Unification' Congress of the RSDLP in the spring of 1906, Latvian and Russian social democrats were closer than ever. The German-

Russian Bolshevik Ludwig Martens (later famous as the Bolshevik representative in the USA in 1919 and 1920) was certainly shipping weapons from Hamburg to the Russian Empire in 1906,[80] so he may have been shipping them via north-east England in the hope of avoiding surveillance on the part of the Russian secret police. Yet Litvinov's own account of his gun-running activities in the year 1906 makes no mention of England or Scotland and speaks only of his efforts to convey weapons from western Europe to the Black Sea coast of the Russian Empire via Bulgaria.[81] Some evidence, furthermore, gives the impression that Latvians really were despatching weapons entirely on their own account in 1906 and 1907. A Bulgarian who acted as a weapons purchaser for the Bolsheviks in Liège in 1906 refers to buying on the part of 'the representative of the Latvian social-democratic party' as if it were a separate operation.[82] The senior Latvian social democrat Iakov Kovalevskii (Jēkabs Kovaļevskis) describes a more or less wholly Latvian gun-running operation centred on Belgium and Hamburg which fell apart in 1906.[83] Thus, Al'fred Nagel' may have been trying, in his work with Fischer, to revivify Latvian work which had been underway for some time.

Fischer did not lose interest in the Russian revolutionary movement after the exposure of his gun-running in the middle of 1907. Indeed, he must have departed for the Fifth Congress of the RSDLP in London the minute the trials of his associates in Newcastle came to an end. At the congress he talked to Lenin about British politics and discussed ways of getting back to Russia with a friend he had made in Archangel in the late 1890s. Some of the cartridges which he had been transporting in 1906 and 1907 seem to have come to light on the beach at Blyth in north-east England in August 1914, when, naturally, they were thought to be a cache for incoming Germans.[84]

As to the other protagonists in this chapter, Robert Spence Watson remained hostile to the tsar until his death in 1911, accusing him of ruling by 'brute force' in June 1907, writing to the British authorities (at Kropotkin's instigation) when Nikolai Chaikovskii was arrested in Russia in December 1907, and protesting when the tsar came to Cowes in 1909.[85] Charles Flynn recedes into the shadows. The Russian Embassy in London made another unavailing attempt, in the wake of Fischer's gun-running, to get Britain to stop armaments reaching Russian revolutionaries from British ports.[86] Latvians continued to operate in Britain, impelling the Russian ambassador in London to write to the Foreign Office about them in 1907 and in 1908, and perpetrating a wages heist in Tottenham in 1909 as well as the Houndsditch jewellery raid of December 1910 (the latter culminating in the notorious 'Siege of Sidney Street' of January 1911).[87] Fischer's Latvian contact, Al'fred Nagel', may have subsequently offered his services to British counter-intelligence, for a Latvian with this name was arrested in Moscow for spying in 1924 and executed there the following year.[88]

More important than these details, though, are the political positions which Spence Watson and Fischer exemplified. They stood for different views of the way forward in Russia. Spence Watson's outlook was more or less that of the Russian Kadets. Fischer was a Bolshevik with a dash of the Socialist-Revolutionary about him. Studying the reactions of these people and their associates to the Russian Revolution of 1905 serves to show that political ideologies were diverse in Britain in the early twentieth century, that they were diverse in ways which matched the diversity in Russia, and perhaps that political consensus was coming to an end in western Europe, just as it was in the east.

Acknowledgements

I am grateful to Mabel Weiss for permission to quote from the Spence Watson Papers at the Robinson Library of the University of Newcastle upon Tyne, and to David Soskice for permission to quote from the Stow Hill Papers at the House of Lords Record Office.

Notes

1   'Dr R. Spence Watson to the Friends of Russian Freedom', *Free Russia*, Vol. 16 (1905), No. 2, p. 13.
2   *Newcastle Evening Chronicle* (26 January 1905).
3   D. Mackenzie Wallace, *Russia* (London, 1877).
4   For British documents on the Dogger Bank incident see G. P. Gooch and Harold Temperley (eds), *British Documents on the Origins of the War, 1898–1914* (London, 1928–36), Vol. 4, pp. 5–41. On the earliest stages of Britain's mistrust of Russia see J. H. Gleason, *The Genesis of Russophobia in Great Britain: A Study of the Interaction of Policy and Opinion* (Cambridge, Mass., 1950). On Anglo-Russian relations in Central Asia and China at the end of the nineteenth and beginning of the twentieth centuries see Keith Neilson, *Britain and the Last Tsar: British Policy and Russia, 1894–1917* (Oxford, 1995), pp. 178–264.
5   On Russian émigrés in nineteenth-century Britain see, for example, Monica Partridge, *Alexander Herzen: Collected Studies* (Nottingham, 1988), pp. 17–44, 145–57; Martin A. Miller, *Kropotkin* (Chicago, 1976), pp. 160–80; and Donald Senese, *S. M. Stepniak-Kravchinskii: The London Years* (Newtonville, Mass., 1987).
6   London, National Archives (Public Record Office), HO 144/545/A55176.
7   HO 45/10254/X36450, sub-file 31, Salisbury to F. R. St John (12 October 1898) (copy).
8   Ibid., sub. 116.
9   HO 144/757/118516, sub. 1, 3, 15.
10 Ibid., sub. 47, 51.
11 David Saunders, 'Tyneside and the Making of the Russian Revolution', *Northern History*, Vol. 21 (1985), pp. 259–62.
12 Fisher, *V Rossii i v Anglii: nabliudeniia i vospominaniia peterburgskogo rabochego (1890–1921gg.)* (Moscow, 1922), p. 57. Kropotkin first spoke in Newcastle at the behest of Joseph Cowen in 1882 (Saunders, 'Tyneside', p. 267). Between 1886 and 1896 he spoke four times to the Tyneside Sunday Lecture Society, which was founded by Spence Watson: Tyneside Sunday Lecture Society, *Annual Report (1916–17)* (Newcastle upon Tyne, 1917), pp. 13–14, 17.

13 John A. Garrard, *The English and Immigration, 1880–1910* (London, 1971), pp. 23–7.

14 Bernard Porter, *The Origins of the Vigilant State: The London Metropolitan Police Special Branch Before the First World War* (London, 1987), p. 116.

15 HO 45/10254/X36450, sub. 58 (23 November 1898).

16 HO 144/757/118516.

17 Neilson, *Britain and the Last Tsar*, pp. 237, 267.

18 W. Harrison, 'Mackenzie Wallace's View of the Russian Revolution of 1905–1907', *Oxford Slavonic Papers (New Series)*, Vol. 4 (1971), p. 82; see also W. Harrison, 'The British Press and the Russian Revolution of 1905–1907', *Oxford Slavonic Papers (New Series)*, Vol. 7 (1974), pp. 75–95.

19 Percy Corder, *The Life of Robert Spence Watson* (London, 1914), p. 298. On Stead's journey to Russia in the late summer and autumn of 1905 see Joseph O. Baylen, *The Tsar's 'Lecturer-General': W. T. Stead and the Russian Revolution of 1905* (Atlanta, 1969); and A. N. Zashikhin, 'Uil'iam Sted i proval ego "missii" v Rossii osen'iu 1905 goda', in V. I. Startsev (ed.), *Nauchnaia biografiia – vid istoricheskogo issledovaniia* (Leningrad, 1985), pp. 67–82.

20 HO 144/272/A59222B, sub. 2, Spence Watson to Sir Matthew White Ridley (Bensham, 17 December 1897).

21 Ibid., sub. 12, Spence Watson to Earl Grey (Bensham, 17 April 1898).

22 Robert Spence Watson, 'England as the Refuge of the Oppressed', *Free Russia*, Vol. 15 (1904), No. 7–9, p. 70.

23 Ibid.

24 See Saunders, 'Tyneside', pp. 272–3.

25 Soskice replaced Feliks Volkhovskii as editor of *Free Russia* on 2 June 1904: *Free Russia*, Vol. 15 (1904), No. 6, p. 68. On Spence Watson's pericarditis, see his letter to Soskice of 7 August 1905 ('In the past 5 months I have six times come to the very gates of death'): London, House of Lords Record Office (HLRO), Stow Hill Papers, SH/DS/1/Box 10/Wat/item 12.

26 Ibid., items 6 and 7, telegram and letter from Spence Watson to Soskice (Newcastle, 24 January 1905).

27 Ibid., item 13, Spence Watson to Soskice (Newcastle, 24 August 1905).

28 Robert Spence Watson, 'The Russian Puzzle', *Free Russia*, Vol. 16 (1905), No. 8–10, p. 93.

29 HLRO, SH/DS/1/Box 10/Wat, item 18, Spence Watson to Soskice (Bensham, 24 October 1905) – also published in *Free Russia*, Vol. 16 (1905), No. 11, pp. 110–11.

30 HLRO, SH/DS/1/Box 10/Wat, item 21, Spence Watson to Soskice (Bensham, 3 November 1905).

31 Ibid., item 22, Spence Watson to Soskice (Newcastle, 16 November 1905).

32 Ibid., item 23, Spence Watson to Soskice (Newcastle, 12 December 1905).

33 Dr Robert Spence Watson, 'The Aliens Act, 1905', *Free Russia*, Vol. 17 (1906), No. 1, pp. 1–2. Soskice's activities in Russia between 1906 and 1908 are described in Barry Hollingsworth, 'Benckendorff's "Bête Noire": *The Tribune* and Russian Internal Affairs, 1906–1908', in William Harrison and Avril Pyman (eds), *Poetry, Prose and Public Opinion: Aspects of Russia, 1850–1970* (Letchworth, 1984), pp. 106–32.

34 The *Newcastle Daily Chronicle*'s leaders on Russia in 1905 included 'The Russian People' (2 May), 'The Baku Horrors' (8 September), 'The Tsar and Peace' (20 September), 'The Russian Revolution' (30 and 31 October), 'A Free Russia' (1 November), 'The Russian Atrocities' (22 November), and 'The State of Russia' (21 and 29 December).

35 *Newcastle Daily Chronicle* (11 September 1905).

36 *Newcastle Evening Chronicle* (4 February 1905).

37 *Newcastle Daily Chronicle* (2 May 1905).
38 *Newcastle Daily Chronicle* (9 May and 5 June 1905).
39 *Newcastle Daily Chronicle* (11 September 1905).
40 *Newcastle Daily Chronicle* (13 November 1905).
41 The *Newcastle Evening Chronicle* (23 November 1905) carried a long report of the meeting from which all subsequent quotations in this paragraph are taken.
42 Eliyahu Feldman, 'British Diplomats and British Diplomacy and the 1905 Pogroms in Russia', *Slavonic and East European Review*, Vol. 65 (1987), No. 4, p. 600.
43 G. Fisher, *Podpol'e, ssylka, emigratsiia: vospominaniia bol'shevika* (Moscow, 1935), pp. 161–2 (cf. Fisher, *V Rossiii*, p. 58). According to a British businessman who was born in Russia in 1853 and spent the whole of his working life there, 'The Rothschilds, as is well known, have never participated in any loan to the Russian Government': Maxwell S. Leigh (ed.), *Memoirs of James Whishaw* (London, 1935), p. 127.
44 *Newcastle Evening Chronicle* (23 November 1905), from which all subsequent quotations in this paragraph are taken.
45 Norman McCord and Richard Thompson, *The Northern Counties from AD 1000* (London and New York, 1998), p. 339.
46 Carol Ann Devlin, 'Congenial Ally or Threatening Rival: The Newcastle-upon-Tyne Labor Movement, 1900–1914' (Syracuse University Ph.D. thesis, 1991), pp. 140–202.
47 McCord and Thompson, *The Northern Counties*, p. 339.
48 Fisher, *V Rossii*, p. 72.
49 D. I. Antoniuk *et al.* (eds), *Perepiska V. I. Lenina i rukovodimykh im uchrezhdenii RSDRP s partiinymi organizatsiiami 1905–1907gg.: Sbornik dokumentov v piati tomakh* (Moscow, 1979–91), Vol. 1, Book 1, pp. 161–2.
50 *Rossiiskii Gosudarstvennyi Arkhiv Sotsial'no-Politicheskoi Istorii* (RGASPI), f. 351, *op. 1, ed. khr. 22, l. 6.*
51 David Saunders, 'A Russian Bebel Revisited: The Individuality of Heinrich Matthäus Fischer (1871–1935)', *Slavonic and East European Review*, Vol. 82 (2004), No. 3, pp. 625–54.
52 Fisher, *V Rossii*, pp. 72, 89.
53 Most of the information in this paragraph comes from Fischer's letters of 1905 to the 'Committee of the Overseas Organization' of the Bolsheviks: Antoniuk, *Perepiska V. I. Lenina*, Vol. 1, Book 1, pp. 108–9, 161–2, 203–5; Vol. 2, Book 2, p. 253; Vol. 3, Book 1, pp. 56, 101, 296–7. For a letter from Alekseev to N. K. Krupskaia in which he describes his visit to Newcastle see ibid., Vol. 3, Book 2, pp. 287–9. For evidence of the official Bolshevik recognition of Fischer's Newcastle cell see *Proletarii*, No. 8 (4 [17] July 1905). For the meeting Fischer organized on behalf of Russian Jews at the Newcastle Socialist Institute and the presence of the *Ermak* and the *Smolensk* in the Tyne, see the *Newcastle Daily Chronicle* (28 August, 23 October and 11 November 1905). See also Fisher, *V Rossii*, pp. 71–3, 88–9.
54 HLRO, SH/DS/1/Box 10/Wat/items 7 and 8, Spence Watson to Soskice (Newcastle, 24 and 27 January 1905).
55 S. G. Hobson, *Pilgrim to the Left: Memoirs of a Modern Revolutionist* (London, 1938), pp. 126–8. Hobson and Chaikovskii were probably funded by Akashi, the Japanese military attaché in Stockholm, whose near-contemporary official account of his subversive activities during the Russo-Japanese War is to be found in Akashi Motojirō, *Rakka ryūsui: Colonel Akashi's Report on His Secret Cooperation with the Russian Revolutionary Parties during the Russo-Japanese War*, ed. by Inaba Chiharu, Olavi K. Fält and Antti Kujala (Helsinki, 1988), pp. 33–53.

56 See especially S. M. Pozner (ed.), *Pervaia boevaia organizatsiia bol'shevikov 1905–1907gg.* (Moscow, 1934), pp. 257–83; Michael Futrell, *Northern Underground: Episodes of Russian Revolutionary Transport and Communications through Scandinavia and Finland, 1863–1917* (London, 1963), pp. 66–84; Antti Kujala, 'The Russian Revolutionary Movement and the Finnish Opposition, 1905: The *John Grafton* Affair and the Plans for an Uprising in St Petersburg', *Scandinavian Journal of History*, Vol. 5 (1980), No, 4, pp. 257–75; and Akashi, *Rakka ryūsui*, pp. 47–52, 163–4.

57 FO 371/122, ff. 521–38, 544–7 and HO 45/10333/137609: files which include Grey to Sazonov (3 February 1906); the Customs to the Home Office (9 March 1906); a Home Office minute of 13 March 1906; and a Foreign Office minute of 18 September 1906.

58 HO 45/10349/147444.

59 See FO 371/122, ff. 539–44.

60 William H. McNeill, *The Pursuit of Power: Technology, Armed Force, and Society since A.D. 1000* (Chicago, 1982), pp. 238, 262–3, 271. See also Marshall J. Bastable, *Arms and the State: Sir William Armstrong and the Remaking of British Naval Power, 1854–1914* (Aldershot, 2004), especially pp. 136–42.

61 HO 144/757/118516, sub. 3.

62 University of Newcastle upon Tyne, Special Collections, Spence Watson Papers: Feliks Volkhovskii to Robert Spence Watson (Lausanne, 2 January 1906).

63 Fisher, *V Rossii*, pp. 89–90; Fisher, *Podpol'e*, pp. 153–8.

64 Pozner, *Pervaia boevaia organizatsiia*, p. 22.

65 Felipe Fernández-Armesto, *Civilizations* (London, 2000), p. 368.

66 Andrejs Plakans, 'Peasants, Intellectuals, and Nationalism in the Russian Baltic Provinces, 1820–90', *Journal of Modern History*, Vol. 46 (1974), No. 3, p. 460.

67 *Justice* (25 March 1905–28 July 1906).

68 FO 371/322, f. 388, Chief Constable of Newcastle to the Home Office (10 April 1907); and ibid., f. 423, Home Office to the Foreign Office (11 May 1907). See also the *Newcastle Daily Journal* (10 April 1907), in which Keast was said to be 'a man about 30 years of age, of medium height, stoutly built, and with Jewish features', but in which a draper named James H. Jackson is reported as saying: 'It had been suggested to him that Keast was a Polish Jew, but if that was the case he must have been in the country for a long time, for he speaks excellent English.'

69 The Russian Consulate's translation of this letter into English is to be found in FO 371/122, f. 550, and FO 371/322, f. 390.

70 The information in this paragraph comes from FO 371/322, ff. 386–428; HO 144/1010/145334, sub. 3, 5; *Sunderland Daily Echo* (2–16 April 1907); the *Newcastle Daily Journal* (4 April–10 May 1907); the *Newcastle Daily Chronicle*, 4, 10, 18 April, 2 and 10 May 1907; *Newcastle Evening Chronicle* (10 April–9 May 1907); *Newcastle Weekly Chronicle* (20 April 1907); the *Scotsman* (Edinburgh, 16–19 April 1907); the *Glasgow Herald* (10 July 1907); *Forward* (Glasgow, 8 June and 6 July 1907); the *Daily Mail* (3 and 5 April 1907); *The Times* (10 April 1907); *Justice* (London, 11 May 1907), which is the reprint of an article called 'The Cartridge Mystery' by Thomas Denvers from the May 1907 issue of *The Keel* ('the organ of Tyneside Socialism'); and *Justice* (22 June 1907), which includes an address by Denvers to 'a fairly good audience' at Methil in Scotland. On an 'Al'fred Nagel'' who worked for the Second International in Brussels, see Pozner, *Pervaia boevaia organizatsiia*, p. 207.

71 Graham Johnson, *Social Democratic Politics in Britain, 1881–1911* (Lewiston, N.Y., 2002).

72 *Newcastle Evening Chronicle* (1 May 1907); *Glasgow Herald* (10 July 1907).

73 Denvers, 'The Cartridge Mystery'.

74 Ron Grant, 'British Radicals and Socialists and their Attitudes to Russia, c. 1890–1917' (University of Glasgow Ph.D. thesis, 1984), pp. 174, 182 (n. 111).

75 H. W. Lee and E. Archbold, *Social-Democracy in Britain: Fifty Years of the Socialist Movement* (London, 1935), pp. 148–54.

76 McCord and Thompson, *The Northern Counties*, pp. 288, 347.

77 John Leslie, 'Russian Revolution, Anarchism, and the Leeds "Convention"', *Justice* (5 September 1918). Leslie had been 'organising secretary of the Scottish District Council of the [Social Democratic] Federation' in 1898 and was at that time an enthusiast for the doctrine of 'class war': Johnson, *Social Democratic Politics*, p. 143.

78 Fisher, *V Rossii*, p. 90.

79 Ia. P. Krastyn', *Revoliutsiia 1905–1907 godov v Latvii* (Moscow, 1952), p. 48.

80 *RGASPI, f.* 124, *op.* 1, *d.* 1210, *l.* 6 (from an autobiographical note by Martens).

81 M. Litvinov, 'Transportirovanie oruzhiia v Rossiiu', in Pozner, *Pervaia boevaia organizatsiia*, pp. 103–10.

82 B. Stomoniakov, 'Zagranichnaia organizatsiia po dostavke oruzhiiu v Rossiiu v 1905 godu', in ibid., p. 94.

83 *RGASPI, f.* 124, *op.* 1, *d.* 887, *l.* 11 (from an autobiographical note by Kovalevskii).

84 *Newcastle Daily Chronicle* (24 August 1914). The last of the Newcastle gun-running hearings of 1907 took place on Thursday 9 May. Four days later, the London *Times* reported 'The arrival of Russian Socialists in England with the object of holding a party congress'. Fischer described his experience of the Fifth Congress in *V Rossii*, pp. 91–2, and in 'Ob Il'iche', *Staryi bol'shevik*, No. 1 (1930), pp. 124–5.

85 Robert Spence Watson, 'Government by Brute Force', *Free Russia* (June 1907), pp. 1–2; University of Newcastle upon Tyne, Special Collections, Spence Watson Papers: SW 1/10/22, Kropotkin to Spence Watson (London, 14 December 1907) about Chaikovskii; FO 371/327, f. 291, Spence Watson to Sir Edward Grey (no date, but stamped 20 December 1907); *Free Russia* (July 1909), p. 11.

86 FO 371/322, ff. 429–36.

87 FO 371/326, ff. 172–90; Donald Rumbelow, *The Houndsditch Murders and the Siege of Sidney Street* (London, 1988 [first published 1973]).

88 Pozner, *Pervaia boevaia organizatsiia*, p. 207, n. 3; David King, *Ordinary Citizens: The Victims of Stalin* (London, 2003), p. 26.

Index

Active Resistance Party (Activists) of
  Finland 84, 87, 88–9
agriculture 35–8, 80–2, 137–55,
  200–3, 205; *see also* peasants
Aksel'rod, P. B. 219, 225, 253
Aladin, A. F. 203
Alekseev, Vice-Admiral E. I. 107
Alekseev, General M. V. 7, 94–118
Alekseev, Nikolai 267
Alexander II 82, 159
Alexander III 8, 58, 82
anarchists 40, 47, 262–3, 269
Apanaev, Abdulla 119, 122, 124, 125,
  131
Arendt, Hannah 34
Arkhengel'skii, A. M. 182
Armenians 48–9
Armstrong, Lord 269
Arnol'd, G. A. 187
artels 28 n25, 39
'Artem' *see* Sergeev, F. A.
Artem'ev, N. A. 182, 185, 187, 188
Artsybashev, Mikhail 18
assassinations *see* terrorism
Autonomists 197, 198
Azef, Evno 272

Baku 38, 45, 47–8, 121
Bakunin, Mikail 30 n47, 234
Baltic Germans 55–8, 60, 65–7, 72–4
Baltic provinces 6, 17, 40, 55–78,
  268–73
banquet campaign 122, 181
Basanavičius, Jonas 59
Bashkirs 121
Bat'ianov, General M. I. 97
Batumi 38, 43
Bebel, August 63
Bel'gard, A. V. 65

Belorussians 58
Bely, Andrei 5, 18, 19, 26, 29 n37
Benevskaia, Mariia 16
Bez zaglaviia group 185, 199
Bialystok 204–5, 211
Bil'dering, General A. A. von 96
Biriliev, A. A. 205
Black Hundreds 46, 49, 161–2, 167,
  169, 171, 204
Bloody Sunday 2, 12 n9, 14, 27, 38, 45,
  64, 88, 160, 260
Blok, Aleksandr 19, 29 (n. 40)
Bobrikov, N. I. 83, 84, 86, 89, 90
Bobrinskii, Count V. A. 49
Bogdanov, A. A. 219, 224, 227
Bolsheviks 2, 39, 40–1, 160, 162,
  177–8, 180–91, 218–40; *Vpered*
  group of 180, 186, 226, 228
Breshko-Breshkovskaia, E. K. 22
Britain 10–11, 260–78
Bulygin, A. G. 65, 105
Bunakov, I. S. 199
Bund 62, 64, 66, 68, 70, 168, 177, 180
Burtsev, V. L. 263, 264

Catholic Church 58, 74
Caucasus 6, 17, 40, 48
Chaianov, A. V. 139
Chaikovskii, N. V. 268, 273
Chechelev Republic 50
Chekov, Anton 35
Chernov, A. V. 145–6
Chernov, V. M. 19, 199
Chernyshevskii, N. G. 61
Chirvinskii, N. P. 182
Chita 50, 107, 111
civil society 45–6
Constitutional Democrats *see* Kadets
Cowen, Robert 262–3

crime 15, 49; *see also* smuggling,
    terrorism
Currie, Daniel 271, 272

Dan, Feodor 235
Dashnaks 48
Deich, Lev 24
Democratic Reform Group 197
Dillon, Edward J. 11
Dogger Bank incident 261
Dolgorukov, Prince Pavel Dmitrievich
    197
Dolgorukov, Prince Petr Dmitrievich
    198
Domaszewicz, Andrius 61–2
Donbass 36, 38, 48, 169, 171
Dorpat (Iur'ev, Tartu) 60
Dostoevsky, F. M. 22
Dubnow, S. M. 8, 156
Duma *see* State Duma
Dragomirov, General M. I. 97
Dzierżyński, Feliks 62

Ekaterinoslav (Katerynoslav) 38, 40, 49,
    50, 163–4, 169
Emancipation Edict (1861) 58, 110,
    137, 138, 243
émigrés 14, 16, 218–40, 260–74
Engels, F. 252–3
Epshtein, Lev Isaakovich ('Stepan') 160
Ermolov, A. S. 206
Estonia 6, 55–7, 60, 65–6, 71–2, 74–5;
    socialist movement in 63–4
Estonian National Progressist Party 71
Ezerskaia, Lidiia 23

Figner, Vera 165
Finland 40, 79–93, 232, 268
Finnish Diet 82, 83, 90
Firsov, G. A. 141
Fischer, Heinrich 260, 261, 262–3,
    266–74
Flynn, Charles 260, 261, 267
France 10–11
Frederiks, Baron V. B. 205, 207
Frumkina, Fruma 23, 25
Fukushima, Major-General Yasumasa 105

Galeev, Galimdzhan 119–25, 131
Galeev, Salikhdzhan 119, 124, 125, 131
Gapon, Father G. A. 12 n9, 45
Gasprinskii, Ismail Bey 126–7, 128,
    130

Geiden, A. F. 206, 207
Geiden, Count P. A. 198, 206
Georgia 40, 43–4
Germany 10, 55, 57, 63, 101
Gershuni, G. A. 27 n15
Gertshenstein, Ia. G. 202–3
Giers, A. N. 65
Gippius, Zinaida 18
Gol'denberg, Grigorii 159
Goremykin, I. L. 201, 202, 204, 205,
    207, 212
Gorky, Maxim 224, 233
Gots, Abram 16
Gredeskul, N. A. 198
Grey, Sir Edward 264, 268–9
Grigor'ev, Vaska 165
Guchkov, A. I. 208
Guria 40, 43–4
Gurko, V. I. 201–3, 211

Harbin 107, 108–9
Helphand, Alexander *see* Parvus,
    Alexander
Helsinki 87, 88
Herzen, Alexander Ivanovich 50, 61, 97
Hobson, S. G. 268
Hung hu tze 99
Hutchinson, Robert 271

Ianovskii, E. M. 186
Iaroslavl' 170
Independent Jewish Labour Party 44,
    48–9, 86; *see also* police socialism
industrialists 46, 68, 269
International Socialist Bureau 236
Irkutsk 50, 108
Ittifak 121, 122, 126, 131, 134 n13
Iuzovka 41, 49
Ivanov, S. A. 187
Ivanovo-Voznesensk 47
Izkhaki, Gaiaz 120
Izvol'skii, A. P. 205, 206

Jacobson, Carl 59
Jadidism 129, 132–3
Jaunlatvieši see Young Latvians
Jews 23, 31 n76, 48, 204, 265–6; in the
    Baltic provinces 57, 61, 66; in
    Khar'kov 156–76; pogroms against
    8, 48–9, 156–76, 178, 204–5, 211,
    265–6
Jogiches (Tyszka), Leo 61, 62
John Grafton affair 268

Kadets 8–9, 46, 106, 181, 196–217, 224
Kamalutdinov, Zia 128
Kant, Immanuel 16
Kapsukas, Vincas 68
Katerynoslav *see* Ekaterinoslav
Katkov, M. N. 58
Kaufman, P. M. von 205
Kaul'bars, General A. V. 97
Kautsky, Karl 219, 223–4, 228, 252, 253
Kazan 7, 50, 119–36
Keast, Thomas Dugger 270, 272
Kharkiv *see* Khar'kov
Khar'kov (Kharkiv) 8, 47, 50, 156–76
Khomutov, P. 121
Khrustalev, P. A. *see* Nosar, G. P.
Kiev (Kyiv) 5, 41, 48, 156, 158, 159, 162, 164–7, 171, 177–95
Kiev Polytechnical Institute 177–91
Kishinev 165, 265
Kliucharev, A. S. 128
Kokoshkin, F. F. 198
Kokovtsov, V. N. 10, 205–6
Kolo 197, 210, 211, 212
Kondrat'ev, F. A. 47
Konopliannikova, Zinaida 21
Kovno (Kaunas) 55, 57, 68, 69, 73
Krasin, L. B. 225, 272
Krasnoiarsk 50
Kremenchuk 163
Kremer, Alexander 61
Kropotkin, D. N. 159, 273
Kropotkin, Prince P. A. 262–3
Krupskaia, N. K. 223, 232
Kryzhanovskii, S. E. 106
Krzhizhanovskii, G. B. 225
Krzhizhanovskii, G. M. 180, 186, 187
Kudirka, Vincas 60
Kuropatkin, General A. N. 95, 97, 98, 100
Kursk 49
Kuzmin-Karavaev, V. D. 198
Kyiv *see* Kiev

landlords 35–6, 37, 38, 42–3, 56, 137–55
Laqueur, Walter 5, 13
Latvia 6, 55–7, 58–9, 74–5, 268, 270; socialist movement in 62–64
Latvian Social Democratic Party 64, 65, 66, 67, 68
Lenin, V. I. 2, 5, 9, 34, 36, 37, 115, 180, 218–40, 246–7, 253–4, 267, 273; as author of *The Development of Capitalism in Russia* 219; *One Step Forward, Two Steps Back* 222–6, 233, 236; *Our Differences* 219; *Two Tactics of Social Democracy in the Democratic Revolution* 230, 233, 236; *What is to be Done?* 219, 220, 223
Leont'ev, P. M. 58
Levitus, Aron 160
Liao-yang 99
Liapunov, Lieutenant-General M. N. 102
Libau (Liepāla) 56, 64
liberals 1, 5, 8; in the Baltic provinces 64, 66, 69, 71–2; in Kiev 177–95; *see also* Kadets, Octobrists
Linevich, General N. P. 97–101, 103, 107–11
literacy 42, 46
literature 18–19, 22
Lithuania 6, 55–7, 66–7, 68–9, 71–3, 74–5; national movement in 59–60; socialist movement in 61–2
Lithuanian Democratic Party 60
Lithuanian Social Democratic Party (LSDP) 62, 67, 71
Litvinov, M. M. 272–3
Lomonosov, Iu. V. 177–95
Lunacharskii, A. V. 224, 247
Lutheran Church 59, 60, 65, 67, 74
Luxemburg, Rosa 62, 219, 225, 253
L'vov, N. N. 201

McKean, Robert B. 254
Mackenzie Wallace, D. 261, 264
Maksudi, Khadi 125
Maksudi, Sadri 131
Manchuria 5, 6, 84–118
Martens, Ludwig, 272–3
Martov, Iu. O. 61, 219, 223, 225, 253–4
Martson, General F. V. 95
Martynov. A. S. 253
Marx, Karl 6, 140, 252–3
Mehring, Franz 253
Meller-Zakomel'skii, General A. N. 113, 115
Mensheviks 11 n3, 24, 40, 43, 50, 162, 178, 180, 186, 191, 219–40, 241–59
Miakotin, B. A. 199
Miliukov, P. N. 46, 186, 197, 206–11, 243
Minsk 44

Mitau (Jelgava) 57
Moiseenko, Boris 16
Morawski, Alfons 61
Morozov, Savva 46
Moscow 5, 6, 39, 41, 45; uprising in 2, 108–9, 110, 112, 234, 236
Mukden, battle of 95, 98, 99
Muromtsev, S. A. 197
Muslims 7, 119–36, 162, 164, 167–8, 197, 210

Nabokov, V. D. 198
Nagel', Al'fred 270, 272–3
national minorities 4–5, 6, 7, 16–17, 119–36, 197, 211
Nazarov, Fedor 16
Newcastle upon Tyne 260–78
Nicholas II 2, 7, 10, 42, 60, 83, 89, 94, 95, 104, 111–12; and the Bulygin rescript 105; and the State Duma 205, 206–11; *see also* October Manifesto
Nietzsche 18, 24
Nikolaev 42
Nikolai Nikolaevich, Grand Duke 101, 207
Nizhnii Novgorod 50, 120, 124
Nosar, G. P. 242, 246, 250
Noskov, V. A. 225
Novomirskii, Daniil 40, 47
Novorossisk 49–50

oblastnichestvo 50
Obolenskii, I. M. 87
October Manifesto 8, 10, 43, 48, 69, 71, 106, 109, 121, 156, 178–9, 188–9, 226, 229, 243
Octobrists 197
Odesa *see* Odessa
Odessa (Odesa) 12 n9, 36, 38, 40, 45, 47, 48, 49, 165, 167, 171, 265
okhrana see police
Old Finns 84
Oranovskii, Major-General V. A. 105
Orel 49
Orenburg 129, 130
Orthodox Church 17, 28 n24, 59, 167, 200
Ostrogozhskii uezd 137–55

Palitsyn, General F. F. 112, 114
pan-Islamism 126–31
pan-Turkism 126–31

Pares, Bernard 263
Parskii, Colonel D. P. 95
Party of Democratic Reforms 198, 199, 203, 206, 209
Party of Peaceful Renewal 197, 198, 201, 206
Party of Socialists–Revolutionaries *see* Socialists–Revolutionaries
Parvus, Alexander 10, 243, 244, 245, 254
peasants 1, 7–8, 28 n22, 35–8, 41–2, 137–55, 243, 251–3, 255–6; in the Baltic provinces 55–7, 64–9, 72–4; in Finland 85; peasant commune 36–7, 44, 61, 253; peasant revolts 42–4, 68, 121, 137–55; *see also* agriculture
Peasant Union 42, 197, 255
People's Party of Order 49
Pereleshin, D. A. 137
Peshekhonov, A. V. 199
Petrunkevich, I. I. 203
Pikhno, D. I. 165
Pleve, General P. A. 111
Plehve, V. K. 12 n9
Plekhanov, G. V. 218–30, 236–7, 238
Pliekšans, Janis (Rainis) 63
Poale-Zion 160, 168
Pobedonostsev, K. P. 60
Pogorelko, A. K. 170
pogroms *see* Jews
Pokrovskii, M. N. 39
Poland 17, 40, 58, 112, 212
Poles 55, 58, 61–2
Polish insurrection (of 1863) 56, 57–8, 68, 74
Polish Socialist Party (PPS) 62
police 15, 25, 46, 119–36, 145–6, 159, 160, 165, 166–7, 181, 182, 185, 248, 262–72
police socialism 12 n9, 44–5, 47, 86; *see also* Zubatov, S. V.
Poniatowski, S. A. 198
Popular Socialist Party 185, 199
populist movement 35, 36, 50, 61, 158–9, 180
Portsmouth, Treaty of 101, 105–6, 107
Postalovskii, D. 228
press 58, 59–60, 107–8, 122, 123, 163, 243–6
priests 43, 167
Protsenko, V. N. 165–6
Pugachevshchina 137, 161
Putilov works 38

Putin, Vladimir 4

Radstig, A. A. 185
railwaymen 41, 46, 49, 69, 161–2,
  169–71, 177–95
railways 36, 38, 47, 49, 56, 106–7,
  108–9, 112, 115, 181, 183–4
Ratner, M. B. 188
redemption payments 37, 43–4, 148 n4
Rediger, A. F. 205, 207
Rennenkamf, General P. K. von 115
Reval (Tallinn) 56, 65, 69–70
revolution of 1905: historiography of
  1–4, 13–14, 23–4, 34–7, 39–40,
  137–40
revolutions of 1917 2, 7, 9, 75, 94–5,
  103–4, 229, 232, 256
Riga 56, 57, 63, 64, 68, 69, 202, 268
right-wing organizations 49; *see also*
  Black Hundreds
Rogozinnikova, Evstiliia 21
Rostov-on-Don 38, 50
Rozhestvenskii, Admiral Z. P. 102
Russification 58–61, 83–4, 130–1
Russo-Japanese War 6–7, 13, 26, 38,
  42, 94–118, 261
Ruzskii, A. P. 183
Rykov, A. I. 228
Ryshkov, S. M. 198

St Petersburg 5, 6, 21, 38–9, 41
St Petersburg Soviet 161, 234, 241–4,
  246–51, 256
Sakhalin 102, 108
Salisbury, Lord 262
Samara 43
Saratov 43, 46, 47, 129
Sazonov, S. D. 268, 269
schools 42, 60, 66, 68, 74, 119–36,
  141, 158
Scotland 57, 71, 268, 270, 271
Sennitskii, Lieutenant-General V. V. 170
Sergeev, F. A. ('Artem') 160, 161, 169,
  171
Shaevich, K. 45
Shakhovskoi, Prince D. I. 198
Shanin, Teodor 37
Shapozhnikov, G. N. 198
Shaufus, N. K. 205
Shcheglovitov, I. G. 205
Shendrikov, Ilia 47–8
Shendrikov, Lev 47–8
Shershenevich, G. F. 198

Shipov, N. S. 206, 208
Shirinskii-Shikhmatov, Prince A. A.
  205
Shlikhter, A. G. 179, 180–3, 186–91
Shmidt, N. P 46
Shtof, A. A. 205
Shuliavka 178
Shvanebakh, P. Kh. 205, 207
Siberia 50, 102–3
Simbirsk 129
Siping 97–9, 105, 110
Slavophiles 58–9, 60
Šliūpas, Jonas 59
smuggling: of literature 58, 59; of arms
  268–74
Sobolev, General L. N. 106
Social Democracy of the Kingdom of
  Poland and Lithuania (SDKPiL) 62
Social Democrats 9, 15, 27 n11, 40–1,
  46–8, 121, 218–40, 272–3; in the
  Baltic provinces 61–4, 66, 69–70; in
  Britain 260–78; in Finland 84, 85–6,
  87, 88, 90–2; in Khar'kov 159–62,
  168–71; in Kiev 177–95; and the
  State Duma 196, 199, 203–4, 211,
  236–7; *see also* Bolsheviks,
  Mensheviks
Socialists–Revolutionaries 16, 19, 21,
  22, 25, 40, 89, 121, 160, 162, 177,
  178, 180, 197, 224, 243; Combat
  Organization of 16, 23, 25, 40
Society of Friends of Russia 260, 264
Solomon, V. A. 185, 187
Soskice, David 264–5
soviets 49–50, 70, 178, 189; *see also* St
  Petersburg Soviet
Spence Watson, Robert 260, 261, 262,
  264–6, 267–8, 271, 273–4
Spilka *see* Ukrainian Social Democratic
  Union
Starynkevich, K. S. 170
State Duma 1, 7, 10, 42, 106, 125,
  131–2, 196–217
Stead, W. T. 264
Stishinskii, A. S. 201–3, 205, 211
Stolypin P. A. 8, 126–7, 130, 205, 206,
  207, 270–1
strikes 3, 8, 10, 38, 40–1, 44–46, 48,
  49, 121, 161, 177–8, 181–3, 244; in
  the Baltic provinces 64–6, 67–8,
  69–71; in the Far East 107–11, 115;
  in Finland 87–90
Strizhevskii, M. V. 120, 127–8

Struve, P. B. 27 n5, 197, 230
Stučka, Peteris 63
students 40, 41, 63, 119–26
Sture, Lidiia 25
Sumy district 43, 47
Sungari river 99
Swedish Party (of Finland) 84, 85, 86, 91

Tallinn *see* Reval
Tambov 198
Tatars 119–36
teachers 43, 70, 119–26
terrorism 5–6, 13–33, 40, 61, 87, 262, 270–1
Tettau, E. 98–9, 100
T'ieh-ling 95–6
Tiflis (Tbilisi) 48, 49
Tikhvinskii, M. M. 182, 185, 187
Tocqueville, Alexis de 6, 35
Totleben, E. I. 170
trade unions 45, 46–7, 91, 180, 181–3, 187, 248
Trepov, D. F. 206–11, 248
Trotsky, L.D. 5, 10, 24, 241–59; theory of 'Permanent Revolution' 10, 241, 250–4
Trubetskoi, Prince E. N. 181
Trudoviks 196–204, 209, 211, 212
Trusiewicz, Stanislaw 61–2
Tsushima Straits, battle of 95, 101–2
Tuckum 72
Tula 49
Tyneside 260–78

Ufa 121, 125, 128, 129
Ukraine 6, 36, 40, 44, 48–9, 156–76, 177–95
Ukrainian Social Democratic Union ('Spilka') 177
Ulianov, A. I. 218
Ulianov, V. I. *see* Lenin, V. I.
Ulianova, M. I. 218
Union of Liberation 199

Union of 17 October *see* Octobrists
Union of Unions 46, 177–95
universities 45, 60, 63, 122–3, 158, 161, 164, 177–8
USA 10–11, 57, 71

Valdemars, Krišjānis 59
Valentinov, Nikolai 41
Vasilev, B. P. 165
Vikzhel 47
Vileišis, Petras 66
Vil'na (Vilnius) 44, 55–7, 61–2, 66–9, 73
Vilnius *see* Vil'na
Viriatino 36
Vladivostok 110, 112–13
Vodozov, V. V. 199
Volga–Urals region 35, 40, 119–36
Voronezh 7, 41, 137–55

Wilbur, Elvira 139–40
Williams, Harold 263
Wilton, Robert 263
Witte, S. Iu. 8, 57, 67, 101, 106, 156, 250–1
women 16, 39, 43, 90
workers 1, 16–17, 38–9, 40–2, 44–9, 161–2, 169–71, 242–3, 246–55; and anti-Semitism 48–9, 159; in the Baltic provinces 57, 62–5, 69–71; in the Far East 107–10; in Finland 86–7; *see also* strikes, trade unions
Woytinsky, Wladimir 41

Young Finns 84, 86, 91
Young Latvians (*Jaunlatvieši*) 58–9, 60

Zakharov, Colonel 107, 109, 111
Zasulich, Vera 225
zemliachestva 28 n25, 39, 41
zemstvos 131, 137–55
Zheleznov, V. A. 188–9
Zubatov, S. V. 12 n9, 86